RISING UP,
LIVING ON

ON DECOLONIALITY a series edited by
Walter D. Mignolo and Catherine E. Walsh

On Decoloniality interconnects a diverse array of perspectives
from the lived experiences of coloniality and decolonial thought/
praxis in different local histories from across the globe. The series
is concerned with coloniality's global logic and scope and with
the myriad of decolonial responses and engagements that contest
coloniality/modernity's totalizing violences, claims, and frame,
opening toward an otherwise of being, thinking, sensing, knowing,
and living; that is, of re-existences and worlds-making. Aimed at a
broad audience, from scholars, students, and artists to journalists,
activists, and socially engaged intellectuals, On Decoloniality
invites a wide range of participants to join one of the fastest-
growing debates in the humanities and social sciences that attends
to the lived concerns of dignity, life, and the survival of the planet.

RISING UP, LIVING ON

Re-Existences,
Sowings,
and Decolonial Cracks

CATHERINE E. WALSH

DUKE UNIVERSITY PRESS
Durham and London 2023

© 2023 DUKE UNIVERSITY PRESS | All rights reserved
Printed in the United States of America on acid-free paper ∞
Designed by Aimee C. Harrison
Typeset in Portrait Text Regular and Fengardo Neue (Loïc Sander)
by Westchester Publishing Services

Library of Congress Cataloging-in-Publication Data
Names: Walsh, Catherine E., author.
Title: Rising up, living on : re-existences, sowings, and decolonial
cracks / Catherine E. Walsh.
Other titles: On decoloniality.
Description: Durham : Duke University Press, 2023. | Series: On deco-
loniality | Includes bibliographical references and index.
Identifiers: LCCN 2022033987 (print)
LCCN 2022033988 (ebook)
ISBN 9781478019527 (paperback)
ISBN 9781478016885 (hardcover)
ISBN 9781478024156 (ebook)
Subjects: LCSH: —Latin America. | Postcolonialism—Latin America. |
Social movements—Latin America—History. | Black people—Civil
rights—Latin America. | Indigenous peoples—Civil rights—Latin
America. | Traditional ecological knowledge—Latin America. |
Women—Crimes against—Latin America. | Feminist theory—Latin
America. | BISAC: POLITICAL SCIENCE / Colonialism & Post-
Colonialism | SOCIAL SCIENCE / Gender Studies
Classification: LCC JV51 .W35 2023 (print) | LCC JV51 (ebook)
DDC 325/.3—dc23/eng/20220923
LC record available at https://lccn.loc.gov/2022033987
LC ebook record available at https://lccn.loc.gov/2022033988

Cover art: Blanka Amezkua and Pedro de La Rosa, untitled work
(Blanka's silhouette, raised arms and wearing a skirt), 2014. Acrylic
on amate (bark) paper, 15.5 × 23 in. Courtesy Blanka Amezkua.

For María Lugones, ancestor-spirit,
the conversations begun moons ago and
those that continue now with your tango
en la luz de la luna.

In memory of bell hooks, Diane Nelson, and Gustavo Esteva.

CONTENTS

GRATITUDES

Gratitude seems a more appropriate word than *acknowledgment*. My desire here is not just to acknowledge, recognize, and give credit. More deeply, it is to express my heartfelt appreciation and thanks to those who have accompanied me in this experientially grounded venture of living-writing/writing-living.

Several years ago, I came across the Brazilian writer Conceição Evaristo's concept-term *escrevivência*, a portmanteau of *escrita* and *vivência*. This is life written in one's experience, an experience that, of course, is never solitary or lived alone. And, at the same time, it is writing that writes the world in which one thinks, feels, struggles, and lives. My first gratitude, then, is to Evaristo for this concept-as-praxis. She gave me not only a way to name the weave of writing and living that I have long felt but also a way to write living and live writing, most especially in these pandemic-ridden times. In the almost two years that I dedicated myself practically full time to this book, writing became a force of light and life to create, construct, reflect, relate, and re-member; to resist, persist, exist, re-exist, and sow life despite and in the fissures and cracks of a system that intentionally drives hopelessness, fear, individuation, division, violence, and death.

I offer special gratitude to my ancestor-guides, some named in this book and others not, all of whom continue to make felt their guidance, teachings, and presence. Gratitude to the orishas who walk with me, opening paths, flowing sweet and salt waters, and imparting energies and vital force. *Axé*. Gratitude to the Pachamama of these Andes that adopted me as one of her own. And gratitude to this very special place that is Guápulo, with her chorus of birdsong that greets the red-orange dawn ascending each day from behind Cayambe's snow-capped volcano, her peace in the midst of urban chaos, and her brighter-than-bright and larger-than-life moon that seems to give reason, sense, and meaning to cycles of everyday existence—mine and those of the beings, human and otherwise, that make my-our space in Guápulo a special place of serenity and care, of loving and living.

Gratitude *sentipensada* for the encounters, conversations, and relations of comradery, friendship, and shared thinking with so many, too many to name. However, and in the context of this book and series, I would be amiss to not mention Walter Mignolo. My gratitude to Walter for the twenty-five years and growing of constant talk, thought, and decolonial colabor. And my gratitude to the "we" of decolonial complicity thinking-and-doing increasingly visible and present throughout the globe. It is a "we," of course, that is neither fixed, nor organized, nor stagnant; it is dynamic, heterogeneous, plural, expansive, and continually made.

DECUL—the endearing name that students gave to the regional-international doctoral program in Latin American (inter)cultural studies born in 2002 in Quito—is part of my *sentipensada* "we," of the gratitudes woven from the mind and heart that extend to five generations and the intergenerational community that endures. Here special gratitude goes to Adolfo Albán, who first as DECUL student, then as assistant, later as professor-accomplice-colleague, and all the while as artist-intellectual-activist-friend, introduced the praxistic concept of re-existence so central to this book and to the life struggles present in Abya Yala and the world.

Gratitude to the Fanonian thinkers who continue to inspire, most especially to Nelson Maldonado-Torres for the many conversations and the shared decolonial conspiring, in attitude, practice, and thought—much of which is reflected in the pages of this text—and to Lewis Gordon and Jane Anna Gordon, who, each in their own way, have taught me through their life practice, texts, and organizational work in the Caribbean Philosophical Association about the concrete possibilities of existence otherwise.

Gratitude to the Stellenbosch Institute for Advanced Studies (STIAS) for the opportunity, as research fellow in July-August 2018, to begin conversations and thought with South Africa. Gratitude to the Black Panthers' former minister of culture Emory Douglas for the conversations in Chiapas and later in North Carolina about the role of art in revolutionary struggle. Gratitude to María Lugones, Betty Ruth Lozano, Sylvia Marcos, Kosakura, Tsaywa Cañamar, Albeley Rodríguez, Raúl Moarquech Ferrera Balanquet, Daniel B. Coleman, and PJ DiPietro, among many others, for the ongoing dialogues on the complexities of that thing called "gender." Gratitude to Gustavo Esteva, who recently began the journey of reencounter with his ancestors, for the days spent at his home in San Pablo Etla, Oaxaca, in 2018 and the intense talk and thought on Freire and Illich. And gratitude as well to Vilma Almendra, Violeta Kiwe, Manuel Rozental, and René Olvera from the collective weave that is Pueblos en Camino, to the *compas kurdxs*, and to the many other activists and community-based leaders in this Abya Yala and beyond who refuse silencing and death by sowing life.

A special word of gratitude to those friends who read and commented on pieces of the book as it was being born and crafted: Nina Tepper, Ángel Burbano, Paulina Peñaherrera, PJ DiPietro, Alicia Ortega, Yamila Gutiérrez, Marcelo Fernández, Elizabeth Huanca, Patricia O'Rourke, and Michael Handelsman. Gratitude as well for the book-related reflections and discussions made possible with faculty members and participants in the Caribbean Philosophical Association's 2021 Summer School and the 2021 Maria Lugones Decolonial Summer School, and with so many others in the numerous on-line exchanges, encounters, seminars, and events of 2020–21. Together we fractured, traversed, and defied isolation, separation, and distance.

Gratitude to the artist Caleb Duarte for sharing images of the Zapantera Negra project of EDELO (En Donde Era La ONU), to Sofia Menses for her help with the bibliographical organization, to the two reader-evaluators for thinking with me in their wonderful comments and suggestions, and to the Mexican artists Blanka Amezkua and Pedro de La Rosa for permission to use, as the cover of this book, their artwork painted by La Rosa on legendary *amate* (bark paper) inside the silhouette of Amezkua's body; I am honored. A deep word of gratitude as well to the team at Duke Press: to Aimee Harrison for her amazing cover design; to Ale Mejía for her assistance and presence; to project editors Annie Lubinsky and Jessica Ryan and to copyeditor Erin Davis at Westchester Publishing Services; and most especially to Gisela Fosado. Gisela's intellectual astuteness and critical eye, along with her enthusiasm, patience, and dedication, have made both this book and our series On Decoloniality labors of co-relation, co-affection, and shared care, qualities seldom found in academia's market logic of publication.

Finally, gratitude to all who accompany me and those whom I accompany—each in our own territory, calendar, and material and spiritual space and place—in sowing life in these times of destruction, dispossession, violence, war, and death, in making and widening fissures and cracks in coloniality's seemingly impenetrable wall, and, above all, in rising up re-existences, invoking and convoking those that came before, and giving force to the otherwises present-past that resist and persist living on.

BEGINNINGS

The world needs other stories.
—CORINNE KUMAR

How many stories have we been told?[1] How many stories have been shrouded, silenced, and untold? And what about all those distorted stories that form part of the master narrative, the myth of nation-state, universalism's political discourse, and coloniality's global project all wrapped up as one? Those stories constitutive of the enduring colonial legacy and devastation, and most especially the enduring legacy and devastation that is the colonization of the mind? The Pakistani feminist Corinne Kumar reminds us of these stories, while calling forth the many others that we need to exist and re-exist in a world where existences outside and in the fissures and cracks of the dominant story line are denied.

I seek these latter stories, the herstories and theirstories, the stories recounted and shared, the stories that are mine, and all those constructed walking with others present and past. I seek the stories that unsettle and that crack coloniality, that re-member that which has been dis-membered, and those that weave decolonizing paths. Of course, the stories in and of themselves are not enough; yet their gathering is part of the beginnings.

I grew up in a white, working-class family of mixed immigrant origins. From the time I can remember, the origin stories that I was told made evident not only the difference in roots—Irish, rural Nova Scotian, peasant Lithuanian—but also the lived tensions among them. For my father, who proudly identified with the male genealogy of the first, there was a hierarchy of whiteness and social status at play in which the latter two—reflection of the female lineage—were constantly demeaned. Moreover, and as occurs in many families, there is another ancestry that remained negated. This, as I have come to learn in more recent years, is tied to the historical presence of free Black people in Nova Scotia, including in my paternal grandmother's own genealogy.

My childhood was lived in two small towns in central Massachusetts, one beside the other and both on lands dispossessed from the Nipmuc Tribal Nation.[2] I never knew this story of the land until now. As I was finishing this book, I realized that I had never been told—nor had I asked—about the memory-life that gave origin to this territory-land. A search brought me to a 2016 article in a local newspaper that led me to a detailed research study published in the *International Journal of Historical Archeology* and to the Nipmuc Nation's webpage.[3] The story is fragmented and it is long. I will only retell here some of its pieces.

Magunkaquog—what in 1846 became Ashland, the town where I lived from the age of about three or four until eighteen—was the seventh of fourteen "praying plantations" or "praying Indian villages" established by the English missionary John Eliot between 1650 and 1675 to aid in the conversion of the Indian population. As the Nipmuc Nation details, Eliot believed that by removing the Native peoples from their tribal villages and creating towns for them, the Natives would eventually forsake their "ungodly" ways and emulate the English. Here "the native people were forbidden to practice their traditional ways, wore English style clothes, lived in English style homes and attended the Puritan church." The reasons for voluntarily moving to these towns were varied, including "protection from Mohawk attacks, curiosity about English ways, economic survival, education, and the availability of food and clothing."[4] While many Nipmuc made strategic alliances with Eliot and later with the English colonialists—even fighting on their side in the various wars—these alliances did not eliminate the lived reality of colonial violence, including the ongoing dispossession of Nipmuc lands, nor did they necessarily wipe out the Nipmuc's own agency, spirituality, cosmology, knowledge, and sense of collective subjectivity and being.

Still, and although the story is fragmented, what is known says much about the patterns and deep roots of settler colonial power and dispossession. In 1715 Harvard University "bought" Magunkaquog. "Harvard's knowledge of the Magunkaquog community is not surprising given the close association between Eliot, the college, and its charter mission to Christianize the Indians." Yet the reasons for the "purchase" are not totally clear. Stephen Mrozowski, Holly Herbster, David Brown, and Katherine Priddy suggest that they were most likely tied up with a "larger political drama" between New England leaders, missionaries, and the English government.[5]

The deed of the "sale" of Magunkaquog's eight thousand acres (the original of which is still housed in Harvard's archives) included fifteen Native signatories, one of whom was found dead the following day, hung by his own belt. Evidence suggests not only that a group of the Nipmuc Nation opposed the deal but also that the purchase itself was shrouded in illegalities and questions of settler colonial power. Harvard held on to the property until the mid-eighteenth century, leasing parts to English colonists for farming. It seems, however, that the "Christian Indians" stayed on the land, even after it passed into private ownership in 1749.[6]

What does it mean to grow up on dispossessed land, I ask today, land that, according to this archaeological study, included—not far from my childhood home—a Nipmuc meetinghouse and its religious-spiritual grounds? And why were these stories of land and life never mentioned in school and generally obscured—at least for me and, I suspect, for most if not all non-Nipmuc town residents—for practically three hundred years? Is this not part of the master narrative, the global project of colonization-civilization that replaces memory with distorted *histories* that endure in and through a colonizing of the mind?

As is probably the case throughout Turtle Island (North America), the violences of ongoing settler colonialism and dispossession have continued with the years. In 1917 the Nyanza Chemical Plant and Waste Dump was constructed on thirty-five acres of these same Nipmuc lands, where it continued until 1978. Nyanza became in 1982 one of the first ten "superfund" sites designated for cleanup by the Environmental Protection Agency. As an agency report details, Nyanza generated "large volumes of industrial wastewater containing high levels of acids and numerous organic and inorganic chemicals, including mercury, leading to soil and groundwater contamination. Over 45,000 tons of chemical sludges generated by Nyanza's wastewater treatment processes, along with spent solvents and other chemical wastes, were buried on site."[7] The area with the largest amount of buried waste and exposed sludge is referred to as the Megunko Hill section, the same hill on which the Nipmuc meetinghouse once stood.

I don't recall hearing about the plant or its dangers when I was growing up in the 1950s and 1960s. Yet it was there in close proximity, behind the high school and next to a baseball field where many played and where many cooled off in or ice-skated on the multicolored waters of the small adjacent pond, a chemical water pool. Today the grave health problems suffered by many who were Ashland residents during Nyanza's operation and its aftermath, including my own family, are increasingly known. Nonetheless, the deeper significance for the Nipmuc Nation is most often rendered invisible. I can't help but ask whether the plant's destruction of land, water, and life is not part of the continual colonial legacy of violation, denigration, and dispossession.

There are some voices, however, that are weaving the relation. In my search, I came across mention of the artist Dan Borelli's project of Ashland-Nyanza that endeavors to give presence to the social history long hidden. In 2016 Borelli inaugurated a memorial healing garden on Megunko Hill in between where the meetinghouse and the chemical dye plant once stood. At the inauguration, members of the Nipmuc Nation performed a healing ceremony in this garden, a ritual of forgiveness,[8] a ceremony of memory, re-membering, and re-memorialization, of putting together the fragments and pieces that colonial violences have dis-membered.

I now know that I carry this story of colonial violence in my body and my mind, not by choice but by land, inheritance, and birth, and by obliviousness and ignorance without question. Encountering these pieces hidden and not known to me until now is a gift; a gift that opens cracks in the oblivion that coloniality perpetuates and delivers, and the innocences it enables and allows. Although I left Ashland in 1970 and have not returned since, the colonial weight of its story is now part of my herstory. Reclaiming the balance of this, and of all the stories that I—and *we*, including the readers here—have not been told, is a necessary step in understanding that coloniality is not a metaphor, to paraphrase Eve Tuck and K. Wayne Yang.[9] It is embodied, situated, and lived. Whether we like it or not, it is constitutive in a myriad of ways of who each one of us is: of those whom coloniality works to oppress, those whom it works to privilege, those whom it works to co-opt and capture, and all those who find themselves among or in between oppression, privilege, co-optation, assimilation, inclusion's ephemeral promise-hope, or western modernity's civilizing project, universalizing grip, and imperializing frame.[10]

While coloniality is everywhere, it is differentially embodied, situated, experienced, and lived. Indigenous peoples, African descendants, people of color, and women—most especially women of color—know this all too well, especially when their very existence and humanity are questioned, dismissed, and denied. Yet how often do those not marked by the colonial difference recognize their situatedness, embodiment, experience, and envelopment in coloniality's matrices of power, including its societal structures, institutions, and knowledge frames, and recognize the plurality—rather than unicity—of world-senses and lifeways? I am not suggesting rhetorical acknowledgments of settler guilt, as if such acknowledgment could somehow ameliorate colonial history and reconcile colonial blame.[11] Rather, I am referring to the work to be done to disrupt, transgress, and break apart—to crack—coloniality's permanence and hold, work that necessarily entails, following George Yancy, an unsuturing of "whiteness as the transcendental norm."[12]

All this is part of the project of this book. Its idea began a number of years ago. However, its situated, embodied, storied, and lived character made it, for all too long, a work always in process and progress, a praxis within—rather than about—existence difficult to compose on computer or paper.

Several years ago, I put a hammer next to me on the desk. The hammer keeps present the doing of cracking and the labor of crack-making; that is, the work to be done in the multiple contexts and situated spheres of lived life (including, but not only, in teaching, writing, and the university), the work of doing *with* and that of thinking *with and from*—not studying *about*—other crack makers, and the situated-embodied work with and from myself. And the hammer reminds me that to crack coloniality means, first off, to crack and fissure the coloniality that is part of me. It is to recognize how coloniality has invaded and permeated my existence and being without permission, approval, and most often without my awareness or recognition. It is to comprehend how coloniality is naturalized in/as existence itself. And it is to consciously struggle to disrupt this naturalization and totalization, including—to paraphrase Kumar—its institutionalization and universalization of the supremacy of the white, the European, the US "American," the Christian, the West; an institutionalization, universalization, and violence "nationalized" in territories throughout the globe.

Coloniality

Coloniality is the concept that the Peruvian sociologist Aníbal Quijano introduced in the late 1980s and early 1990s to refer to the constitution of a model and pattern of domination and power that began in 1492 with the so-called conquest (read: invasion) of the Cross and Crown, the colonization of the lands referred to today as the Caribbean and Latin America, and the subsequent reordering of the world with Europe at the center.[13] The ideas of race and gender were—and are—fundamental to the coloniality of power; its social classification and othering of populations; its control of labor, subjectivity, authority, and knowledge; and its constitutive entwine with modernity and capitalism, both of which took form with and through coloniality starting in 1492. The practices and policies of genocide and enslavement, the pillage of life and land, and the denials and destruction of humanity, spirituality, and cosmo-existence became the modus operandi of this model of western Christian civilization that later traveled the globe.[14] As I argue in this book, systemic racism and heteropatriarchy are component parts, as are the binaries that profess to fix and determine both gender and nature.

Coloniality, as such, is not a descriptive term to refer to the practices of domination in and of a colonial past. It is part of the hidden stories, the local histories that became and continue to become global designs.[15] Coloniality is the complex matrix or matrices of power that, in its constitutive inter-weavings with capitalism, patriarchy, and the ongoing project of modernity, continues to configure and reconfigure, to control and order existences, knowledges, nature, and life throughout the world. In this sense, *coloniality* is not a modern replacement word for *colonialism*. Rather, it is a decolonial conceptual framework, logic, and analytic for understanding and interven-ing in the systems and structures of power in which all of us are part, systems and structures deeply marked by race, gender, and heteropatriarchy, as well as class; by the dispossession of bodies and land; and by western rationality as the only framework and possibility of existence.

Coloniality in no way precludes or erases the specifics of settler colonial-ism as it has been constructed and lived, most especially in what the settlers named Canada and the United States. While settler colonialism is distinct from the coloniality of power established in sixteenth-century South and Central America, its patterns of power and systems of violence—including genocide, pillage, dispossession, expropriation, enslavement, racialization, and dehumanization—are, without a doubt, related. In fact, and as Rich-ard Gott argues, Latin America is, in many ways, also a white settler society since Europeanization, the importation of European migrants, and the ex-termination of Native peoples were central parts of the nineteenth-century history of many nations, including Chile, Argentina, Paraguay, Uruguay, and Venezuela.[16] Coloniality is, in this sense, an analytic that connects the broader struggles of Indigenous nations in the North and South, a connec-tion that builds what Emil Keme refers to as the "transhemispheric Indig-enous bridge" that is Abya Yala (or Abyiayala) and in which the plurality of territories, memories, stories, and struggles remains.[17]

My approach to coloniality in this book offers and invites such connec-tions. Moreover, it brings together my own processes and experiences of learning to unlearn and relearn, and of social, political, educational, epis-temic, and existence-based questioning, unsettling, unsuturing, and strug-gle lived first in the United States and, in the last almost three decades, in Ecuador. I recognize and think *from and with* these territorial groundings, which is distinct from studying or writing *about*. And, at the same time, I contemplate the global nature of the colonial matrix of power and the threads woven with decolonizing struggles throughout the world.

Cracking coloniality, in this sense, and as I will show throughout this text, references the decolonial work that exists, is taking place, and needs to be done. It is not about decolonization as a linear process or point of arrival, or as a metaphor that, as Tuck and Yang rightfully argue, all too often "supplants prior ways of talking about social justice, critical methodologies, or approaches which decenter settler perspectives," with little or no regard for how decolonization wants something different from these forms of justice, criticity, and critique.[18] To crack coloniality means, for me, to open fissures in this totalizing system or matrix of power, and to widen further the fissures that already exist in coloniality's supposedly impenetrable wall. The fissures and cracks are about the situated and embodied questions and work we need to do with ourselves and about the questions and work to be done with respect to social structures, institutions, and practices, including those related to knowledge; to being, becoming, and belonging; and to existence itself, particularly in these present times. The fissures and cracks evidence actionality, agency, resistance, resurgence, and insurgent forms of subjectivity and struggle; they are the spaces of creation against and despite the system, of hope against despair, of life living up against coloniality's present-day project of violence-dispossession-war-death all intertwined; of re-existence in times of de-existence. The fissures and cracks are not the solution but the possibility of otherwises, those present, emerging, and persistently taking form and hold.

Existence, Re-existence, and Existences Otherwise

Coloniality necessarily raises existential questions that are situated in life, in the lived contexts of being in a world—and being-in-the-world—when one's very existence is continually threatened and called into question. Frantz Fanon spoke to this problem well, as have a number of contemporary Africana philosophers of existence, most especially Lewis R. Gordon, Sylvia Wynter, Paget Henry, and Nelson Maldonado-Torres. As many anticolonial, decolonial, and community-based feminists, and feminists of color, including Corinne Kumar, M. Jacqui Alexander, María Lugones, Laura E. Pérez, Rita Segato, Gloria Anzaldúa, Gloria Wekker, Sylvia Marcos, Saidiya Hartman, Aura Cumes, Breny Mendoza, Ochy Curiel, Lorena Cabnal, Oyèrónké Oyewùmi, Leanne Betasamosake Simpson, Tsaywa Cañamar, and Betty Ruth Lozano Lerma, among others present in this text, have made clear, these struggles of and for existence are rooted not only in the problem of race but, more crucially, in the intimate ties of racialization, heteropatriarchy, and gendering. Likewise, they are about reconstituting relationality with and among the human, nonhuman, and spiritual worlds.

As such, I ask, what might it mean to take seriously Pérez's plea to "unthink and rethink braver, more truthful, and more deeply human understandings of being and existence"?[19] "To move past the boundaries of alienation" and toward "the promise that oppositional knowledges and political mobilizations hold," as Alexander suggests, enabling crossings and relation between the secular and sacred, the human and nonhuman, the embodied and disembodied, between tradition versus modernity, "us" versus "them," and the many other oppositions and separations of existence and everyday life?[20] And, following Gordon, how are we to understand the existence-based questions conditioned by Blackness—especially those "premised upon concerns of freedom, anguish, responsibility, embodied agency, sociality, and liberation"—as realities and questions of humanity, of struggles to live on evoking and invoking those that came before?[21]

All of these questions interweave with mine. While the queries I raise in the pages that follow are many, there are two principal ones that orient and guide: How are we to sow and grow existence, re-existences, and existences otherwise in, from, and making decolonial cracks, opening toward and revealing radically distinct arrangements of knowing, theorizing, thinking, and doing, and of being, becoming, belonging, and living in relation, particularly in these present times? And how are we to understand this embodied and situated praxis as constitutive of the necessary and ongoing processes of learning to unlearn that which coloniality has naturalized and inculcated, and of learning to relearn from, with, and in coloniality's decolonial and decolonizing outside, borders, fissures, and cracks?

My reference to existence here takes me beyond ontology. Like Fanon, I am not interested in the individual and individualized construct of *Being* or in the phylogeny of the species.[22] I am also not interested in Eurocentered constructions of ontological existence that, all too often, find their ground in what Emmanuel Chukwudi Eze describes as a capitalist metaphysics of consciousness and domination.[23]

My concern instead is with social existence, with sociohistorical, socioherstorical, and sociotheirstorical considerations that—and not unlike Fanon's sociogeny—point to and are constitutive of existential struggles of and for life, struggles that emerge out of the negation, denial, and subjugation of one's existence; struggles resisting, existing, re-existing.

Re-existence is an actional idea that has its roots in the long horizon of struggle of Black and Indigenous communities. It was the Afro-Colombian artist-intellectual Adolfo Albán Achinte who introduced the term at a public event in Quito in 2005, making clear the way it interpolates and undoes coloniality's semblance of total and totalizing power. As he explains, re-existence refers to "the mechanisms that communities create and develop to invent daily life and power, in this way confronting the hegemonic project that since colonization until our present day, has inferiorized, silenced and negatively made visible existence.... Re-existence puts off center the established logics in order to look for, in the depth of cultures—especially Indigenous and Afro-descendant—the keys to forms of...organization and production that permit the dignifying and reinventing of life and its continued transformation."[24]

For Albán, it is in the specific context of the construction of Black subjectivities that re-existence takes meaning and form. "My argument," says Albán, "is that the enslaved did not just resist the system of enslavement, they configured a particular form of existence as a project of society and life, a project that is still evidenced today in Black ancestral communities. Black peoples fought for freedom and in this struggle they developed ways to exist, that is to be in the world in the condition of subjects."[25] Re-existence, in this sense, is part of the long horizon that continues into the present in racialized and discriminatory societies. It implies "living in 'other' conditions,"[26] to exist and not just resist—to re-exist resisting and to resist re-existing—to re-elaborate and build projects of society and life in adverse conditions, and to surpass and overcome these circumstances, resignifying and redefining life in conditions of dignity and self-determination: a re-existence as subjects and with others in radically distinct terms, confronting at the same time the biopolitic that controls, dominates, and commodifies subjects and nature.[27]

In a somewhat similar sense, the Brazilian geographer Carlos Walter Porto-Gonçalves began in 1998 to refer to what he termed "r-existence," this explained in a later text as "the spaces that were never conquered by the colonial invader...the spaces of freedom in the midst of slavery/servitude...that serve as bastions of r-existence; that is, a resistance that is not simply a reaction to the invader, but a form of r-existence because it incorporates new horizons of ethnic and peasant communities' own senses reinvented in these circumstances. These communities resist because they exist; therefore, they r-exist."[28]

Of course, the use and conceptualization of the term did not necessarily begin or end with Albán and Porto-Gonçalves. The Oxford online dictionary maintains that the word *re-existence* first appeared in the mid-seventeenth century, in the work of the philosopher, poet, and theologian Henry More (1614–87). Its meaning: "renewed or resumed existence"; "a new or further existence."[29] Nonetheless, what interests me here is re-existence's praxical and actional intentions and inventions; that is, the ways that people are sowing and resowing life, cultivating the possibilities of an otherwise, of social, cultural, political, epistemic, ethical, and existence-based affirmation.

How is re-existence rising up and living on today in societies deeply marked by the systemic violences of racism, gendering, Christianity, and heteropatriarchy? Of the continual dispossession of bodies, land, knowledge, and life in Native territories throughout the world? And what about the pluriversal of existences past and present that defy, contest, unsettle, and crack coloniality and its continual configuration and reconfiguration of power, including—but not only—in the colonial institutions of education, schooling, and state? These are some of the crucial questions and concerns of the book that you have in your hands.

Modes of Writing and Organization

As I said at the outset of this introduction, this book is situated and embodied; it could not be otherwise. Consequently, its modes of writing are by no means usual. They too are situated, embodied, grounded, experienced, and lived, part of what Conceição Evaristo describes as *escrevivência*, a "writing engaged, committed to life, to living," and to the relation with lived reality; a writing-living that denounces, disturbs, and calls out from one's own historic processes and subjectivity.[30] The modes, moreover, assume a serpentine rather than lineal movement. I meander in and out of autobiographical narratives and narrations, personal letters and conversations, lived accounts, and weavings of thinking with authors, artists, students present and past, ancestor-guides, intellectual militants and activists, and political-epistemic, collective, communal, and community-based subjects, processes, practices, actions, and movements. In this weaving, I make no hierarchical distinctions; all are thinkers. The writing, in essence, is part of the cracking and of the existences and re-existences rising up and living on, processes within which I endeavor, through a pedagogy of questioning of sorts, to actively engage you, the reader. My writing, in this sense, intends to stir up, to unsettle, to implore, and to defy inaction and indifference.

The text is organized into five chapters. While each affords connections to the next, they can also be read and pondered on their own. I begin in chapter 1 with the force of cries, the presence of cracks, and their connections. They are cries of outrage, indignation, and dignified fury, mine woven with others; cries that denounce, define, and scream out against the present-day intertwinement of violence-dispossession-war-death and the targeted de-existences present and taking form; cries that detail coloniality's mutations, changing strategies, and reconfigurations, including in the time of COVID-19. Here the clamor of shared cries sounds the impetus and will to struggle, to resist and re-exist and not just survive. With these cries come the cracks, the debilitating of the wall, and the praxis of fissure.

Chapter 2 asks about and walks the intermeshed processes of decolonizing and deschooling. It is a narrative of sorts, thought and told through fragments of my own ongoing story of learning, unlearning, and relearning. I conceive the fragments as pieces of cloth, written on over many decades. The fragments are not meant to be pieced together into a whole since that would suture, close up, or bring to a finish not only the narrative but also the ongoing character, process, and doing of praxis and pedagogy that, in and through the chapter, unfold and take form. With the fragments, pieces of my own asking and walking, existences and educations otherwise take on lived form.

Chapter 3 traverses the binaries and boundaries of gender, race, nature, and knowledge. It is concerned with the intertwinements that coloniality/modernity has made and continues to make between and among these axes and their binaries of power. And it asks about the present-past practices, philosophies, and modes of lived existence that resist, persist, and re-exist, disrupting and transgressing what Alexander refers to as the "existential impasse," reassembling what belongs together.[31] In these ways, the chapter opens toward what often cannot be seen; these are the cracks but also the profound relations and interconnections that enable and call forth distinct ways of being, sensing, and thinking, and, most especially, of making and doing a feminist politics grounded in life, spirituality, and relationality.

Chapter 4 is concerned with the undoing of nation-state, acknowledging that state formations—whether neoimperial, neoliberal, progressive, or increasingly corporate—are what the Kurdish leader Abdullah Öcalan calls "the spine of capitalist modernity" and "the cage of natural society."[32] Moreover, they are central pegs—with and through their binaries, borders, boundaries, and forced incorporation of peoples and land and, relatedly, their structures, institutions, knowledges, and practices—in the maintenance, configuration, and reconfiguration of coloniality's global order. Here I ask about how the nation-state's naturalization and universal hegemonic hold is being undone from the land, on the ground, and with and through plurinational propositions. While the reflections open toward processes of thinking and doing in various territories of the globe, they give centrality to those I have been most closely engaged with in the Andes.

The book closes in chapter 5 with thoughts on, from, and with sowings, resowings, and cultivations of existences and re-existences. It gives attention to the prospects of growing an otherwise, a something else within the extant cracks. And it considers the ongoing decolonizing work of fissuring and cracking. In so doing, it weaves relation with the chapters that come before while, at the same time, offering reflections on how concrete, situated, and embodied subjects are planting life where there is death; making seedbeds of decolonial doing, thinking, and existing; practicing the sowing; and reconstituting the sense, hope, and possibility of life.

A short epilogue added in June 2022 as notes to readers shares some of the commotion lived as I finished the book's final review, opening reflections on the realities of these times, on present-past intertwinements, on territorial interconnections, and on relations of corporalities, subjectivities, and struggles for dignity and life in the lands that I, you, and we call home.

I invite the reader not only to peruse the pages that follow but also to engage with the text, to make it your own, adding your cries, questions, walking paths, traversings, undoings, plantings, and, above all, stories. As Kumar reminds us, *"The world needs other stories."* But it also needs more people with hammers, more folks from different territories of the globe willing to assume and become part of the collective work and praxis of cracking coloniality's wall, opening, widening, and connecting the fractures, fissures, and cracks, which are the re-existences rising up and living on.

Cries and Cracks

1

> Who decides who's dangerous enough to die?
> ... Survival has always been a covert operation ...
> The death of a people has never gone silent
> in the chamber of life ...
> ... We are seeds cracking concrete,
> for liberation is the only air we can breathe ...
> ... Who decides who's dangerous enough to die?
> —ALIXA GARCÍA AND NAIMA PENNIMAN, *Climbing Poe Tree*

Who decides who's dangerous enough to die?[1] Is this question not at the crux of existence, of indignation and dignified fury, and of life-based struggle in these current times?

The radical poetic query of Alixa García and Naima Penniman in their powerful spoken-sung song seems to say it all. Here, as they have done over the past two decades in their spoken word, hip-hop, multimedia theater, and popular education project Climbing Poe Tree, García and Penniman name reality, harness "creativity as the antidote to destruction,"[2] and give force and credence to the cries and cracks that enable us to re-exist and not just survive.

My "us" here does not presume a sameness of struggle, nor an equivalence of histories, herstories, theirstories, and lived conditions, especially when some—and not others—beget presumptions of danger and related likelihoods of death. While the nexus of systemic racism, systemic heteropatriarchy, systemic white supremacy, and systemic economic greed (i.e., capitalism) gives cause to the presumptions and likelihoods, it also gives reason to the covert operation of and for life. My "us" in this sense opens toward the multivocality of cries, the multiplicity of struggles, and the plurality of crack-making and crack makers who make (re)existence their aim and ground against the violence, dispossession, war, death, and de-existence of these present times.

I recall María Lugones's emphasis on the I → we, on the movement between the solitary and collectively social as resistance's two sides. For Lugones, this movement draws from a sense of intentionality, active subjectivity, and "tense inside/outside/in-between conversations, interactions that take in and also disrupt, dismantle, dominant sense."[3] It is about the constant asking of how to politically move with others, "without falling into a politics of the same, a politics that values or assumes sameness or homogeneity; without mythologizing place; attempting to stand in the cracks and intersections of multiple histories of domination and resistances to dominations."[4]

This chapter is about these cracks, and it is about the cries, mine in political movement and relation with others. It takes root in the spaces, places, and contexts in which I live, struggle, think, ask, and walk, in the moving to resist the present-day projects and practices of violence-dispossession-war-death all intertwined—including, as I will explain, the targeted de-existence that in 2020 began to take on new form—and in the moving to create and construct re-existence within, from, and making cracks.

I begin with the indignation and the dignified fury that spawns the cries.

Indignant Cries
and Dignified Fury

"I think, then they disappear me," says the graffiti on the wall. The words first appeared on Mexican building and Facebook walls in late September 2014. Quickly they crossed territories and borders. The graffiti was—and is—a cry; a cry against the forced disappearance of the forty-three students from the Ayotzinapa teacher-training school, and a cry for freedom and life where daring to think means disappearance and death. "Who decides who's dangerous enough to die?" García and Penniman's spoken-sung query-cry continues to resound in my mind.

It was September 26, 2014. Municipal police and other forces of Mexico's narcostate brutally attacked three buses of students from the Ayotzinapa Rural Teacher-Training School in the southwestern Mexico town of Iguala.

Three students were killed, eight were wounded, and forty-three were made to disappear.

A year later, and in commemoration (against oblivion) of the first-year anniversary of the Ayotzinapa massacre and disappearance, José Elizondo and Karla Ávila wrote the following words:

> When thinking to question, to claim, to build, becomes a threat to the *guardians of silence*. When the bullets go through the insurgents' throats by right. At this moment, "I think, then they disappear me." At that moment the jailers of thought shoot with live ammunition. And the words become the last breath of those who only know how to cry FREEDOM. Because no longer "I think then I am." Because reason does not find reasons to so much madness. Because I no longer "think then I exist." Because thinking has become a revolutionary act. Because thinking has become a threat to the monitors of the single thought. And for that, they disappear me. And because of that, they disappear us.[5]

In the days and weeks following the Ayotzinapa attack, the collectively anonymous phrase "I think, then they disappear me" organized social protests; it was the cry that refused to be silenced. The British trip-hop band Massive Attack projected it on a huge screen at its mammoth concert in Mexico City's Condesa Park the week following the occurrence. The phrase-as-cry traveled. At my university in Quito, Ecuador, we put it on the walls in a "happening" of protest, memory, and support for the forty-three disappeared, for those killed, and for those who managed to survive.

The phrase certainly does not need interpretation. However, its lived significance was made clear in the account of Omar, one of the survivors. Through a telephone connection with those of us gathered at the Quito event, he recounted in detail the story of horror that began on the night of September 26 and continued into the early hours of the following day. As Omar made clear, it was not a random attack but rather a conscious assault on the school of rebellion, resistance, and critical thought that is the Ayotzinapa school of rural teacher education.

Ayotzinapa was founded in 1926 by the teacher Raúl Isidro Burgos as part of a state project for massive public rural education, a project that quickly became a tool for social transformation. In Mexico, probably more than anywhere else in Latin America, rural teacher schools have been—and continue to be—a place for thinking, rethinking, and giving action from below to education and existence understood as necessarily intertwined. From its outset, Ayotzinapa was a seedbed for revolutionary thought, social consciousness, and community-based struggle in this peasant region, one of the poorest in the southwestern state of Guerrero. Genaro Vázquez and Lucio Cabañas, among other well-known revolutionary teachers and guerilla fighters, studied at Ayotzinapa.

In recent times, Ayotzinapa students have played crucial roles in the struggles against neoliberal education reform, educational commodification, and the alarming levels of institutional violence and repression in Guerrero. Moreover, in their teacher-training school and well beyond, most especially in communities and community-based education, these militants walk an educational praxis that challenges the system and its dominant institutional aims and frames. Education here is about existence and re-existence; it is about sowing dignity and life in these times of violence-dispossession-war-death. And this is precisely the reason for the disappearance, elimination, and extermination.

While many throughout the region dared to cry out in response, public educational institutions in Mexico, including and most especially universities, were complicit in their policies and practices of silence and silencing. In fact, I experienced this myself several weeks after the incident in an event organized by a large "autonomous" university in celebration of Enrique Dussel's eightieth birthday and his legacy of critical-political thought. Ayotzinapa was absent in the opening remarks and first presentations; no one mentioned the horror or the political-epistemic-existential significance of what had just recently occurred. When it was my turn to speak, I publicly expressed my fury and indignation at the silence. A university authority sitting by my side whispered in my ear that we were not to speak about this incident here. I refused to be hushed. A group in the audience left the auditorium. Others stood and applauded. As I came to learn, my refusal of silence had lived consequences. In the days following, I was targeted outside the university. The message was made crystal clear: be silent or suffer the consequences. All of this together—the Dussel event and that which transpired afterward—marked a public "coming out" of my own *gritos*, or cries. In the years hence, they have only become louder and stronger.

I now write crying out. Crying out I write. I can't write, speak, or think otherwise. Those that know me can confirm that I hardly ever raise my voice. My way of expressing feelings of frustration, indignation, anger, pain, and horror is other. However, I can no longer contain this screech and scream that are born deep inside and that come out through the pores and orifices of my body like a rumble. My organs as a whole, led by my heart and soul, yell NO! They cry out for dignity, and they cry out for existence and life.

My cry is both product and reflection of an accumulation of experiences and of sentiments felt and lived. Ayotzinapa and this "autonomous" university only hastened their overflow. Yet the fact that now, in 2022, the whereabouts of the forty-three are still unknown and their remains still unfound gives further credence to the cries that, of course, are not just mine. They are the refusal of many throughout the world to be silenced.

It was in the decades of the 1970s and 1980s that my cries began to take form. This was in the United States, as I detail in chapter 2, most especially in contexts of social struggle with other women militants, with social movements, and with racialized and ethnicized communities. In the mid-1990s they extended to the situated context of Ecuador, my place of labor and life since then. Here, in this small Andean nation, the cries have taken on multiple dimensions, some of which I could not have previously imagined.

One of the dimensions has been with respect to state. While the focus of much of my militancy in the United States was related to state—against state and federal government policies of discrimination and for social justice and racial, gender, cultural, and linguistic rights—state per se never aroused deep emotions, nor did it engender much hope. By the mid-1970s, the revolutionary prospect and hope that many of us in the United States held in prior years—and aimed at the dismantling and transformation of the US nation-state—had already waned.[6] Cuba, of course, remained a central referent. However, since I did not experience the revolution or the processes of state remaking firsthand, they remained only as referents celebrated and contemplated from afar.

The so-called Left turn of the first decade of the twenty-first century in South America opened other lived horizons. With the shared project of twenty-first-century socialism, the call for state refounding, and subsequent new radical constitutions as base and support, Ecuador, Bolivia, and Venezuela marked new and hopeful paths. It seemed as if "revolution" was in the making in an amalgam of the state and the people. Not only was I close to what was occurring, but in Ecuador I was actively involved as an invited adviser to the citizen-based Constitutional Assembly (2007–8), specifically in the conceptualization of a plurinational and intercultural state, and the concretion of Afro and Indigenous collective rights. All of this was part of what Ecuador's then-president Rafael Correa began to publicly refer to as the "Citizens' Revolution."

While the participatory processes of the Constitutional Assembly afforded important learnings, the Citizens' Revolution had, as I was to later witness, little of revolution in the critical sense. It was a top-down-conceived and top-down-run project. With the goal of ending poverty and moving Ecuador toward modernization and material prosperity, the "revolution" advanced what it referred to in later years as a new model of state-controlled capitalism. China replaced the United States as principal financial partner, and a neoextractivist economy became the motor for economic advancement.

Despite the Constitution's recognition of "Nature's rights"—the first constitution in the world to make Nature with a capital *N*, understood as Pachamama, Mother Nature, or Mother Earth, the subject of rights—the destruction, pillage, and dispossession of Nature became the norm during Correa's ten-year reign. Oil, large-scale mining, hydroelectric plants, and massive palm-oil cultivation, among other extractive industries, along with other extractivisms—including the extraction and marketing of ancestral knowledges—became the modus operandi of the destruction, pillage, and dispossession. With this also came the ascent of an authoritarian statism and patriarchal-paternal-colonial logic of governance, power, and control. Here the silencing of political critique; the attack on feminisms, sexual diversity, and the so-called ideology of gender; the criminalization of protest; and the labeling and incarceration of Indigenous leaders as "terrorists of the state" wove in and out with a myriad of other violences at once territorial, sociopolitical, epistemic, racialized, ethnicized, and gendered. Among other political acts, Ecuador's historical legacy of Indigenous-conceived and Indigenous-run bilingual education was dismantled, and over ten thousand community-based schools were closed. Huge "millennial schools" were constructed far from the communities themselves, and without public transportation. Here, the policy of intercultural and linguistic integration—supported by a standardized curriculum in Spanish only—was designed to contribute to the breakup of what in the 1990s and early years of the 2000s had been the strongest Indigenous movement and force in Abya Yala or the Americas.

For me, these years of Ecuador's so-called progressive state were particularly crucial. They gave a very different lived context and sense to my cries. In contrast to the past, my cries were now not just against institutions, government, or the system as such. Instead, they were in relation and response to a lived reality that traversed much of daily life, fractured the transformational hope posited in governments termed "Left," and extended to my sphere of labor and life in the university.

Some years back I began to speak and write about the growing "hurt, pain, and smell" in Latin American universities. They smell, I argued, for their growing complicities with capitalism: a capitalism re-realized in the name of modernization and effectuated, in great part, through geoepistemic and sociocultural extractivisms, in addition to the extractivisms of both Nature and nature, the latter understood, from the western point of view, as I describe in chapter 3, as natural resources to be dominated and controlled by man. And they cause hurt and pain "for their dehumanizing character and practice that both—universities and governments—perpetuate in their interior, including in their modernizing politics, practices, and propositions. Such inclination distances them from the lived social and cultural existence and reality of the vast majorities. At the same time, it demands discipline in face of the necessities and interests of the market and the (trans)national state, thus encouraging old and new forms of dehumanization and dehumanity." They also hurt for what the Venezuelan thinker Edgardo Lander calls their "intellectual somnambulism," part of what the Argentinian scholar María Eugenia Borsani refers to—in the dialogue that she and I have sustained—as "the silence that becomes accomplice, the apathy and indifference placidly installed, since awhile back, in the universities and the humanities." All this is part of what I call "dehumanity and dehumanities."[7]

During Correa's government, the reform of higher education policy and law put universities at the beck and call of the state, required to respond not only to the state's scientific and technological needs and demands but also to the state's politics of vigilance, discipline, and control. For Arturo Villavicencio, former head of the state office of higher education, this meant "the creation of a university fragmented in absurd typologies, with limited and hierarchical academic spaces" and models that discredit national education while reifying that of the first world and its supposedly "universal" knowledge. An academic capitalism-colonialism is at play, argued Villavicencio, that denies the history and experience of the Ecuadorian university, as well as the very notion of university itself as a public space for debate, discussion, analysis, and criticism.[8] While this trend has been present for quite a while in Europe and the United States, it is much more recent in Latin America.

My university took a radical position in resisting this model and imposition. Yet, most often, the resistance was ruled from the top down, from a script of resistance that demanded confrontation in the manner of the old paternalist-patriarchal Left. Blind obedience and silenced consensus became both script and norm. My questions and questionings were multiple, as were my cries: Resist government actions to strengthen the university's internal regime of power? Resistance in exchange for what? Resistance from whom, for whom, and for what? The questions and cries—mine and of a small collective of faculty—were met with discipline, harassment, a wide genre of threats, and in my case even violence. Physical and verbal intimidations and the vandalizing of my car are only a few of many examples.

Resist not to destroy but to build, I said; that is, an ethical, critical, and dignified resistance *against* authoritarian regimes of control and power, and *for* conditions of existence otherwise. Before my eyes, the shared critical project that initially constructed this house of studies—my home-place of doing-thinking-teaching-acting during twenty-plus years of my life—began to crumble. My cries were profound, most especially because they were related to a space/place/project that I had fought for and believed in. Often, the cries remained stuck in my gut, vibrating in rebellion and defense;[9] vibrations that took a toll on my health and well-being.

The university and the politics of higher education, of course, are only part of a much larger despair. The collective hope born with the 2008 Ecuadorian constitution, deemed by some as the most radical in the world, turned into collective anguish. The wager placed in the State (with a capital letter), in the possibility of its intercultural and plurinational refounding (a wager also present in Bolivia's 2009 constitution), and in the imagining of a different social order of life, existence, and collective well-being with Mother Nature faded during the Correa years. The effective viability of large-scale social struggle also waned, this the result, in large part, of government efforts to capture and co-opt social movement leaders, divide and rupture organizations, fragment communities, and imprison all those who dissent. Of course, such state incidence is not simply national; it is part of the region-wide aim and strategy of the capitalist-extractivist-heteropatriarchal-modern/colonial system that endeavors to break the social weave and weaken and debilitate social struggle in order to exercise what the Zapatista Subcomandante Insurgente Galeano has called "destruction/depopulation and, simultaneously, reordering/reconstruction."[10]

Such strategy, effect, and action provoke, for many, anguish, fear, and despair. So too does the search for answers to the praxistic questions of what to do and, more critically, how to do it. That is, *how* to create, make, and walk processes and practices—pedagogies as essential methodologies, Paulo Freire would say—from the fissures or cracks of this matrix of power increasingly understood by many in this Abya Yala of the South as the systematic practice of violence-dispossession-war-death all intertwined. Before turning to the cracks, let me explain a bit more about this intertwinement, its manifestations and cries, the ways in which it marks new mutations, strategies, and configurations in the coloniality of power and, relatedly, opens toward a project of de-existence enabled by COVID-19.

VIOLENCE-DISPOSSESSION-WAR-DEATH

In 2008 Nelson Maldonado-Torres wrote about the "paradigm of war" and its deep connection "with the production of race and colonialism as well as the perpetuation, expansion, and transformation of patriarchy."[11] For Maldonado-Torres, this paradigm constructs particular ways to conceive humanity, knowledge, social relations, and the social order central to modern life and the modern world. "Violence and war ... are not contingent results of particular historical projects, but constitutive dimensions of dominant conceptions of civilization and civilizing processes," he argues, dimension-conceptions that do not just define but also advocate for the elimination of "the Others," those who disturb, threaten, and resist this "civilization."[12] Dispossession is part and parcel of these dimensions and processes. Recalled are the words of the Nishnaabeg intellectual Leanne Betasamosake Simpson: "The intention of the structure of colonialism is to dispossess."[13]

In Abya Yala South, or what many continue to refer to as Latin America— but certainly not here alone—the project of war and its practice have been strengthened in recent years, leading to what many Indigenous and Black communities experience and understand as the deeply woven relation of violence, dispossession, war, and death, all tied to the interests and avarice of capital and the project and logic it constructs, perpetuates, and maintains.[14] Vilma Almendra, Nasa-Misak activist-thinker and community-based leader from Colombia's Cauca region, reminds us that "with the installation of the Conquest, the warlords, as the merchants of the word, the sellers of life, the plunderers of the common goods and much more," began the processes and practices of submission, contempt, fragmentation, dispossession, violence, war, and death.[15] Such processes and practices continue today as part of the "strategies of the death project: submission with terror and war, submission with legislation of dispossession, submission with the recruitment and cooptation of social movements," Almendra says.[16] This in a country where despite the so-called peace accords signed in 2016 between the Colombian government and the Fuerzas Armadas Revolucionarias de Colombia (Revolutionary Armed Forces of Colombia), more than one thousand community-based leaders were assassinated between 2016 and 2020. In 2020 the assassinations averaged one a day, continuing without respite in 2021 and 2022.[17] Here what some have called "paramilitary capitalism" combines with the power and interest of drug lords, state-based and international mafia, and most especially the United States. For Almendra, all this accompanies "ideological submission in order to colonize the territory of the imagination ... so as to guarantee and legitimize the economic model of capitalism at the service of the transnationals."[18] In Manuel Rozental's words, "The only certainty today is death; life is just a possibility."[19] Submission, dispossession, death; how can we not cry out?

On March 3, 2016, shortly after I began this book, Berta Cáceres was assassinated. Cáceres, Lenca leader and founder in 1993—along with a dozen other women and men—of the Consejo Cívico de Organizaciones Populares e Indígenas de Honduras (Civic Council of Popular and Indigenous Organizations of Honduras), was a tireless fighter against transnational corporations and neoliberal extractive policies, and a defender of Mother Earth and life. Upon receiving the 2015 Goldman Environmental Prize, Cáceres affirmed that the armed repressive apparatus in Honduras protects the interests of transnational corporations linked to the powerful economic, political, and military sectors of the country. And she declared that neoliberal extractive policies have led to an increase in persecution, violence, repression, criminalization, dispossession, and forced displacement of communities.[20] Cáceres was victim of the same violence that she denounced, a violence that in the same week ended the life of four peasant leaders in Cauca, Colombia, and, less than two weeks later, Nelson García, another Honduran environmental activist from the civic council.

Cáceres, García, and the Cauca leaders are only a few of the many in a long list that continues to grow each day: the list of the eliminated in the project-war against existence and life, a project-war that marks the disposables for their gender, their sexuality, their condition of impoverishment and racialization; for their struggles in defense of their lands, rivers, forests, and dignity against the greed, destruction, exploitation, and interests of capital. This project-war is a component part of what the Zapatistas referred to in 2015 as the "capitalist hydra," with its continually regenerating heads.[21]

Many of us know someone on the list of those to be eliminated or someone "they" are about to add. I am thinking of the Peruvian peasant leader Máxima Acuña (2016 winner of the Goldman prize) in her ongoing fight against the Conga mega-mining project;[22] the Mapuche leader and community-based authority Relmu Ñamku in her struggles against Chevron and fracking in Patagonia, Argentina;[23] the Afro-Colombian activist and lawyer Francia Marquez (2018 winner of the Goldman prize) in her fight against gold mining and for ancestral rights as community leader and legal representative of the Communitarian Council of La Toma in Cauca;[24] and Alexa Leonor Mina and Mery Yein Mina, members of the Afro-Descendant Women's Mobilization for the Care of Life and Ancestral Territories, among many others. I am thinking of the assassination of Yolanda Maturana, defender of the environment against illegal mining, by hooded men in her home in Pueblo Rico, Risaralda, Colombia, on February 2, 2018;[25] the gunning down in a public Rio de Janeiro street on March 14, 2018, of Mariella Franco, Afro-Brazilian politician, human rights activist, lesbian, feminist, and self-identified child of the favela; and the assassination of the Nasa leader and Indigenous governor of Cauca, Cristina Bautista, on October 29, 2019. These are just a few names of the thousands threatened or killed since I began this book. To them we can add the long list of the African American men and women assassinated by police in the United States and elsewhere, a result of the systemic anti-Black racism that knows no bounds.

The violences are often unimaginable. This is the case of the special terror that hundreds of Black women continue to face in the territory-region of the Colombian Pacific, many already eliminated simply because they are women and carriers of the struggles of and for existence-life. I recall the specific case of Sandra Patricia Angulo, documented by the Afro-Colombian women's collective Red Mariposas de Alas Nuevas (Network of Butterflies with New Wings): "What they did to Sandra Patricia Angulo in Buenaventura, they did to us all. It hurts us to know that she defended her life until the end, and it hurts to know that she was hunted by five men, who united to degrade her, to make her suffer, according to them to punish her and give her a lesson; machos, macho killers, machos who take advantage of a woman alone whom they chase and hunt down. How long Buenaventura? Until when Colombia?"[26]

Particularly present is Mayra Sofía Medina Lozano, daughter of the Afro-Colombian decolonial feminist, former graduate student, and friend Betty Ruth Lozano. Sofía, whom I have known since she was a child, was gang-raped by members of the militant social organization of which she was part. In a ten-page public letter of denunciation written six years after the incident, she describes in detail what occurred, her continuing cries of fury and indignation, and her demands to the named assailants for reparation. Almost two years later, there is still no reparation or response. As Betty Ruth said in the October 2020 email that accompanied Sofía's public letter of denunciation, "The rape of women is part of the colonizing project that has been imposed as a 'culture' that holds the victim responsible and is materialized in a high number of women who are sexually assaulted in all social spheres and in places where we believe we are safe with our 'comrades in struggle' who end up being exonerated. We see them as our comrades in struggle while they see us as objects for the satisfaction of their desires."[27]

In an interview published in 2016, the public intellectual and Argentine scholar Rita Laura Segato referred to the "pedagogy of cruelty" growing throughout Latin America. Segato was specifically referring to the Guatemalan context (although it certainly does not end there) and to the case known as Sepur Zarco. Here agents of the state submitted a group of fifteen Mayan Queqchi women to sexual and domestic slavery over the course of six years in what was designated as a military barracks of "rest" after first disappearing their husbands because they aspired to the titles of their ancestral land. All this was during the same period in which Guatemala was engaged in so-called peace processes.[28] For Segato, the anthropological and gender-based expert in the case, the pedagogy of cruelty is an expression of the para-state sovereignty and control characteristic of the new, unconventional forms of war. Expressive cruelty is a strategy of reproduction of the system that is "particularly effective when applied to the body of women."[29]

This trial—historic for exposing a crime of gender as a crime of state—staged the operation of the pedagogy of cruelty on the body of women as the battlefield. The respective sentences of 240 and 120 years of imprisonment to the two responsible military officers are, without a doubt, important milestones, including for their emphasis on "the multiple forms of war that are deployed against women today, making their bodies the main territory of contention."[30] As Segato explains, "A very important aspect of the material, moral and community reparation that they [the women] claim, understood from their own perspective, is that the State, through this exemplary sentence, publicly declares and establishes their innocence, an indispensable condition for the community to reintegrate them and for reconstituting and healing the social weave." Moreover, "the most impressive thing was their great courage all this time, without being scared—for the enemy never ceased to be truculent—and without desisting."[31]

In conversation with Segato, I ask whether, besides the pedagogy of cruelty to which these women were subjected, they did not also exercise their own pedagogy of resistance-existence of and for life. With this question I am remembering the meaning that Paulo Freire gave to resistance-existence in his book *Pedagogy of Indignation*. The physical and cultural survival of the oppressed, Freire said, is not rooted in resignation or adaptation to the destructive wound of being or in the denial of life; rather it is based on rebellion against injustice—rebellion as self-affirmation—and on physical resistance to which we can add cultural resistance; that is, "the resistance that keeps us alive."[32] In thinking with Freire, Enrique Dussel emphasizes the "action-which-is-becoming-ethical-transformative consciousness: liberation," whose ethical, material process and objective is life.[33] For Freire, "Existence is life that knows itself as such,... life that questions itself, which makes itself vision, ... speaking of itself and of others around it, to pronounce the world, to unveil and to hide truths." This is the rebellion-resistance-existence that struggles to make the world ethical, says Freire, ethics as "a necessary consequence of producing human existence, or of extending life into existence."[34]

Recalled here is the re-existence of which Adolfo Albán Achinte speaks, as mentioned in the introduction to this book: the mechanisms and practices that seek to redefine and resignify life in conditions of self-determination and dignity.[35] Is all this not part of these women's pedagogy, their pedagogy of struggle—of outcries, screams, reverberations—of and for life?

Cries are not just reactions and expressions of fright. They are also mechanisms, strategies, and actions of struggle, rebellion, resistance, disobedience, insurgency, rupture, and transgression up against the imposed condition of silencing, the ongoing attempts to silence, and the accumulation of strategic silences. Cries gather silences and reclaim and recapture kidnapped voices along with denied subjectivities, with bodies, nature, and territories violated and dispossessed.[36] As Maldonado-Torres sustains, the cry of fright of the colonized is not simply an expression of horror and terror. More critically, it can be understood as a practice and intervention that is political, epistemological, ontological-existential in nature, and that points toward, conjures up, and guides decolonial attitudes as well as the idea and possibility of decolonization.[37] Is not the collective cry "I can't breathe," which rapidly spread after George Floyd's violent death under the knee-choke of a white police officer, an example of such practice and intervention?

My cry, of course, is not the same cry as that of the women and men who have lived and live the colonial wound and its entanglement of patterns of power that racialize, impoverish, violate, dehumanize, and deterritorialize. I do not cry out "for" them. They have their own cries. My cries are part of a related and relational fright. It is a cry against the capitalist-extractivist-heteropatriarchal-racist-modern/colonial system that is killing us, though not necessarily all in the same way. And it is a cry in the face of a despair that despairs, that deprives us of hope; a cry toward the what to do and the *hows*: how to think, act, fight, and scream out in and from my space-place and contexts, and with other contexts and collectivities that struggle from the "belows," margins, and fissures of the dominant system.

I must dislodge and move the cry, make it come out of my gut and chest, and feel, listen to, and walk its vibration. In this way, it stops being just mine. It begins to move with what the sound artist Mayra Estévez calls the "sonorities of resistance and of bond against the diminishment of life," and it begins to replicate.[38] "Leave the skin of [my] cry. Get into the world's skin through my pores," Glissant poignantly said.[39] All of this is part of a plural and diverse we—Lugones's I → we and what Glissant called the relational I—that, with and from the distinct contexts "of below," does not stop resounding. I can no longer—we can no longer—hold back the indignation and fury, and the horror and pain with respect to all these acts still present and near, in face of the project-war of death that is in full operation, and up against what the Zapatistas referred to in 2015 as the storm rapidly approaching, which now is here.[40]

In 2015 activists in Mexico spoke of 150,000 dead, 50,000 disappeared, and 50,000 kidnapped. How many today? In an event in early 2019, Lluvia Cervantes, a Mexican feminist-activist friend, said the official numbers in late 2018 were the same as the unofficial ones of 2015; however, not mentioned by the state are the more than 36,000 unidentified bodies that somehow appeared in 2018.[41]

I recall my five-city speaking tour in Mexico in November 2018, and especially the part in which I had to travel alone for a number of hours by bus. To make the time go by and to let my inner cries and fears out, I began to write notes. Here are some translated into English.

As I gaze through the bus window, I see the trailer trucks, one after the other, eating the landscape and the road. I remember what some friends told me a few days ago: that the trucks carry many "things," including the bodies of the disappeared, some still alive, and others not, piled up for hours, days, months, or years.

I recall their description about the refrigerated trucks that began to appear a few months ago in the neighborhoods of various cities; trucks that call out with speakers for people to come out of their homes to see if one of their disappeared is among the bodies piled up and frozen inside. Perhaps they are the same trucks that take the bodies to medical schools; corpses-specimens for universities of "excellence," for "scientific" study in what we continue to call "higher" education. Meanwhile, the television on the bus (just like the screens at the airport) projects advertising about the "magical tourism" promoted by the federal government of Peña Nieto. Visit these "magical" towns (read: Indigenous) and see the beauty of nature, say the voice and image on the screen; here the Indians can even give you a "cleansing" of the evils of urban tension and stress. (I can't help thinking that the "cleansing" of government and its evils would be a much better business!)

. . . It is November, and although AMLO (Andrés Manuel López Obrador) has not yet assumed the presidency, his projects are circulating in the media. One of them: the "Mayan train" is bound for southern Mexico, passing "inevitably," some say—and "conveniently," I say—through Zapatista territories. A train that would take tourists to enjoy nature and "pristine" beaches (not yet Cancunized), to consume the water that is almost nonexistent, and to "tour the misery" of the "Mayan" peoples. Even the name bothers, as the Zapatista Subcomandante Moisés argues; it imposes their (i.e., the government's) naming as if it were ours while, at the same time, homogenizing Mayan-speaking peoples: Tsotsil, Tzeltal, Tojolabal, Chol, Mam. Of course, it is not surprising that the Mayan train project does not have a prior, free, and informed consent of the peoples as required by the Constitution. What are these constitutions for, anyway? I can't think of a country in the region in which the constitutions (no matter how progressive they seem) have really defended the rights of ancestral peoples.

Meantime, the trailer trucks keep passing by the window. I don't recall ever seeing so many trucks, none with a company name. I am traveling now to Querétaro from Aguascalientes, the place where the International Philosophy Congress was held, this time and for the first time with a visible participation of feminist philosopher-thinkers. There they told me that before I arrived, a series of graffiti-like messages appeared in strategic places of the event and its university headquarters: calling to "kill the Feminazis." How much gender violence today in academia, including in the academic fields of the so-called humanities and social and human sciences? In the academia I know, as in society in general, there is an almost total impunity that interweaves with oblivion, silence, and I don't-care-ism. I suspect it is happening in most of the world. The humanities serve—consciously or not—as perpetuators of the growing dehumanities of territorialized, racialized, feminized, gendered, epistemic violence; lest we forget the networks of trafficking, commercialization, and sexual exploitation, the elimination of social leaders and of urban peripheral youths.

The bus is approaching Querétaro and I see the "Beast" pass by, the colloquial name of the train that continues to take thousands of Mexicans and Central Americans to the North every day. This is the journey to the "still-promised land," to the border, or "nonborder," as many activists have begun to call it; a journey, promise, and borderland that replicates and repeats inhumanity, dehumanities, and dehumanizations. I remember what I saw in Mexico City a few days ago: the migrant caravan of Hondurans and other Central Americans. I heard the screams of fear and terror after more than one hundred people—including children and elderly—were disappeared and then made to reappear a few days later, climbing out of trailer trucks of terror, just like the ones I see from this bus. I can't help feeling the horror.

My cries well up inside. I think of the multiple violences experienced and the forms, practices, and projects of dispossession embodied and reflected in the bodies forced to flee: Mexico, Honduras, Guatemala, and also Nicaragua, where twenty-six thousand people, most of them women, were forced to flee just between April and October 2018. I think of the pedagogies of cruelty, including on the northern side of the border/nonborder, where immigrant children are held in cages. And I think of the violences lived in this war of death that characterizes the everyday life of so many throughout the Americas and the world; a war that terrorizes, angers, frightens, and silences.

As the bus parks at the station, the Mexican trailer trucks of terror continue to move around in my head. I have to stop these notes for now, yet I know the musings on the complexity of this well-equipped war will not end when I get off the bus; with its intricate collection of devices, weapons, tools, and actors that—although they may change face, strategy, and national territory—maintain similar purposes and objectives, the war made project has come to radically alter how I (and of course the vast majority) think about and struggle for existence and life.

Now, and as I go back to these notes, I am reminded of how the Zapatista Subcomandante Insurgente Galeano explains the global character of this war.

The war also comes in the shields and clubs of the different policemen in the evictions; in Israeli missiles that fall on Palestinian schools, hospitals, and civilian neighborhoods; in the media campaigns that precede invasions and then justify them; in the patriarchal violence that invades the most intimate corners; in the heterosexual intolerance that stigmatizes difference; in religious fanaticism; in the modern markets of live human flesh and its organs; in the chemical invasion of fields and countryside; in the contents of the media; in organized and disorganized crime; in forced disappearances; in government impositions; in the pillage and dispossession disguised as "progress." In sum: in the destruction of nature and humanity.[42]

The extreme silences of individualism and indifference and the ruptures of community, organizational, and collective weaves and of the fabric of political-social struggle are just some of the alterations that characterize the current moments, the result and effect of a hegemony of ideology and thought that invades all spheres of existence. It is no coincidence that women are a central target of the attack, particularly if we consider that women are today leading many of the struggles against this violence-dispossession-death-war and the capitalist-heteropatriarchal-modern/colonial system (see chapter 3).

María Lugones argued in 2012 that the contemporary violence against women and the growing levels of feminicide have to do with "the total devaluation of work and of the bodies that previously produced surplus value and now are worthless."[43] *Femicide* is the term usually used to refer to the deaths of women by men who kill them because they are women, while *feminicide* refers to all the violence committed against women and their self-determination, including state violence resulting from omission and negligence.[44] In recent years, feminicides-femicides and violence against women throughout the world have significantly grown. In 2018, the BBC reported an average of 137 femicides a day in the world.[45] Depending on the country, it is estimated that between 60 percent and 90 percent of homicides of women are femicides. In 2019 South Africa declared femicide a national crisis when nearly three thousand women were murdered between 2018 and 2019.[46] Yet few countries in the world—including the United States and European countries—use the words *femicide* and *feminicide* in any legal capacity. Latin America is the region with the most laws, and with some of the highest rates.[47]

I refer to those women who die practically every four days in Peru, every three days in Bolivia, every fifty hours in Ecuador, every thirty-one hours in Argentina, 54 women per month in Honduras, 4 a day in Colombia, 10–12 a day in Mexico (with a 145 percent jump in cases between 2015 and 2019), and 15 a day in Brazil (5,500 per year, of which more than 60 percent are Afrodescendant women, with Brazil being the fifth-highest country of femicide-feminicide in the world).[48] Those are some of the known figures. The reality is much worse, with an over 100 percent growth in 2020 in many Latin American nations.[49] Equally alarming is the fact that an estimated 90 percent of the crimes remain in impunity.

While feminicide-femicide is often thought of as violence relegated to peripheries; to border cities like Ciudad Juárez, Mexico; or to endemic regions like Latin America or Africa, it is also an ever-present and growing crisis elsewhere. In 2017 the US-based Violence Policy Center reported close to two thousand women killed by men in the United States. The Women Count USA: Femicide Accountability Project reported a similar number in 2018, the majority killed by current or former partners. Women under twenty-nine years of age and women of color are the majority of victims, with Black, Native American, and transwomen the most affected.[50]

Undoubtedly, feminicide-femicide is a tool of capitalism, heteropatriarchy, and coloniality intertwined and a result of the imbroglio of violence-dispossession-war-death. Throughout the world today, women in general, and especially young women, peasant women, and Native and African-descended women, are considered disposable. They are targets of elimination, subordination, capture, silencing, exile, and deterritorialization before the bulldozer-excavator matrix of power.[51]

While Latin America is said to be, after Africa, the region with the highest level of feminicide and violence against women in the world, it is also the region with one of the greatest levels of attack on so-called gender ideology, the term used by evangelicals and conservatives in government and the Catholic Church to label feminisms and the promotion of gender and sexual diversity. In a 2018 opinion piece in the *New York Times* Spanish edition focused on the new marriage between evangelicals and conservatives in Latin America, Javier Corrales explained in clear terms the perverse logic at work: "When experts argue that sexual diversity is real and gender identity is a construct, evangelical and Catholic clergy say that it is not about something scientific, but about an ideology. Evangelicals like to emphasize the word 'ideology' because it gives them the right, they argue, to protect themselves—and especially their children—from exposure to those ideas," Corrales says. "The gender ideology allows them to cover up their homophobia with a call to protect minors. The political beauty of 'gender ideology' is that it has given the clergy a way of rethinking their religious position in lay terms: as parental rights. In Latin America, the new Christian motto is: 'With my children, do not get involved.' It is one of the results of this collaboration between evangelicals and Catholics."[52]

In the last decade, laws have prohibited the discussion of gender issues and sexuality in education systems in Brazil, Panama, Paraguay, and Peru, and campaigns have been present in Ecuador, Colombia, Chile, Argentina, Mexico, Costa Rica, and the Dominican Republic, to mention only some countries.[53] In Colombia, campaigns linked "gender ideology" with the peace accords between the government and the Revolutionary Armed Forces of Colombia; the argument is that these accords give emphasis to "gender ideology," including feminist rights and the rights of the LGBT community, and therefore should not be supported. In Ecuador, former "progressive" president Rafael Correa made the elimination of gender ideology in schools and universities one of the aims of his "Citizens' Revolution."[54] As the campaigns against gender and sexual diversities increase, so too do the numbers of cases of sexual abuse of children. In 2017, the same year that Peru passed its law against gender ideology, there were twenty-five thousand reported cases of sexual abuse against children, many in schools.[55]

Latin America is by no means alone. Anti–gender educational policies are in place globally. In the United States, Alabama, Louisiana, Mississippi, Oklahoma, and Texas maintain what are popularly referred to as "no promo homo laws" that include both anti-LGBT and anti–gender ideology curricular legislation and controls.[56] Such policies are also present across Europe, where, according to some, religious politics increasingly intersect with rising populism and nationalistic anxieties.[57] Feminist theorists Andrea Peto and Agniezka Graef maintain that anti–gender ideology policies are particularly intense in Eastern Europe, where "the 'gender ideology' code is a vast void, a big basket filled with multiple issues—such as education on gender and sexuality, same-sex marriage, feminism and trans rights. This amalgam is very adaptable, which permits—in different contexts or at different times—any one of these issues to be the target of attacks."[58]

Yet, as Piro Rexhepi poignantly argues, what is at play is ever more complex if one considers how the debates about gender and LGBT rights bring to the fore a series of simple opposites of not just patriarchy/gender equality but also secular/religious, modern/traditional, and East/West. To these we can add the binary white/of color. All these binaries are in operation in the debates of gender and sexual diversity rights in Eastern Europe, inextricably tied, as Rexhepi explains, to the European Union's eastern enlargement processes taking place. It is in this sense that "decolonizing queer critique in Europe requires not only merging the post-colonial with the post-socialist critique of Europeanization, but also exposing how Islamophobia figures in main-stream queer rights debates in the 'center' as well as in the 'periphery' of Europe." Here "queer communities are normalized, depoliticized and co-opted into hegemonic neoliberal structures through the exclusion of other identitarian dimensions, such as class, race, and religion," Rexhepi says, enabling and perpetuating the making and marking of Muslims as Europe's others.[59] In this logic, *queer Muslims* is a misnomer.

Of course, this use of gender and LGBT rights as a multiculturalist strategy of nationalist inclusion/exclusion is not limited to Europe. The United States' promotion of "homonationalism" to mark a distinction between US-national lesbians and gays (most especially those who are white) and racialized "others" and Israel's promotion of gender and LGBT rights as what Sarah Schulman refers to as a "deliberate strategy to conceal the continuing violations of Palestinians" are clear examples.[60] Certainly we can ask the question of how such laws and rights—in their conceptualization, legislation, and application in most if not all of the world—benefit some over others, all too often ignoring and maintaining systemic racism and the complex, interlaced forms of systemic domination and oppression that for many are constitutive of everyday life.

In this sense, pro–gender diversity laws and anti–gender ideology policies seem to have something in common: both serve state interests, mark criteria and discourses of inclusion and citizenship, and enable—whether intentionally or not—the violences of modernity/coloniality. While secularism (understood from the perspectives of modernity and the West) accompanies the first, Christianity—that is, traditional (white, western) Christian values—marks the second, including its aim to intervene in the secular realm of laws and state. In Europe and increasingly in the United States, Islam is considered a social-political-racialized-religious threat to both. At play, without a doubt, are differing (but related) visions and projects of recivilization and progress that further reify and hegemonize the West and its power to globally define what lives and whose lives matter.[61]

Brought to mind is the rise in recent years of new alliances between evangelicals, the conservative arm of the Catholic Church, and ultrarightist political parties, an alliance of the Bible and cross, of capitalism, and of white governance, supremacy, and armed violence. In the Americas, Jair Bolsonaro in Brazil is a particularly visible case in point. The 2017 reelection of Sebastian Piñera in Chile (with four evangelical pastors as his campaign advisers) is another case in point, along with the campaign declarations of Colombia's Iván Duque in 2018 that he would uphold and promote Judeo-Christian thought; Duque's presidential win was greatly aided by the approximately one million votes he received from Colombian evangelical parties. To this we can add the US-backed coup in Bolivia that ousted Evo Morales in October 2019 and installed the evangelical fundamentalist Jeanine Áñez as president as she held a Bible over her head. All have worked to fuel not just heteropatriarchy but also systemic racism, land grabbing, takeover and plundering, and state-sponsored violence-dispossession-war-death. Let us not forget the presence of such alliances in Donald Trump's first campaign and election, most specifically in the persona of Vice President Mike Pence,[62] and the explicit visibility of the alliances in the 2020 campaign, where the pact among the Bible, guns, and white governance was proudly and unabashedly put on show, including after Joe Biden's win, and in direct voiced opposition to the cries and movement Black Lives Matter.

However, the evangelical partnerships and alliances are not only with the Right. Colombia's front-runner for the 2022 presidential elections, the progressive Gustavo Petro, has revealed evangelical alliances.[63] Such alliances, as I will mention later, also exist in Venezuela with Nicolás Maduro and Mexico with López Obrador. As evangelical communities and political parties increase in numbers, what are we to expect in terms of politics in coming years?

How are we to read these times, I asked in early 2019 as my cries became more frenetic, and what do they suggest about the mutations and changing configurations and strategies of the colonial matrix of power? While I knew then that the intertwinement of violence-dispossession-war-death was real, I sensed the need to more specifically name the mutations and reconfigurations that I was witnessing and experiencing in daily life. The Zapatistas' call in 2015 for critical analysis and thought with respect to the capitalist hydra and its capacity of regeneration—analysis and thought crucial for the praxis of struggle and resistance—reverberated in my head. Along with it was Aníbal Quijano's argument that the coloniality of power is not static but instead dynamic in project and nature.

―――――――

COLONIALITY'S MUTATIONS, CHANGING STRATEGIES, AND (RE)CONFIGURATIONS

In May 2019, and as the first anniversary of Quijano's passing approached, I decided to write him a letter.[64] I began by sharing my belief—a belief that I suspected he shared—that the coloniality of power is not the same today as it was when he first began to describe it more than thirty years ago. Also not the same are the forms of domination, control, silencing, destruction, exploitation, repression, discrimination, violence, dispossession, and elimination. I began the letter from a question-suspicion: *If, as you forcefully argued, Aníbal, what we understand as coloniality took shape in what we now know as "Latin" America, becoming a model and matrix of global power, are we not facing once again, I ask, the centrality of this region in forging an even more complex matrix, in which the intricate entanglement of racism, global capitalism, heteropatriarchy, Christianity, and modernity/coloniality is taking on new extremes and forms of inhumanity and dehumanity?*

Latin America seems to be the eye of the storm, I said, the region and place where the terms, strategies, practices, and pedagogies of violence-dispossession-war-death are being tested and refined, and where the multiple heads of the hydra are acquiring an indestructible, mutant, and indistinct force. I thus proceeded to sketch some of the new strategies, configurations, and mutations that I considered as central in 2019. I share them here as I wrote them in the letter:

1 *The denationalization of the nation-state. In a paper presented in 1991 entitled "Will Latin America Survive?," you predicted, Aníbal, the denationalization of nation-states as part of the global trend of capitalism, population reclassification, and the recrudescence of the coloniality of power. You warned about the social and political conflicts that could come along with it, without naming its substance or content.*

Today, almost thirty years later, the denationalization you spoke of has already occurred. José Ángel Quintero Weir, Anuu-Wayuu intellectual from Venezuela, says it clearly: "The nation-state has died, and we did not kill it."[65] *Today it is in the throes of death decreed by the large corporations and the new stage of capital accumulation. Thus, we can speak of the corporate state, or the state association or state corporation, whose institutions work for the benefit not of "society" (another concept-reality that you mentioned in this same text) but of big capital and the income of the governments (of both "Right" and "Left") that hold them. If there is no Nation (of course we can ask if there once was), and if the national state is increasingly a fiction, how to analyze and what to do against the patterns of State, government, and authority? I would love to hear your thoughts on this, my Aníbal.*

2 *The new configurations of the military-police apparatus. Here I am referring to the so-called public security or citizen security designed to advance and protect the interests of the corporate state, dissolving the distinctions between what is legal and not legal, and facilitating the institutional framework and institutionalization of dispossession and the practices of violence-war-death. The federal-military intervention of Rio de Janeiro and the militarized cities and communities in Colombia (Cali, Buenaventura, Cauca, where racialized and feminized violence and death only increase) are examples. Another is the new configuration of public security-militarization in Mexico, under the "progressive" government of López Obrador.*

3 *The growing political-religious-heteropatriarchal alliance. As we well know, my dear Aníbal, there is a long history of political-religious alliances in Latin America, including the partnerships of Nelson Rockefeller, the Summer Institute of Linguistics, and the CIA (1920–60),*[66] *the targeted actions in the 1980s against liberation theology, and those in the 1990s against sexual and reproductive rights. However, the current alliance is somewhat different. The goal: to intervene (as a shared force) in secular law but also in "national" governments, spe-*

cifically in the reconfiguration of the state as an association-alliance of global "moral" interest (read: antifeminist). Brazil's Bolsonaro regime, the Duque-Uribe duo in Colombia, Piñera in Chile, Morales in Guatemala, the base of evangelical support for López Obrador in Mexico, and the active participation of churches and evangelical leaders in the current conflict in Venezuela (with the Congress of Christian Movements for Peace and its seventeen thousand churches in support of Maduro, and the powerful Evangelical Council of Venezuela in support of Guaidó, a council with clear international economic and political links). At the same time that this alliance is consolidated in the region, feminicides and transcides have reached horrific levels.

4 *New extractivist economies, including of knowledge.* For you, dear Aníbal, knowledge has always been a central axis of the coloniality of power. For this reason, I dare to ask how you would see today the new centrality of knowledge as a productive matrix and an economic-cultural organizer of society. I am referring to the "cities of knowledge" (based on the model of the Songdo City of Knowledge in South Korea) where, as is the case of Yachay in Ecuador and Pachuco in Mexico (both built on expropriated ancestral lands), extractive industries and education meld in benefit of the (corporate) state. Here, high-quality universities, research centers, and institutions jointly promote a culture and economy of knowledge through a focus on the "life sciences"; that is, technologies related to pharmaceutical and bio-drug industries, and biodiversity and genetic resources, with attention as well to the nanosciences, energy and petrochemicals, and hydrocarbons. Is it of any doubt that extractivism and knowledge are key battlefields of the coloniality of power?

5 *Dehumanities and UNIversities.* I believe that for most of us, including you, Aníbal, the role of higher education in advancing the present order-disorder is clear. Today UNIversities, from Mexico to Argentina, are complicit in the institutionalization of a global model that, under the pretexts and slogans of excellence and innovation, commercializes knowledge and education in ways fundamental for this global project. With the corporatization, transnationalization, and dehumanization of public higher education come new complicities with the project of violence-dispossession-war-death. The examples are many; participation in research projects of genetic bioprospecting and the financing of public universities with funds from extractivist industries are just two.

Faced with all these realities, the social and human sciences are shortsighted and silent. Some say that their own survival consists of keeping their gaze inside, within themselves, distancing themselves from social reality, from the demands *of real people who fight against war and for life, by the demands of humanity against inhumanity and dehumanity. Our colleague María Eugenia Borsani has called this part of the growing presence of dehumanized, dehydrated human and social sciences, on their way to their own death.*[67]

In fact, the death of humanistic and social careers has already been announced. The most recent case is Brazil, where the government announced in April 2019 the cessation of educational investment in the social and human sciences, seeking its elimination due to its lack of utility. Of course, that goes hand in hand with the "cleansing" campaigns of what the Bolsonaro administration refers to as communists, gays, Blacks, Indians, vagrants, and women whores, a campaign that reestablishes "traditional universal values."

The installation in Latin America of the "Global University"—often with this name—is one more manifestation of strategies, mutations, and configurations. I am not referring only to the productive trend that began a few years ago, based on global standards of student, administrative, and teacher evaluation and productivity, but to a new model and institution linked to the evangelical political-financial power and its alliances, centered on "universal" values and a utilitarian curriculum functional to the global, productive, technical, technological, and professionalizing order-disorder, and often online to avoid the "problem" of human relational contact. Is this not one more example of the war-project already on the way to recolonize humanity?

Finally, there is one more strategy-configuration-mutation to mention:

6 *Total dispossession. That is, in the words of José Ángel Quintero Weir, the last dispossession after the storm, the dispossession of everyone from below: Indigenous people, campesinos or peasants, Black communities, local cultures, the urban poor, and many, many more, all those outside the power of corporate states and governments, and their politics and economics, all of us who are struggling for life in the face of growing hopelessness, inhumanity, and dehumanity.*

In October 2019, several months after my letter to Aníbal, all that I mentioned in it passed from the sphere of suspicion to palpable truth. It began in Ecuador in the first weeks of what is now popularly referred to as "Rebellious October." From the mountainsides, Amazonian forest, and Pacific coast, tens of thousands of Indigenous people began to arrive to the capital city of Quito, responding to the national Indigenous organization's call for mobilization against neoliberal government policy. In Quito, tens of thousands more from government-opposed social sectors, organizations, and movements joined the action in what became the largest Indigenous-led uprising in the history of this country. In what follows, I share my notes written several weeks after.

ON THE OCTOBER AWAKENING(S) AND THE CONDOR

These notes, written in November 2019, began as a need—my need—to reflect on the two-week peoples' rebellion and protest in Ecuador, a rebellion-protest that I lived and that for months after continued to trouble my body, mind, spirit, and soul. Different from many of the analyses circulating in the "critical" intellectual world, these notes are not intended to impose a singular interpretation, assume an authoritative voice, simplify the occurrences, or make the events, mobilizations, and movements the object of study. They are notes written from my cries and felt-thought, and they are organized into three parts.

I *A month has gone by since Ecuador's "October Awakening." I am referring to the "awakening" of massive social protest in what was probably the largest Indigenous-led uprising and national strike ever in this Andean-Amazon-Pacific plurination. While tens of thousands marched from the provinces to the capital city of Quito, thousands also occupied provincial government offices, blocked roads and commerce, and "shut down" the country's operation, all in response and resistance to state- and International Monetary Fund (IMF)–imposed economic policies, including the presidential decree that eliminated fuel subsidies.*

The fact that this protest-awakening was led, in large part, by Indigenous women has not been sufficiently acknowledged. Also not acknowledged—in the media or in Indigenous organizations themselves—is the role of women in re-thinking, re-creating, and sowing movement, politics, struggle, and life today (in Ecuador and the region), in "awakening" protest, resistance, and re-existence in these times of capitalist-heteropatriarchal-colonial oppression, violence, destruction, and death.

But I am also referring to another "awakening," that of state-authorized and state-led repression and violence. Without a doubt, the state awakening in Ecuador was driven by the March 2019 letter of intention with the IMF and its demands of economic, social, and tributary structural reforms. The fact that these reforms violate national and international economic, social, and cultural rights and threaten the very existence of the majority of the population is reason enough for protest, as is the unconstitutionality of the letter of intention itself, which was signed by President Lenin Moreno without prior congressional approval.

Contrary to what it may seem, the "state awakening" is not of the nation-state or national state as we know it. Rather, it is of what Quintero Weir calls the state corporation or the corporate state constitutive of the new and emergent stages of global capitalist accumulation and interest.[68] It is an awakening—a making visible in Ecuador—of new strategies and configurations of the colonial matrix of power, in which, as I have argued, the denationalized corporate state and the military-police apparatus or complex are part.

In this sense, Ecuador evidences what some of us have suspected for a while: the nascent awakening or rebirth of the condor. My reference, symbolically, is to the huge vulturelike bird native to the Andes and thought to be almost extinct. Literally, it is to Operation Condor, the US-backed clandestine campaign that began to take form in the 1960s under John F. Kennedy against the "Cuban threat" and continued throughout the Johnson, Nixon, Ford, Carter, and Reagan administrations. The antecedents, of course, can be traced back to CIA operations decades before, to Nelson Rockefeller's avarice for oil, and to the relations both together established with military dictators and in the region. The mission of Operation Condor was to eradicate Soviet, communist, and socialist influence and ideas, and to suppress—through state-implemented violence, repression, and terror—social opposition and movements, including Indigenous movements, that threatened capital's interests and neoliberalism's advance. The governments of Argentina, Chile, Uruguay, Paraguay, Bolivia, and Brazil were the principal members, although Ecuador and Peru also formed part.

Is not the October Awakening evidence of the condor's rebirth and of an Operation Condor II taking form?

I am not suggesting a repeat of fifty-plus years past, but instead a new chapter or sequel. The configuration, actors, alliances, and strategies today are certainly not the same, lest we forget the presence throughout the region, particularly in Mexico and Colombia but not only there, of narco, paramilitary, and state pacts and formations; that is, of state corporatizations in which both extractive interests and global capital—and their obvious ties—are constitutive parts. The present-day complicities and configuration are not only attributable to the United States, although without a doubt the US government and its allied corporations and "multilateral" institutions (the IMF, International Development Bank, World Bank, Organization of American States, etc.) remain central to the game. The complicities of and configurations with global capitalism are also within Latin American countries themselves. They were present (often with distinct forms and players) in the former "progressive" governments of Lula in Brazil, the Kirchners in Argentina, and Correa in Ecuador. And they continue today in Bolivia, Venezuela, Nicaragua, and Mexico, despite the denial by much of the *traditional Left. In countries of both the Right and Left, oligarchies and elite, big business, and the church (i.e., evangelical-political alliances that include conservative Catholics and Opus Dei), to name just a few, foster and maintain the complicities and configurations. The co-optation and in-corporation of local governments and community leaders, most particularly Indigenous and peasant leaders, are part of the plan, giving a much more complex and diverse face to the plan-project-operation present and taking form, but also enabling one of the strategic aims: the serious debilitation and fragmentation of communities and social movements. For all this and many more reasons that we are yet to discover, the new condor plan is much more complex than its predecessor.*

The October Awakening is of the condor now in movement and flight. And, at the same time, it is of the people in rebellion and re-existence-based movement. Ecuador was the beginning. Then came Chile, where student-led protests against neoliberal policies and for a constitutional assembly and a new people-based constitution have brought millions of all ages to the streets in a pacific and dignity-based rebellion without the need of figureheads or leaders. The response: brutal state repression and violence, levels of which were last seen with Augusto Pinochet and Operation Condor. In the televised words of President Piñera, "We are in a war against a very powerful enemy: the people." While the violence in Santiago (televised and on social media) is evidence, what is not seen in the media or press is the even more brutal state-authorized and state-led violence, dehumanization, and extermination in Wallmapu, the territory-communities of Mapuche peoples.

Bolivia came next. There, the inconsistencies and suspected fraud of the October 20, 2019, national elections awakened and pushed rebellion, a peoples' response to the complex social and political tensions long brewing and exacerbated by the Evo Morales–Álvaro García Linera government, including its political-patriarchal authoritarianism, extractivist economy, fragmentation and weakening of social movements, and imposition of another presidential term after a peoples' referendum said NO. The rebellion took to the streets, not in a simple polarization of those for and against Morales, but in a much more complex amalgam of struggles, forces, interests, and visions politically, culturally, and socially grounded, and with differential ideas and practices of (pluri)nation, government, democracy, people, and power. In this mix, the rapid escalation of chaos, confrontation, and violence was not (or not only) state led as in Ecuador or Chile. Its impetus instead appears linked, in great part, to the "civic" opposition, whose regional extreme-right elite, neoliberal and conservative religious interests, and anti-Indigenous, racist, and fascist postures have long worked to keep internal colonialism and coloniality alive. Here it is not just the levels but the forms of violence: the dehumanizations of Indigenous leaders and authorities, especially women, the hunting down of government members, and the burning of homes, among others, that recall and continue the colonial enterprise's long horizon in its internal and global project and form.

With the resignation of Morales on November 10, 2019, some say the "coup" began. Others, including Morales and García Linera, argue that it was constitutive of the effort to discredit elections. And others contend that the anger, indignation, and social discontent surrounding the elections and the suspected fraud provided the perfect moment to put in action the overthrow that members of the conservative Bolivian opposition, with the support of the United States and the Organization of American States, had been preparing. The "taking out" some years back of Manuel Zelaya in Honduras (orchestrated by the United States and the Organization of American States) is brought to mind.

The self-proclamation on November 12 of the white, blond, ultra-right-wing, and religiously conservative senator Jeanine Áñez as interim president, and her publicly declared goal "to pacify the country," is indicative of that which is ahead. "I dream of a Bolivia free of Indigenous satanic rituals, the city is not for Indios!" she said in an April 14, 2013, tweet now recirculating. Another on June 20, 2013: "May the Aymara new year not shine of ALBA! Satanic, no one replaces God!" With the Bible held high, she rejoiced tonight (November 12, 2019) in front of the presidential palace. The Bible and the banner of "democracy," a democracy without a doubt conceived in and controlled from the new colonial configurations and strategies especially visible in Latin America today, in which the alliance of evangelical religion and politics are a component part. A democracy designed to bring Bolivia back into the fold, making sure that all that threatens its advance—especially Indigenous peoples, peasants, popular sectors, youths, feminists, and outspoken women, and the ideas, practices, and knowledges that challenge western, conservative, religious values—will be dispelled, controlled, dominated, eliminated, and exterminated. Can we doubt the condor's rebirth, presence, and flight?

II   *The sounds of gas bombs and of helicopters overhead twenty-four hours a day still ring in my ears, along with the high-pitched roar of the war planes that flew over Quito for four hours a day the week following the twelve-day October uprising-strike-awakening. A show of military might or just "practice," as the official news claimed, for an air force day of commemoration? The resonances invade my dreams, along with the lasting images of levels of police brutality, state repression, and violence never before been seen in this Ecuadorian plurination.*

Why the excessive force of police and military against thousands of people—women, men, youths, and children, Indigenous, Black, mestizo, urban, and rural—the vast majority in pacific protest? How are we to comprehend the grave and disproportionate use of gas bombs not just on the streets but also in declared "peace zones," including the Arbolito Park, communal kitchens, and the Salesian Polytechnical University, where more than five thousand women, children, and elderly were housed each night? What about the use of horses to disperse and trample (images that recall the Spanish invasion more than five hundred years past), of government pronouncements (without evidence, of course, and as also have occurred in Chile and Bolivia) that blame Cubans and Venezuelans for the destabilization? And what about the public declaration by the Ecuadorian minister of defense, trained at the School of the Americas and part of the right-wing government of León Febres Cordero (a key collaborator in Operation Condor), a declaration that authorized the use of all means necessary, including lethal weapons, to protect strategic installations and the state? "Do not forget that the Armed Forces, proudly, have the experience of war," he said.[69]

The words of Ecuador's president Lenin Moreno at the November inauguration in Quito of the 174th session of the International Human Rights Commission afford a similar tone: "One of the characteristics of the modern democratic state is its reserve on the monopoly of the use of force . . . the use of force of the state that permits the existence of pacific societies. This situation required the use of force."[70]

While lethal weapons were not employed, the disproportionate violence had its toil; the October statistics: 12 dead, 11 mutilated by the impact of gas bombs, 1,340 wounded in incidents with public forces, 1,152 jailed;[71] as I continue to work on these notes a month later, the numbers are still increasing.

Of course, the statistics don't tell the stories of those assassinated, brutally beaten, tortured, kidnapped, disappeared, trampled, gassed, gravely wounded by rubber bullets shot short-range, or illegally held without respect for human rights, the Constitution, and legal due process. They don't evidence the racism. And they don't reveal the complicities: hospitals that shut out the wounded, police who attacked street-based medical brigades, the Catholic bishop who, in the city of Riobamba, closed the door of the cathedral to the funeral procession of an assassinated Indigenous leader, to name just some.

Neither the statistics nor the political analyses circulating internationally recount the pain and horror of that lived; the physical, psychological, emotional, and economic toil and effects—then and now—for individuals, families, and communities; the lack of reparation; or the rampant escalation of anti-Indigenous racism in government discourse, the press, and conservative, elite, and some middle-class *sectors. Instead, and all too often, these analyses, written from a distance, contribute to the dehumanization, to the inhumanity and dehumanity(ies) authorized and avowed, and to the idea that politics and political struggle (still too often conceived in simplistic Left-versus-Right terms) trump existence. The recent report on human rights during the October Indigenous uprising and national strike published by the Alliance of Organizations for Human Rights, with its focus on the testimonies of those women, men, youths, and children whose lives have been gravely affected by the state-authorized violence, provides a human and humanizing context for revealing that which occurred.[72]*

III *It is October 13, 2019. The long-awaited "dialogue" between Indigenous organizations and government begins, an example of sorts of how negotiations might and should take place in this plurinational state (recognized as such by the 2008 constitution). In adherence with the Indigenous movement's demand, the dialogue is televised on all national channels. The several-hour session ends with President Moreno's revocation of Decree 883, which was to eliminate state subsidies on gasoline. With the revocation came the announcement that a new decree would be negotiated.*

Thousands of Indigenous women and men celebrated in the Casa de Cultura (the national "House of Culture"), with many other protest participants and supporters joining in the surrounding streets. Yet it was a Pyrrhic victory of sorts, important without a doubt in ending the eleven-day protest and the rounds of violence, but insufficient in eliminating the hovering presence of the IMF and its demands of structural reform and country control. Insufficient in addressing and repairing the violences committed by state forces, and insufficient in attending to the causes of growing impoverishment, violence (especially against women), and territorial contamination, displacement, and dispossession, the result of an extractivist economy that knows no limits and claims no harm. Insufficient in making the Constitution, deemed by many as the most radical in the world (with its recognition, among other things, of Nature's rights), a document of praxis.

While government-organized dialogue continues with some sectors, the Confederation of Indigenous Nationalities of Ecuador and the Indigenous movement, along with other social organizations and collectives, have taken their own path in the plurinational Parliament of the Peoples. The parliament's proposal presented to the government on October 31, 2019, makes clear the problem: the sacrificing of society in order to meet the indicators of economic growth and the demands of the capitalist system. "Change in the civilizing perspective, ... transition from a capitalist vision toward a new form of relation among society, nature, and production, ... more coherent, ethical and human public policies" are the guiding principles of this important document that outlines a plan of economic, political, social, and tributary reform that is people and community focused and structural in scope. Government representatives, including the president, rejected the plan outright.

In the televised words of the newly named head of the armed forces, the indirect message to this proposal and the Indigenous movement was clear: "We will not permit the imposition of a model that goes against the basic terms of democracy." Is it just coincidence that his words came on the same day as Jeannine Añez's self-proclamation as president of Bolivia in order to restore "democracy," or the day after Trump proudly announced that Latin America is returning to democracy and that only Venezuela and Nicaragua are left?[73]

Not coincidence, I argue, but part of the plan, of the October (and now November) awakenings and the condor (and his Operation II) now in regional movement and flight.[74]

TARGETED DE-EXISTENCE(S)

As the reader well knows, 2020 ushered in the world pandemic of COVID-19. Life everywhere is no longer the same. There is much that could be said about the pandemic's roots and ties, most especially in terms of capital-driven interests, but that is not my principal concern here. Instead, I continue with the reflections and cries that find ground in coloniality's mutations and reconfigurations, and in its project of violence-dispossession-war-death. In another letter written to Quijano on the second anniversary of his death (May 31, 2020), I began to describe how I saw a targeted de-existence taking form. Here are some excerpts from the letter:

I *It is March 2020, the first month of the virus-pandemic-quarantine in Ecuador. Messages begin to arrive from folks I know in the Ecuadorian Amazon. They tell me about the militarization of the region, the surveillance and control measures, and the prohibitions against the movement of Indigenous leaders, including—for those residing in urban areas—the return to their forest communities. They also tell me about the large military presence in the oil and mining areas. It seems that safeguarding or protecting companies, their activities, and their workers is the military's main function. Militarization is not intended to protect the Amazonian peoples and nations from COVID-19; rather, it appears to have contributed to contagion and spread. Although the military has prohibited the movement of leaders, it has allowed, according to what I am told, the free movement of young people from the communities to the bars, discotheques, and peri-urban brothels (the places of greatest contagion). They have also allowed the free movement between and within Indigenous communities of workers and technicians of the extractivist companies. Many agree that this is how the spread of the virus began among the smaller Indigenous nations or nationalities (Siona, Secoya, and Waorani) in the north of the Amazon, where there are large oil concessions, and in the south, where mining projects are located in the territories of the Shuar and Achuar nationalities, both recognized for their strong warrior resistance.*

I cannot stop asking you, my dear Aníbal, if we are not facing an exacerbation of the coloniality of power, an exacerbation that recalls the strategies and actions of more than five hundred years ago, those that today point to the de-existence of Amazonian Indigenous peoples, facilitating extractivism's totalizing advance. The magnitude of what is happening is unimaginable. In the daily news, the Amazon receives no mention; moreover, urban citizens are told that the pandemic is in full decline. I give you some more examples.

On April 7, 2020, one of the worst socio-environmental disasters in the last fifteen years occurred in the Ecuadorian Amazon: a spill of at least 15,800 barrels of crude oil that was dispersed into the Quijos, Napo, and Coca Rivers, affecting access to water and food for more than 150 communities and approximately 120,000 people in three Amazonian provinces.[75] Although there were warnings from scientists, environmentalists, and community organizations about the serious erosion occurring—related, in large part, to the construction of the Coca Codo Sinclair hydroelectric dam—neither the government nor the public and private oil companies involved took preventative measures to protect pipelines and communities.

The Communal Federation and Union of Natives of the Ecuadorian Amazon, the Confederation of Indigenous Nationalities of the Ecuadorian Amazon, bishops of the provincial-based vicariates, and a number of affected persons presented a demand for protective action in light of the serious situation of vulnerability, not only due to the contamination of water as the principal food source but also due to the crisis aggravated by the COVID-19 pandemic.[76] Within the lawsuit, they also requested the restoration of all the affected components of the ecosystem, comprehensive reparation for the affected people, and guarantees of non-repetition, since there is an imminent risk of a new rupture. The judicial process continues to drag on to this day. Meanwhile, the threat of death to these Indigenous communities is real.

In an alert that circulated on social networks, several communities denounced the decrease in food rations (made available by one of the oil companies), specifically in the communities that gave testimonies in the protective action hearing.

Moreover, and as the Communal Federation and Union of Natives of the Ecuadorian Amazon's president stated, "if before there was a problem with food, now it is impossible to feed the family, as if that is not enough, they are making people who do not know how to read sign an act where they expressly state that they have no reciprocal right to formulate any claims." With this alert, human rights organizations demand that the company and the state cease the harassment and extortion that the communities are experiencing. Undoubtedly, this is one more sample of the practices and policies of the current coloniality that point not only to control and domination but also to the de-existence of Amazonian peoples and the forest of which they are—we are—part.

At the end of May, another alert from the Alliance of Human Rights Organizations was circulated, this one about the recent opening of a new oil route in the Yasuní National Park. Perhaps you remember, Aníbal, about the struggles that began during the government of Rafael Correa to keep crude oil underground in this park, which has the greatest environmental diversity in the world and is home to Native peoples in voluntary isolation. As the human rights report indicates, "The satellite images unequivocally show the construction of this new highway, which, from March 15th, when clearing was not yet generated, until May 6th, has caused 2.2 km of penetration into the Amazon rainforest, which requires a large amount of movement of workers and materials, contrary to any common sense at this time of pandemic."[77] I cannot stop asking about de-existence and extinction and, in a related way, about the interests that determine existence, de-existence, and extinction in these times.

Of course, Ecuador is not alone. The policy and practice of de-existence extend to the entire Amazon. As I write (May 2020), there are indications of more than twenty thousand Indigenous people infected with COVID-19 in the Amazon.[78] Brazil, due to its size and territorial extension, stands out. According to a study by the Oswaldo Cruz Foundation, the mortality rate for Indigenous people hospitalized with COVID-19 in Brazil is 48 percent, far exceeding that of any other group. Brazil is the second country, after the United States, in the number of infections and deaths, and number one in the world in terms of Indigenous contagion. The Conselho Indigenista Misionero (Indigenist Missionary Council) calls for an international complaint to the Inter-American Commission on Human Rights against the Bolsonaro government for the flagrant case of genocide.[79]

An editorial makes clear that the reality and intention "are the dispossession of Indigenous people, their extermination, and, relatedly, and in conjunction with powerful actors, the destruction of the Amazon." The editorial goes on to cite Harvard University professor Bruno Carvalho, who asserted (in the

New York Times) *that we are going to have to get used to living without the Amazon. Organizations like the World Health Organization have also made statements about the imminent risk of extermination. "Extermination, as the President of Brazil has openly stated, is the intention of his policy for the Amazon. To complete the picture, garimpeiros, drug traffickers, and all kinds of extractivist mafias and armed actors are, through violence, assassinating, stripping away, dispossessing, and occupying territories that later pass into the hands of agribusiness and transnational mining, logging, hydroelectric, and oil companies, among others."*[80]

Burning the Amazon, as began with force in 2019 and continues in even greater proportions today, is part of "the comprehensive public policy of dispossession and conquest with blood and fire." In the words of the Yanomami leader Davi Kopenawa Yanomami, "All this destruction is not our mark, it is the footprint of the whites, your trace on earth."[81]

COVID-19 is, without a doubt, a stamp of this footprint, the one that is accelerating the de-existence of millenarian peoples, knowledges, and the Amazonian forest. As occurred during the so-called conquest, this disease is facilitating the genocidal occupation of the Amazon.

What does all this suggest, my dear Aníbal, regarding coloniality? During these days I have this same question going around and around in my head, including whether the concept of "coloniality" is the most appropriate to analyze what we are experiencing today, with the COVID-19 pandemic, the extreme greed of capital, and the new configurations of power all combined. Of course, the Amazon is not the only place where this virus of violence, greed, extermination, and power is present and taking shape. But it is central, as the lungs of Mother Earth, especially since its de-existence denotes the de-existence of all life.[82]

Since I wrote this letter to Quijano, the situation has worsened, with thousands of people and thousands of acres of forest affected throughout the Amazonian region. Meantime in Ecuador the demand for protective action filed by communities and organizations continues without resolve as 2021 ends. According to community-based leader Veronica Grefa, the response of state and company officials could not be viler: "The oil spill has been beneficial, the company and state contend; communities have received food, have been given work, and even rights that they did not have before like, for instance, access to piped-in water. After fifty years of oil extraction and exploitation," Grefa argued, "we know this is about money and profit with no care for lives. The devastating effects of this last spill now threaten our existence."[83]

The threat, of course, travels from territory to territory. Just now, as I was finishing the revision of this chapter (October 17, 2021), an emergency email appeared from the Brazilian decolonial activist-geographer Carlos Walter Porto-Gonçalves:

> Another tragedy hits the Serrinha Indigenous Village of the Kaingangs, in Rio Grande do Sul. News from an hour ago. This is an emblematic conflict arising from the introduction of the lease of indigenous land to plant soybeans, which has been dividing the indigenous people and massacring those who persevere in defending their way of life, their territorialities. This is not a specific issue that involves indigenous peoples, but a mode of modern-colonial capitalist development that involves several other groups with their rage to exploit the metabolic conditions of life reproduction to transform them into exports of goods while deterritorializing indigenous peoples, peasants, riverside dwellers, quilombolas and other groups who come to live in precarious conditions on the outskirts of urban areas where they begin to fight for bone carcasses to eat. It is a systemic crime, the one committed in Serrinha against the Kaingangues and, as such, deserves a systemic response in which we all act, bringing the strength of each one's pain.

Throughout Abya Yala, the strategies and evidence of targeted de-existence—raced, gendered, territorialized, and generational—are increasingly widespread. In Wallmapu, the Mapuche territories of what are called Chile and Argentina, children and youths are now the targets of state and extractivist company violence. In the three months of a massive national strike led by youths in Colombia in 2021, nonviolent protest was met with extreme state violence; assassinations, rape, disappearances, and the torture of youths were the authorized mode of control.[84] As 2021 came to a close, body parts of those dismembered continued to appear in the rivers that pass through the city of Cali. The elimination of Black youths at the hands of police in the United States and the disproportionately high numbers of African American deaths due to COVID-19 are also indicative of the targeted de-existence of these present times. Throughout the Americas (as well as elsewhere in the world), the COVID-19 pandemic has not only magnified the depth of racial inequalities but also enabled racially targeted police violence. In Brazil, for instance, before the pandemic it was twenty-one times more likely than in the United States for a Black person to be killed by police;[85] in the first half of 2020 the number of deaths at the hands of police had grown by more than 43 percent.[86] Colombia and Honduras are not far behind. Yet the issue is not so much the numbers—since all Black lives matter everywhere—as it is "the historically woven storyline" that creates the structure, dynamics, and narrative practices of racism, a story line in which existence itself is in constant tension and question.[87]

I am reminded of Saidiya Hartman's discussion of the paradox of agency and existence within the extreme circumstances and objective conditions of enslavement. That is, "existence as the space of death, where negation is the captive's central possibility for action, whether we think of that as the radical refusal of the terms of the social order or these acts that are sometimes called suicide or self-destruction, but which are really an embrace of death."[88] In her historical novel *Jonatás y Manuela*, Luz Argentina Chiriboga also makes evident the operation of this paradox and collective embrace among enslaved women in the region now known as Colombia and Ecuador; in essence, a uniting of cries within a freedom-based action of re-existence through death, of living on in an-other spiritual realm and world, with the ancestors and all those who came before.[89]

While the long horizon of cries that constitute collective memory is certainly not forgotten, the present-day cries of existence that I give voice to here are for dignity and life in the here-and-now, up against the entanglement of violence-dispossession-war-death that constitutes coloniality in its extant and ongoing mutations, configurations, and forms. De-existence today, as I understand it, is both consequence and component of coloniality's mutations and reconfigurations. It takes the entanglement and its related cries to a deeper and more complex level in which selective extermination is the project and aim—that is, the selective extermination of groups of people deemed not useful to the system's ambitions and identified as obstacles to its planned advance; the "disposables." At play is the extermination not just of human lives but also of histories, herstories, and theirstories, of collective memory, ancestral knowledges, and grounded social and political thought. Moreover, for many Indigenous and Black ancestral communities, it is the extermination of existence as life with and on the land, and among and with all living beings, the extermination of Mother Earth. De-existence, of course, is not new. It has always been constitutive of the colonial project and the genocides, ethnocides, ecocides, and epistemicides perpetuated by this project over five-hundred-plus years in the so-called Americas, as well as in other territories of the globe (the Holocaust being a case in point). However, and as I have argued here, de-existence today seems equally if not more nefarious in its current manifestations and venture in which race, gender, sexuality, land, and intergeneration (elders and youths) are the targets, with the COVID-19 pandemic a useful tool of authority, control, violence, demo-bilization, and death.

THE CLAMOR OF SHARED CRIES

I scream. You scream. We scream and cry out. The decibels, the echo, and the resonance rise in crescendo. They mix, mesh, move, and communicate with other cries, human and those of other beings: land, water, rivers, oceans, mountains, forests, and sky. They combine with those past: the ancestors whose presence and memory continue alive. And they join and fuse with the cries of all those who refuse to be silent against the projects of de-existence and violence-destruction-dispossession-war-death. They are cries of horror, pain, valor, outrage, fury, indignation, and self-affirmation. And they are cries of, from, with, and for existence and life, for a re-existing, reliving, and living-with in conditions of dignity, hope, peace, and justice. They are cries that call out, implore, and demand a thinking-feeling-doing-acting. Cries that clamor for practices that not only resist but also resurge, in-surge, inter-vene in, transgress, and create; practices, pedagogies-as-methodologies, and praxes of creation, invention, configuration, and coconstruction—of the what to do and the hows—of struggles, routes-walks, and sowings of and in the fissures and cracks of the capitalist-modern/colonial-anthropocentric-racist-heteropatriarchal order-disorder.

It is the cry that moves us. The cry that refuses to be silent and stay lodged inside. The cry that seeks accompaniment and pushes and persuades ac-tions to undo the cry. We know the cry in and of itself is not enough; it is impetus, and it is the will to struggle and resist, to re-exist and not just survive.

I am reminded of Edouard Glissant's wise and poetic words: "Leave the cry, forge the word. It is not to renounce the imaginary or the underground powers, it is to assume a new duration, anchored in the emergence of the peoples," he said.[90] Glissant's lucid call was not to more theory, more ideology, or one idea of the world. Instead, it was to "the tremendous tangle, which is not about falling into lamentations, or surrendering to unbridled hopes. [It is about] The word to world cries in which the voice of all communities has reach." Moreover, and as he went on to argue, it is also about "the accumula-tion of common places, of deported cries, of deadly silences that verify that the power of the states is not what really moves us, an acceptance that our truths do not marry with power."[91] So the cries, the word, the places come together, in and for existence, in and for life.

I return to Alixa García and Naima Penniman's powerful spoken-sung words that began this chapter. "Who decides?" Certainly, we can ask, together with these self-identified soul sisters, not only who decides who's dangerous enough to die but also who decides to be part of the covert operation that is survival. Who decides to enable and sustain the chamber of life? And who decides to join with other seeds in breaking silence, cracking concrete, and breathing liberation? Who decides? Do you decide?

Cracks and Crack-Making

I awake to the subtleties of light breaking through the early morning brume, to the strength of the equatorial sun opening cracks, some large enough to permit view and others just small slits of featherlike beams, both—and each in their own way—giving presence to the possibility of the day rising. It is the subtlety of light rather than the clarity of day that guides and teaches me. I am referring to the light that peeks through the brume, illuminates the shade, and brightens that which all too often goes unseen. Recalled are the lyrics of Leonard Cohen's song "Anthem": "There is a crack in everything, that is how the light gets in."[92]

The light present in the cracks is—and at the same time—the result and possibility of the crack-making. Both together have come to orient my standpoint, space, and place of view, my life labor and praxis. And both together continue to alter and pluralize perception and sight, but also ways of knowing, thinking, sensing, being-becoming, and envisioning. While I still find solace in the clarity of day and, in a related sense, sustain hope's light for social change, the solace, clarity, and hope are increasingly less certain, less unencumbered, and less clear. It is not the clarity of a singular path that I seek. Nor do I find myself tied to the juxtapositional binaries of light versus dark, day versus night, and hope versus despair.

I recall Gloria Anzaldúa's poignant title *Light in the Dark* and her calling us to the task "to light up the darkness."[93] For Anzaldúa, and as I will take up in more detail later in this chapter, the work is to intervene, disrupt, challenge, and transform existing power structures, particularly those that limit and constrain us as women. It is to "heal the sustos resulting from woundings, traumas, racism, and other acts of violation," lighting up and "navigating the cracks [as] the process of reconstructing life anew."[94] Thinking from and with this reconstructing, and, in a similar vein, from and with re-existence—this understood as the processes, most especially of those historically excluded, racialized, gendered, stigmatized, and silenced, to construct and reconstruct life in conditions of dignity—moves me away from singular paths and lineal world views or horizons.

With the cracks, I have come to rethink hope. No longer do I sustain the HOPE in capital letters that I once held in my younger years, associated with the total overthrow and the overall transformation of capitalism and the dominant order. That is the unbridled hope that Glissant mentions in the quote discussed earlier. No longer do I maintain in my gut and heart the all-encompassing and utopic HOPE that another world is possible. This latter phrase, the slogan of the World Social Forum, is for me today just a slogan rooted more in discourse than in the daily praxis of women and men—or those who identify as neither or both—who struggle in the margins and cracks of this system to re-exist and resist, to re-create existence and sustain life in dignity and relation.[95] "Other worlds already exist," said a flyer that someone passed to me at the 2005 World Social Forum in Porto Alegre, Brazil, "the problem is that most of you don't see them." Recalled is the Zapatista proposition and project: "A world in which many worlds fit."

My wager today—in praxis and in this book—is in and for the lowercase hope, the hopes engendered, enabled, and constructed in the cracks and fissures of the system and dominant order. It is in and for the ways *muy-otras*—very others—of thinking, knowing, being, feeling, sensing, doing, loving, and living that exist despite the system, interrupting it, contesting it, transgressing it, and making it rupture, fissure, and crack.

I haven't stopped wanting fundamental change, nor have I stopped struggling for it. As the Zapatista Comandanta Dalia says, "If we don't struggle, the capitalist system is going to continue until it does away with all of us, and there will never be change."[96] In these times of pandemics—of COVID-19, systemic racism, white supremacy, and gendered violences and feminicide, among others—and their project of what I described earlier as de-existence, Comandanta Dalia's words ring particularly true. So too do those of the Subcomandante Insurgente Galeano: "Our rebellion is our NO to the system, our resistance is our YES that something else is possible."[97]

My personal-political proposition and venture are with this "something else," what I understand and refer to as the *otherwise*. It is with sensing, seeing, perceiving, and recognizing its presence, struggle, and emergence most especially in the system's cracks. It is with sensing, seeing, perceiving, and recognizing the fissuring and crack-making, both in the present and with respect to long historical, herstorical, and theirstorical horizons. And it is with contributing to the cracking, to the making and the connecting of cracks.

ENCOUNTERING THE CRACKS

Of course, I have not always recognized the presence and significance of the cracks. I think it all began around ten years ago.

One morning, as I was leaving my house in Guápulo, a centuries-old barrio built into a ravine—native territory of the KituKaras and now an uninvited part of the capital city of Quito—I encountered a phenomenon: two yellow flowers growing in a crack in the stone-cement wall that borders the stone-cement stairs (figure 1.1).

In the daily routine of climbing the 125 steps that lead to the street, I never saw or maybe never paid attention to the cracks. My eye always went to the totality of the steps and the wall and the solidity of the stone, not to its crevices and fissures. It was the living flowers that captured my attention and guided my eye to what had previously gone unseen. Did their seeds somehow crack the stone and concrete, I asked, and how did the seeds get in there and

1.1 Flowers in the crack, Guápulo, Ecuador. PHOTO: CATHERINE WALSH, 2013.

find the sustenance to grow? Was the flowering not a signaling of the presence and possibility of existence against all odds, of hope against hopelessness? How many cracks had I passed by unnoticed, and how many cracks had I seen but simply forgotten? One that I had chanced upon several years before came to mind. It was the crack made by a tree that had burst through the asphalt paving of a fairly new road on Ecuador's Afro-Pacific coast. I remembered my amazement that no one had cut down this tree growing in the middle of the street, that it had been left there to naturally flourish as if it were there that it belonged, forcing the cars to go around it. However, it was the novelty of the tree and not the presence of the crack that caught my attention then. The roots of life that had somehow taken form below the surface went unconsidered in my mind, as did their insurgent force that broke through breathing life.

With the encounter of the blooming crack on the wall, my perception began to change. My sight moved toward the fissures. I remember soon after seeing a seed sprout a green leaf in a sidewalk crack as I walked by. I became enthralled with the life present in the cracks and, similarly, with the significance and possibility of the fissures in both a real and metaphorical sense. If, as those who work in construction argue, the crack is a break that can spread throughout the entire width of the constructive element, leaving it useless for its intended structural function, could this not also apply to the dominant system of power? I began to wonder. The crack weakens the structure, weakens the wall; as such, could the crack not also weaken the structure of the wall that sustains the systemic intertwinement of coloniality, capitalism, racism, and heteropatriarchy? Are the cracks not suggestive of decolonial potential and possibility?

In 2014 I published a short text—"Pedagogical Notes from the Decolonial Cracks"—that began to explore this idea of thinking with and from what I was beginning to understand as decolonial cracks: the fissures in the modern/colonial order.[98] At that point I did not realize that there were many others also thinking with and from the cracks, most especially with respect to the global and totalizing nature of the system and the possibility of debilitating and weakening its wall.

DEBILITATING THE WALL

It was René Olvera Salinas, a Mexican activist close to the Zapatista struggle and my graduate student at the time, who introduced me to the work of the Mexican-based collective Grietas (Cracks). "Although our walk always exists on the edge of possibility, it exists. . . . We widen a bit more the crack that we inhabit in the wall of economic and political impossibilities," says the collective. "And we make the fracture deeper within capitalism's great wall. In the end, we make room for all that opposes the systemic and existential shock that demobilizes the desire and will to change the world."[99] Grietas is not just a collective project but also a social endeavor; "from our marginality we want to communicate with other cracks, with other cries, words, and thoughts that feed the hope that other worlds, without exploitation and depredation, are possible." Moreover, it is with this "other" premise that "we house ethical, theoretical, aesthetic reflections about a politics that is very other, together with artistic creation, sociological imagination, anthropological rage, the 'other' history and the 'other' geographies, anti-capitalist economy, rebellious philosophies, social psychology, thought spoken out loud, and recuperated memories, wrenching away fear and repression." In this sense, "we give space to all that which opposes the systemic and existential shock that immobilizes the desire to change the world."[100]

For those involved in this collective, the cracks and crack-making are, of course, not simply individual endeavors but, relatedly, part of the long horizons of social struggle from below, including contemporary creative rebellion, resistance, and resurgence that strive to rupture the system from its margins and outside. In an interview-conversation with members of the collective, I explained the difference I saw between defensive resistance *against* capitalism and the coloniality of power, and the insurgencies of Indigenous movements since the 1990s, particularly in Ecuador and Mexico, these understood as offensive postures and actions that propose, create, and construct. Insurgency in this sense, as I argued then, does not limit us to the notion of re-volution; that is, of "turning over" the entire current state of affairs, as if it were possible to simply leave behind the old and replace it with the new. Insurgency, instead and more complexly, pushes an understanding of the permanent continuum of struggle and change. It refers to the processes and practices of constant creation, invention, strategy building, and action through practice that intervene in and fissure the system, and work toward the building of radically distinct possibilities of existence and living.[101]

While I did not say so in the interview, I understand now that the cracks and crack-making are, without a doubt, part of this insurgency. They are insurgent acts; the consequence of resistances and insurgencies exercised and in motion. Cracks open and take shape in struggle itself, in uprisings, rebellions, and movements, but also in the creative and everyday practices of people endeavoring to create and construct something else. They are part, it seems, of what the Kurdish activist Dilar Dirik describes, following the fundaments of the Kurdistan liberation movement, as "the idea of working 'despite of' what is happening around you. In other words, to act through practice."[102]

I am thinking of practices that disrupt the capitalist, racialized, heteropatriarchal, anthropocentric, and westernized logics of modernity/coloniality, including the "monologue of modern-western reason."[103] That is the logic-and/as-reason that works to define knowledge and thought as within the productive, totalizing, and universalized sphere of the "West"; a sphere marked by color, gender, sexuality, geopolitics, and Christianity, by the supposed superiority of Man over nature, and by the negation of ontological-existential, epistemic, and spiritual-cosmogonic relation. As a monologue, its intention is to exclude, to ensure the solidity of its spheres and walls, and to make sure that any epistemic-existential fissures that may appear are quickly eliminated or patched over. The enigma, of course, is that this monologue knows no territorial or political boundaries. It crosses continents and consolidates itself in domains associated with the so-called Right(s), as well as with much of the so-called Left(s), each in their various systemic manifestations and forms. More often than not, neither is able to fathom, imagine, and comprehend the presence and force of the cracks, or the practices of crack-making that are being shaped, constructed, created, and lived despite the modern-western-colonial logic-and/as-reason and its systemic and structural matrices of power.

Totalizing views have always been part of the problem with regard to not only the system but also its transformation. It is precisely because of capitalism's totalizing character that revolutionary postures have historically called for its total overthrow and transformation. Such postures permit neither the release of political action, as the Mexican deprofessionalized intellectual Gustavo Esteva contends, nor the recognition of the cracks below and their hope-filled force and possibility. "In anti-capitalist struggle . . . we cannot free up or release political action as long as we maintain a vision of capitalism that immerses us in that paranoia, in its perception as a unified, homogeneous system that occupies all the social space and from which nothing can escape."[104]

This paralyzing vision—what I referred to earlier as HOPE in capital letters—is nourished by and feeds into the idea that the only way to dismantle the world-system is in its entirety. The Left educated in this tradition, says Esteva, "either struggles continuously against a specter, or it continuously postpones the real struggle against capitalism, because it has not managed to conjure up the strength needed to face the giant that its imagination conceives." For Esteva, "this posture disqualifies and discounts all possibility that a non-capitalist reality exists. And it rejects all anti-capitalist struggles deemed (or perceived) as partial, and, even more, those that pretend to be located beyond capitalism."[105]

It is necessary, says Esteva, to "leave the intellectual and ideological jails, and liberate hope from its intellectual and political prison"; that is, to construct "new forms of transformational struggle."[106] For me, such arguments recall Paulo Freire's call made toward the end of his life, "to reinvent the forms of political action, ... to reinvent the ways to fight, but never stop fighting."[107] We have to "look for new paths of struggle, new forms of rebellion."[108]

In the book *El pensamiento crítico frente a la hidra capitalista* (Critical thought up against the capitalist hydra)—the result of the 2015 Zapatista seminar and seedbed of thought with this same name—the subcomandantes "SupMoisés" and "SupGaleano" argue the need for new forms of struggle.[109] In the face of capitalism's multiple and changing heads—the "capitalist hydra" capable of mutating, adapting, and regenerating itself—we need new forms and methods of struggle, resistance, and rebellion, they argue. In the face of the catastrophe or storm that is coming, "things are changing and the *compañeros* and *compañeras* are changing the forms of struggle. We need to change in order to survive."[110] In this pursuit of change, the Zapatistas put into practice their methodology-pedagogy of walking, asking, and cracking. Asking, one walks. Asking and walking, one also cracks history's wall. "If there are no cracks, then we will make them scratching, biting, kicking, hitting with hands and head, with the entire body, until we succeed in making history the wound that we are as Zapatistas." The danger, of course, is to stop working on the crack, they contend, because then the wall will heal itself; the task is not just to widen the crack but, equally important, to make sure the crack doesn't close. "What is important is the crack." Moreover, "while we may want to bring down the whole wall (of history and the system), it is enough to make a crack in it. ... Rebellion in the world is like a crack in the wall, ... what it wants is to debilitate the wall in such a way that it falls down itself."[111]

Durito, a small beetle that uses glasses and smokes a pipe, a protagonist in many of the late Subcomandante Insurgente Marcos's stories, also has much to say about the wall and the cracks:

Now flattened, the powerful have placed the world as if it were a wall that divides some from others. But it is not a wall as we know it, no. It is a wall laying down. That is to say, there is not just one side and another side, but also an above and below.... The wall and those above weigh a lot, and those below disagree, murmur, and conspire. What's more, the great weight has caused a big crack in the wall.... Those below, that is to say the immense majority of humanity, try to peek through the crack to see what weighs so much and, more than anything, to find out why they have to hold up this weight.... The rebellion in the world is like a crack in the wall: its first sense is to peek through and lean out the other side. But this weakens the wall and ends up fracturing it completely. Rebellion goes way beyond what can be considered modern "change," that which takes advantage of the crack to sneak over to the other side. Those above, consciously or unconsciously, forget that through the crack, everyone cannot pass. Rebellion, on the other hand, goes much further. It doesn't pretend to peek through or, much less, lean over to the other side. Instead, what it wants is to weaken the wall in such a way that it ends up falling apart and, thus, there is no longer one side or another side, neither an above nor a below.[112]

The crack, in this sense, is not the solution in and of itself. It is part of the strategy, the pedagogy-methodology, and praxis. This seems to also be what the British intellectual and longtime Mexican resident John Holloway suggests when he says that "the cracks are also questions, never answers." As he explains in his book *Agrietar el capitalismo* (*Crack Capitalism*), "It is there that we begin, from the cracks, the fissures, the schisms, the spaces of negation-and-rebellious-creation ... of an-other doing. The crack is an insubordination of the here-and-now, not a process for the future."[113] The importance of the crack is in its own making, in its being and doing. For Holloway, this is the method and the practical-theoretical activity of the crack: to throw ourselves physically against the wall and at the same time to stop, reflect, and look for cracks or faults on the surface. These two activities are complementary, Holloway says. In this way, "theory only makes sense if it is understood as part of the desperate effort to find a way out, to create cracks that contest the apparently unstoppable advance of capital, of the walls that are pushing up toward our own destruction." Moreover, and as he goes on to argue, "the opening of cracks is the opening of a world that presents itself to us as closed. The method of the crack is a method of the crisis: we want to understand the wall, but not from its solidity, but instead from its cracks."[114]

Understanding the wall not from its totality but from its cracks—that is, from that which debilitates the wall itself—requires, of course, shifts in thought, posture, and gaze. The invitation here is to learn to unlearn the totalizing frame and gaze; to reorient the sense, eye, thought, goal, and struggle toward and from the cracks.

While Holloway's invitation and reflection are with respect to capitalism and conjure forth, in theory and practice, what some may consider as a fairly traditional Marxist view, the fact that they find ground in, derive from, and think with Zapatista analysis, perspectives, and struggle is important to note. For Holloway and for the Zapatistas, capitalism is about the control of existence itself. The fact that colonial difference is not necessarily the foundation of Holloway's thought (nor necessarily that of Esteva) is not my concern here. My interest, more broadly, is with disrupting the totalizing frame and gaze of the dominant system, of which capitalism is a component part. And it is with opening the muse with respect to the cracks and the shifts they push and pose in seeing, sensing, and thinking.

SEEING, SENSING, AND THINKING FROM THE CRACKS

"To explore the cracks between (and in) the worlds, we must see through the holes in [consensual] reality," Gloria Anzaldúa said. For Anzaldúa, "seeing" is another type of perception. "We must empower the imagination to blur and transcend customary frameworks and conceptual categories reinforced by language and consensual reality,... to access other 'realities,'... to celebrate the thresholds between the worlds, integrating polarities, mastering dualities."[115]

Of course, Anzaldúa is one of many who think and speak from the colonial wound, one of many concerned with the seeing and perceiving, the transcending and undoing of the customary frameworks and conceptual categories constitutive of the dominant classificatory system, the matrix of colonial power, and their overarching paradigm of western civilization. Brought to mind are W. E. B Dubois's pronouncement in 1903 of the problem of the twentieth century as the problem of the *color line*, Frantz Fanon's description sixty years later of the logic of "Man"/nonwhite Native as an invariant absolute, and Aimé Cesaire's call for decolonization as the work from the cracks of western Christian civilization.[116] Also recalled is Steve Biko's critical, analytic interrogation: "Can we in fact crack this cocoon, you know, to get whites away from the concept of racism?"[117] For these decolonial thinkers, but also for the Jamaican-born philosopher Sylvia Wynter, it is the code of "Race" and the classificatory dehumanizing principle of white/ Black (with their associative logics of rich/poor, human/less human, being/ nonbeing, superior/inferior) that organize socio-systemic hierarchies and subjective understandings.

In a letter written to her colleagues in the humanities at Stanford University shortly after the brutal police beating of Rodney King in 1993, Wynter spoke to the problem of these subjective understandings—what she calls "inner eyes"—made evident in the classifying acronym NHI used by Los Angeles public officials. NHI means "no humans involved." Its reference, as Wynter explains, is specific: "young Black males who belong to the jobless category of the inner-city ghettos."[118] Her letter begins with the question, Where did this system of classification come from? And it goes on to detail its roots, (re) production, and perpetuation, including in the present order of knowledge disseminated in the global university system and by its academics and intellectuals. "It is only by the 'trained skills' which we bring to the ordering of such facts [i.e., facts consistent with the dominant system of values], that intellectuals as a category are able to ensure the existence of each order's conceptual framework, which we rework and elaborate in order to provide the 'inner eyes' by whose mode of subjective understanding, each order's subjects regulate their behaviors, for both enormous good and evil."[119]

The inner eyes reflect and refract; they give shape, substance, and form to the ways we see, perceive, and read reality and the world. As Wynter makes clear, they determine the ways we see—or pretend not to see—the violences of systemic racism, racialization, dehumanization, and the invariant absolutes of hierarchical and oppositional classification. Moreover, they govern the ways we maintain, uphold, or contest this classificatory system.

For Wynter, the eruption of the liminal category of NHI in South Central Los Angeles opened a horizon toward a "new frontier of knowledge able to move us toward a new, correlated human species, and ecosystemic ethic."[120] It is in this horizon, correlation, and knowledge, in the perception and sight that they open up and the inner eyes that they proffer, that I sense the interconnectedness of Wynter and Anzaldúa.[121]

In *Light in the Dark*, Anzaldúa considers the shifts in her own seeing and perception—that is, in her inner eyes. She describes her movement beyond the border position, posture, perspective, and theory that characterized her earlier work; beyond the either/or. It is a move, she says, toward "a third point of view, a perspective from the cracks as a way to reconfigure ourselves as subjects outside binary oppositions, outside existing dominant relations."[122] As Anzaldúa explains, "Las rajaduras give us [mestizas] a nepantla perspective, a view from the cracks, rather than from any single culture or ideology. This perspective from the cracks enables us to reconfigure ourselves as subjects outside the us/them binary," she says. "Dwelling in liminalities, las nepantleras cannot be forced to stay in one place, locked into one perspective or perception of things or one picture of reality. Las nepantleras refuse to turn right onto the dominant culture's assimilation/acquiescence highway. They refuse to turn left onto the nationalistic-isolationism path demanding that we preserve our ethnic cultural integrity. Instead [we] construct alternative roads, creating new topographies and geographies, . . . [experiencing] multiple realities."[123]

Taken together, the situated arguments and propositions of Anzaldúa and Wynter deepen the significance of the cracks, opening perspectives that I had not previously considered. My initial interest with the cracks was as spaces that contest the system and the modern/colonial matrices of power—including invariant absolutes, hierarchical binaries and oppositions, and the maintenance of consensual reality—and that construct possibilities of the otherwise or something else. Wynter's emphasis on subjective understanding as inner eyes affords another dimension and horizon of sight and perception in both the maintenance and fissure of the system, and in the ways we—as concrete subjects—see and perceive reality, and act in and upon it, including with respect to the sight, perception, and action from and in the cracks and fissures. For Anzaldúa, in a distinct but related sense, the cracks also offer different ways of defining self, deciding group identity, healing wounds, and building relation.

In my thinking with both women, I have come to understand the cracks as part and parcel of an existence integrally and relationally understood. This existence in the cracks crosses and links the social, political, ontological, corporal, epistemic, and spiritual, as well as the individual and collective. It is an existence that is neither static nor stable, but always being and becoming. Here existence, re-existence, and (re)existences are fashioned, molded, and constructed in and through processes of struggle that cross, link, and intervene in all these spheres, transgressing, healing, sowing, cultivating, connecting, and creating.

"Cracks in the discourses are like tender shoots of grass, plants pushing against the fixed cement of disciplines and cultural beliefs, eventually overturning the cement slabs," Anzaldúa says.[124] Cracks open light and flower hope in spaces and places that seem impenetrable and solid. I think of the flower that appeared in my stone-cement wall, and the two green leaves that sprouted in the asphalt of a city sidewalk. I recall the spoken-sung words of

Alixa García and Naima Penniman that opened this chapter: "We are seeds cracking concrete, / for liberation is the only air we can breathe." Similarly, I think of Tupac Shakur's poem "The Rose That Grew from Concrete," which a friend recently brought to my attention:

Did you hear about the rose that grew
from a crack in the concrete?
Proving nature's law is wrong it
learned to walk without having feet.
Funny it seems, but by keeping its dreams,
it learned to breathe fresh air.
Long live the rose that grew from concrete
when no one else ever cared.[125]

Individually and together, the decolonial cracks open up and reveal irruption and interruption, beginnings, emergences, and possibilities, opening toward existences so very other that they make life despite—and interrupting and rupturing—the very conditions of its negation.[126] For many, and possibly for most, these cracks pass unnoticed, unseen, and invisible, outside the spheres of perception, attention, and vision. This is, in large part, because of the myopic nature and naturalization of modern life and living. But it is also due to the inability of most to imagine and comprehend the other-modes that exist and could exist in the fissures; that is, to imagine, comprehend, sense, and see what cannot necessarily be seen, or that which the colonial-capitalist order does not want us to see. The cracks require a refining of the vision and eye and of the senses and sensibilities in order to see, hear, listen to, and feel the otherwise being and becoming. Suggested are the words of the Afro-Brazilian slam poet Luz Ribeiro, "Through the crack I saw dreams of the whole horizon."[127]

CRACK-MAKING AND THE PRAXIS OF FISSURE

My interest is not only in what lights up, awakens, blossoms, and unfolds in the cracks. More critically, it is in how the fissuring is done; that is, in the labor and toil, thinking-doing, and praxis of cracking. I am referring to the strategies, practices, and pedagogies-as-methodologies of excavation and creation; those that make, deepen, and widen the fissures, and those that open and let us see through the holes, begetting, as I argued earlier, different perspectives, dimensions, horizons, hopes, and views. This is the praxis of fissure, the social, political, epistemic, spiritual, artistic, poetic, performative, creative, territorial, and re-existence-based insurgencies that rupture, fracture, and crack systemic totality(ies), giving presence and credence to that denied while at the same time enabling a "something else."

The examples are many and present in almost all spheres of life. I think of my own efforts to crack the western-centric postulates of knowledge in the university, to fissure the self-contained nature of academia and its protective walls, and to move and think with collectives, organizations, and communities in which crack-making and the praxis of fissure are constitutive components of thinking, being, analyzing, theorizing, doing, and living. As I will argue later here and in subsequent chapters, these efforts are, for me, necessarily tied to the decolonial hows; that is, to the pedagogies-as-methodologies and methodologies-as-pedagogies of doing decolonizing work, not just with others but also with ourselves. But before turning to such considerations (and the base they afford for the chapters to come), let me explore a bit more about the significance of the cracks and the praxistic arts of cracking.

ARTS OF CRACKING   In 2007 the Colombian artist Doris Salcedo fractured the floor of the Tate Museum of Modern Art in London. She entitled her 167-meter- (548-foot-)long crack *Shibboleth*, drawing from a passage in the Old Testament that tells how members of one tribe killed those of the other who pronounced that word in a different way, and evoking Paul Celan's poem of the same name. "Shibboleth, in Hebrew, is a word that simply means 'ear,' 'ear of wheat,'" but, as Salcedo explained, Celan's use extends its significance to the universal nature of the Holocaust, and to belonging and exclusion in different societies. Salcedo's *Shibboleth* crack finds base in the violence of her native Colombia and the violences that Europe perpetuates with respect to third-world peoples. "What the work tries to do is to mark the deep division that exists between humanity and those of us who are not exactly considered citizens or humans, to mark the profound difference, literally bottomless, between these two worlds that never touch, that never meet," she contended. "The space that the work marks is a negative space, which is the space that, ultimately, we people from the third world occupy in the first world." It is about racism, understood "not, let's say, as a symptom of a malaise suffered by first world society, but rather as the disease itself."[128]

Of course, the crack is also in the institution of art itself. "The museum and art in particular have, throughout history, played a very important role in defining an ideal of beauty, an aesthetic ideal," Salcedo said, and "that ideal is defined so strictly, so restrictively, that all non-whites are left out. So, Shibboleth is a critique of art, art history, the museum and, obviously, society in general." While art is powerless in the face of death, Salcedo maintained, "it has an ability to bring life that has been desecrated to the human field and give it a certain continuity in the life of the viewer." Recalled are ongoing experiences elsewhere, including those in movement and space of the New York City–based Decolonize This Place.[129]

The collection of the late African American artist Jacob Lawrence's panel paintings *Peering through History's Cracks: American Struggle*, exhibited at New York's Metropolitan Museum of Art in fall 2020, also gives centrality from a different eye and art of cracking to the inhumanities and dehumanizations of race. Here Lawrence makes visible and visceral the histories that systemic racism's totalizing frame and gaze have propagated and denied.[130] In this exhibit-intervention, the visual images of enslavement and its violences combine with the artist's captions written below, together telling the "other" histories of the cracks. "Is life so dear or peace so sweet as to be purchased at the price of chains and slavery?" says one, citing the "founding father" and slave owner Patrick Henry in 1775 (Panel 1, 1955). "I cannot speak sufficiently in praise of the firmness and deliberation with which my whole line received their approach," Andrew Jackson is quoted in another as saying in New Orleans in 1815 (Panel 25, 1956). Here Lawrence's eye and brush focus on the only thing left standing: a wall built by enslaved people, with the massacred bodies of these people piled high below.[131] Of course, the impetus and invitation here are not only with respect to the cracks that Lawrence opens but also, and more crucially, in relation to the cracks that continue to connect. The contemporary connection with the movement, mobilization, and existence-based cries of Black Lives Matter could not be clearer.

Recalled is another connected crack, this one instigated and led by the Black Panthers' minister of culture and artist Emory Douglas and Caleb Duarte of the EDELO (En Donde Era La ONU) arts collective and entitled Zapantera Negra. Here the aim was to connect the anticolonial, revolutionary politics of the Panthers and the Zapatistas, including both movements' critical uses of art and aesthetics within their struggles.

It was in December 2013 at the Zapatista Escuelita (Little School) in Chiapas that I met up with Emory; we were both first-grade students in this experience of learning autonomy and liberation. Emory was sitting in front of me on one of the wooden benches that filled the rustic auditorium of the Morelia Caracol, and which faced the stage where a group of about ten or twelve Zapatista women and men leaders were seated, ready to speak to us during this opening and welcoming session of the school. Each of the couple hundred students present had by our side our *votan*, or guardian-teacher; this was a young Zapatista woman or man of adolescent age who was to accompany us twenty-four hours a day for the next week, facilitating our learning and aiding in translation from Tojolabal or Tzotzil to Spanish. I noticed that the fellow student in front of me on the bench was struggling to understand the Spanish translation of his *votan*, and I suspected that he was English speaking and from the United States. When I offered to translate to English, he gratefully accepted, and as we presented ourselves, I recognized the familiarity of both his name and face. I asked, Had we met before? Without responding, he began to show me a collection of images on the computer that he had on his lap. I immediately remembered where I had seen them and him before; Emory was the artist of the Panthers' newspaper, a paper that I was recruited to distribute in 1971 at the University of Massachusetts–Amherst. He told me of the Zapantera Negra project that had its base in the small city of San Cristobal de las Casas, and its collaborative work with a number of communities in mutual learning, mural art, and thinking the political-aesthetic relation between Zapatistas and Panthers.

1.2 Emory Douglas in Oventic, Chiapas, Mexico. PHOTO: CALEB DUARTE, 2012.

Figure 1.2 shows Emory alongside a Zapatista-painted mural in Oventic, one of the community-based sites of autonomous government.

For those unfamiliar with the critical role of art and culture in both movements, I offer a brief history. First, it is important to recall the intimate relation between the Panthers and the Black Arts movement in the United States. Emory was the person who brought both together. As Bobby Seale—founding chair and national organizer of the Black Panther Party—explains, Emory was crucial in advancing a revolutionary culture "which was about the need to give the people more economic, political, and social empowerment." As the political party's minister of culture, "Emory was not only the dedicated Revolutionary Artist of our sixties and seventies protest era, . . . his artistic flavor was the revolutionary humanistic reflection of the sixties mood, our aspirations, and the demands for our constitutional, democratic, civil/human rights." Emory had charge of getting out the weekly newspaper, which, at its peak, circulated more than four hundred thousand copies a week. It was largely Emory's drawings and graphics, says Seale, "that communicated and helped the average protestor and grassroots organizer define the phenomena of who and what our oppressors were. Emory's leadership and art further reminded us and called us to action to try and make that phenomena, those oppressors, act in a desired manner."[132] Certainly the naming and caricature of the "pig"—synonymous with the police who occupy communities, brutalize people, and violate peaceful protesters' rights—still remains steadfast today.[133] Recalling these images and their political importance, the actor and film producer Danny Glover writes, "The images were images the community embraced. They were so right on and so appropriate for the struggle at hand at that time, and a sense of self-determination ensued from those images that Emory created."[134]

Second, it is important to understand the vital role of art and culture in the Zapatista struggle, particularly since the establishment of autonomous municipalities in 1994 and of the Caracoles in 2003 as the regional form of autonomous organization and "good government." Throughout Zapatista territory, community-based mural art tells the story of the historical leader Emilio Zapatista and of the present-day struggles of autonomy and liberation. In this mural art, Zapatistas are sometimes armed with weapons, and sometimes armed with revolutionary furor, hope, practice, and praxis, along with ancestral millenarian knowledges. I recall the image painted on the outside wall of the elementary school that I visited in 2009 in Oventic, my first visit to Zapatista territory and to one of the sites of its "good government" (figure 1.3). As the words say, "In the Autonomous Zapatista

1.3 Zapatista primary school, Oventic, Chiapas, Mexico. PHOTO: CATHERINE WALSH, 2009.

Schools children are educated in the spirit and collective consciousness of the world."

The weave of art and culture does not stop there. In the letters written by Subcomandante Insurgente Galeano to the philosopher Luis Villoro in 2016, Galeano argues that "the arts (and not politics) are those who dig into the depths of the human being and rescue its essence. As if the world were still the same, but with the arts and through the arts we could find the human possibility among so many gears, nuts and springs grinding with bad humor."[135] Here the concept and practice of collective autonomy is key: "The social plane is the power, since its creation depends on sharing, both in the collective making and in the collective share."[136] In the opening of the December 2019 *compArte* encounter of film and filmmakers—part of what the Zapatistas call their ongoing praxis of "seventh art," which in their words is art from and of the cracks—Galeano referred to the arts as the seed in which humanity will be reborn.[137] The Zapatista spokesperson Subcomandante Insurgente Moisés explained why and how art can birth a new world: "For us women and men Zapatistas, art is studied by creating many imaginations, by reading in the gaze, by studying in the act of listening, and in practice...with our resistance and rebellious being."[138] Such is the art and arts of cracks.

Given the centrality of art in the praxis of struggle and rebellion in both the Panthers and the Zapatistas, I was intrigued with the idea of the Zapantera Negra project and wanted to know more. Since Emory and I were assigned to spend the next days in different communities, we decided to meet up again in San Cristobal after the school ended. There I got a chance to learn about the project and about EDELO—also referred to as "where the United Nations used to be"—a house of art in movement and intercommunal artist residency that began in San Cristobal in Chiapas as part of an initiative led by Caleb Duarte and Mia Rollow. "Inspired by the 1994 Indigenous Zapatista uprising, where word and poetry are used to inspire a generation to imagine 'other' worlds possible," EDELO investigates "how ART, in all its disciplines and contradictions, can take the supposed role of such institutional bodies: in creating understanding, empathy, and to serve as a tool in imagining alternatives to what seem [sic] to be a harmful and violent system that we have come to accept."[139]

Among the many images I saw at the Zapantera Negra exposition, one particularly stood out. That was the Zapantera Negra poster designed by the Mexican artist Omar Insunza, better known as "Gran OM." This poster (figure 1.4) shows the connected but not fused faces of Zapantera Negra, an image that expresses the relational connecting of two revolutionary movements and what could be understood as two revolutionary, decolonial, and decolonizing cracks.

For me, the significance of Zapantera Negra is not only in the images and art produced but in the art of fissuring historical separations still present throughout the Americas between Indigenous and Black peoples and their struggles, and the praxis that this entailed and implied, including with respect to the learnings that both struggles—each in its own place, space, territory, generation, and time—afford to each other. In this sense, it seems that not just this shared project but also EDELO's ongoing use of art as a tool to imagine alternatives (reflected most particularly in Caleb's creative expression) and Emory's continuing justice-focused activist (art)work in the last decades with youths are clear manifestations—at least for me—of the possibility, power, and potential of the praxis of fissures and the art and arts of cracks.

1.4 Zapantera Negra poster, 2012. AUTHOR: GRAN OM. SCREEN CAPTURE: CALEB DUARTE.

In the body-mind texts and performances of Daniel B. Coleman, I see and sense an-other art of crack-making and an-other praxis of fissure. Self-identified as a "mixed-Black, transmasculine non-binary, queer and tender radical" who thinks with body and moves with mind,[140] Daniel weaves—in performance, pedagogy, and word—a praxis of transfeminist embodiment and transgender corporealities that suspends "the scopic regime of legibility" and creates "an erotic ancestry of flesh."[141] Here the cracks are part and parcel of Daniel's body-based thought-mind movement; that is, of the making, connecting, relating, and inhabiting of cracks that, of course, are not Daniel's alone. I see and sense similar cracks in the body-mind work of the interdisciplinary artist, writer, curator and Mariel survivor Raúl Moarquech Ferrera Balanquet. In his performance of and written reflections on "Mariposa memory," Raúl makes visible lived relationalities of present-past in which the ancestors and ancestral memory fissure the dominant frames of existence, life, and the living.[142] Together both Raúl and Daniel, and each in their own way, have taught me over the years—since we first met in 2012—about the praxis of fissure and the sensibilities present and made possible in the cracks.

The performative action of the Oaxacan Muxe Lukas Avendaño affords another example of crack-making praxis, one that not only transgresses gendered binaries but also visibilizes and denounces the violences of forced disappearance. In "Where Is Bruno?," a performative action to find his brother Bruno Alonso Avendaño Martínez, disappeared on May 10, 2018, in the locality Santo Domingo Tehuantepec, Oaxaca, Mexico, Avendaño "addresses the possibilities of 'appearing'... in the desolate social and political landscape, connecting artistic practices and political strategies that denounce and make visible: disappeared bodies, and forced disappearance?" Here Avendaño's performative action opens questions that are the cracks (thus recalling the words of Holloway quoted earlier): How to represent those who are invisible? And how to make the disappeared (re)appear?[143]

Amid the pain that is the violence-dispossession-war-death that many Indigenous territories know all too well, Violeta Kiwe Rozental Almendra, a six-year-old from Colombia's Cauca region, gives life to the memory of struggle of Cristina Bautista, Nasa leader and governor, and Violeta's friend, assassinated on October 29, 2019. In her book *Cristina Bautista: This Land's Bleeding Flight* (in its English-language version), Violeta draws for other children her visual narration of Cristina's struggle and life, and its violent end by the assassins in this war. The script added by her mother, Vilma Almendra Quiguanás, only compliments Violeta's illustrated narration.[144] Is this not one instance more—this time of a child and for other children—of the praxis and pedagogies of fissure that sow life in the midst of massacres (more than eighty-eight in Colombia in 2020 alone) and death, making lived memory a force that cracks the oblivion that pushes us to forget?

I could go on. I think of the 2020 massive mobilizations that began with the assassination at the hands of police of the African Americans George Floyd and Breonna Taylor, and that brought to the world's attention what Black communities have known for centuries: the danger of being a Black person in white peoples' world. That is the systemic racism, anti-Blackness, and dehumanization that somehow "remain hidden in plain sight."[145] In the United States, but also in cities throughout the globe, the movement, mobilizations, and cries of Black Lives Matter continue to rupture the hiddenness, urging attention, sight, and sense and undoing the seeming solidity of the institutionalized—and clearly related—regimes of citizenship, whiteness, and legal rights. The attacks, as 2020 ended and 2021 began, on the Capitol Building in Washington, DC, and in cities throughout the United States by white supremacists wielding arms—all pushed forth and sanctioned by then-president Trump—are evidence of the deeply entrenched systemic and structural character of racism and its present-day lived project of violence-war-death in the United States as well as elsewhere.

In November 2020, João Alberto Freitas was beaten to death in Porto Alegre, Brazil, by white supermarket security guards, one of whom was a military police officer. In May 2020, and in another Brazilian city, police brutally killed fourteen-year-old João Pedro Matos Pinto in his house, firing more than seventy high-caliber bullets. Afterward, they admitted they had entered the wrong property in search of drug traffickers.[146] These Joãos are two people more in the Trump-aligned order of President Jair Bolsonaro, an order that eliminates, at the hands of police, more than fifteen Afro-Brazilians a day (according to official accounts), the majority youths. "Afro-Brazilians make up over half of the country's population, but they are still fighting for their right to live," says a news report.[147] Of course Afro-Brazilian women and men don't need a news report to tell them what they know all too well.

The cracks are not the solution. However, they are part of the actions, strategies, and determinations to resist, exist, and re-exist. How many more can I and you, the reader, reference and name? I think of the "Land Back" struggles in Turtle Island that weave with the Native struggles of land present in all of the colonially invaded territories of six continents and in which the ongoing lived legacies of "conquest," settler colonialism, internal colonialism, and coloniality intertwine, including within the legacies of apartheid that continue in South Africa. But I also think of the struggles that transgress the imposed boundaries and totalizing myth of nation-state, most especially the ongoing work-in-struggle of the Kurdistan Communities of Women in Syria, Turkey, Iran, and Iraq. Here the praxis of women's communities, particularly in Rojava, is planting radically different seeds of society and democracy, while at the same time fissuring patriarchy through the autonomous organization of women in all spheres of life, including in governance without state, in education, and in the social sciences. As I will describe in more detail in later chapters of this book, this agency—including in the women-thought science of jineology—sows re-existence in spaces, places, and territories that crack the dominant order and liberate life.[148]

I mention all these examples because they show that the work of crack-making—the arts and praxes of fissure—are not metaphorical abstractions, academic constructions, or imagined possibilities. They are real-life practices that, sometimes with and at other times without explicit reference to cracks, cross the situated, contextual, and strategic fields of struggle against the capitalist, racist, heteropatriarchal, colonial system or matrix of power and its multiple manifestations, actions, and effects; real-life practices that struggle for an otherwise of existence and being-becoming, of re-existence and life.

ON THE CRACKS AND THE HOWS OF DECOLONIZING PRAXIS

Some may say that I am obsessed with the cracks. They are probably right. Since I first came across the crack on the stone-cement wall and later encountered others whose thinking and doing also found resonance, meaning, and place in the cracks, my sense of ground, purpose, and connectedness has grown. What has become especially clear is the relation of cracks with decolonizing work; the cracks are part of the how and hows of decolonial praxis.

The cracks, as I have said, are not the solution in and of themselves to coloniality's permanence and hold. Rather, they are part of its weakening and debilitation, on the one hand, and the opening toward its otherwise, on the other. It is in this way that I think of cracks and crack-making as essential strategies and tools of the "decolonial hows," strategies and tools not of the master, to recall Audre Lorde's well-remembered phrase: "The master's tools will never dismantle the master's house."[149] As Lewis Gordon pointed out in his opening talk at the Caribbean Philosophical Association 2021 Summer School, how we read Lorde is important. Not only masters have tools, said Gordon, and it is seldom the masters who build houses. The tools we need are to build: to build ideas, to build other and better houses that shift the supremacy and centrality of the master's thought and house.[150] For me, the cracks and crack-making are part of these tools; tools that fissure the centrality and unicity, and that open up and open toward other possibilities; tools that inventively craft methodologies-as-pedagogies and pedagogies-as-methodologies of decolonizing creation, prospect, praxis, and construction. It is in the cracks where the building often begins, and where the decolonial how and hows of the otherwise take form.

My reference to pedagogy here is not in the sense of schooling. For me, and as I will describe in more detail in the next chapter, pedagogy is a productive sociopolitical practice and process, an essential and indispensable methodology, based, as Paulo Freire argued, in peoples' realities, subjectivities, histories, and struggles.[151] But my understanding does not stop there. I recognize Freire's limits, including his ideological-political orientation too often rooted in western emancipatory postures, visions, and paradigms, a rootedness that Native authors such as Sandy Grande and Linda Tuhiwai Smith have well described.[152] This orientation is the same that Freire himself criticized at the end of his life, that which did not let him see with clarity racialized, heteronormativized, and patriarchal structures, lived experiences of coloniality, and struggles for autonomy, self-determination, and decolonization.

While I find connection with Freire's understanding of pedagogy as indispensable method, the relation of the political and pedagogical, and the pedagogical nature of social-political struggle, pedagogy per se is not the subject, object, or central axis of my concern here.[153] My concern instead is rooted in the existence-based *hows* of fracturing coloniality's project and hold—including, as I mentioned in the first part of this chapter, coloniality's ongoing mutations and reconfigurations—and it is rooted in the decolonizing processes, practices, and praxis that work to enable, create, construct, and make possible otherwises, or a decolonial something else.

It is here that I find special resonance with Frantz Fanon's praxistic postulates that take existence, decolonization, liberation, and humanization—and not pedagogy—as the actional foundation.[154] For me, Fanon is not a voice of the past who, as some seem to believe, has little relevance for the present. His careful thinking on *how* to unravel the complex existential entanglement that is colonialism-coloniality, and most especially its structural base of racism/race, remains essential today. With the introduction of sociogeny or sociogenesis—referred to by some as a principle and science for humanity—Fanon not only exposed the connection between the inferiority complexes suffered by many Black and colonized peoples and the colonial structure of social and societal oppression but also opened considerations toward the pedagogical-methodological *hows*.[155] Fanon's central concern was with the actional; that is, with processes and practices that push a recognition of the lived nature of the problem, and the necessary decolonial work to loosen and disengage it. His project was to build and enable self-determination, self-liberation, decolonization, and rehumanization, and/as "a change of skin." In this work of and toward a decolonial and decolonizing how, Fanon seemed to advance his own praxis of fissure. Not only did he teach us *about* the colonial problem; even more crucially, he urged actionings *with* (not *on*) others to crack the lived nature of colonial reality and colonialism/coloniality's existential foundation, shedding light on the zone of nonbeing not seen and planting seeds of re-existence. In this sense, I find a special affinity and alliance with Fanon.

Of course, and as I will show in other chapters, Fanon and Freire are only two among many others, including, and most especially, the Afro-Caribbean feminist and spiritual teacher M. Jacqui Alexander. In her powerful book *Pedagogies of Crossing*, Alexander allies herself with Freire's comprehension of pedagogy as method. Yet, and at the same time, she defines her project as crossed by other dominions that take her beyond the confines of modernity and the imprisonment of what she refers to as modernity's "secularized episteme." Alexander's project is to "disturb and reassemble the inherited divides of Sacred and secular, the embodied and disembodied," through pedagogies that derive from the "crossing," this conceived as a signifying and existential message, as a passage toward the configuration of new ways of thinking and being.[156] While Alexander does not name the cracks, the passage and configuration, along with her analytic perspective and arguments, seem to suggest related paths, paths that once again bring to the fore colonial wounds and the need for healing.

Alexander affirms that "colonization has produced fragmentation and dismemberment at both the material and psychic levels." And she argues that "the work of decolonization needs to make room for the deep yearning for wholeness, a yearning that is both material and existential, both psychic and physical, and which, when satisfied, can subvert and ultimately displace the pain of dismemberment." The problem, as she makes clear, is that anticolonial and Left liberation movements seldom understand this yearning and need. "What we have devised as an oppositional politic has been necessary, but it will never sustain us, for while it may give some temporary gains (which become more ephemeral the greater the threat, which is not a reason not to fight), it can never ultimately feed that Deep place within us: that space of the erotic, ... of the Soul, ... of the Divine."[157]

As I think with Alexander, I sense the presence of fissures and cracks that open toward that which is not seen—or, more critically, that which the dominant order does not want to be seen—in this case, the spiritual, the sacred, and the multiple instances and terrains "where its shades are inscribed."[158] As Alexander fractures secularism's assumed totality and hold, she opens spaces of and for the crossings and connections of subjectivity, collectivity, and the divine, for the spirits and ancestors who walk with us. In so doing, she guides decolonial and decolonizing hows of re-membering and reassembling relational wholeness.

Is this not what the practice-based work of decolonization and its praxis of fissure is, at least in part, all about? That is, the connecting and interweaving of cracks, cries, and also plantings in ways that do not just debilitate the wall but also enable re-relation with those beings and ontological-existence-based practices and ways of life and living that continue to exist beyond the wall, outside and/or in the borders, margins, limits, and crevices of its structure.

This, in essence, is the focus of that which follows. It is a journey of sorts that moves not in lineal but serpentine motion, with no clearly defined endpoint of arrival. The journey is the movement, that which continuously engages the questions of decolonizing hows and of existences otherwise, walking and asking, crying and cracking, and thinking, doing, and acting *with*, planting and cultivating the seeds of otherwises that flower rebellion, breathe liberation, and generate what Fanon referred to in the *Wretched of the Earth* as a "new thought" and "change of skin."[159]

Asking and Walking 2

"Asking we walk"
    the asking in itself challenges the master imaginary:
    it challenges master narratives, master's houses
    houses of reason, houses of science
    universal truths of privilege, of property, of power, of politics.
    ... Continuing *to ask, to listen, as we walk;*
    seeking ... searching ... creating ...
    finding sacred mountains everywhere.
    —CORINNE KUMAR

I begin with the wise words of the Pakistani feminist Corinne Kumar, written as part of the introduction to her three-volume anthology *Asking We Walk: The South as New Political Imaginary.*[1] As Kumar explains, the words of her title are the wind from the South as new political imaginary: "The Zapatistas of Chiapas offer a new imaginary: in their struggle for their lives and livelihoods, and for retaining *lifeworlds*, in their profound and careful organization, in their political imagining do not offer clear, certain, rigid, ideological, universal truths, sum up their vision in three little words: *Asking, we walk.*"[2]

It is the idea, practice, and praxis of asking and walking / walking and asking that guides this chapter. Without a doubt, these thoughtful actions have much to do with the never-ending processes to decolonize and deschool. Deschooling and decolonizing, as I understand them, are coconstitutive. Together they point to the ongoing work to disrupt and transgress, to crack, break apart, and break free from the master imaginary, the master's house, and the master plan: from the structures, institutions, logics, and universal truths that attempt to order, discipline, and control minds, bodies, spirits, and souls, and to shape, organize, and rule social existence. I recall the words of the insubordinate priest and anarchist thinker Ivan Illich: "Not just education but also social reality has come to be schooled.... Not just education but also society as a whole need to be deschooled."[3] To paraphrase him: *not just education but also existence need to be deschooled.* How to ask and walk these processes is part of my interest here.

I write the chapter as fragments of and from my own ongoing story. It is a narrative of pieces and parts of learning to learn, unlearn, and relearn; of struggles with, in, and through social existence and education; and of experiences lived, felt, and thought with others. The chapter is not meant to be an autobiographical account. I conceive it instead as a pedagogical conversation of sorts, a telling of fragments as I muse, walk, and ask in the company of you, the reader, and in the company of many others with whom I have learned to unlearn and relearn in this incessant ask and walk that is existence in the midst of coloniality.

The fragments are just that. They are bits and pieces of a story; a story that is never mine alone, since it is interwoven in life and living with others. I imagine the fragments as pieces of cloth written on over many decades. The cloth, in some cases, has begun to fray and show its age. Some of the letters have begun to fade, so I carefully write over them again, this time maybe with a clearer stroke of the pen.

With each piece of cloth and each relettering, I recall the paths walked, the faces of those who guided and accompanied me and of those who endeavored to deter me and divert the path, or to try to make linear and straight its serpentine movement. Brought to mind are my incessant questions, the asking that has accompanied my walking and my search for and making of walkable paths. Re-membered are the deeply felt sentiments of lived— and necessarily linked—reflection, thoughtful action, and actional thought etched as a watermark of sorts on each piece of fabric. Evoked as well are the moments, processes, and experiences of my own learning to learn, and unlearn in order to relearn, of my continuing endeavor to decolonize and deschool, and, relatedly, of my preoccupation, venture, sowing, and cultivation of and for existences and educations otherwise.

The fragments are not meant to be pieced together into a whole. I am not interested in stitching a quilt, at least not right now. I fear that this would suture, close up, or bring to a finish not only the narration here but, more importantly, the ongoing character, process, and doing of decolonial praxis and its intersubjective and collective sense and stance. My fragments are just that; they are pieces that I loosely assemble with a coarse yarn, pieces that can be taken apart, rearranged, and strung up to move in and with the wind. They are pieces that call forth and call for those of others, including students, community members, activists, educators, authors, and friends with whom I have learned, unlearned, and relearned; with whom I have thought, asked, and walked; and with whom these processes and movements continue. But they are pieces that also summon, incite, and invite you, the reader, to think about your own stories. What are the particular fragments or pieces that come to mind, most especially those that conjure up, point to, and conjoin efforts, hopes, and experiences that have sought and seek to decolonize and deschool? I am beginning to imagine many pieces of cloth each with bits and pieces of your testimonies and narratives that accompany mine. And I am beginning to imagine the conversations that might follow.

The chapter, in this sense, is conceived as a pedagogy unfolding and taking form. Here, I am thinking with Paulo Freire's notion of pedagogy as an essential and indispensable methodology. And, relatedly, I am thinking with M. Jacqui Alexander's understanding of pedagogy "as that which interrupts, transgressing, disturbing, dislocating, and inverting inherited concepts and practices"; pedagogy as the psychic, analytic, and organizational methodologies that we use to make different conversations and solidarities possible; pedagogy as an ontological and epistemic project tied to our very modes of being.[4]

As such, the pedagogy-methodology/methodology-pedagogy that takes shape in this chapter seeks to mark a difference and distance from—a transgressing, disturbing, dislocating, and inverting of—the dominant, inherited, and linked institutions of society, education, and school. In so doing, it heeds Illich's call, made almost fifty years ago, to deschool society. For Illich, deschooling meant taking radical action against the modern capitalist "schooling" of our hearts, bodies, minds, and values, and for the liberation of "other" ways of learning and living. The problem, for him, was with the accelerated global degradation and modernized misery of society, existence, and life. And it was with the direct relation of this degradation and misery with the nature of modern social institutions and their practice of lifelong institutionalization.[5]

In fact, after *Deschooling* was published, Illich began to take this proposition further, rejecting not just schooling but education. "I moved from the criticism of schooling to the criticism of what *education* does to a society, namely, foster the belief that people have to be helped to gain insights into reality, and have to be helped to prepare for existence or for living."[6] This tenet, developed further in Illich's subsequent "In Lieu of Education" and explored in detail more recently by Gustavo Esteva, opens avenues of reflection and action on the complicity of education—on its idea, institution, conditions, and practice—with dependence, notions of progress and development, consumerism (including of knowledge), and capitalism's global project.[7]

I will return later to some of the precepts and arguments of this negation and proposition and their practice and experience today. However, my interest first is with the ways schooling, understood as the authoritative control, discipline, and domination of "hearts, bodies, minds, and values," underscores my own education and existence-based struggles, and I suspect, the struggles of many of the readers here. The problem, as I see it, is with the ways schooling comes to regulate social institutions and lives. The question that follows, then, is how to liberate other ways of existing, re-existing, learning, relearning, and living. While this problem and this question necessarily start with ourselves, they do not stop there. Existence, as learning, always necessitates relationality and correlation, to use Sylvia Wynter's term;[8] that is, a praxis of interhumanness, of being human as praxis.[9] How we construct this praxis, with whom, and what for—with what project of existence and/as humanity—are crucial concerns in that they can mark colonial conduits or, differentially, decolonial pathways. These are the concerns that underlie this chapter, its narrated fragments, and its continuous reflection on the praxical work to be done; that is, the work toward the interwoven pedagogical imperatives of decolonizing and deschooling, which, of course, are component parts of the cries and the work of cracking coloniality's wall.

Fragments That Resist, Insist, and Persist

TALKING BACK:
REBELLING AND QUERYING SCHOOL

My relationship with schooling and its institutions has always been problematic.

When I was growing up in the United States, many of my teachers said my constant questioning of both them and textbooks was going to lead to no good. I was "too smart for my britches," some said, and too defiant of the rules and rituals. My refusing, for political reasons, to pledge to the flag beginning at about ten years old—and then writing an essay about the reasons for this defiance—is one of many examples.

My father went off to war as an adolescent, never graduated from high school, and for many years was a wage laborer. At home he exerted his authority, often in violent ways, over my mother, my much younger sister, and me (but not my brother). I was the oldest. And, as he often told me, I was the problem; the reason for family conflict. All would be much better, he said, if I wasn't there. Spending weekends and school vacations at my grandparents' home was a partial solution. With adolescence the situation worsened. My emerging manifestations of rebellion, dissidence, independence, and critical thought were met with aversion, reprimands, and continual punishment, an appropriate response, he told me, for a girl who refused to be docile, "ladylike," and silenced, a girl who insisted and persisted in rebelling, querying, and talking back.

My mother was an English teacher in the local small-town public high school, a job she began around the time I was about to reach high school age. Her hope was to return to the intellectual world she had left with marriage and children, improve the family's economic situation, and gain some independence from my father. She supported my intellectual curiosity. However, its rebellious and dissident nature was, for her, a special cause for concern; concretely, her fear was what it might mean for her emerging teaching career if I—the defiant and too-outspoken daughter-student—were to attend her school. Thus came the decision to make an economic sacrifice and send me to a Catholic high school in a larger, neighboring town. Besides my mother's fear, there was the hope of both her and my father that Catholic education would "school" me. However, my social and political questioning of the system only grew, and with it began a nascent questioning of gender, race, and class. Let me explain.

The distance between the school and my home was several miles. There was no direct public transportation, and the indirect route not only took me way off course but also cost me several days of going without lunch; that is, in the infrequent times when I had lunch money. On days that I could not find a ride home, I most often had to walk. One day I discovered a shortcut that took me through a Puerto Rican neighborhood. As the days went by, the residents began to recognize me and I them; often we would exchange greetings. All this seemed a normal part of my routine; that is, until I was called to the principal's office and severely reprimanded by the principal-priest for associating with "them," though he never named who the "them" were. His words opened my eyes to a social reality I had not heretofore considered in my sheltered, white, small-town life; that is, to racism and the stereotypes that accompany racialization. I was putting myself into great danger, he said; their neighborhood was definitely out-of-bounds for a good Catholic schoolgirl. How could it be that I had been seen talking and, so he claimed, "drinking with them"? My parents were called in and I was threatened with expulsion. The reprimands, disciplining, and "schooling" continued at school and at home.

However, the "lesson" was not the one expected. Instead, and with the help of a radical young parish priest interested in the theology of liberation, I began to study how social and political power constitute and sustain "the system." And I began to learn about the relationship of capitalism and the Catholic Church, and the complicities of both in constructing and maintaining poverty, racism, sexism, and patriarchy. In August 1968 (when I was about to enter my junior year), this priest took a group of us to a Catholic Youth Conference in Chicago, held during the same dates as the now-famous Democratic National Convention. There, I personally witnessed the police brutality in the park, directed most especially at African Americans and women. My eyes were opened further. And my learning, unlearning, and relearning began to take form.

The last two years of high school became more conflictive and problematic; not only did I query more, but my questions and thought were more directed at the complicities of the institutions of religion and education. The threats of expulsion continued. Somehow my mother's constant pleas to the authorities to keep me in school, coupled with my honor society grades, helped to get me to graduation. In contrast to the majority of my classmates, who went on to attend Catholic or other "respectable" private colleges, I chose—to the consternation (but not surprise) of the educational-religious authorities—a large public university known for its radical politics. My father was happy to get me out of the house.

RISING UP AND TAKING BACK

This was 1970: the time of the Vietnam War, Students for a Democratic Society, the Weather Underground and the Panthers; of racial and sexual politics; and of revolutionary preparedness, study, organizing, and hope. The university—*this* university (the University of Massachusetts–Amherst; UMass) and in *this* time—provided the context, place, and space for me to begin to probe the why, what, and how of the work to be done, a probing that meant shared militancy, collectivity, and coalition;[10] in essence, a learning-doing of rising up and taking back with others. With other women I discovered an existential energy and force. We took back our bodies and our ways of loving. And we rose up in a multiracial feminist coalition against the patriarchal and raced military apparatus and its capitalist war project. One action that I particularly recall is the night we climbed in the windows of the campus ROTC building, startling the recruits, taking over the building, and converting it into a women's center. With this coalition and with other radical organizations in which I was involved, we broke down the walls of classrooms (in a metaphoric sense) and made political praxis the proposition, process, and goal. It was in these contexts that I first heard the words of Angela Davis and the repeated phrases of Sojourner Truth, listened to and read the poetry of Audre Lorde, and read the texts of Rosa Luxemburg, Karl Marx, Frantz Fanon, and Paulo Freire. Within our political study groups, the interest was with how each contributed to what we understood as the rebellion and revolution at hand.

After two years, I decided to leave the university. Not only had the economic struggle to pay tuition and housing become too much, but also rising up no longer seemed enough. I needed to explore ways to live against and despite the system, and in its margins and cracks; in essence, taking back an existence otherwise in the world. In the years following, I experimented with communal and cooperative living, practiced subsistence farming, participated in a feminist women's health collective, and opened an alternative school. While in the university, I was never sure about a field of study; I moved from sociology to anthropology to organic farming and dappled in dance and art. Education and teaching were never considerations. However, without my taking conscious notice, both somehow appeared in my walking path.

"TEACHING TO TRANSGRESS"?

It began slowly.[11] I had to pay rent in the collective house where I was living. The only job opportunity that came through was as a part-time teacher's aide in a privately run kindergarten. I lasted less than six months; the discipline, control, and forced indoctrination of the children into formal schooling horrified me. With this "experience," I landed another job in a progressive early childhood center. There I began to appreciate the curiosity of young children to learn while doing. With these experiences and a whole series of questions as impetus and guide, I decided to put my energies to work in making a different kind of school for young children in donated space in an urban multiracial neighborhood. Conceived as a parent cooperative, the school worked to build—together with the children (two and a half to six years old) and their parents—an antiracist and antisexist process and practice of participatory learning, doing, and decision-making. Together we built a playground; made furniture, books, and materials; and crafted a learning environment where thinking and doing were interwoven with reflection and analysis with and on the social world. As I understand it now, the "school" worked to decolonize and deschool; to decolonize and deschool my own preconceived notions of education, and to guide the shaping of a process, practice, space, and place where children were free to be, but also where difference, diversity, and discrimination (in terms of race, gender, class, family structures, etc.) were part of shared inquiry, analysis, and discussion.[12]

I still vividly recall one example pushed by the tears of Buffy, a dark-skinned five-year-old girl, in response to a younger white boy's remarks about her Afro–Puerto Rican father and white mother, and her linguistic movement between Spanish and English. With all of the children and myself seated together on the floor, we listened to Buffy as she recounted what had occurred, described how she felt, and said what she had to say about it. Then we listened to the boy's explanation of his remarks and why he had made them. Together as a group we began a collective reflection on the incident, on the problem of racialized violence and its various forms, and on the ways whiteness and the English language were naturalized and normalized. Thinking about it now, I recall a phrase from J. Nozipo Maraire's novel *Zenzele*: "It is funny how little children can intuitively understand so much."[13] For weeks, racism, discrimination, and stereotyping became the explicit guiding force of the curriculum always in construction, and a permanent part of our critical thought and reflection about the social world with the children and also in workshops with their parents.

The incident experienced by Buffy, along with many other experiences lived and encountered in this educational space, raised questions that I could not answer. How does the dominant social structure work, setting up in a myriad of ways racial, sexual, and class borders, limits, and boundaries? How are racism and sexism learned and internalized at such a young age, including among children whose families actively work to combat either or both? How might we create spaces of learning, thinking, and doing with others in community that challenge the social structure and its derived social practices, including those of formal schooling? It was this questioning that led me back to the university in the evenings. What I sought was not "higher education" but a space with others of shared and reflective reading, debate, discussion, and thought.

The undergraduate degree that I eventually finished was in sociology and human development, not education. I wanted to more deeply understand the social sphere in order to intervene in it, not to be part of the educational system. Yet, on the advice of a counselor, I took several education courses in order to obtain a teaching certificate just in case I might someday need it. What I did not know then was that one of the requirements for the certificate was student teaching within the system, in a school chosen by university officials. The alternative school I had started did not count, although by now it had a string of student teachers from a number of local colleges. I refused the university's choice of a school because it was all white. I needed to continue to learn unlearning—in effect "un-suturing"[14]—the "normalcy" that accompanies whiteness; such learning, unlearning, and unsuturing, I believed, could not happen in an all-white school. They offered me another possibility: a practicum in an international school in London or in Quito, Ecuador.

So began in 1977 my Ecuadorian connection and relation. I was initially assigned to the second grade. My expectations—part of my naïveté regarding the US system of international schools abroad—were shattered on the first day; the very traditional curriculum, the very traditional head teacher, and the very traditional environment of this elitist school made me want to get back on the plane and go home. The tensions were mutual. Yet, because of the contractual obligations for my semester stay, I was somehow able to negotiate a counterteaching space outside the traditional classroom that used my training in modern, jazz, and African dance.[15] What was supposed to be a semester stay in Quito turned into two years; from teaching dance I went to working as a cook in a vegetarian bohemian restaurant. It is in Ecuador that I learned Spanish. And it is in Ecuador that my questions about the structural inequalities of the capitalist-driven world-system grew. I began to realize how little I really knew and how much I had to learn, unlearn, and relearn.

LEARNING TO UNLEARN AND RELEARN

With my questions I returned to the same university that had helped radicalize me a decade before. This time it was to a master's program focused on bilingual education and made up almost entirely of Puerto Rican faculty and students. Certainly the reality of this program and the region were not typical of most of the United States. Brought first as migrant farm labor in the

1950s and 1960s, western Massachusetts's Boricua or Puerto Rican community became permanent with time, continually growing given its proximity to New York City's *guagua aerea* (air bus) with the island. At the university there was a consolidated Puerto Rican intellectual class grounded in antiracist and anticolonial politics.

I still vividly recall one of my first courses in the program. I was the only non–Puerto Rican in the class. It was in the second or third session that the professor asked me to stand and explain to her and my forty or so classmates why I was there. What was my interest as a white student, she asked, and how could I possibly contribute to a Puerto Rican–based education? While it was not the first time I had had to confront the reality of whiteness and white privilege, it was probably the most difficult and dramatic, with the whole class waiting for my answer. My response took a while as I struggled with the vulnerability, fear, and tears welling up inside. I don't remember my exact words, but rather the sentiment and gist, which have stayed with me ever since. Both had—and have—to do with the hard processes of the unsuturing, of learning to unlearn in order to relearn, and the social, moral, political, ethical, epistemic, and human responsibility that this implies. That is, the responsibility and obligation to use the privilege that I carry on my skin to work against structural oppressions, work that simultaneously takes place inside and outside educational institutions, and alongside educators, students, parents, and communities.[16] It is the responsibility and obligation to use my whiteness in what I understand today as opening, making, and widening cracks, all of which necessarily entails the never-ending processes of decolonizing and deschooling, including—and most especially—of myself.

It was in the context of this program, the Puerto Rican community in which I became actively engaged in spaces of both daily living and popular education, and later in Puerto Rican communities and shared educational projects throughout the US Northeast that I began to learn about colonialism. Colonialism not as an abstract theory or a condition of the past but as a constitutive part of the unique lived and ongoing reality of Puerto Ricans as both US citizens and colonial subjects, what Kelvin Santiago-Valles calls a "subject people."[17] How colonialism works in and through schooling became one of my central concerns, including in my subsequent doctoral work.

One day in 1980 I received a call from a lawyer associated with the Puerto Rican Legal Defense and Education Fund. He asked if I might be interested in working with him, the fund, and a community-based organization on an educational and language rights case in a majority–Puerto Rican elementary school in Bridgeport, Connecticut. The essence of the case was the abysmal distance between the curriculum and the sociocultural and sociolinguistic reality of the students. Could it be, he asked me, that schooling perpetuated the colonial condition, a perpetuation in which language played a crucial part? And could we work together, using the legal system and courts, to decolonize language and education in this school? I was fascinated by the idea and challenge and, of course, accepted at once. With community leaders, parents, and the lawyers, we built the case and won. To my knowledge, it was the first time that the relationship among education, language, and colonialism was argued in US courts, most especially with regard to Puerto Ricans.[18] I was subsequently appointed as the court monitor and, over the course of several years, worked with community leaders and teachers to shape a pedagogical and curricular process that endeavored to undo in this context and setting—or at least fissure or crack—colonialism's ongoing framework and operation.

In my doctoral research, I delved more into how the past and present realities of colonialism intersect in schooling and how language plays a major role in these processes. I was especially interested in the cognitive and sociosemantic processes of bilingualism in Puerto Rican children and the ways in which English carries a colonial weight that affects how these children think about their communities, their families, and themselves. My concern was also with the ways language and meaning inform pedagogy and shape both the conditions under and the struggles through which Puerto Rican students come to know. The National Association of Bilingual Education awarded the dissertation first prize. Some years later, it became the focus of my first book, along with added considerations on how Puerto Rican and Latinx students perceive the contradictory nature of schooling and how to think with them in building, from their lived realities, what we termed then—and, as I will describe later, in concert and colabor with Paulo Freire— "critical pedagogy."[19]

During these years, I experienced difficult and intense processes of learning, unlearning, and relearning; of constantly putting into question and tension what I thought I knew in order to begin to know with and from realities radically different from those of my own upbringing, existence, and education. Crucial in this process was my intellectual-political guide, doctoral thesis director, and "boss" in the Horace Mann Bond Center for Equal Education, where I worked during the years of my master's and doctoral study, Meyer Weinberg. Meyer was a veteran of the 1960s civil rights movement in Chicago, a highly recognized intellectual-activist in antiracist and desegregation struggles, and an educational historian by trade. In order to comprehend the depths of structural inequalities in the United States, one has to understand the relation of present and past, he argued, a relation deeply marked by race and capital, and in which education and schooling have always had a central role. How to confront these structural inequalities not just in theory and rhetoric but in concrete practice was the challenge that Meyer pushed me to assume, a challenge that, in essence, had to do with political-pedagogical praxis.

COMING TO POLITICAL-PEDAGOGICAL PRAXIS

After finishing my doctorate in 1984, I was asked to stay on as a faculty member and coordinate a statewide project (part of a regional Northeast consortium with Brown University) focused on the training of bilingual educators and on collaborative work with "language minority" communities (i.e., Latinx, Haitian, Cape Verdean, Chinese, and Southeast Asian).[20] These were times in which the changing complexion of US society—most especially with respect to Latinos/as and the rapid growth of immigrant, refugee, and non-English-speaking communities of color—and the deepening of structural inequalities in labor, housing, health, and education urged reflection, action, and organized struggle. How to think about this struggle inside and outside the context of schools and schooling, how to begin to weave threads of relation with experiences elsewhere, and how to shape and mold political-pedagogical praxis—and with whom and what for—were some of my many pressing questions.

Freire was a central force in helping me move my questioning toward pedagogical praxis, toward what he called the pedagogy of questions. Several colleagues and I were able to negotiate with Harvard University (where Freire was in residence for three years) for him to spend a semester a year at UMass (1984–86). Our interest was to open and stimulate reflection, discussion, and dialogue on political-pedagogical praxis.

Since my first encounter in the early 1970s with *Pedagogy of the Oppressed*, Freire had been an important force in my thought and practice, a guide in understanding and making education a sphere of political action. For Freire, education is not limited or restricted to schools. It includes and extends to, in a much broader sense, social, political, epistemic, and existential contexts where "leaders and people, mutually identified, together create the guidelines of their action," an action at once political, educational, and of liberation.[21] Practice and praxis, in this sense, had to be grounded in peoples' own social-political analysis of the lived realities and conditions—internal and structural-institutional—of domination, marginalization, subordination, and oppression, Freire argued; an individual and collective consciousness-building necessary for humanization, politicization, liberation, and transformation. Here it was Freire's emphasis on the incessant struggle to recuperate humanity denied, and to build a human and humanizing ethics in and with the world—which included the educator's own learning to be with relation to and against one's own being—that gave practical-theoretical ground to my thought, reflection, and action.

To come to know in person Paulo and Elsa, his first wife, was a gift that I hold closely to my heart. On many an afternoon during the cold winter months, we would sit together with a pot of tea, he sharing his political-pedagogical experiences and (re)learnings to be—including in Latin America, Cape Verde and Guinea Bissau, Geneva, and the United States, most especially, in the last case, with women and communities of color[22]—and me reflecting out loud about my much more limited sphere of political-pedagogical learning, questioning, and struggle. I remember how Paulo was not afraid to show his vulnerability and emotions, and how easily he cried. The tears, he said, were a reflex reaction of the connection of his heart and mind. They were genuine expressions and manifestations of love, hope, humanization, and liberation entwined.

Together, Paulo and I cofacilitated seminars and open dialogues with colleagues and students in the university and workshops within the Puerto Rican community's program of popular education. In 1986, along with Deborah Britzman and Juan Aulestia, we organized at UMass the First Working Conference on Critical Pedagogy. Paulo, Maxine Greene, Meyer Weinberg, Stanley Aronowitz, Patti Lather, Henry Giroux, Peter McLaren, Ira Shor, Peter Park, Madeleine Grumet, and many others, including collectives of activists, educators, feminists, cultural workers, and others from throughout the United States and Canada, came together to debate, discuss, and share perspectives, postures, and experiences of transformative pedagogy and social struggle and/as praxis. Paulo's thought, writings, and dialogical presence served as the guiding force in what then began to be positioned as "critical pedagogy," a network and movement of sorts that I identified with until my permanent move to Ecuador in the mid-1990s.

This movement-network came to build—into the 1990s and with teachers, students, youths, and community leaders and activists—multiple spaces of critical questioning, relation, debate, and reflection, as well as of intervention and action, aimed at analyzing and confronting the racialized, classed, and gendered relations and realities of schools and society, and at conjoining social and educational change. The voices were diverse, some tied to intellectual interests within the academy and others rooted in lived processes on the ground.

I recall in particular the voices and theorizing analyses of a group of high-school-age youths, part of the Oxnard, California–based Students for Cultural and Linguistic Democracy (SCaLD) formed in 1992 by present and former Mexican, Chicanx, and Vietnamese students. "How can we talk about just changing schools? Schools reflect society," argued Rosalba, a member of SCaLD. "No matter what structural or instructional changes we put in place, they are always temporary. What we really need to be talking about is how to set up a system that cultivates something different."[23]

Adriana, another Mexican student from SCaLD, was also particularly clear in her analysis of the ways that teaching, curriculum, and schooling are intricately connected to the unequal social world: "We need to deconstruct the Eurocentric model of curriculum. To look at the relation between power and knowledge in the classroom and within the curriculum, not only as teacher or student but as both—to understand how both teachers and students understand that relation. . . . About the way certain kinds of knowledge are taught to us, introduced to us. . . . About why everything is centered on an individual perspective, about self-interest. . . . About how we could be using knowledge to understand what's going on in the world and in our own communities."[24]

In SCaLD's collectively written text "Reclaiming Our Voices," these youths sum up their reason for coming together: "Never again will we walk away and let the voices of our people stay forgotten." There they describe "Education" as the problem. "We know from experience that there is little or no connection between our real lives and education." The human aspect of teaching and learning is neglected; the system works to dehumanize, they say. "All throughout this country, every day, students are being hurt by the authoritarian, oppressive, traditional educational system. The destructive impact of the system is most severe in the lives of multiethnic students; the implanting of servility and silence is coupled with discrimination and institutionalized racism."[25]

Against this reality, SCaLD began a collective process that they called critical pedagogy in action. "Collective action occurs when students and community realize that injustice prevails, not freedom, and that the power to transform society is theirs," they argue. "Without the authoritarian system of education, students explore a foreign curriculum, a curriculum made up of their life histories and cultural truths. Voicing, dialogue, and collective sharing help [us] create a collective experience that gives [us] the strength to question [our] social situation." For them, critical pedagogy was not a method but a way of life. Furthermore, as they go on to say, "Critical Pedagogy gave us the opportunity to discover hidden voices to understand and to look more critically at what was going on around us. With these voices we began to challenge oppression and raise the awareness of parents and the community so that educational transformation could be possible. With Critical Pedagogy, education is not limited to the classroom. What happens in the classroom is a model for what needs to happen in the outside world. Learning is living and as students we learn by changing the way we live."[26]

I met members of SCaLD in the early 1990s in the Southern California desert at one of the critical pedagogy summer schools organized by the California Association of Bilingual Education. A group of SCaLD students, along with their teacher Bill Terrazas and Los Angeles activist Joyce Watts, were invited participants. I still remember the students' intervention that opened the first day of the weeklong experience. Through a participatory sociodrama, they depicted the realities of their everyday lives in the context of an educational system that worked to silence, negate, and oppress, and, relatedly, a social structure that endeavored in all too many ways to subjugate and dehumanize them, their families, and their communities. They engaged all of us adults in the room in the drama and forced us to locate ourselves and take a position.

So began our dialogue that continued throughout the day and all night. In front of a small bonfire under the desert sky, these young women and men recounted to Joyce and me their lived experiences as sons and daughters of mostly undocumented farm workers and, in many cases, as members of organized gangs: affiliations, as they detailed, necessary for survival. They shared their physical, symbolic, and heartfelt wounds and scars, the violences lived, and the everyday fears of elimination. And they talked about their strategies of resistance, persistence, and existence, as well as about the political pedagogies and practices of collective learning that had come to symbolize and make possible hope and life in and out of school.

As the sun began to rise, they asked Joyce and me to become "advisers." As they explained, this meant being there to listen, to dialogue (not judge), and to be part of shared reflection. In my case, as I lived on the East Coast, it meant ongoing telephone contact (these were the times before internet) and spending at least a week with them each year. Over the next several years, and until my permanency in Ecuador no longer permitted it, I kept this pledge. Moreover, SCaLD became part of the collaborative project of

Puerto Rican and Latinx youth researchers that Carmen Mercado (Hunter College), María Torres Guzmán (Teachers College), and I had begun in the Northeast in the early 1990s. In this Northeast and Southwest exchange, including as conference presenters—one year even interrupting the professional solemnity and academic authority of the American Educational Research Association—these adolescent researcher-educators shared their critical assessment of schooling, the stark disparity for students of color between education and real life, and the ways that they individually and collectively perceived, proposed, and worked to make social and educational change in and out of schools. Together, they wove threads of relational possibility and planted seeds of resistance, persistence, and life.

For me, at this time, the incessant and continually emergent question was not about transforming the institution of schooling. I did write about and struggle with the idea of educational reform, believing that education could and should make a difference in people's lives and not simply reproduce and maintain the colonial, raced, gendered, capitalist, and patriarchal order. But my deeper questions were about *how* to build spaces of collective learning and of praxis—of analysis-reflection-action—that could lead to concrete change in the lives of students, communities, and educators. *How* to work both inside and outside the educational institution, *how* to use the system against the system, and *how* to support the active agency of youths, parents, and communities in this work, process, and struggle were persistent queries.

As I understand now, the questions and experiences of the *hows* were, without a doubt, part of my own coming to political-pedagogical praxis. They were not about me as teacher-savior enabling the awareness and critical consciousness of what Freire referred to as the oppressed, but instead about my learning to unlearn in order to relearn, including with respect to my role, responsibility, participation, thinking and doing, and praxis. Critical pedagogy was one chapter, a chapter that I later came to take distance from, in part, because of its western-centric frame, as I will explain later. Another chapter was in the use of the legal system and courts; the use of the system against the system.

After the Bridgeport case, I continued to work collaboratively with legal advocacy organizations, including the Puerto Rican Legal Defense and Education Fund, the Lawyers' Committee for Civil Rights, the NAACP Legal Defense Fund, and the Multicultural Education and Advocacy Project, the last being the only nonprofit legal advocacy organization specializing in the defense of the educational rights of linguistic minority and immigrant children. Here the collaborative work started on the ground; that is, in, from, and with the community.

In Massachusetts, for instance, bilingual parents, community organizers, and community leaders began to come together in community assemblies, meetings, and workshops to discuss the violences, negations, and discriminations that children and youths faced in the schools. And they began to ask about and explore their legal rights. In the late 1980s, they formed PUEDO (Parents United in Education and the Development of Others), a statewide organization run by parents that the Multicultural Education and Advocacy Project and the university center that I then directed helped support by paying the salary of a community-based organizer. One of PUEDO's central concerns was to fight for the educational rights of the community's children. Here and in local community meetings, we—several lawyer-activists, community organizers, and I—were asked to facilitate workshops on linguistic and educational rights, to help generate and build processes of documentation of what was going on in schools and support organized action.

The examples are many. In Lynn, Massachusetts, for instance, Dominican mothers climbed on the bus with their children in the morning, paying no heed to the English-speaking bus driver's demands that they get off, and then sat in bilingual classrooms observing what went on and taking mental or written notes. High-school-age youths gave testimony in the community meetings, speaking of the discrimination, the dehumanizing treatment, and the lack of education they received in school, including from "bilingual" teachers who were white and had no community-based interest or ties. All these observations became a key part of community sessions, discussions, and analysis and, over time, came to give form to the legal demands. In this case, as in others, my community involvement was strategically and collectively "erased" when the litigation went to court. I then "reappeared" as an educational expert presenting to the judges the disparate educational conditions for limited English speakers in the particular school or school district in question. After the cases were won and judges sought a court-appointed monitor to ensure implementation, lawyers presented my curriculum vitae. And so it was, in case after case, that I assumed the work on the ground with students, teachers, and administrators in schools to change not just policy but practice.[27] In Lynn, for instance, I spent almost three years working directly in the classroom with a group of high school students deemed "problematic" by the school administration because of their rural Afro-Dominican backgrounds, limited formal schooling, and lack of literacy skills. Together we used photography, sociodrama, and video to document their struggles on the streets, in nightlong factory work, and during the day in school. They made and published photo-novels, produced videos, and presented to authorities a revision of the school rules (most of which, because of my court-appointed authority, were accepted).

Together we were clear about the political and strategic nature of this pedagogical work and the shared endeavor of praxis—of critical reflection-analysis-action—with respect to their lives and the institution of schooling. To stay in school and graduate was, as they clearly contended, an enormous struggle against the lure of drugs and gangs, and the economic hardships of daily life, often without parents or family support. Yet for most, the goal was to graduate and get the degree. Using the legal system against the educational system was one way—at least in this time, context, school, and dissident community-based practice—to give voice to students' and parents' concerns; to break the patterns of violence and silence present, perpetuated, and maintained by schools; and to cultivate dignity against ignominy and denigration.

Of course, the legal system and courts were not the only venue of my work with communities, students, and educators to create radically different spaces of learning, to build political-pedagogical praxis, and to transgress—or open fissures in—the institution of school. One of the experiences that I especially recall is that created with Haitian educators in the Boston public schools. In 1988, up against an influx of Haitian adolescent students from rural areas with limited or no formal schooling, Haitian administrators and teachers asked for my advice and support. Together we worked without any additional funds to develop and put in place a Freire-inspired literacy program in Kreyol and English, rooted in students' sociocultural contexts, lived experience, and everyday realities in both Haiti and the United States.[28] This program, later adopted in New York City and Miami, continued for more than ten years because of the dedication of its teachers,[29] until bilingual education was dismantled by conservative forces in Massachusetts and the nation. It served as a culturally and socially rooted space of learning within, despite, and against the still-colonial system of schooling; a space of learning with dignity for living and life. It also served to push further my own understandings of the decolonizing and deschooling possibilities of political-pedagogical praxis.

I began my experience as an educator by rejecting the formal education system, sharing, in a sense, Ivan Illich's position against universal education through schooling but also believing in the possibility of alternative spaces of learning. Yet over the course of the years just detailed, I learned of the strategic importance of work not just outside but also within educational institutions. Brought to mind are the words of Janja, an Afro-Brazilian educator, feminist, and capoeira master: "There are spaces of education that defy schooling, and some of these spaces are in the buildings that we call schools."[30]

It was from within schools and with students, parents, and critical educators that I learned of my obligation—that is, my social, political, and ethical responsibility—to use my skin privilege to simultaneously work inside, outside, and against. Such responsibility and/as stance brings to the fore what I have described elsewhere as "strategic shifts, tactical moves, and an intertwined complex of relations that transgress and traverse power domains, all postured and understood as forms of struggle *against* the dominant order."[31]

How to make these shifts and moves, with whom, and in what contexts were part of my own continually evolving inquiry; that is, my asking, walking, and learning that, in many ways, shared Illich's posture against the modern capitalist "schooling" of our hearts, bodies, minds, and values, and for the liberation of "other" ways of learning and living. While it was Freire and not Illich who was my primary referent then, my rereading of Illich today helps reveal threads of connection.

As Illich claimed, the modernized misery of society, existence, and life has to do with the nature of modern social institutions and their practice of lifelong institutionalization. "Health, knowledge, dignity, independence, and creative labor are all defined as little more than the performance of institutions that claim to serve these purposes," he said.[32] From this perspective, advances and improvements are dependent on the greater allocation of resources; more and better services; more and better institutions; more and better administration, governments, policies, and laws; and more and better institutionalization.

Up against this reality, Illich's hypothesis and argument in *Deschooling* were that society can and must deschool itself. For him, the path of change was not in institutional or educational reform. And it was not in institutionalized or educational alternatives. Rather, it was in the simultaneous effort of dismantling these institutions as a practice of freedom, and of building a radically distinct societal project. As he concluded, "Deschooling will inevitably blur the distinctions between economy, education, and politics, on which the stability of the present-day world order is founded."[33] Illich later took a radical distance from education itself, and with it a distance from the precepts and perspectives of his longtime friend Freire. "I went from the criticism of the school to the criticism of what education does to a society," Illich said; "that is, to promote the idea that people need to receive help to prepare themselves to exist or live.... Therefore, in spite of its good and solid tradition, I had to move away from the approach of *concientization* [in Freirian terms, the awakening of critical consciousness] and adult education whose main spokesperson was Paulo during the 60s and early 70s, not only in Latin America but throughout the world."[34]

Illich met Freire in Brazil. "We hit it off immediately and became good friends. Then, a year and a half later, he was in the military police jail.... I brought him to Cuernavaca, and there we edited and published his first book outside of Brazil. We made the first translations of his writings and circulated them throughout the world." Despite the differences that emerged between the two over time, the long friendship between Illich and Freire remained untouched. "I remember Paulo with immense affection, but also as somebody who more and more wanted to save the credibility of educational activities at a time when my main concern had become a questioning of the conditions which shape education in *any* form, including *conscientizacão* or psychoanalysis or whatever it might be."[35]

I understand Illich's perspective and heed it. Yet it was in the work with students and communities in US urban public schools that my learning to unlearn and relearn began to take crucial turns. It was in these contexts that I learned the significance of what Lewis R. Gordon calls the "pedagogical imperative of pedagogical imperatives."[36] And it was in these contexts that I learned the significance, possibility, process, and practice of collective praxis. For me, public education per se was not the problem, particularly urban public education. The problem was with schooling's institutionalized project and frame that reproduced systemic racism, structural inequalities, and a singular white, western, and most often masculine viewpoint of knowledge and the world. Freire was an important referent and guide then. I never thought of his work as an approach or model to be applied, but rather as ideas, strategies, and tools useful in the shared endeavors of teachers, students, and communities to question and to change the conditions and circumstances of learning, being-becoming, thinking, and doing.

Yet as I began to spend an increasing amount of time in the early 1990s in Ecuador, my referents began to change. Bit by bit, the bases of what I thought I knew began to become undone, and with them the guides and referents that had accompanied me in my processes and practice. In what follows, I share some of the fragments of my story in its walking and asking from North to South.

Fragments That Continue
to Walk and Ask

"We make the road by asking," Freire once said. This thought, adapted from the celebrated phrase of the Spanish poet Antonio Machado ("Se hace camino al andar," literally translated as "You make the way as you go"), opens Freire's "speaking" book with the founder of the Tennessee-based Highlander School, Myles Horton.[37] It gives the book its title and, in so doing, it names its project: spoken reflections on the paths of struggle; on the doing, making, and walking; and on the asking that never rests. In essence, this is what Freire referred to in other texts as the "pedagogy of the question."[38]

In a radically different calendar and geography, the now "defunct" Zapatista spokesperson Subcomandante Insurgente Marcos continued his ongoing conversation with Viejo Antonio, a wise elder.[39] "In order to know and walk, one must ask," Viejo Antonio explained. "The questions serve to learn how to walk, and not to stand still."[40] As I mentioned at the outset of this chapter, "Asking, we walk" is the Zapatista political-pedagogical vision-stance-project and the political imaginary and guide adopted by the self-described "pilgrim of life" Corinne Kumar in her edited three-volume collection. This, for Kumar, is "an invitation to a deeper dialogue from our differences, from our many worlds, continuing *to ask, to listen, as we walk*, seeking new paths to justice; searching new ways to peace; creating new imaginaries; finding sacred mountains everywhere."[41]

It is the idea, practice, and project—the pedagogical praxis—of walking and asking that especially guides this chapter's second part. While my asking and walking are certainly present in the fragments shared in the first part, it was in the move and movement from the United States to Ecuador in the mid-1990s that my paths of walking and asking—and with them of learning, unlearning, and relearning—experienced radical shifts. In Latin America—or rather, what I prefer to name Abya Yala South—the processes to decolonize and deschool were to become even more intense. As I said earlier, what I thought I knew and whom I thought with were not only challenged, they were unraveled and undone.

UNRAVELINGS AND UNDOINGS

The unraveling and undoing began in the early 1990s before my permanent migration. Since my first stay in Ecuador in the late 1970s, I had returned for short stays practically every year. My Ecuadorian partner's deep involvement with the Confederación de Nacionalidades Indígenas de Ecuador (Confederation of Indigenous Nationalities of Ecuador; CONAIE) introduced me to the realities and struggles of the Indigenous movement and opened paths of conversation. In 1993 I spent nine months in Ecuador collaborating with CONAIE and conducting research—at CONAIE's request—on the sociopolitics of Indigenous bilingual education, including the conflict between, on the one hand, missionary, oil company, and state interests and, on the other, community-based vision and practice.[42]

In Ecuador, Indigenous bilingual education is the result of decades of political community-based struggle. Unlike anywhere else in the Americas, it had semiautonomy with respect to the state. From its official recognition in 1988 until 2014 when the Correa government dismantled it, this model of schooling—referred to as bilingual intercultural education—had national Indigenous organizations at the center of its conceptualization, organization, and administration within the state. However, as might be expected, this semiautonomy was always in dispute, most especially because of its political challenge to the white-mestizo establishment and the national educational model officially named "Hispanic education."

During this time, both CONAIE and the Amazon-based Organization of Indigenous Peoples' of Pastaza asked me to be part of their processes to conceptualize projects of Indigenous higher education. Together, these initial experiences put in tension and question what I thought I knew, unraveling any possible sense of correspondence with the referents, contexts, and realities that heretofore had oriented and guided my knowings, learnings, unlearnings, and relearnings in the United States.

Part of this questioning, tensioning, and unraveling was in relation to Paulo Freire. Here, in the fragment that follows, I share some of my personal notes of reflection written to Paulo in recent years; they are notes that evidence my making of other paths, asking and walking.[43]

_____

MAKING OTHER PATHS: NOTES TO PAULO

The last time I saw and spoke to you in living person, Paulo, was at your seventieth birthday celebration at New York's New School for Social Research in 1991. Hundreds of us gathered to celebrate you. You were beaming with joy and love. Nita, your new wife, was by your side, and as you spoke, you cried. You cried for the joy in once again finding love after the death of your first wife, Elsa. And you cried because crying—as loving—is an emotion and a feeling that is constitutive of being human and, of course, of humanizing pedagogies as well; as such, crying need not—should not—be hidden. With this action, you reminded us that being a critical educator and thinker means being with and in the world. It means understanding oneself in a constant process of becoming where the "critical" is not a set postulate or an abstract of thought. Rather, it is a stance, posture, and attitude, an actional standpoint (something that Frantz Fanon understood well) in which one's own being and becoming are constitutive to the acts of thinking, imagining, and intervening in transformation; that is, in the construction, creation, and "walking" of a radically different world.

For me, this celebration and meeting also had significance in my own walking. I was beginning my immigration—in body, spirit, and mind—from North to South, from the United States to Ecuador. This meant starting to move from paths well known, from the sites of struggle, activism, and political-intellectual-pedagogical work that for so many years were home. And it meant starting to separate from the collectives and walking partners with whom these paths and work had been imagined, crafted, and created.

At your birthday event, I spoke to you briefly of my move. Later, I wrote to you in São Paulo, where you then were, about the movement I felt it entailed and about the uncertainties and challenges of finding walking paths, directions, and partners. Your response could not have been more pedagogical. You told me to just walk, to walk questioning and asking . . .

In Ecuador, my understandings of the spheres of pedagogy began to expand. Over time, I came to more deeply understand pedagogy in the frame of sociopolitical struggle. And I began to become more cognizant of the pedagogical nature of this struggle. You referred to this in a sense in Pedagogy of the Oppressed *when you talked about the educational nature of the contexts of struggle, and the inseparableness of the pedagogical and the political; that is, the political action that involves the organization of groups and popular classes in order to intervene in the reinvention of society. Here, you argued as well that "political action on the side of the oppressed must be pedagogical action in the authentic sense of the word, and, therefore action with the oppressed."*[44]

Your concern in Pedagogy of the Oppressed *was with an educational praxis of reflection and action that endeavored to work against oppression and for liberation. In this sense, your position was hopeful. Yet while it certainly had roots— your roots—in Latin America, its class-based focus seemed somehow out of place with what I began to witness with respect to the postures and struggles of communities and social movements in the Andes and South and Central America.*

Ecuador's Indigenous movement was, at the end of the twentieth century, considered the strongest in Abya Yala and possibly the world. Through its multiple uprisings, mobilizations, and politically educational actions, I came to see Indigenous resistance as much more than a resistant response to and against oppression. As the Kichwa intellectual and historical leader Luis Macas told me in 2001, the struggle of Indigenous peoples is about decolonization; that is, to confront the structural problem of the "colonial tare," which means to resist but also to fight for and contribute to the building of decolonial conditions and possibilities. Here, resistance proffers movements—pedagogical actions, if you will—not just of defense and reaction but also, and more importantly, of offense, insurgence, and (re)existence circumscribed in and by the continuous construction, creation, and maintenance of the "otherwise."

Of course, coming to this recognition and comprehension has itself been part of my own political and pedagogical processes. My collaborative work throughout the 1990s with the Indigenous movement at their request pushed me to think from, alongside, and with a radically distinct politics and lived praxis grounded in the intertwinement of collective identity, territory, cosmogony, world-sense or view, spirituality, and knowledge. This intertwinement challenged not only many of my western beliefs but also the western tenets of my "critical" thought, pedagogy, and politics.

At the center of these collaborations and my own emergent praxistic muse was "interculturality," one of the key ideological principles of CONAIE's political project first introduced in 1990. In contrast to western multiculturalism or even what Peter McLaren has called "revolutionary multiculturalism,"[45] CONAIE defined interculturality as a political process, practice, and project of fundamental structural and institutional transformation. In this context, interculturality meant—and means—not only horizontal relationality but also, and most importantly, the rebuilding (in decolonial terms) of a vastly different social project for all.[46] Understanding and thinking with and from interculturality as a political and epistemic project became the organizing focus of my work and writing in ongoing conversation for many years with the movement and its leaders. It displaced and replaced, if you will, our shared interest and project of critical pedagogy.

These learnings with the Indigenous movement began to trace and mark out different paths of walking and of asking. Popular education and critical pedagogy had taught me about the centrality of experience and of what you, Paulo, called epistemological curiosity. Yet it was through the conversations and collaborations with Indigenous leaders and communities that I started to doubt what I thought I knew. Could it be that my emergent perceptions were correct, that critical pedagogy and popular education were, in many ways, still western-modern postures, practices, and constructions? Was not their "criticalness," I asked, postured primarily in western terms, from western theory, and from within modernity itself? What about modernity's outsides? And what to do about the dominant geopolitics of knowledge, this understood as the universalization of a western-centric (Euro-US-centric) definition, frame, logic, and approach to knowledge—rational knowledge—that effectively denies and negates other sites, modes, and practices of knowing and of knowledge production?

This is not to say that your referents, Paulo, were only of the West, or that western modernity was necessarily your project. Certainly your reflections on and your ruminations with Cape Verde and Guinea Bissau are evidence of this. In fact, it was after your lived experiences in Africa and with communities of color in the United States that you began to question your own western and Marxist biases that for many years had made you unable to see how the ideas of race and gender and the practices of racialization, gendering, and heteropatriarchy operate within a colonial matrix of power that is not just class based. Your last books, most especially Pedagogy of Hope, are reflective of this questioning, opening, and self-critique.

Still, critical pedagogy in its theoretical formulations then—and in its resonances as "revolutionary" critical pedagogy today—remains in project, thought, and paradigmatic assumptions a western, anthropocentric, and largely Marxist-informed endeavor. The Native intellectual Sandy Grande reminds us of this in her writings on "Red pedagogy." For her, "revolutionary critical pedagogy remains rooted in the Western paradigm and therefore in tension with indigenous knowledge and praxis." Moreover, critical pedagogy typically defines "the root constructs of democratization, subjectivity, and property . . . through Western frames of reference that presume the individual as the primary subject of 'rights' and social status."[47]

In the Andes, I began to see the radical distinctiveness of an Indigenous-thought project in which culture, cosmology, spirituality, wisdom, knowledge, land, and nature and/as life interweave self-determination, decolonization, mobilization, and transformation. And I began to see coloniality and the lived colonial difference as constitutive of pedagogies otherwise, pedagogies that modernity, western critical theory, and even you, Paulo, did not directly consider or address. I guess this was the beginning of my distancing from critical pedagogy, western critical thought, and you; of my search for and my making of new and different paths, asking and walking.

In the years since, ongoing collaborations with Afro-descendant movements, struggles, processes, and projects have pushed further my unlearnings and my re-learning to learn alongside, from, and with knowledges and ways of being in the world that modernity and western ideologies have rendered invisible and continue to negate. This, of course, has engendered shifts in my reading and writing, in the choices of whom to dialogue with, and in the how, what, and why of such dialogue and its implications for practice and praxis.

For many years, your texts that had traveled with me to Ecuador remained untouched on the shelf. Not just the books but also their—that is to say, your—tenets, foundations, and pedagogical postures seemed foreign and somehow out of place. In Ecuador and throughout the region, the weight of what Luis Macas called "the colonial tare" was all over, as was the force of social, political, epistemic, and existence-based struggle. My learning and relearning, particularly during the first decade, were intense as I grappled with my own being and becoming here in Ecuador, with what and whom to read and think, and with how to walk asking. I discovered Andean Indigenous and African-descended thinkers—Dolores Cacuango, Fausto Reinaga, Manuel Quintin-Lame, Manuel Zapata-Olivella, and Juan García Salazar, to name just a few—and the significance of orality and oral literatures. You became, Paulo, just a memory at best. I remember when I received news of your passing; I cried for the memories and learnings lived, and I cried because I had already, some time before, let you go. Our paths had parted.

There is much I could share about the unexpected ways that new paths emerged in the making throughout the last half of the 1990s. I won't detail all of this to you here. Suffice it to say that Indigenous leaders first, and later Black-movement leaders, asked for my accompaniment, gave me tasks, and pushed me to walk asking. A space, place, and pathway also took form in what was then the most progressive university in Ecuador, a regional Andean university with strong ties to social movements. And, at an event in Bolivia in the late 1990s, Walter Mignolo and I crossed paths. It is Walter who introduced me soon after to Aníbal Quijano and a group of Latin American intellectuals who were beginning to think with Quijano's concept and analytical framework of the coloniality of power. So began another walking and asking in what came to be known as the modernity/(de)coloniality working group. In all of these walkways, Paulo, my distancing from you grew.

Yet, about a decade and a half ago and in ways also not planned or predicted, my walking—which was never linear—took new serpentine curves. New askings related to the political-epistemic insurgencies and decolonizing processes of social movement struggle also surfaced. I think it was my emergent questioning of decoloniality's how and hows that pushed me to muse about pedagogy once again. Are not the struggles, practices, and actions of communities, movements, and collectives marked by the colonial difference, not just political but politically pedagogical, I asked? Are they not grounded in, and do they not assemble, a methodology-and/as-pedagogy of praxis—of analysis, reflection, and action, and of reanalysis and re-reflection in order to better act? And are they not also concerned with and enveloped in the on-

going pedagogical-methodological question and imperative of the how(s) of existence and re-existence?

These questions—this asking and walking—were provoked, in part, by two Afro-Caribbean thinkers: Frantz Fanon and M. Jacqui Alexander. I remember, Paulo, when we read together Fanon's Wretched of the Earth *in one of our cofacilitated seminars at UMass-Amherst. It was my second reading; the first was in 1971 in a study group organized by a cell of the Panthers that I was invited to attend. While Fanon was one of your referents, mentioned in* Pedagogy of the Oppressed *and more present in your later texts—most especially* Pedagogy of Hope *and* Pedagogy of Indignation—*I don't think you ever really thought with Fanon. Moreover, I don't believe you were able to perceive and recognize his pedagogical existence-based stance, a stance grounded not only in humanization (also one of your central concerns) but, much more radically, in the intimate relation of rehumanization and decolonizing liberation. Here, sociogenesis and deracialization form part of a methodological-pedagogical posture and practice that transcends education and schools. With Fanon, I found connection to Malcolm X's call to undo the enslavement of minds, Manual Zapata-Olivella's summons to remove the mental chains, and Juan García Salazar's invitation to unlearn "casa adentro" (in-house) that which white dominant society and education have taught, in order to learn again from collective ancestral memory. Moreover, and with Caribbean Fanonian thinkers, most especially Sylvia Wynter, Lewis R. Gordon, Paget Henry, and Nelson Maldonado-Torres, I began to understand the interconnectedness of pedagogy and praxis with lived being, existence, and ancestrally rooted philosophy or thought.*

But it was Alexander who brought me back to you. In her powerful book Pedagogies of Crossing, *Alexander allies herself with your understanding of pedagogy as method. Yet she defines her project as traversing other realms that take her beyond the confines of modernity and the imprisonment of what she refers to as its "secularized episteme."*[48] *Her aim is to "disturb the inherited divides of the Sacred and the secular, the embodied and the disembodied," through pedagogies that are derived from "the Crossing," this conceived as a signifier, existential message, and passage toward the configuration of new ways of being and knowing. It is her conception and use of pedagogies here that particularly enticed me.*

[Pedagogies] as something given, as in handed, revealed; as in breaking through, transgressing, disrupting, displacing, inverting inherited concepts and practices, those psychic, analytic and organizational methodologies we deploy to know what we believe we know so as to make different conversations and solidarities possible; as both epistemic and ontological project bound to our beingness and, therefore, akin to Freire's formulation of pedagogy as indispensable methodology. Pedagogies [that] summon subordinated knowledges that are produced in the context of the practices of marginalization in order that we might destabilize existing practices of knowing and thus cross the fictive boundaries of exclusion and marginalization.[49]

In this text, Alexander seems to be thinking both with and beyond you, Paulo. She locates her perspective of pedagogies as akin to yours; that is, of pedagogies as indispensable methodologies of and for transformation. And, at the same time, she reveals the limits of the psychology of liberation that, of course, was constitutive of your work. Yet, in so doing, she does not reject you. Rather, you, Paulo, are part of the crossroads she evokes and invokes, of the crosscurrents of genealogies, theorizings, politics, and practice that she fashions, of course not for your contribution to feminism, sexual politics, or the sacred, but rather for your political signification and use of pedagogy in concept and praxis.

It was Alexander who helped me more clearly grasp the pedagogical nature and imperative of efforts and struggles of decolonization. I found resonance, solace, meaning, and accompaniment in her positing and posturing of pedagogies as methodologies, and I sensed the ties with my own insistence in the queries and practices of the decolonial hows. I also found a distinctive way to engage you, Paulo, and your thought that was not about compartmentalization; that is, locating you simply within modernity and the western Left. Instead it was about moving beyond the existential impasse and divide that coloniality has proffered.

This "finding" made me realize your continued presence all these years, not as authoritative voice but as grandfather, ancestor, and pedagogical-political guide. After reading Alexander, I returned to your texts, rereading them all, pondering the difference of our paths as well as the crossroads, the points of encounter, disencounter, and reencounter that break the linearity of time and sketch spiral and serpentine movements. I let myself walk and ask alongside, with (rather than against) you, allowing the differences, disagreements, frictions, and tensions to be present, learning from them while at the same time opening and making other paths. And I let myself muse while I walk and ask, about the fragments past and present that assemble, disassemble, and reassemble paths; about the paths themselves, discovered, crafted, carved out, and hewn in the making with no preconceived notion of destination or direction; and about those beings, spirits, and forces that make and mark the paths, that accompany me and those whom I choose, in distinct moments and contexts, to accompany. Is all this not part of the pedagogy and liberation of hope and heart to which you referred, Paulo, in your last years? More broadly, is it also not part of a liberation of being, becoming, thinking, knowing, and doing in

relation—or what Wynter calls "correlation"—that can come with the pedagogical
praxis of walking and asking with its learnings, unlearnings, and relearnings?

As I assemble these fragments of notes and questions to you, Paulo, and ponder
the moments of divergent and traversing paths, I think of other elders with whom
I have walked and asked, and who particularly pushed my learnings, unlearnings,
and relearnings. And so I leave for now the fragments as notes shared here with you
(and with the reader). Their essence and heartfelt sense are not only on the page;
they are sketched and resketched on various pieces of colored cloth that I have sewn
together with rough stitches, allowing me to re-assemble and to re-member.

UNLEARNING IN ORDER TO RELEARN (AGAIN)

It was March 1999. I don't remember the exact date. Three men appeared
at the door of my office at the Universidad Andina Simón Bolívar in Quito.
One was Juan García Salazar, and the other two were *palenqueros*, leaders of
a *palenque* in Ecuador's Pacific province of Esmeraldas, part of the African-
origin ancestral territory of the Gran Comarca.[50]

I had only seen you, maestro-hermano Juan,[51] once before. It was at a national
event I had organized several months earlier with representatives of the Black move-
ment focused on the newly passed (December 1998) constitution, the first official
document in the history of this nation to recognize the existence of "Black or Afro-
Ecuadorian peoples." The event's aim was to explore with Black leaders the signifi-
cance of the Constitution's related recognition and naming of Afro-Ecuadorian
collective rights. One of the speakers, also from the Esmeraldas province, acknowl-
edged your presence in the majority-Black audience of well over five hundred. Do
you remember, maestro-hermano Juan? He referred to you as the self-identified
"worker of the process of Black communities" and the central figure in the Pacific re-
gion's struggle for collective territorial rights. As the microphone went from hand to
hand until it reached you standing in the midst of many in the back, the auditorium
grew silent. Your short intervention made clear the issue at hand. "Our rights are
ancestral-territorial," you said, "they are rights that existed long before the forma-
tion of the Ecuadorian state that now comes to name, define, and control us. Our
collective existence has continued despite state and despite its political and social
institutions. Neither the state nor the Constitution give us existence or rights." As
you went on to explain with regard to both entities, "The fact that we Black peoples
were added on as an afterthought to the article that identifies the collective rights of
Indigenous peoples is evidence once again of the negation of our ancestrality, differ-
ence, and existence. Hundreds of years ago Black and Indigenous people were allies

against colonialism and the state, but today Indigenous leaders are part of the state, actors in the state politics of recognition and inclusion. This should not be our route," you argued. "For us Black peoples the fight ahead is on two fronts: it is to strengthen 'in-house' our collective sense of belonging as territory-based ancestral peoples, not as citizens of the state, and it is to strategically use the Constitution, defining our own meanings of collective rights and our own determinations of their application, most especially with respect to territory, identity, culture, and our own education, in order to continue the work casa adentro *[in-house] and, at the same time, begin the work* casa afuera *[out-of-house]."*

I listened in awe to the clarity, radicalness, and force of your words, always spoken in the collective voice. And I observed, also in awe, the respect that you, a charismatic yet humble leader, wielded. The power of your words and presence left me overwhelmed; I did not even try to approach you.

As such, I was not only shocked to see you at my door but also a bit scared to know why you had come. "We have come to propose and to talk; close the door, sit down, and listen," you said as you and the other two leaders entered. "We have been watching you for some time, we know of the accompaniment that you have given to the Indigenous movement, to leaders and communities," you stated, "and we are here to say that now it is our turn. We have an encargo *[a task or charge] to give you. Do you accept?" When I asked what it was, your response was that I did not have to know, I just had to answer yes or no. My mind began to run back and forth, to think about what this task could be, and to worry about the possible implications in terms of time and work; I was evidencing—at least within myself—a mind-frame and self-focus that were still colonized, westernized, and schooled. Somehow, I halted the internal back-and-forth and said yes. "OK, now go and bring the rector of the university here," you said. "We want to make an agreement." Since the hierarchy of the university was still quite small and accessible at this time, I was able to find the rector—a leader in the Socialist Party and member of the 1998 Constitutional Assembly involved in the writing of the articles pertaining to (Indigenous) collective rights—and bring him to my office. The proposal that you put on the table and that we agreed to that day was that the university would provide an open space for national monthly meetings of Black organizations and Black community leaders focused on debating, identifying, and defining their understandings of collective rights. The university would offer the space without participation or intervention. And I would be the point person to facilitate the logistics of organization, invitation, and communication. I would be allowed to attend the meetings—to accompany—but I would not be allowed to talk. As you later told me, this was part of the task: my learning to unlearn from and with Afro-Ecuadorian perspectives.*

So began the process and practice of expanding tasks and charges, accompaniment, and relation with you, maestro-hermano Juan, that extended over almost twenty years, until your passing from this world to that of your ancestors in 2017. The initially agreed-on meetings-workshops continued for a year and a half with the attendance of over eighty leaders and organizational representatives each month. With time, you not only increased my responsibility and charge but also made it a practice to reflect with me, after the sessions, about the debates and perspectives, and about the vast differences in thought between those who maintained their existence and roots on, in, and with collective memory and ancestral territory, and those occupying individualized urban lives and space. While together the Black community could identify a shared stance in-house, the differences, divergences, conflicts, and tensions within the community were great, you told me, often spurred on by the promises of modernity, progress, development, and the lures of state-sponsored social inclusion, what you called "representative inclusion." Some urban Black leaders described you as too radical, as overly entrenched in the past, and as unwilling to open toward and accept the "rewards" of citizenship. But for those rooted in ancestral territory and community, you were the hermano *and* maestro *who manifested their existence-based thought; you were the appointed guardian of collective memory and oral tradition.*

In 2002 you gave me another charge: to make a home for the more than three thousand hours of oral testimony and narratives of elders compiled in rural communities over more than thirty years by you and other Black activists, as well as over ten thousand photographs. The Fondo Documental Afro-Andino (Afro-Andean Documentary Fund, a collective memory archive) was thus born, conceived, as I am sure you recall, in a legal memorandum of agreement as a collaborative project between the collective Procesos de Comunidades Negras (represented by you) and the Universidad Andina Simón Bolívar. With this agreement, the university agreed to not only house but also classify and digitize the materials in order to enable their use in the Black community, by educators and researchers, and by the public at large. While the materials were to be housed in the university, this was only "in trust"; the Black community retained and retains ownership. You stipulated that I was to be the person from the university responsible for the Fondo, and you and I were to work together in coordinating its project. With the support of a small team over the first five years, we were able to create educational materials from the archive for use by community leaders and teachers, hold workshops focused on what you referred to as ethnoeducation—that is, Afrocentric community-based education outside the sphere and control of the Ministries of Education, formal schooling, and the state—and advance the work of digitization, eventually completed in 2014 with the help of staff from the university's library. Over the years, you continued to add more testimonies and interviews to this living archive, the largest in Latin America, coordinated today, in concert with your wishes, by me and a community-based council that you named before your passing.

With a relation cultivated over years and that few understood, we developed our own methodology-pedagogy of colabor. The goal was to make collective memory walk, especially among the younger generations and in contexts beyond rural communities. We began to write conversing and to converse writing, each with our own voice and designated font. I understood my role here not as self-defined or self-determined. It was a role fashioned and created by forces outside me; a charge, of sorts, never fully articulated but implicitly understood by you, maestro-hermano Juan, as a pedagogical imperative in which we each carried an obligation and responsibility to sow and cultivate collective memory, to put it on paper for future generations, and, in so doing, to help make it walk.[52] My role here was never as "author" but as an appointed catalyst, asking, thinking, conversing, and writing with. Our numerous published texts made cracks in the framework and mindset of academic scholarship. While we were most often obliged, for copyright reasons, to sign the texts (varying the order of our names), their decolonized and de-schooled praxis remained. This praxis is especially evident in our last book, written in three voices and fonts: yours, mine, and Abuelo (Grandfather) Zenón, the real and symbolic ancestor-elder of the Black Pacific territory-region.[53] Through the years, you taught me to learn, unlearn, and relearn with Abuelo Zenón, an elder-ancestor who, while not physically present, continues to walk collective knowledge and memory, "allowing African descended peoples to be where we were not," Zenón says. Zenón speaks in the present tense, you told me. He is of the present that is at the same time future and past; as such, his word is the word of the community, the territory or land, and the ancestors who still walk with us.

Maestro-hermano Juan, you were (and still are) my teacher, my elder, and, as you argued over and over, my family. A family not of blood—blood does not ensure anything, you said—but a family planted and cultivated from the heart. The many charges you gave me over the years—too many to detail here—had a purpose. As you explained to me in your last years, the purpose, in part, was to push me to learn unlearning and relearning. "I watched you unlearn and relearn, and I saw how you assumed all this with commitment, respect, obligation, and affection, always understanding its collective, not personal or individual, sense," you once told me. "We [I, the elders, and ancestors] put your commitment, engagement, and obligation to test. Never did I imagine that it would be a white woman, a woman not even born here, who would become the person with whom to entrust all these encargos and with whom to share, sow, and cultivate the knowledges of generations," you said, laughing. "The ancestors work in ways that we do not always understand. They es-

tablish responsibility and obligation, a responsibility and obligation that they gave you and that you must retain."

The encargos *that you, maestro-hermano Juan, left me are many. However, the greatest ones are to learn to unlearn in order to relearn this new way of being and walking with you and, relatedly, to relearn to take care of, sow, and cultivate the seeds of collective life-memory, the collective life-memory that is Juan García Salazar, now ancestor-guide alongside Abuelo Zenón.*

The pieces of cloth that I gather are stained with tears. Sometimes the tears make the ink run. I let it dry and then write over it again. They are fragments, I remind myself. The stories are too long to fit here. Moreover, they are not mine to own or tell, but part of a collective creation that is here and not here; that is, a creation in ongoing relation that crosses secular and sacred divides, walking, asking, learning, unlearning, and relearning (still and again).

DECOLONIAL CRACKING IN THE UNIVERSITY

I carry pieces of cloth with me in my bag. They remind me of the many fragments that I have not yet jotted down. But they also remind me that the fragments are not just snippets of narratives lived, but also part of the ongoing struggles and crucial work that continue, including in the university. The pieces of cloth are part of me, the questions, and paths.

I am not an academic. That is not my identity or identification. I have always been clear about that. Still, I have been a university professor for nearly forty years. If I consider myself an intellectual militant, or a militant intellectual, and not an academic, how is it that I have managed to stay working in the educational institution? I recall bell hooks's words and share their sentiments: "It has not been easy for me to do the work I do and reside in the academy (lately I think it has become almost impossible) but one is inspired to persevere by the witness of others." Moreover, as hooks argued, "the classroom remains the most radical space of possibility in the academy. . . . I celebrate teaching that enables transgressions—a movement against and beyond boundaries. It is that movement which makes education the practice of freedom."[54]

The fragments in the first part of this chapter allude to some of my struggles with schools, and to some of the efforts of decolonizing and deschooling both institutional spaces and myself. I guess I could say that in those years in the United States, I managed to both make and find fissures in the system that enabled me to simultaneously move outside, inside, and always against it. In

Ecuador, this movement took on new forms and challenges, most especially in the university. The pieces of cloth keep accumulating; I select only those that help understand the context, challenges, inspiration, and perseverance.

It was 1996. I was contacted by a small group of professors in what was then the emerging project of the Universidad Andina Simón Bolívar's Ecuadorian campus. They asked me to give a talk on postmodernism, postcolonialism, and their difference. This was my first contact with institutionalized higher education in Ecuador.

After the talk came invitations to offer short modules for educational professionals, many of whom were Indigenous, and a trimester-long course on interculturality and social movements in the newly inaugurated Latin American studies master's program comprising students from throughout the Andean region. This university, particularly then, professed a vision and project closely tied to Andean social movement politics and perspectives. It also encouraged a certain level of intellectual creativity, activism, and progressive thought, which, as I came to understand some years later, meant neither challenging authorities nor diverting from the institutionally inscribed and defined politic and perspective. After the students asked me to offer a part two of the course, the rector convinced me to assume a full-time position. This university, he said, was the perfect home for my intellectual militancy, for my growing relations with social movements, and for creating and developing graduate programs grounded in Andean social realities and struggles. How could I say no?

I signed the contract in January 1999. That was the year that ended with the crash of the national economy, the installation of dollarization, and the moratorium and loss of solvency in a number of banks. Many people lost their life savings. Our salaries dropped in value, and I was left with about thirty dollars a month for the next several years until the economic system began to recuperate. Ecuador's then-president was overthrown by the populace, the second in what came to be three popular-based overthrows and nine presidents in a period of ten years; as was the case with the overthrow several years before, I was again on the streets with the masses. No other Latin American country has been able to overthrow presidents like Ecuador has, enabled by the strength of the Indigenous movement and the strength of a popular people-based force. To live these overthrows, uprisings, and revolts gave a concrete sense to resistance, insurgence, and rebellion, and to the dynamism and power of the masses that, in my US experience, I never thought possible. Of course, this is not to simplify or idealize these processes or shroud the complicated racialized and gendered violences and tensions within. It is rather to highlight and note that politics in this small plurination cannot be conceived without reference to social resistance, insurgent agency, and struggle.

How to think *from* and *with* these struggles, instead of studying *about*, was my inquiry-based proposition, first in the master's and later in the doctoral program. How are we to build with students processes of theorizing and thought grounded in lived experience and in the social and political realities of the region? How are we to make central the conceptual, analytic, epistemic, and existence-based theorizations, postulates, and contributions of those typically absent in the academy, in syllabi, and in reading lists in Ecuador and in the region, most especially Indigenous and African-descended authors, women in general, and Indigenous and African-descended women in particular? And how are we to shift the geopolitics of knowledge and reason, disrupting and indisciplining the hegemony, dominance, and predominance of the Global North and West, recalling Fanon's cry (in *Wretched of the Earth*) that the European game is definitely finished, and it is necessary to find something else? These were a few of my many questions made praxis.

Despite the institution's progressive rhetoric, it maintained in practice what Nelson Maldonado-Torres refers to as the white liberal establishment and white academic field.[55] My posture, pedagogy, and praxis caused discomfort, hostility, and, on many occasions, outright opposition among the then all-white-mestizo and predominantly male faculty. For many, if not most, social movements had a place on the street and, possibly, as objects of study. The idea that these movements and the people and communities within them produce knowledge was considered absurd; so too the historical leader Luis Macas's contention that the Indigenous movement was/is not just social but also political and epistemic.[56] To think with this knowledge; its present, past, collective, and ancestral production; and its thinkers meant decolonizing, transgressing, and disrupting the canons not only of the social sciences and humanities but also of critical Latin American thought, which was then, and in many ways still is, mostly white-mestizo and male. It also meant having few if any allied colleagues within the institution.

My intellectual militancy took on an insurgent stance. While I have used the concept of insurgency to refer to the struggles and actions of Indigenous and Afro-descendant communities, collectives, and movements in the region, I can also understand my agency in this sense. More than a defensive posture *against*, insurgency, for me, is indicative of a propositional and insurgent offensive *for*, a *for* that necessarily is struggled and crafted with others. As I have argued elsewhere, "It is in the *for*, in the postures, processes, and practices that disrupt, transgress, intervene and in-surge in, and that mobilize, propose, provoke, activate, and construct an otherwise, that decoloniality is signified and given substance, meaning, and form." In this sense, "my conceptualization of insurgency is simultaneously political, epistemic, and existence-based; insurgency urges, puts forth, and advances from the ground up and from the margins, other imaginaries, visions, knowledges, modes of thought, other ways of being, becoming, and living in relation. . . . More than a simple renewal, restoration, or revival (of knowledges, life-practices, and re-existences), insurgency denotes the act-action of creation, construction, and intervention that aims towards an otherwise."[57]

What has this meant for me in the university? The fragments of ongoing insurgent creation, construction, and intervention, and the accompanying fragments of ongoing struggle—including with respect to the various forms of material, epistemic, and symbolic violence that I have experienced in this institution of higher education over many years—are many, too many and too complex to tell here or fit on the pieces of cloth. Yet it was early on (in 2001), in the design and development of a regional Andean doctoral program, that my insurgent act-action of creation, construction, and intervention began to take tangible form.

In the scheme of higher education, doctoral programs are usually not considered spaces of indiscipline, insurgence, or decolonizing praxis.[58] However, the context and conditions that gave base to this program were by no means typical. I recall well the challenge and charge that the rector gave me in late 2000: to develop a doctoral program (the first in Ecuador) focused on the social, cultural, and political reality of South America's Andean region, a challenge-charge made even more complex by the limited availability of financial resources and of faculty within the institution who held a PhD. I took the challenge-charge as an opportunity to create and construct a program that, in its conception, organization, and practice, has worked to make decolonial cracks in this institution and in the framework of doctoral study.

The story is long, and it certainly is not mine alone to tell. It is a narrative of shared insurgence with others in community and in coalition, most especially with students. I choose only a few of the fragments to share here, organizing them by the overarching questions that have guided this program-project from the outset. A few vignettes help reveal as well the praxical sense of that asked, learned, and lived.

WHAT, WHY, AND WHAT FOR?   What to call this program and why, with what propositional aim, focus, and politics of naming? Given the newness of graduate study in Latin America then, and particularly in Ecuador, program validity, accreditation, and approval meant not breaking but extending the academic fields recognized in and by the West. And who better to do this, university officials said, than a professor native to the United States and with thirteen years of US university experience? Without a doubt, both the task and charge given to me were strategically conceived and planned.

The idea was to build on the transdisciplinary program in cultural studies that I had begun within the Latin American studies master's shortly after being hired. With its international acceptance as a transdisciplinary area of study, cultural studies was a strategic way of naming study and reflection from the region that wove social, cultural, and political thought, knowledge, and struggle. It took seriously Stuart Hall's argument that political moments produce theoretical movements, and his invitation to think cultural studies as a situated political-theoretical project. "Not that there's one politics already inscribed in it. But there is something at stake in cultural studies, in a way that . . . is not exactly true of many other very important intellectual and critical practices."[59]

For all of these reasons, a doctoral program in cultural studies seemed to make sense. However, with the emerging presence of postmodern versions of cultural studies in the region, the politics of this naming required deeper deliberation. The problem was, on the one hand, with the replication of the depoliticized (text-based) model of cultural studies prevalent in the United States and, on the other, with Latin American defined versions—reflected particularly in the work of Nestor Canclini and Jesus Martin Barbero—still largely rooted in western modernity's shrouding of the colonial matrix of power and, with it, race, heteropatriarchy, and gender.

As a way to open this deliberation, I organized a seminar with a group of South American and Andean-focused intellectuals from the humanities and social sciences, piggy-backing the seminar with a meeting of the modernity/coloniality collective. What was at stake in naming cultural studies in this context of the Andes? Why move away from the tradition typical in the Andes of studies *about* culture, toward a thinking *from and with* the relational connections of culture, politics, and knowledge? And what for? Could this doctoral program work to interculturalize theory, knowledge, and thought within a framework and practice of decolonizing praxis that called into question the modern/colonial supposition that knowledge is only produced in academia and by academics, which, in the then-context, were predominantly white, male, and western focused? And what might this mean in terms of the program of study and research? These were some of the fundamental and foundational questions that pushed the reflection, dialogue, and debate. The seminar, of course, was intended not to provide answers but rather to make evident the tensions, possibilities, and challenges. It also helped establish a collective base of dialogue and support.[60]

WHO AND WITH WHOM?   The *who* of students and faculty, and the *with whom* to think, engage, and dialogue were also central concerns. The proposition was to convoke midcareer students from throughout the region who, besides meeting the academic criteria, had a strong base of lived experience, including in sociopolitical and cultural processes, organizations, or movements. The hope was for critical intellectuals who situated their thought in Abya Yala and the Andean region and who had knowledges and perspectives historically left out of whitened, westernized institutions.

The twenty-two accepted students who made up the first group met all these criteria and more. As I came to learn, there was another element present that I had neither sought nor expected. This was a sensibility *sentipensante*—a felt-thought—that broke the objective, individualized, and individualizing rationality so typical of graduate study. I still vividly recall the class session that finished the first week of my introductory course. After five continuous days of intense four- to five-hour reflection, discussion, and debate, one of the students asked the members of the group how they felt, suggesting a collective evaluation of and reflection on the first week. What occurred was in no way anticipated or expected. One of the students broke out in a weeping cry that continued nonstop for several hours. His tears—provoked in part by the separation from his three-year-old daughter—spurred other tears, and at one point most everyone, including me, was crying. Each of us spontaneously began to express—in the midst of tears, cries, and embraces—our deeply felt sentiments-thoughts about the space created and in construction, and about life fragments left behind in the contexts, communities, and countries of origin. The intensity of the week increased even more. In this scenario, the students began to knit a collective relation in which emotions, sentiments, hopes, and lives; sociopolitical activism, militancy, and struggle; and the program's focus, pedagogy, and praxis came together. In this cohort, and in those that have followed, learning, unlearning, and relearning have become shared endeavors of the body, spirit, mind, and heart, transgressing academia, the classroom, and the finality of degrees.

In each cohort, at least one child has been part of this collectively constructed process. Diana Sofía, the daughter of the father who had wept, is one example. Some months after her father's initial tears, Diana Sofía came to be part of the program-community, continuing this relationship for more than ten years, first accompanying her father's and later her mother's doctoral study. One day when she was about ten years old, after several days of sitting in on Edgardo Lander's course on capitalism and the coloniality of knowledge and taking notes, Diana Sofía raised her hand. After several attempts to capture Professor Lander's attention, she spoke out: "Professor, I have my hand raised because I want to ask a question." At first the professor thought she was just kidding and went on talking. But with Diana Sofía's insistence, he took notice. "For the last twenty minutes you have been explaining the concept of the coloniality of knowledge, but I still do not understand it," she said. "Could you please explain it more clearly?" Other students seconded Diana Sofía's request. Thanks to her, Lander made his explanation clearer. I wonder if he still remembers.

As can be imagined, the *who* of faculty was a crucial question. It was crucial in an epistemic sense. And it was crucial in a social, political, and existence-based sense. Not only did faculty members have to have a PhD (not common in the region then) and a strong base of teaching and research experience, they also had to think from the region and with its realities, peoples, movements, and struggles. "Criticalness" meant not reproducing but instead questioning and cracking the hegemonic hold—prevalent in the Latin American academy—of Eurocentricity and western modernity.

Initially I turned to those whom I knew in the Andean region and several Latin American colleagues in the United States. Many, but not all, shared the perspective of modernity/coloniality. Most considered themselves part of the collective creation and construction of the doctorate as a colearning endeavor. All were willing to break vertical relations, coming to see the students as colleagues in the guided—and always intense—processes of debate, discussion, and learning from the region and in dialogue with elsewhere.

With Afro and Indigenous intellectuals and social movement leaders among the student body from the outset; women (mestiza, Afro, and Indigenous) gradually increasing in presence; and other diversities—of geography, territory, sexuality and gender identities, physical capacities, lived experiences, and political and discipline-oriented postures—each cohort has built the spaces of reflection, dialogue, and learning in its own ways, weaving connections with those who came before them. In ways totally untypical of doctoral study, the graduates have become the elders or grandparents, the aunts and uncles, and sisters and brothers who continue to be present in this community named by the first group as DECUL (*doctorado en estudios culturales latinoamericanos*). One generation takes care of another. It is this inter- and transgenerational community that welcomes and orients each consecutive cohort. Community members have become professors in the program, intellectual guides, and parts of dissertation committees. Of course, such collective and community-based relations are part of the decolonial fissuring or cracking of the individualized, degree-oriented structure and "schooled" arrangement of doctoral study and its universal, westernized, and westernizing tenets and epistemological focus. Here the fundamental question of whose knowledge—of whom to think with and how—underscores a praxis that does not negate the situated and positioned contributions of the West or Global North, but begins first with the situated and positioned contributions of Abya Yala South.

HOW(S)   The third fragment of this DECUL narrative is captured in the praxical question of the *how(s)*. How are we to learn to unlearn and relearn, and, relatedly, how are we to construct pedagogical-methodological processes of colearning in and out of the classroom? How are we to think *from and with* (and not study *about*) knowledges grounded in territory and place, in collective, individual, and intersubjectivities, and in sociopolitical, epistemic, and existence-based struggles, critiquing and challenging the systemic racisms and heteropatriarchal structures—material, epistemic, embodied, spiritual, and symbolic—that continue to order and "school" academia and the social sphere? And how are we to keep present and continually make tense our own suppositions and belief systems, subjectivity, privilege, and place in these processes and practices?

For me, such interrogations point to the need, on the one hand, to radically change—in essence, to deschool—the classroom milieu, including the professor-centered ambiance, the academic competition-oriented relation among students, and the ways that learning, thinking, theorization, and analysis typically occur. Here the practical *hows* are multiple. They include, among other considerations, making the classroom a shared place and space for interrogating lived realities, subjectivities, and experiences; building a comradery, complementarity, and relationality of thought; and engendering the collective construction of praxis. In my courses, for instance, students typically take turns organizing (in small groups or pairs) the first part of the four-hour class session. Such organization includes the use of generative questions grounded in the topic of discussion and the readings, and contemplations, examples, and activities that situate, position, and ground the topic, ideas, and thought. My role, in the second part of the class, is to push the theorizations, analysis, reflection, debate, and discussion a bit further, enabling, in the third part, a collective conceptual-analytical mapping that we build on from session to session, often taking over not just the white boards but also—with newsprint—the walls and sometimes even the ceilings. Food and drink, initially my doing, and then a collective sharing, give us nourishment throughout the long sessions and afford a practice of making and doing community.

All of this has been part of my pedagogy-as-methodology-as-praxis. However, it was only recently and because of the teachings of Wilmer, a blind student in the last doctoral cohort, that I began to recognize its visual centricity. How could we rely not only on the eye but also on the conscious use of other senses? The problem, as Wilmer has taught us (that is, both professors and fellow students) is not with the lack of sight but with modernity/coloniality's ocular-centrism—what Joaquin Barriendos calls the coloniality of seeing[61]—and what Wilmer refers to as "the empire of the gaze." As Wilmer explains, "The gaze constitutes in ontological terms the existence or non-existence of the human being in a way that oversizes the eye and places it in a privileged place of sociocultural determination. Modernity, through its systems of representation, feeds the hegemonic sense of a visual culture, where the eye defines knowledge, truth, reality." Negated, subjugated, and ignored is the use—most especially, but not only, in graduate studies—of other senses, including hearing, listening, sound, sense, and touch, senses that complement and extend that of sight and work to fissure the "modern civilizing pattern,... the hegemonic regime and the empire of the gaze."[62]

Of course, the questions of the *hows* extend to research as well, to the creation and building of decolonizing methodologies-and/as-pedagogies. Here there is certainly no model or manual to follow. However, there are a series of considerations—including, for instance, the basic need to make evident throughout the investigative and writing processes one's own subjectivity, intersubjectivity, relation to the subjects and contexts involved in the study, and relation to the research problem itself. This means putting up front the varied complexities of insider and outsider research and concerns of embodied privilege tied to skin color but also to academia. As Linda Tuhiwai Smith poignantly describes, the problem is not just with white intellectuals researching Native communities, but also with "native intellectuals" trained in the West or westernized institutions, including those engaged in "producing 'culture.'" For Smith, "these same producers and legitimators of culture are the group most closely aligned to the colonizers in terms of their class interests, their values and their ways of thinking."[63]

Second, it means negotiating relation as a process in which all of the subjects involved necessarily have a say in the *what, why, how, with whom*, and *what for* of the study, and in the processes, practices, products, and results beyond the written thesis itself, a document typically of little or no use to grassroots contexts and communities. I am not referring here to the naming of a research paradigm—participatory action research, collaborative research, or critical ethnography, for instance—or to "method" per se, which, as Fanon reminds us, carries the colonial weight of subjection and objectification, most especially of subjects, peoples, and communities of color.[64] My reference instead is to the real-life processes and relationships of questioning, of embodied interrogation and negotiation among human beings, including the tensions, conflicts, and even rejections that are frequently part of the process.[65] For me, these relations and processes are part of the pedagogy-as-methodology-as-praxis of research and, as such, need to be a central part of written narratives and researcher reflections in which the first-person *I* is not to be avoided but made central.

Third, it means continually recognizing that knowledge is always local, situated, and positioned, which, in essence, entails a continuous questioning of one's own analysis and interpretations. Such questioning follows María Lugones's argument that "no slice of reality can have a univocal meaning,"[66] and, relatedly, her call for intersubjective attention and a cross-referencing of one's own different realities. As Lugones explains, such cross-referencing is necessary for emancipatory work. It is part of a moral integrity that maintains present the problems of duplicitous interpretation and of self-deception, both which can easily make the researcher an oppressor. "The one in self-deception could, but does not cross-reference," Lugones argues, does not consider and engage "memories of him or herself in more than one reality."[67] Brought to the fore here as well is what Bagele Chilisa refers to as the decolonization process of research. That is, "conducting research in such a way that the worldviews of those who have suffered a long history of oppression and marginalization are given space to communicate from their frames of reference." And, relatedly, "'researching back' to question how the disciplines . . . through an ideology of Othering have described and theorized about the colonized Other and refused to let the colonized Other name and know from their frame of reference."[68]

Of course, understanding that knowledge is always situated and positioned also requires an intentional effort to break the theory-practice divide. That is, to take distance from the notion of theory as a singular or universal truth, and to make the activity of theorizing or theorization part of the ongoing process and practice of thinking from and with subjects, contexts, and experiences, as well as with authors and texts, "exposing the problematic influence of the western eyes."[69] Recalled is Chela Sandoval's idea of "theory uprising."[70] It is in and through these processes and practices that methodology becomes pedagogy becomes praxis.

In no way am I suggesting that these considerations take away the colonial impositions and colonizing force of research and of academic institutions. I am also not making claim to a decolonial doctorate, a decolonial research program, or decolonial dissertations. Such use of the decolonial threatens to not only institutionalize it but also wrest it of its active subjectivity and agency. Rather, my argument here, as has been the case throughout this chapter, is for the ongoing decolonizing work that can be done—that *is* being done, that needs to be done, and that we need to do—within educational institutions, the place where I, as many of you, spend a large part of my time and energy. I am referring to the work that opens fissures and cracks, including in the established standards of graduate study and research, standards that are part of the systemic and systematic colonizing of knowledge, bodies, and minds, and of the systemic and systematic racisms and epistemicides that are co-constitutive of educational structures, standards, and institutions.

However, and precisely because it disrupts, displaces, and transgresses hegemonic standards and the disciplined comfort of many professors, administrators, and even students in other programs, this doctoral project has been, over the years, a constant target of backlash; that is, of vigilance, interrogation, and violences (including symbolic, epistemic, and gender and race based). As such, all of us—I am referring to both students and faculty—have learned to be simultaneously tenacious and strategic, as well as doubly rigorous in both an academic and decolonizing sense, meeting and far surpassing the established standards that pretend to judge, evaluate, compare, and discredit us and our university-based work (including theses and research).[71] In the twenty years of the DECUL program-project-community, all of the attempts to break us and to school us have failed.

The pieces of cloth accumulated over the years here are not just mine. They are those as well of close to a hundred present and former students and a handful of faculty who have made DECUL the community that it is. Together we have reinforced and opened further this decolonial crack. And both together and alone the graduates have continued the work of crack-making in other institutions and educational spaces throughout the region. Of course, the cracks themselves are not solutions. Their aim is not to re-form (or reschool) the institution but to rupture its totality, weaken its wall, and collectively build ways of thinking, theorizing, being-becoming, sensing, and doing that engender and enable existence(s) and education(s) otherwise, against, despite, and beyond the system. Cracks are not and cannot be eternal; permanence would mean, in essence—and most especially in the case of DECUL—institutionalization, becoming part of that which they endeavor to disrupt, transgress, dismantle, and undo.

I finish this section with one last remnant of cloth. It has drawings, not words. In one drawing, the DECUL crack is filled with sprouting seeds and budding and blooming plants rising up from the crevices. The DECUL community surrounds it. The drawing signifies the end of the DECUL program with this last promotion (2019–24), at least in this university and under my direction.[72] Visible in the background are several university authorities, elated by the decision, with their buckets of cement prepared. They think that by patching over and filling the fissure, the collective agency that opened and maintained the crack will disappear. What they don't realize, however, is that we are seeds, we are sowers, and we are cracks. I draw another image on the cloth. It is of seeds taking root and flowers beginning to bloom within a whole series of cracks and fissures that extend across cement and stone walls and earthen territories, weaving in and out, making and showing their relationality and connections, resisting and (re)existing, and continuing the work to decolonize and deschool.

Existence Deschooled:
Junctions and Reflections

My fragments are coming together. While I could go on adding more, I stop and begin to go back and look over the phrases, the drawings, and the text written here. As I read and reread, assemble and reassemble the pieces as cloth-text, I realize that the voices, perceptions, standpoints, and consciousness present are not necessarily the same. To paraphrase M. Jacqui Alexander, the ideological *I* has shifted and transformed. The *I* now is not the same as decades past, although there are threaded inflections and connections. In Alexander's words, the "modulations are about an opening that permits us to hear the muse, an indication of how memory works, how it comes to be animated."[73] I also think about María Lugones's notion of the I → we, which "does not presuppose the individual subject or collective intentionality of the collectivities of the same." As Lugones notes, intentionality and intention "get redrawn, refashioned historically and intersubjectively"; the shared company changes, as does the interactive multiple sense and movements of complex sociality.[74]

My fragments are just that, pieces in the muse of being and becoming always in relation with others. They are intricately tied up with processes of learning, unlearning, and relearning, and with ongoing lived struggles to decolonize and deschool, asking and walking. Now, with this written text, I imagine a canvas of sorts taking form. The canvas is an open backdrop. As with the fragments loosely sewn together and strung up, it too is mobile and moves with the wind. The difference is in size: long strips that form the continuous pages that are transposed here. The difference is also in aim; the strips-as-pages give background, meaning, context, and a sense of lived existence to the smaller squares in the foreground.

As I read and reread, I think about what I have left out, most especially the experiences of existence deschooled that I have witnessed and, for short periods, shared. I know I cannot include all. Yet there is one that definitely needs to be here: it is the powerful and poignant experience that I briefly mentioned in chapter 1: that of the Escuelita Zapatista.

It all started with the special invitation I received from the Subcomandantes Insurgentes Marcos and Moisés to participate during the last week of December 2013 as a first-grade student in the Zapatista "little school." Autonomy and freedom were the thematic threads. The "teachers" were the Zapatista communities themselves and most particularly the youths, those born, raised, and educated in the Zapatista struggle. Each "student" was assigned a *votán*, literally translated as "guardian-heart of the people"; the *votánes* were young women and men who served as guardian-teacher-translator-interpreter-guides, accompanying us twenty-four hours a day. The mode of learning was existential. And it was experience based, an "experience" that was radically different from any I had had before. It brought to the fore the complexity, difficulty, and lived sentiment of unlearning, the first step in beginning to relearn, but also the lived sense of existence deschooled. I was genuinely a first grader; all seemed new, different, and outside my frame and practice of knowing, doing, learning, and living.

The thousand students—from children to elders and from all over the world—gathered first at the Universidad de la Tierra (University of the Earth) in San Cristobal de las Casas in the Mexican state of Chiapas, where we were assigned to one of the then-five *caracoles*, the regional centers of Zapatista "good" government and organization in the Lacandona forest. After a several-hour trip by bus and truck, my group of several hundred arrived to the *caracol* of Morelia, where we were received by hundreds of Zapatistas of all ages in a ceremony led by the *comandancia* of women, men, and those who identified as neither. The Escuelita had begun.[75]

After a night of sleeping among many on the cement floor of the local school, we climbed onto the numerous pickup trucks that were to take us with our *votánes* to our assigned communities. The political tensions and threats of danger were real. The trucks were followed and filmed by military forces. The small village that my partner and I were assigned to was coinhabited by paramilitaries and government-allied forces. Seven churches—the majority evangelical—conducted low-intensity warfare with speakers blasting biblical messages into the late hours of the evening. We were the only "students" in this community.

The "school" consisted of the Tzotzil family with whom we stayed and our *votánes*. My *votán* was a fifteen-year-old girl. She was the one who explained to me my assigned tasks: to work in the kitchen from dawn to midday and to study with her in the afternoons the Zapatista textbooks we were given. Because of the danger lurking outside, I was not to leave the house. This was not what I expected of the "school," and with the days my frustration grew.

Yet what I did not realize then was the weight of my own subjective rationality and logic, and the encumbrance of my so-called feminist political consciousness. The fact that I had to spend hours shucking corn and removing it from the cob in the kitchen, with little or no other contact outside this "women's" space, seemed antithetical to the notions of freedom and autonomy that I was supposed to learn, most especially with regard to Zapatista women. Bit by bit and through occasional translation from Tzotzil to Spanish, my *votán* began to give me a glimpse at what was really transpiring in the kitchen space, including the ways that women in this community used the kitchen as their collective meeting and existence-based space and place. The conversations and shared work were not trivial or inconsequential, as I wrongly assumed; they were simultaneously social, political, and freedom and autonomy based.

Once again, this time in a particularly difficult sense, I was forced to unlearn, decolonize, and deschool, including with respect to my own beliefs, precepts, and understandings of freedom and autonomy. Through the shared practices of daily living, this "Escuelita" pushed me to more deeply think about the complex ways that autonomy and freedom are struggled for, signified, and lived in a particular way by the Zapatistas in this village (where they are a minority) and more broadly in all of Zapatista territory. We must not forget that Zapatista communities run their own systems of education and health care, accept no state services (not even electricity or water), and are communally self-sufficient, including in terms of food. Their three-tiered "good" government (a contrast with the "bad" government of state), made up of women and men with equal power, is based on the belief that "the people rule and government obeys." In this sense, freedom and autonomy are part and parcel of a pedagogy and practice of existence decolonized, deinstitutionalized, and deschooled. It was only later, months after the experience in the Escuelita, that I began to understand this.

I am once again reminded of the paraphrased words of Illich with which I began this chapter: *Not just education but also existence need to be deschooled.* What does this deschooling imply, mean, and suggest?

For the Zapatistas, the practice of deschooling has involved the negation of the presence and interference of state; it is autonomy and freedom from capitalism and coloniality's project, rationality, and logic, and from all of the institutions that work to control, discipline, and "school" bodies, hearts, and minds as well as existence itself. For many Indigenous peoples and nations, and for many activists throughout the world, such practice offers a basis for possibility and hope, a source of and for learnings, and a cause for alliances in struggle.

For me, the experiences over many years of unlearning and relearning with and from the Zapatistas (not just in the Escuelita but also in other contexts and more broadly) have been crucial in helping to ground and make real the significance of an "otherwise." That is, in the territorial context of Zapatista existence-based struggle, a being-becoming, sensing, thinking, theorizing, analyzing, asking, walking, constructing, and living that work incessantly to confront the colonial-capitalist hydra, organize resistance and rebellion, and build a collective force in and through existence "to explain, understand, know, and transform reality."[76] The Zapatista invitation and provocation is not to reproduce their experiences, actions, and thought, but to think, ask, and walk with and alongside them, recognizing the shared need "to make more and better seedbeds" in many calendars and geographies. That is, not to collapse the struggles or territories into one but to do the work of organizing, sowing, cultivating, and connecting resistance and (re)existence. Deschooling, in this sense, calls forth the social, political, and human act and actions of existence, of re-existing *with*, in conditions of dignity, freedom, and autonomy from the dominant logic and institutional practices that work to individualize, control, separate, and divide.[77]

I return to my fragments, pieces, and strips of cloth-text, to the I-we differentially and intensely marked throughout. I reflect on the junctions, and on the re-memberings of that which time and context (evidenced in the first and second parts of this chapter) seemed to dis-member. My interest, as I said at the outset, is not to make a quilt, at least not right now. I fear that by sewing it all together, I will lose the movement and force a cohesiveness, centering, completion, suturing, and close in, of, and on myself. A quilt would force the individual *I*, disenabling the mobility of crossings—what both Alexander and Lugones refer to as learning each other—and with it the possibilities of a taking in of others and their fragments and pieces, including those of you readers here.[78]

In all of this, I have come to understand, maybe as many of you have, that the fragments and pieces are existence itself, never alone but always in relation. The poem "I Am Made of Scraps" of the Brazilian poet Cora Coralina seems fitting in closing:

I'm made of scraps or pieces
Colorful pieces of every life that goes through mine and that I am sewing in my soul.
They are not always beautiful, nor always happy, but they add to me and make me who I am.
In each encounter, in each contact, I am getting older . . .
In each patch a life, a lesson, a love, a nostalgia . . .
That make me more person, more human, more complete.
And I think that this is how life is made: of pieces of other people that are becoming part of the people as well.
And the best part is that we will never be ready, finished . . .
There will always be a scrap to add to the soul.
Therefore, thanks to each of you, who are part of my life and allow me to enlarge my story with the scraps left in me, I can also leave bits of me on the paths so that they can be part of your and others' stories.
And so, from piece to piece we can become, one day, an immense embroidery of "we."[79]

Traversing Binaries
and Boundaries

3

It took five hundred years,
at least in this hemisphere, to solidify the
division of things that belong together.
But it need not take us another five hundred years
to move ourselves out of this existential impasse.
—M. JACQUI ALEXANDER

For all too many years, western modernity and its institutions of control, socialization, and thought tried to instill in me the idea of separation, not relation.[1] Binary-based divisions and categorical boundary-oriented thinking and being were the modus operandi of family, education, science, and the church. They were part of the "natural order," I was told; of existence itself.

I recall the stories of my paternal grandmother that seemed to fracture and fissure this order and mold. In the many hours I spent with her as a child, she would weave tales from her own childhood in late nineteenth- and early twentieth-century rural Nova Scotia, the place where nearby hundreds of maroons had settled years earlier, following, among other paths, the Underground Railroad from the US South. These stories—at least as I remember them—were rooted in the multiple and fluid life-forces of nature. The wind, water, and sky were protagonists, along with the forests, hills, and valleys, the animals and humans. All seemed connected. With her stories, my grandmother transported me to a different world in which I could see myself and sense and feel a freedom that everyday life seemed to negate and deny.

As I grew, this other world became less real, more distant. My grandmother's recountings were imaginary, I was told, fairytales that she made up, although when she was alone with me, she argued otherwise. Together Christianity, my parents, and schools not only made the separations, classifications, and hierarchies increasingly clear, but, worse yet, they naturalized them. To think and act outside this order and its boundaries was not normal.

"Stop acting like a tomboy and act like a girl," was one of my mother's constant reprimands when I was around eight years old. It's not that I wanted to be a boy; I just wanted to be released from the limits of what I was told I had to be as a girl. With the reprimands, of course, came a series of suppositions about gender, gender-appropriate behavior, and gender-based divisions and controls that, as I got older, became more explicit and controlling. As I reached early adolescence, I was continually warned about my relationships with both girls and boys, and always in ways that not only solidified heteropatriarchy but also promoted suspicions, fears, and inhibitions. Classificatory thought was the organizer not only of gender but of almost all spheres of being and life. The freedom that my grandmother's stories had helped me sense, feel, and imagine gradually disappeared.

Questions about and transgressions from these established norms came and went in different moments of my life. Yet it has only been in more recent years that I have begun to consider not only how this normative order affected me but, more broadly, how it is constitutive of the modern/colonial matrix of power and its universalizing model, frame, and condition of existence. With this consideration have come the queries that most interest me today: How have other ways of being, thinking, sensing, and living existed, and how do they continue to exist, persist, resist, and re-exist outside and in the cracks and fissures of the modern/colonial matrix of power and its (re)production in western, Eurocentered civilization?

These queries and considerations have a special relation to my present-day life context. Over the last almost thirty years in Ecuador, my learnings, unlearnings, and relearnings have, in great part, been about existence and relation. They have been about my own re-being-becoming, resensing, re-thinking, and re-existing in connection with—not separation from—this world.

This is not to say that existential relationality does not exist in the United States, or that I never experienced it there. My grandmother's narratives and tales were a part. So too was the relationality I experienced as a young child in the infrequent times I was allowed to spend time with my maternal great-grandmother, a woman of peasant origins who came to the United

States as an adult from her native Lithuania. Since my father forbade me to learn Lithuanian and since she did not speak any English, our relation was mostly nonverbal, built as I accompanied her in tending to her herbal medicinal plants, preparing offerings for her outdoor altar, and even slaughtering and plucking chickens for the daily meal. As I was to learn from my mother and other women in the family after she passed, she was a woman warrior, a sage, and a healer of life.

Sixteen years of close relation as an adult with US Boricuan or Puerto Rican communities taught me more about relational existence, including with respect to forms of spirituality that transgress Christianity's dominant, divisionary frame. Surely the ongoing struggles of First Nations peoples and of African diaspora, Chicana, Caribbean, and many immigrant communities to keep ancestral existence-based philosophies, spiritualities, beliefs, and practices resurgently alive are testaments as well to relationality's presence. However, it is in the United States that existential relationalities and spiritualities have probably suffered the greatest assault. Settler colonialism and the related modern/colonial forces of Christianity, capitalism, and western civilization have largely accomplished in the North what coloniality still has not totally achieved in the South; that is, to separate the secular and spiritual, convert interdependence into individualized autonomy and independence, and denigrate and stigmatize relational beliefs, knowledges, and practices. As the Chicana thinker Laura E. Pérez notes, "Beliefs and practices consciously making reference to . . . the common life force within and between all beings are largely marginalized from serious intellectual discourse as superstition, folk belief, or New Age delusion." Moreover, "even in invoking the spiritual as a field articulated through cultural differences, and in so doing attempting to displace dominant Christian notions of the spiritual while addressing the fear of politically regressive essentialisms, to speak about the s/Spirit and the spiritual in U.S. culture is risky business that raises anxieties of different sorts."[2]

Context, in this sense, is crucial. It is crucial so as to not generalize or collapse into one the lived modern/colonial differences of histories, herstories, theirstories, territory, and geopolitics, as well as the existence-based differences of ancestral-cultural conceptions, practices, and knowledges. And it is crucial in that it marks, positions, and situates subjectivity, embodiedness, and place(s) of enunciation. This necessarily implies continuities and distinctions in my own hyphenated (as connected) present-and-past, including in the lived contexts and geographies of North and South, understood not in binary-based homogenizing and essentializing terms but, following Sandra Harding, as places in the "entangled histories of modernity, colonialism, and capitalism—whether at their origins in 1492 or in the current forms of globalization."[3] While these entangled histories produce important connections, they likewise create familiar global binaries; first world versus third world, North versus South, West versus East, and West over the rest continue to demarcate hierarchies of economic, epistemic, and racial/ethnic enfranchisement and privilege. Although conceived as geographic, these binaries and their hierarchies transcend location; reference to the Souths in the North, the Norths and Wests in the South, and the third world in the first and vice versa are clear examples. As such, Harding's call to not abandon highlighting the hierarchies that the binaries have created and maintained but to use "strategic binarism" as a way to capture and conceptualize valuable tensions makes total sense.[4] It is in this sense that I recognize and engage both the strategic binary and the existence-based difference of living, thinking, sensing, and being in Ecuador as compared with the United States, and, relatedly, the ways this context of difference has, for me, pushed deeper questions and reflections on binaries, boundaries, and divisions, on the one hand, and practices and possibilities of relation, on the other.

How has the colonial/modern difference operated with respect to race, gender, nature, and knowledge? What are the intertwinements that coloniality/modernity has made—and continues to make—between and among these axes and their binaries of power? What are the past-and-present practices, philosophies, cosmogonies, and modes of lived existence that resist, persist, in-surge, and re-exist, disrupting, dismantling, transgressing, and undoing the "existential impasse" that M. Jacqui Alexander refers to in this chapter's epigraph? And how might they help reassemble fluidity and relation? These are some of the many questions that orient the present chapter and, relatedly, my own endeavors to traverse binaries and think from and with postures, practices, pedagogies, and thought that crack coloniality and open toward re-existences and existences otherwise.

The chapter is organized into three parts. The first part is concerned with the ideas of race and gender and their intersectional conception and use as foundational components of the simultaneously modern, colonial, capitalist, and heteropatriarchal structures of power. The second part builds on this discussion, adding Nature (with a capital N) and knowledge to the gender-race intertwinement and divide. It looks at the broad conceptual and relational base of Mother Nature, most especially in Andean, Mesoamerican, and African-origin cosmological practice and thought, and it explores the dual fluidities that transgress modern binaries, most especially those of gender and heteronormativity. It considers how nature (wrested of its relational sense) and knowledge were—and remain—central to the modern/colonial project. And it explores the ways that engenderings and naturings continue to take form, including in community-based contexts where heteropatriarchy and the authoritative positioning of men—including in their use of cosmology—interlace with extractivism and the destruction of Nature as relational existence, as life. Finally, the third part opens reflection on present-day propositions and practices that disrupt, transgress, and move beyond binaries, activating forms of resurgence and ancestral continuity and creating new forms of insurgent relation.

Race and Gender

Race and gender—or, better said, the ideas of "race" and "gender"—have been foundational to the processes of colonization, to the related projects of violence-dispossession-war-death and de-existence described in chapter 1, and to the ongoing matrix of colonial power throughout the globe.

Oyèrónké Oyewùmi argues that in the case of Africa, not radically dissimilar to those of the Americas and the Caribbean, there were two vital and intertwined processes inherent in European colonization. The first was the racializing and attendant inferiorization of the natives, and the second was the inferiorization of females. "These processes were inseparable, and both were embedded in the colonial situation. The process of inferiorizing the native, which was the essence of colonization, was bound with the process of enthroning male hegemony."[5]

In Africa, as in the Americas and the Caribbean, race and gender were essential to the establishment of what Oyewùmi calls a bio-logic, bio-rationality, and body-reasoning; that is, a cultural logic of western social categories based on an ideology of biological determinism that provided the rationale for the organization of the social world.[6] This logic, and its ideas, framework, and processes, arranges the hierarchical and binary-based systems of social classification that continue to operate today. It is a logic that puts white, European-descended, heterosexual men "on top" and establishes criteria of "value," including of humanity, being, rationality, knowledge, sexuality, spirituality, and existence and/as life itself. Race and gender, in this way, have come to form the foundation of how we are supposed to understand, organize, and live life and be in the world.

"Coloniality" is the overriding concept-analytic that names, analyzes, and describes this logic, structure, and ongoing, systematic, systemic, and dynamic matrix of domination and power. Coloniality is inseparable, as Aníbal Quijano argues, from modernity and the capitalist system of power that began with the colonization of the Americas, and the related classificatory processes of race and racialization.[7] In Quijano's conceptualizations, the coloniality of power has its foundation in the idea of "race," the axis from which all other relations of power emanated and emanate.[8]

Yet, as María Lugones has poignantly shown, the idea of "gender" is the other (related) axis of the coloniality of power. "Gender is constituted by and constituting of the coloniality of power," says Lugones.[9] "The dichotomy of man/woman tied to sexual dimorphism and to obligatory heterosexualism forms the 'civilized' face of the colonial gender system and hides its 'dark' racialized face."[10] Here Lugones's contribution is central precisely because it shows how these two "faces" together are constitutive of the colonial/modern system of power that began with the colonial invasion and continues today. Her analysis not only extends that of Quijano but more crucially exposes the meaning, use, and centrality of "gender," something that Quijano never quite understood. Moreover, and as Breny Mendoza forcefully argues, the fact that race—and not gender—continues to be the pivotal idea in the conceptualization of the coloniality of power makes evident how feminist theory, and Lugones's contribution in particular, has not been taken seriously by many male decolonial thinkers.[11]

Both gender and race are present in what Quijano understood as "the historical disputes over the control of labor, sex, collective authority and inter-subjectivity as developing processes of long duration," Lugones explains. However, there is no gender/race separability in Quijano's model. The problem, she says, rests not in Quijano's linking of gender and race—which makes sense—but in his narrowing of gender domination "to the control of sex, its resources, and products."[12] In so doing, Quijano revealed his Marxist roots, his ethnocentric and patriarchal trappings in the dimorphisms of gender and sexuality and, relatedly, what he could not see in his linking of race and gender.[13]

As we will see later in this chapter, race and gender have worked together in complicit ways to hierarchically categorize and classify beings, establishing criteria for who is human and who is not. And, relatedly, they have worked to build the foundations of modern sciences. Gloria Wekker makes this especially clear: "The idea that biological characteristics, the outward appearances and the interiority of bodies, are legible made race and (race-infused) sex/gender and sexuality important building blocks in the classificatory activities that came to characterize the subject matter of the evolving sciences." Hence, and beginning in the early eighteenth century, female genitalia and pelvises, along with skin, skulls, facial angles, and brain mass, "became the obsessional markers of evolutionary progress toward civilization."[14]

EMBODIED ENTANGLEMENTS

While the ideas of race and gender were fundamental to colonization and to the making of coloniality's system of universal social classification, it was the application of these ideas in physical bodies that made raced and gendered inferiorization and domination real. Recalled is Oyewùmi's emphasis on the bio-logic and body-reasoning of the western and westernized social order in which difference is expressed as degeneration. Here "the body is always *in* view and *on view*," says Oyewùmi; the "gaze of differentiation"—of sex, skin color, and cranium size—is a testament not only to the powers attributed to "seeing" in the western world but also to the ways this sight marks difference and establishes and maintains the violence of a raced and gendered social order.[15]

The South African Saartjie Baartman, the "Hottentot Venus," is a particularly violent case in point. Brought to England in 1819 by a Boer farmer and a doctor, Baartman was regularly put on "display" in London and Paris. Her "attraction" for the public and for scientists, naturalists, and ethnologists was her "primitive and pathological otherness;" that is, her protruding buttocks and what was described as her Hottentot apron: "an enlargement of the labia caused by the manipulation of the genitalia and considered beautiful by the Hottentots and Bushmen."[16] Baartman "became 'known,' represented and observed through a series of polarized, binary oppositions. 'Primitive,' not 'civilized,' she was assimilated to the Natural order—and therefore compared with wild beasts, like the ape or orangutan—rather than to the Human Culture." In this way Baartman "was reduced to her body and her body in turn was reduced to her sexual organs. They stood as the essential signifiers of her place in the universal scheme of things."[17]

Yet, as Wekker argues, the story of this and other "Hottentot Nymphae" does not end here. Drawing on a 1917 case study from the Netherlands, Wekker does an intersectional reading of the response of three white female psychiatry patients to the Hottentot Nymphae images and descriptions, a response that, as Wekker explains, eroticized their own gendered and sexual states, projecting these states onto Black women not actually present in Dutch society at this time. "This projection allowed them to inhabit (what was seen at the time as) a less than feminine gender and an active, clitoral, nonheterocentric sexuality. Central to the code is the silent ubiquity of race, that is, Black women with their abject, supposedly unfeminine, excessive sexuality."[18]

For many if not most women of color, race and gender always go together, marking bodies and the gaze of differentiation that coloniality established and continues to construct and maintain. This is true in the so-called Global North, and it is true in the so-called Global South. The effects of this marking are intense and complex, as are the strategies that women use to subvert, dismantle, confront, and undo their effects. In a conversation that we began in January 2020 (some of which she also presented in a conference paper), Romana Mirza offered her own personal account of this marking and differentiation.[19] As a Muslim woman born in the United States and brought up in Canada, where she still resides, Mirza described her life as a triple intersectional, embodied entanglement: of race, gender, and religion, coupled as well, she said, with body size. While growing up, "I had the 'audacity of equality because I was born here,'" she said, quoting the American comedian Hasan Minaj. "Yes, I lived two lives, but it wasn't a struggle or didn't feel that way. I thought if I dressed like everyone else, I would be accepted like everyone else. It was not until much later," she said, "when I started grad school that I learned about white privilege and, in the years since, I have come to see that my life experiences have been a true struggle," in great part against the white, Eurocentered, and Christian female archetype, ideal, and model.

Now, in her powerful research work with other Canadian Muslim women, Mirza makes intersectional identities a force of pride, dignity, and vital strength. Through methodologies and/as pedagogies of digital storytelling and individual and collective reflections on modest fashion, Mirza and these women work to transgress coloniality's external gaze, marking, and dominion of differentiation, assembling and defining their own decolonizing otherwise in body, spirituality, and being.[20]

In a similar vein, Betty Ruth Lozano Lerma makes central the decolonizing protagonism and force of Black women in the Colombian Pacific. For Lozano, in the present-day raced and gendered world, it is impossible to separate the experience of being a woman and being Black. "Blackwoman"—written and spoken as one word—is Lozano's expression of this reality.[21] While Lozano builds on the concept of intersectionality introduced by US Black feminists in the 1990s to describe the interrelation of race and gender along with other forms of domination and oppression, including sexuality and class, she takes us beyond categories and category-based classifications and descriptions. Through her work with and as part of collectives of Blackwomen in the Colombian Pacific, she makes evident, as we will see later in this chapter, how the embodied coupling of race and gender marks the everyday lived struggles and realities of violence, resistance, and (re)existence; that is, of Blackwomen's insurgencies for life.

This embodied coupling forms the foundation of what Lugones refers to as the "colonial/modern gender system." "Though everyone in capitalist Eurocentered modernity is both raced and gendered, not everyone is dominated or victimized in terms of them," Lugones says.[22] This differentially lived reality is what gives substance and form to the colonial/modern gender system, a system that not only obscures the intersections of gender, race, class, and sexuality but also complicates the very idea of gender itself.

The gender system that Lugones maps has what she refers to as both "light" and "dark" sides. Biological dimorphism and heterosexual patriarchy are characteristic of the "light" side; "hegemonically these are written large over the meaning of gender."[23] The "light" side "constructs gender and gender relations hegemonic ally [sic]," ordering the values and lives of white bourgeois men and women while, at the same time, constituting in white heterosexual terms the modern/colonial binary-based meaning of *man* and *woman* and its associated dimorphisms (reason/passion, mind/body, provider/caregiver, public/private, etc.). The "dark" side, in contrast, is filled with all those considered outside the white western(ized) frame, those whom the colonizer has marked as nonhuman or less human. It is on the "dark side" that coloniality's lived violence occurs, including the violences that endeavored to convert Indigenous peoples and enslaved Africans—perceived as nongendered—from animal-like savages into males and females. Females racialized as inferior "were turned from animals into various versions of 'women' as it fit the processes of Eurocentered capitalism," says Lugones, and its heterosexual and patriarchal arrangements of domination and power.[24]

For Lugones, gender, in this sense, is a colonial construction. Gender differentials that define women in relation to men within a frame of binary-opposed, dichotomous, antagonistic, and hierarchical social categories are composite parts of the modern/colonial system.[25] In their thinking with Lugones, Pedro DiPietro says it well: "The meanings attached to 'male' and 'female' are embedded in the social categories and worldviews that collided at the onset of colonization."[26]

Yet while gender's idea and use were, without a doubt, central to the colonial project, its foundational category and ontological conceptualization were constructed in the West long before, including in the Roman Empire, in the dogma of Christianity and the Catholic Church, and in classical Greek thought. The difference, of course, is in the colonial coupling of gender and race and its embodied entanglements, both of which persist throughout the globe today. However, the debate does not end there. It extends to precolonial times and terrains, to precolonial societies and cultures. Thus while no one would probably deny that the colonial invasion launched a regime and regimen of power in which the ideas of race, gender dimorphism, and patriarchy were key, disputes exist among feminists in Abya Yala today about patriarchy's and gender's manifestations, complicities, and beginnings. While this debate is both extensive and complex, a brief look at some of its tenets is useful for the reflections here.

GENDER AND PATRIARCHY

For Lozano, the notion of "gender" has come to be recognized as a category with its own epistemological status, explicative of the social relations between men and women and understood as the cultural representation of sex.[27] Here the ontological base of sexual difference is most often left unquestioned. Gender, in this sense, functions as an ethnocentric category that gives credence to the relations between men and women in western culture. As such, it negates the diversity in conception, form, and practice of being and doing women, shrouding the diverse ways that peoples and cultures think about their bodies and challenge—in their cosmogonies, lifeworlds, and lived practice—the polarized boundaries of masculine/feminine and man/woman that I will discuss later in this chapter. The naturalization of the ideas and categories of both gender and patriarchy within feminism itself is part and parcel of what Lozano calls "the modern colonial habitus." As she argues, "feminist thought, in its most generalized terms, has been confronted by Black, Indigenous, and popular feminisms. The conceptual elaboration of patriarchy has almost always been that of the first world, making it an ethnocentric conception that aims to measure gender relations in all cultures." Moreover, without eliminating ethnocentrism, "gender and patriarchy become ways to subsume and subordinate the cosmogonies of other worlds (Indigenous, Black, etc.), to the known (western) universe."[28]

In this sense, Lozano asks, thinking with Audre Lorde, whether the categories of gender and patriarchy are not part of the master's arsenal of tools—tools of imperial reason—with which it is impossible to destroy his house.[29] Such questioning points to the problems and hegemonic tendencies within feminism itself, including the persistence of Euro-US-centric frameworks, and the continued invisibilization of the differential experiences of Black and Brown women, of bodies not only genderized, ungenderized, and heterosexualized by patriarchal culture but also subject to the politics of racialization and impoverishment.[30]

Many Indigenous women similarly question the ethnocentricity and homogeneity of the gender and patriarchy categories, the historical origins of these categories, and the complex ways they have been used over time. The debates begun two decades ago by self-identified "Indigenous communitarian feminists" in Bolivia and Guatemala opened reflection on gender oppression and ancestral-origin patriarchies, including their junctures with and differences from those of the West.[31]

For Lorena Cabnal, Mayan Xinca communitarian feminist from what today is Guatemala, the construction and presence of a communitarian feminist epistemology in Abya Yala affirms the existence of an ancestral-origin patriarchy "that is a millennial structural system of oppression against native or indigenous women. This system," she contends, "establishes its base of oppression from its philosophy that norms cosmogonic heteroreality as a mandate, so much for the life of women and men and for both in relation with the cosmos."[32] "Heteroreality" is understood here as the ethnic-essentialist norm that establishes that all of the relations of humanity, and with the cosmos, are based in principles and values of heterosexual complementarity and duality that harmonize and balance life.

With the penetration of western patriarchy, Cabnal says, ancestral-origin patriarchy was refunctionalized. "In this historical conjuncture, there is a contextualization and a configuring of our own manifestations and expressions that are home for the birth of the evil of racism, later of capitalism, neoliberalism, globalization and the rest," she argues. "With this I affirm the existence of prior conditions in our native cultures that enabled western patriarchy to strengthen itself and attack."[33]

Similarly, Rita Laura Segato draws from work with Indigenous women when she argues for the existence of two patriarchal moments: "a patriarchy of low impact proper to the world of the community or village" and "the perverse patriarchy of colonial/modernity," with its imposition of a western logic and order, including with relation to sexuality, the body, gender relations, and gendered violence. "It seems to me that gender existed in pre-colonial societies, but in a form different from that of modernity," Segato says. "When this colonial modernity begins to approximate the gender of the community, it dangerously modifies it, intervening in the structures of relations, capturing and reorganizing these relations within while maintaining the semblance of continuity but transforming the sense and meaning of gender and of gender relations."[34]

For Segato, the idea of gender is tied, in part, to the dimensions that have constructed masculinity since the beginning of humanity, part of a patriarchal prehistory of humanity characterized by a slow temporality. This masculinity constructs a subject obliged to conduct himself in a certain way; to prove to himself, others, and his peers his abilities of resistance, aggression, and dominion; and to exhibit a package of potencies—warlike, political, sexual, intellectual, and moral—that permit him to be recognized and named as a masculine subject with a certain hierarchy over the female.[35]

These arguments, along with many others, have pushed reflection on the meanings and practices of gender and patriarchy over time. However, they have also produced disputes and tensions among Indigenous women, some identified as feminists and others who prefer not to use the feminist label.

How are we to know what preintrusion, precolonial, or ancestral patriarchy was? asks Mayan feminist Aura Cumes. How did it emerge? How did it operate? And with what characteristics over five million years? Was the dominion over women the same in all epochs? And what about the response and actions of women themselves? In all of this, shouldn't we also question the universal application of gender and patriarchy as western concepts that may not be applicable to Mayan societies and their cosmovisions?[36]

In a somewhat different vein, Aymaran intellectual Yamila Gutiérrez Callisaya points to the problematic of using modern concepts to describe premodern relations. If Aymaran societies, or *ayllus*, were organized not around male and female bodies but around the complementary cosmological forces of the feminine and the masculine in all of the living—the earth, mountains, waters, sky, plants, animals, and so on—then why insist on using patriarchy, gender, and gender oppression to analyze and describe life before coloniality?[37] Recalled here is Oyewùmi's critique of the preconceived idea of gender as a universal social category, Alexander's stance regarding the colonial project of division, and Irene Silverblatt's argument that, in the Andes, gender could be a metaphor for complementarity and hierarchy, as well as a conduit for the expression of power.[38] In all of this, cannot we also ask about the very categories of masculine and feminine, including their boundaries and limits?

My interest here is not with taking sides, nor is it with presuming to know whether and how what we term today *gender oppression* existed in Native societies before the colonial invasion. Instead, it is with opening reflection on the ways gender and race are constitutive of the colonial/modern matrix of power. And it is with urging thought on how the gender-race imbrication has worked to control, violate, eliminate, shroud, and deny ways of being, thinking, sensing, and living that have existed and continue to exist outside, despite, and in the cracks of this matrix, structure, and system of power. How might we traverse, transgress, and disrupt the binary-based naturalization of gender and race, I ask, a naturalization in which, as we will see in the next section, nature and knowledge are implied and interwoven?

Nature, Knowledge, Gender, Race

For me, it is the coloniality not just of power but also, and possibly more broadly, the coloniality of N/nature that is at the crux of the problem. My use of the capital and lowercase N/n here is crucial in understanding the complexity of coloniality's dual aim and project.

As one of the readers of this text pointed out, the coloniality of nature (in lowercase) makes sense if we understand it as constitutive of the West's binary and biocentric paradigm of control over nature, this defined in and through a western point of view in which the dominion of man (read: European Man) over nature and the commodification of nature as natural resources are crucial cogs in the establishment and maintenance of western Eurocentric rationality. But why Nature with a capital N, this reader asked?

My argument is that while coloniality finds root and ground in the intertwined projects of civilization, western modernity, capitalism, scientific exploration, Christianity and evangelization, development, and education, it does not stop there. It continues to work at the intersection of the cultural, ontological, existential, epistemic, territorial, cosmological, and sociospiritual, imposing a singular paradigm of existence that simultaneously constructs, justifies, and serves the global order and its central civilizing fundaments: western modernity, coloniality, patriarchy, heteronormativity, Christianity, and capitalism all interwoven.[39] It is in this intersection and imposition that a deeper notion of nature and its control emerges, what I posture as Nature, or more specifically Mother Nature, this understood, as many in the world conceive it, as a living entity, indicative of all of existence in relation, and of life itself.

For me, the coloniality of Mother Nature is at the core or nexus of the colonial matrix and of the existential impasse that Alexander named at the outset of this chapter: the "division of things that belong together." The coloniality of Mother Nature, in this sense, links the colonialities of power, knowledge, and being, adding nature to this matrix and in many ways elucidating the coloniality of gender. The idea here is not that there is something internal in Nature (just as there is nothing internal in knowledge or being) that produces or reproduces coloniality. Nature (with a capital N) is not a tool of the colonial project. It is rather what the colonial project has endeavored to dominate, decimate, and control; that is, the domination, control, and decimation of the modes of existence, relationality, and life that continue to exist despite coloniality, despite Euromodernity, and despite the dominion of the West.

Gender—or the modern "idea" of gender as a dichotomous, binary distinction—is, as I described in the last section, an essential and significant instrument in solidifying this domination and imposed order, in rupturing the intimate ties, present in much of the nonwestern world, among beings, human and otherwise, and/as Nature. As Silverblatt reminds us, "Gender ideologies...infuse the fabric of social life; they permeate much of human experience, extending to our perception of the natural world, the social order, and structures of prestige and power."[40]

Thus, it is no surprise that gender and nature (now with a lowercase n) have together been key instruments to reorder, divide, dominate, and control existence, life, and the relational social world. Oyewùmi also makes this clear when she argues that "dualisms like nature/culture, public/private, visible/invisible are variations on the theme of male/female bodies hierarchically ordered, differentially placed in relation to power, and spatially distanced from one another."[41]

In much of Abya Yala, as is probably true in much of the Global South and in Indigenous territories throughout the world, Mother Nature (or just Nature) is a relational concept that signifies and constructs the integral connection of beings, knowledges, cosmologies, land and territorialities, and ways of being-becoming in and with the world; of existence "with." It is not the word Nature that is of interest here, a word that in fact does not exist per se in many Indigenous languages. Cumes, for example, explains that in Mayan cosmogony, "all that the West calls 'nature': earth, stones, valleys, mountains, forests, cliffs, rivers, lakes, oceans, air, sun, moon, stars, all that, has its own life. People are just one thread more in the weaving of *rachulew* [face of the earth], or what others call 'universe.'" In the Mayan sense of life, the word *nature* does not exist; the closest expression to refer to all that which gives existence and life is *loq'olej*, roughly translated as "the sacred."[42]

It is Nature's signification as a living system of social, symbiotic, territorial, and spiritual relation that interests me here. That is, Nature understood as the interdependence of all beings: human, plant, animal, material, terrestrial, supernatural, and those who live on as ancestors. It is an interdependence that does not erase or subordinate difference but instead advances fluid dualities, complementarities, interpenetrations, and interrelations. Nature here is tantamount to what the *Ekobio Mayor* (wise leader-elder) Manuel Zapata-Olivella described as the family of Muntu, this "the sum of the dead (ancestors) and the living united by the word to the animals, trees, minerals, in an undoable knot…, the conception of humanity that the most exploited peoples of the world, the Africans, return to the European colonizers without bitterness or resentment."[43] In the Colombo-Ecuadorian Afro-Pacific, elders argue that this sense of Nature is the result of cultural seeds planted by the maroon ancestors in order to ensure interdependence, relation, and survival. For Juan García Salazar, the personages of "Mother Mountain" (that is, Nature), including the Bambero, Tunda, and Riviel, among other intangible beings that inhabit ancestral territories, are part of this cultural planting that continues to be cultivated and maintained despite coloniality's persistent advance. "The Bambero…ancestral caretaker of the life of the forest and the animals' collective well-being, has the task of distributing with justice and equity the resources of the mother mountain and of punishing those who take more than needed to live with dignity.…The Riviel, caregiver of the waters, continues in his canoe, moving through the rivers and ocean.…The Tunda, woman of a thousand faces, possessor of eternal youth, eternally in love with life, ancestral dancer whose dominions are the ancestral territories of the communities of African origin."[44]

How Nature is conceived, perceived, and lived in different cultural and territory-based cosmogonies and contexts is important. Not only do lived conceptions, perceptions, and cosmogonies of Nature sustain cultural and ancestral continuance, they also create, construct, generate, and assemble life senses and ways of being that defy western modernity's universalized project of anthropocentric, masculine-centric, and secular separation, independence, and no-relation. The problem is when these life senses, their nuances, contexts, collective histories, herstories, theirstories, memories, and lived practice, are collapsed into modern notions of posthumanism, thus negating or simply overlooking the long horizons of decolonial struggle of knowledge and being from and for life.[45]

In her book on ecologies of practice in the Andes, Marisol de la Cadena argues that "it matters what concepts we use to translate other concepts with." With the concept-phrase "earth-beings/nature" constructed in and through her years of conversation with two Andean peasants in Peru, De la Cadena leads us through a complex reflection in which "practices with earth-beings do not necessarily follow distinctions between the physical and the metaphysical, the spiritual and the material, nature and human." Interdependence and relation here are constitutive. For *runakuna* (native Andean peoples), earth-beings (*tirakuna*) are the entities that one's relations and practices make present.[46] Earth-beings, she argues, are more than simply the ancestral spirits of the wind, the mountains, the rivers, and the lakes; they are beings that, together with other beings—plants, animals, and humans—coconstitute Nature as mutual relation, as existence, as Andean life.

The reciprocal relation that is Nature in the Andes is most often understood and expressed as Pachamama. Most directly, Pachamama alludes to time-space and to earth, earth not separate from but integral to the cosmos. In 1613 Juan de Santa Cruz Pachacuti represented Pachamama in a drawing that placed earth, life, planting, harvest, and fertility in cosmological-existential relation.[47] Here, and in the sense of many Andean communities, Pachamama signifies and calls forth the intimate relationality and complementarity of forces—of the spiritual and sacred; of mountains; of the waters of rivers, streams, lakes, sea, and rain; and of the dimensions of land, sky, and the under-earth in concert with the sun and moon—that permit and enable the production of life. Pachamama, in this way, is not only tied to the rituals of planting, cultivation, and harvest. More integrally, it is the entity-force understood as a feminine power dedicated to the care of Nature, to nurturing the interdependence and relation that Nature signifies and creates. And, interrelatedly, it is the entity-force dedicated to the care of existence, being, and life (human and otherwise) understood not in the framework of "uterine production of reproduction that serves patriarchy" but in the frame of interdependence and reciprocal relation within the cosmos "of which humanity is only a small part."[48]

As such, Pachamama and Nature are not exactly one in the same but instead intimately connected, with human beings part of both. Yet while this sense of life and existence persists in the Andes, it is continually confronted by the intervention of western modernity, an intervention that separates humans from nature, denaturalizing the former and desacralizing the latter and the world.[49]

NATURE REDEFINED

The European projects of invasion, conquest, colonization, civilization, and modernity imposed and implanted their own ideas of nature. While these ideas shifted with time and with the eye and interest of the observer, one constant remained: the establishment of a concept and category rooted in the separation of humans and nature; that is, of those considered human who, at the time of the colonial invasion, were white, European, Christian men, and later those who mirrored the racial and civilizational likeness of the invaders. With this separation came a hierarchy of classification in which humanity came to be judged from the colonial gaze and mirror.

One of the early ideas of nature was that imposed by the Catholic Church. In his *Natural and Moral History of the Indies* (1590), the Spanish Jesuit missionary José de Acosta described nature in what are now the Andes and Mesoamerica as God's design. His account of the region's flora and fauna, together with his hierarchical classification of Indigenous peoples, denoted an understanding and a reengineering "of nature as a way of knowing and revering God, its creator."[50] This idea challenged Andean and Mesoamerican cosmologies of creation, of deities, and of their manifestations, and it served as the foundational base for the church-colonizer campaigns of extirpation. The Huarochiri Manuscript in the Andes and Popol Vuh in Mesoamerica were contracted by the church in the late sixteenth century and early seventeenth century for this purpose. However, the fact that both were subverted by their Indigenous scribes, becoming instead the most important historical registers of Mayan and Andean senses of life, is testimony to resistance's creative force and the praxis of decolonial fissure.

Together, the church and the Crown worked to ensure the boundary-based separation of humans and nature through the idea that nature was/is there to be dominated by man. To establish such dominance meant having a precise knowledge of nature and a control over knowledge itself. Grimaldo Rengifo Vasquez's explanation here is particularly lucid: "To know presupposes a distancing between humans and nature, but this situation did not bring the ancients in the West to intervene, but instead to fuse, to assimilate themselves with nature," says Rengifo. "Knowledge in the modern context, however, is different, because man no longer forms or feels part of nature; instead, he sees himself as possessing her and his knowledge is instrumental: it is not knowledge for contemplation, but rather knowledge for the purpose of exploiting a nature that is supposedly there to be dominated."[51]

Renaissance thinkers like Sir Francis Bacon (1561-1626) and René Descartes (1596-1650) reshaped the idea of nature and its epistemological frame. In his *Novum Organum* (1620), Bacon proposed a reorganization of knowledge grounded in the nature-human divide, arguing that "'nature' was 'there' to be dominated by Man."[52] Both Bacon and Descartes separated nature from human society, redefined nature as a collection of elements, some living and others not, and as environments replete with resources that could be observed, manipulated, managed, controlled, and possessed by Man. Rengifo explains it well: "As man distances himself from nature he affirms the notion of the individual, a being separate and opposed to nature."[53] Nature thus became, in Eurocentered knowledge and in Eurocentered minds, anthropocentric in perspective and construction.[54]

Central here was the establishment of one foundational dichotomous binary: Man (read: white, European/European-descended, lettered, heterosexual man as universal "Man") over nature with a lowercase *n*, thus wresting the relational dominion and significance of (Mother) Nature. This binary came to fix the association of nature with the savage, irrational, and wild, including in racialized and, as I will argue later, in gendered terms. Efforts to "conquer" nature and "civilize" the Indians were one and the same. Indigenous peoples were seen as one savage element more of the savage environments that surrounded them and of which they were part.[55] This binary also came to solidify a scientific base for nature within the modern, colonial, and imperial structure of power, including with regard to knowledge production and distribution.

Nature was converted into something radically distinct from that which had existed before in Abya Yala. It became, in the eyes of the colonizers and their European military, religious, political, and intellectual allies and agents, a system and category to be studied, classified, and ordered (against its disorder). Likewise, it was a wild "thing" to be tamed and controlled, a good to be possessed, and a resource to be extracted and utilized; that is, a resource-as-commodity with market value. "Man" held the right of power over and access to these "resources" of which Natives first, and later Africans, were considered part.

Eduardo Gudynas describes the double process that took place: "the transplantation to the new continent of cultures and ideas about Nature, and the transplantation of the instrumental practices to take advantage of Nature."[56] In Walter Mignolo's words, "Coloniality wrapped up 'nature' and 'natural resources' in a complex system of western cosmology, structured theologically and secularly." Coloniality manufactured an "epistemological system that legitimized its use of 'nature'; to generate massive quantities of 'produce' first, and massive quantities of 'natural resources' after the Industrial Revolution."[57] This is the commodification of nature and of life.

Nature, in this sense, came to occupy a pivotal space in the capitalist modern/colonial order. It is an expression and a constitutive part of the dominions of western rationality, knowledge, and science, but also, as we shall soon see, of the structures of patriarchy and of the very ideas of "race" and "gender," including their binaries and systems of social classification.[58]

Moreover, it is the relation created by modern thought between an abstract subject—understood as the universal heteronormative "Man" without a named class or culture—and nature as an inert object that explains the "totalization" of the western world mentioned in chapter 1. Such totalization, as Santiago Castro-Gómez argues, "blocks the possibility of an exchange of knowledges and of the different cultural forms of knowledge production."[59] Eliminated is the possibility of alterity itself; that is, of other ways of living, being, thinking, and knowing distinct from those of Europe and the West.

The incorporation of the natural world into the world of European science, property, and possession was, in this sense, central to the dissemination of power in the territory that the creole elite named "Latin" America. The natural-scientific explorations first led in the eighteenth and nineteenth centuries by Charles-Marie de La Condamine, Carl Linneaus, and Alexander von Humboldt in the Andes, and locally carried out by "New World" elite such as José Celestino Mutis and Francisco José de Caldas in Nueva Granada, further objectified and naturalized nature.[60] By exploring, explaining, classifying, and ordering the natural world, these men—whether intentionally or not—imposed an epistemic and cultural order and control, constitutive of what Mary Louise Pratt has referred to as a "European planetary consciousness." That is, "an orientation toward interior exploration and the construction of global-scale meaning through the descriptive apparatus of natural history, . . . a basic element constructing modern Eurocentrism."[61]

This "planetary consciousness" is, of course, a component part of what we understand today as the universalizing project of western civilization. It is also fundamental to the belief, vital then and now, that the control, exploitation, and use of nature as natural resources, commodities, and environment are a human necessity and right. "The desire to dominate Nature, to change it into exportable products, has always been present in this region," says the Ecuadorian economist-activist Alberto Acosta. "In the early stages of Independence, when faced with the earthquake in Caracas of 1812, Simón Bolívar said the famous words, which marked that time, *'If Nature objects, we shall fight against it and make it obey us.'*"[62] Recalled here is Bacon's contention, mentioned earlier, that "'nature' was 'there' to be dominated by Man,"[63] as well as Maldonado-Torres's discussion of the paradigm of war (see chapter 1).

The desire, right, and conceived need to dominate, control, and appropriate Nature are, in essence, constitutive components of modernity's mode of reason; that is, the global linear thinking that began in 1492 with the start of coloniality and the "modern age." Nature here was made to be (hu)man-centric, to be given meaning and order by Man. The struggle, in this sense, has been with and against nature conceived as barbarism, chaos, conflict, and nonorder, a struggle thought from the context of the spatial and terrestrial as human realms, where order, orientation, and law coincide.[64] In this view, the operation or even the possibility of other logics for understanding, orienting, and being in and with Mother Nature—logics that conceive Nature as the totality and relationality inherent to life itself—are inconceivable and counterproductive. Moreover, they are considered blasphemous and a threat to the modern capitalist order. While posthumanism has opened important critiques of this Man-centered mode of reason and its bifurcation of human and other forms of life—a critique made much earlier by twentieth-century anticolonial Black thinkers like Aimé Césaire, Leopold Senghor, Frantz Fanon, C. L. R. James, and Sylvia Wynter—posthumanist thought remains, for the most part, modern and Eurocentered. It shrouds not only the intimate entwinement of modernity and coloniality—an entwinement that the aforementioned Black thinkers knew well—but also, as both Mignolo and Zimitri Erasmus argue in conversation with Wynter, the relational way that the human is configured and understood outside the western episteme of humanity and its figure of "Man."[65]

In fact, the relational concept, foundation, and lived practice that intimately connects peoples, animals, plants, and land; bodies and territories; the spiritual and the secular; and the dead and living was a central target of the modern/colonial project and its mercenaries or agents. The imposition of a hierarchical binary-based rationality was one of the many modes of domination and control that strove to break relationality, determine social classification, and establish a Eurocentric logic of the "natural" order. Such order—a component part of the interrelated projects of civilization, scientific exploration, Christianity and evangelization, and education—has, of course, justified Man's intervention in and control, domination, and appropriation of N/nature, with, as Mignolo argues, racism and epistemology "part of the package."[66] Moreover, and in a related sense, it has also justified and naturalized Man's control, domination, and subalternization of women; here the feminine, as an inferior and potentially dangerous force, is postured and conceived as closer to and constitutive of Nature/nature (in both capital and lowercase letters).

(EN)GENDERINGS AND NATURINGS

Bacon's famous quote "Knowledge is power" elucidates his belief—shared by the "fathers" of modern science—that reason is male and nature is female, a belief that of course served to justify the domination of the first over the latter. Gönül Kaya of the Kurdish women's movement explains this clearly: "The relationship between abstracted reason and nature, which he [Bacon] discarded as soulless matter, could only be one of mastery, conquest, and seduction. And so his utopia of New Atlantis consisted of an island of men, who make knowledge and science the basis of their power." Bacon's frequent use of the patriarchal family and marriage as metaphors, as well as his participation in witch-hunting, is, as Kaya points out, further evidence of the subjugation and violences that gave root to modern science, and of the gendering-naturing relation.[67] The metaphorical representation of domesticated nature as a domesticated woman has, throughout history, been one more way to naturalize the idea that the irrational wildness of both need to be under constant vigilance, control, and taming.[68]

In *White Innocence: Paradoxes of Colonialism and Race*, Gloria Wekker argues that gender, race, and nature were constitutive components not only in the control over the colonies but also in the development of western science as a transnational endeavor. From Charles Darwin's *On the Origin of the Species* (1859), "with its belief in progress and natural selection" and its cementing "of preexisting ideas about the superiority of the fittest of the races," to the studies throughout the nineteenth and early twentieth centuries of white and Black female genitalia and pelvises "as obsessional markers of evolutionary progress toward civilization," the quest for racialized, gendered, and naturalized hierarchy became solidified as science.[69] Here the ranked distinction—as boundary—between white Europeans and the colonized was not only the object of study; it was also the signifier and sign of the colonial/modern civilizational, economic, political, epistemic, and existential world order.

While nineteenth-century European science was certainly central in the consolidation of this order, we should not forget that coloniality/modernity was born in Abya Yala South several centuries before. How did the intertwinement of genderings, racings, and naturings take form in this context? And how did they endeavor to undo the relationality and fluid dualities that had organized life for millennia?

Sylvia Marcos contends that in Mesoamerica as well as in the Andes, "man and woman, death and life, evil and good, above and below, far and close, light and dark, cold and hot were some of the dual aspects of one same reality. All elements and natural phenomena were construed as a balance of dual valences," she argues. "In this sense and if the divine pair [the dual female and male unit] was the ultimate duality in the cosmic realm, its most pervasive expression in the intermediary human domain was gender."[70]

Of course, we can question whether the modern social category of "gender" is the appropriate word to refer to this relationality given that biological "femaleness" or "maleness" was generally not the constitutive marker of social organization and relation before the colonial invasion. Moreover, if *man* and *woman* are terms handed down to us by western science and imposed on worlds previously conceived and constructed—cosmologically, spiritually, and existentially—from horizontal relationality, symmetrical complementarity, and dynamic, fluid, and nonhierarchical pluralities that are life, then how might we understand coloniality's "before and after"? What are the social, cultural, and cosmo-existential logics, memories, and constructions that organized life in nonoppositional, nongenetically or nonbiologically derived forms? And in what ways does a thinking beyond or a traversing of western conceptual categories—and of the prevailing dimorphism that envelops them—enable us to contemplate and imagine the existence, then and today, of practices and possibilities otherwise?

DUALITY, FLUIDITY, AND THE ANDROGYNOUS WHOLE

Present-day descriptions of precolonial cosmologies, philosophies, and practices of existence in the Andes and Mesoamerica suggest that life was predicated on a balance of related forces understood as feminine and masculine but not in a biological sense. With respect to people, these forces have been described as dynamic, fluid, open, and nonhierarchical. They were not based on anatomical distinctions but rather associated with what people do and their ways of being in the world, ways that were not fixed but in constant movement, shift, modification, fluid equilibrium, and relation, all of which, of course, was not devoid of conflict or power relations.

Gender duality is the modern expression often used to signify this interpenetration of masculine and feminine forces, and to refer to entities (human and sacred) that incorporated female and male characteristics; nuances of combinations and of a continuum or fluidity that easily moved between poles.[71] The feminine-masculine whole in these ancestral cosmologies, but also in African-descended ancestral life senses, practices, and traditions, has been described as a signifier of wisdom and spiritual power, a fundamental component and metaphor of creation, thought, the cosmos and universe, and the individual body regardless of genitals or "sex." Here a dimorphic gender binary was not only absent, it was most probably not even conceived.

Language offers a clear example. In the colonizer's language and project, humans were—and often are still—defined and translated as "men." Deities or spiritual forces became gods, understood and visually depicted as male. However, in many Indigenous languages the idea of the human (including in its application to deities) has no gender. Yoruba, for example, is a gender-free language. Oyewùmi argues that in Yoruba there are no gender-specific words denoting *son, daughter, brother*, or *sister*, nor are there gender-specific names. Furthermore, the categories of *oko* and *aya*—translated in English as "husband" and "wife"—are also not gender specific.[72] Ifi Amadiume's text *Male Daughters, Female Husbands* provides a clear example, showing not only how the African Igbo society and philosophy of existence functioned before the colonial imposition of dichotomous sexual/gender difference but also how practices of matricentricity and genderlessness intertwined.[73]

In the Indigenous languages of Abya Yala, the idea of the human is also not gender specific. *Runa* in Andean Kichwa, for instance, signifies "person" or "persons"; *runakuna* means "persons in existence." Similarly, as Cumes points out in her analysis of Maya K'iche in the sixteenth-century Popol Vuh (or *Popul Wuj*, as she writes it in Maya K'iche), *winaq* is the word-concept that references a being-person based in a plural idea of existence.[74] In ancient Zapotec, *la-ave* referred to people, *la-ame* to animals, and *la-ani* to inanimate beings, with no designation or difference of "she" and "he."[75] Isaac Esau Carrillo Can highlights the word-concept *leti'* in Yucatec Mayan thought as an androgynous pronoun that names a person without identifying their gender. "The daily use of *leti'* does not need to dichotomize the concept of person into western ideals of [man] and [woman]," Carrillo Can argues. "*Leti'* is a way of making memory, as well as a system of thinking about the *Uyuumtsiles*, the ancestral creative forces and energies of the Yucatec Maya cosmos, that also embodies androgynous characteristics."[76]

The original androgynous whole, understood as the source of creation throughout the Indigenous world, exemplified the oscillation and complementary fluidity between the masculine and feminine and its ritually negotiated tensions. In this dynamic equilibrium, there was no clearly defined either-or.[77] A number of testimonial texts of the time document this androgyny and/as complementary fluidity. In the Andes, Felipe Guamán Poma de Ayala's letters and drawings in *Nueva corónica y buen gobierno* (1615) and Francisco de Ávila's sixteenth-century contracted Huarochiri Manuscript are illustrative. Similarly, in Mesoamerica both the Mayan Popol Vuh and the Florentine Codex, the latter contracted in the sixteenth century by the Franciscan friar Bernardino Sahagún and initially developed in Nahuatl based on the testimonies of more than two decades with Nahua elders and documented by Indigenous scribes, also reveal the presence of deities and people considered androgynous or at the same time masculine and feminine.[78]

In the Popol Vuh, for instance, Jun Rakán—understood as the creator—is described as without sex, "or what is the same for us: father and mother at the same time."[79] Ometéotl, the Mexica Aztec creator, is similarly described as androgynous and, as such, at the top of the cosmological order. So too is Viracocha, the divinity of creation in the Andes. The seventeenth-century chronicler Joan de Santa Cruz Pachacuti Yamqui described Viracocha as incorporating what are often considered the opposing forces of gender: "the sun, the moon, day, night, summer, and winter." In his 1613 diagram of Andean cosmology, Viracocha is depicted as an egg-like figure, above which are the inscribed words, "whether it be male, whether it be female."[80]

Other important deities have been depicted as explicitly dual. Examples include the Nahua plumed serpents of Quetzalcoatl-Cihuacoatl, the two-headed serpent of Maya creation—Xpiyakok in its masculine aspect and Xmukané its feminine aspect—and the Andean deity Pachakamak, with its two faces united in one body. It is this androgynous duality—of creation, spirituality, and cultural-cosmogonic order—that gave foundation to the relational sense, knowledge, and ways of being in and with the world of all of life.

As I will describe in more detail in the last section of this chapter, the notions and manifestations of androgynous duality are not necessarily something of the past. Carrillo Can refers, for example, to the continued veneration in the Mayan Tseltal community of San Juan Evangelista Canuc in Chiapas of the deity Me'il-Tatil, understood as the mother-father who directs part of the cosmos.[81] Another example is Carrillo Can himself-herself-theirself, who, until their premature death, spoke and wrote from the lived experience of being an androgynous subject.[82] As Carrillo Can explains, it was in the experience of writing the novel U yóok'otilo'ob áak'ab/Danzas de la noche (Dances of the night) that "this androgynous spirit that lives in me evolved in my narration in a first person's woman's voice, a relational voice that melds the voices of my mother, my grandmother, and my sister with mine and that in the Mayan cosmos-vision and language allows me to be the 'other I' at all times in-relation."[83] For Carrillo Can, this androgynous spirit or force cannot be encapsulated in the modern notion of transgender; its roots are cosmologically ancient.[84]

Pedro DiPietro explains well how the notion of transgender remains rooted in a western paradigm "in which the modern phenomenon of gender identity reduces the sexual realm to the biologically determined binary between male and female, the sociocultural dichotomy between masculine and feminine, and the biomaterial hierarchy of the natural over free will. "Transgender," says DiPietro, "has an additive position within the paradigm since it does not disturb its range." Moreover, it maintains "a biological substrate that seeks a binary marker (trans man–trans woman), and confirms the supremacy of one gender (the masculine) over the other."[85]

The cosmologically ancient androgynous spirit or force is distinct precisely because it traverses and moves beyond binaries, encompassing a whole. The Oaxacan community of Be'ena' Za'a (Zapotec) Muxes are an example that continues from millennial times; here the contemporary work of the Muxe artist and anthropologist Lukas Avendaño (mentioned in chapter 1) is particularly representative.[86] Similarly illustrative is the concept *otroas*, which, as Sylvia Marcos describes, "expresses a theoretical reference that belongs to and is inspired in the philosophical universe of Mesoamerican ancestral legacies, [a reference] today of Zapatista peoples and communities.... The concept *otroas* recognizes the physical, corporal variants and their permanent transit...between one pole and the other.... So say the Zapatistas: 'And why are we going to force them to be men or women and that they have to take one side or the other'?... Why, we can ask, should we have to accommodate the world and our multiple, complex, mixed, heterogeneous, combined, bi-morfo body/self in mutually exclusive [colonial] categories?" *Otroas* names movement; "it names the living of fluidity of body/gender/cosmos."[87] The two-spirited people of the native cultures of Turtle Island are another living millennial example. As the Nishnaabeg intellectual-artist Leanne Simpson notes, two-spirited people were traditionally just a part of the entire community; today they struggle to reclaim this identity with this name and as grounded normativity.[88]

Of course, manifestations of this androgynous wholeness or duality remain present in various regions of the world. In Hindu culture, for example, Ardhanarisvara—the deity of creation—represents the synthesis of masculine and feminine energies of the universe; described as androgynous, Ardhanarisvara is composed of the male principle or god Shivá and the female principle or goddess Shakti.[89] In South Asia, including India and Pakistan, the *hijras*, considered male-female, have maintained their identity and community organization for centuries. Today they are politically recognized as "third gender."[90]

In parts of West Africa—particularly among the Fanti-Ashanti peoples of Benin and Ghana—as well as among descendants of the African diaspora throughout the Americas and the Caribbean, the spider Anansi continues as a central figure in stories and ancestral practices and thought handed down from generation to generation, weaving webs that unite both continents.

Anansi is neither man nor woman, sometimes transiting toward one, the other, or neither. Some say that Anansi is the trickster in West African Vodun. Others say Anansi is related to the Yoruba orisha Esú, Elegua, or Elegba, well known in the Caribbean and recognized in Brazil as the liberator of slaves.[91] Jaime Arocha writes that Ananse (Anansi) traveled in slave ships from Africa to the Americas; as Ananse could walk on top and underneath the water, this spider deity arrived to the jungles of the Colombian Pacific, "and by the thread that Anansi took out of his-her belly, descended down to the mangroves of the swamps."[92] There, according to Betty Ruth Lozano, Anansi has inherited Blackwomen, passing on the indispensable qualities of self-sufficiency, survival, rebelliousness, and audacity, qualities necessary for Blackwomen's re-existence and insurgence in the Colombian Pacific today.[93]

In her description of precolonial Yorubaland, Oyewùmi argues for the presence of non-gender-specific divinities, or òrìsà (orishas), that encompassed both male and female or were recognized in some contexts and localities as male and in others as female. For instance, the god of creation, Olódùmarè, had no defined gender or human representation.[94] Moreover, in the Yoruba and Lucumi pantheons of spirituality celebrated throughout the Americas and the Caribbean today, this androgynous deity of creation (sometimes written as Odumare or Oldumare) remains without human characteristics or gender. Oshumare or Oxumare, the divinity of the sky and the rainbow, is also considered androgynous. Sometimes represented as a cobra, Oshumare signifies the communion between the sky and the earth, half the year masculine and half the year feminine. The examples of orishas who move within a dynamic fluidity of the masculine and feminine are many, including the dual-spirited figure of Chango. Considered the orisha of thunder and often depicted as the most virile and masculine of the orishas, Chango is sometimes described as incorporating the feminine as well. In his classic work *Chango, Gran Putas* (*Changó, the Biggest Badass* in its English translation), Manuel Zapata Olivella describes Chango's humongous penis and later refers to his uterus and breasts.[95]

Such was the African androgynous divinity that I encountered in a shop in Cape Town, South Africa (figure 3.1), and a similar figure from nineteenth-century Papua New Guinea on display in 2018 in Amsterdam's Tropen Museum (figure 3.2).

It seems that throughout the nonwestern world (including the non-West in the now Global North), androgyny, duality, and the fluid movement between "genders," including in sexual practice, were constitutive components of everyday life before the colonial invasions. In fact, they were the norm, as documented by many First Nations intellectuals, including Leanne

3.1 African androgynous divinity, Cape Town, South Africa. PHOTO: CATHERINE WALSH, 2018. **3.2** Androgynous divinity used in funeral rituals, nineteenth-century Papua New Guinea, Tropen Museum, Amsterdam. PHOTO: CATHERINE WALSH, 2018.

Simpson, Ma-Nee Chacaby, Alex Wilson, Qwo-Li Driskill, and contributors to the compilation edited by Driskill, Chris Finely, Brian Joseph Gilley, and Scott Lauria Morgensen.[96]

In his book *Decolonizing the Sodomite*, Michael Horswell uses the term "third-gender subjects" to refer to the *quariwarmi* (men-women) shamans in the Andes, whose performative role and transvested attire did not fit neatly into a male or female designation but instead "negotiated between the masculine and feminine, the present and the past, the living and the dead."[97] For Horswell, "third-gender" is not meant to add another gender to the male/female divide but instead to rupture the bipolarity of western thought. It opens rather than closes and pluralizes rather than singularizes the possibilities of gender-sex identity and practice, recognizing the diverse fluidities and transitivities that existed not just in the Andes but also elsewhere. Moreover, it suggests a notion of complementarity that is less about a forged union or harmony between the sexes, and more about the conflictive and creative tensions that construct interdependence, mediate power and autonomy, and negotiate gender difference as "an invocation of an androgynous whole" in which the culturally specific force of the feminine played a particularly important role.[98] "Without an appreciation of the symbolic, performative role of the feminine and the androgyne," says Horswell, "we cannot fully understand the complexities of Andean gender culture and the negotiation of complementarity in ritual and quotidian contexts."[99] In this context, as I will discuss at the end of this chapter, the Incan *coya* or queen Mama Huaco was a central example.

I recall Gloria Anzaldúa's powerful reflection on the *herencia* (legacy) and state of Coatlicue, not an academic study on the feminine and androgyne as Horswell offers, but "a way of life," a crucial step in Anzaldúa's own lived journey toward mestiza consciousness. "Coatlicue is a rupture in our everyday world," says Anzaldúa, she is "the mountain, the Earth Mother ... the incarnation of cosmic processes" who simultaneously represents "duality in life, a synthesis of duality, and a third perspective—something more than mere duality or a synthesis of duality."[100] With Anzaldúa's detailed description of Coatlicue's visual image, we can appreciate the fluid, complementary feminine-androgynous dynamism, energy, and traversing force of this sacred spirit-goddess, and for this reason I quote Anzaldúa at length:

> I first saw the statue of this life-in-death and death-in-life headless "monster" goddess (as the *Village Voice* dubbed her) at the Museum of Natural History in New York City. She has no head. In its place two spurts of blood gush up, transfiguring into enormous twin rattlesnakes facing each other, which symbolize the earth-bound character of human life. She has no hands. In their place are two more serpents in the form of eagle-like claws which are repeated at her feet: claws which symbolize the digging of graves into the earth as well as the sky-bound eagle, the masculine force. Hanging from her neck is a necklace of open hands alternating with human hearts. The hands symbolize the act of giving life; the hearts, the pain of Mother Earth giving birth to all of her children, as well as the pain that humans suffer throughout life in their hard struggle for existence. The hearts also represent the taking of life through sacrifice to the gods in exchange for their preservation of the world. In the center of the collar hangs a human

skull with living eyes in its sockets. Another identical skull is attached to her belt. These symbolize life and death together as parts of one process.[101]

As Anzaldúa goes on to explain, "Coatlicue depicts the contradictory. In her figure, all the symbols important to the religion and philosophy of the Aztecs are integrated. Like Medusa, the Gorgon, she is a symbol of the fusion of opposites: the eagle and the serpent, heaven and the underworld, life and death, mobility and immobility, beauty and horror."[102]

With Anzaldúa, we can begin to appreciate the feminine force of duality, fluidity, and the androgynous whole. As I will argue later, this feminine-centered conception and order of the cosmos-pluriverse not only cracks patriarchy-coloniality's supposedly universal order but also reveals and constructs a radically distinct sense of being and/in relation that crosses territories and cultures.

In her now-classic text *Moon, Sun, and Witches*, Irene Silverblatt gives us elements to appreciate how what she refers to as the "ideology of gender complementarity" functioned in Andean Incan societies and served as the base from which Mother Nature's order and work were most often interpreted and understood. For Silverblatt, gender complementarity, gender parallelism, and gender alliance were part and parcel of a relational world-sense in which binary divisions, including between the realms of the supernatural and natural, and the dead and the living, had no ground. "Male and female independent forces were also ancestor-heroes and ancestor-heroines of the mortals whose gender they shared," she contends. "Constructing the supernatural with familiar materials, Andean women perceived kinship and descent to follow lines of women, just as, in parallel, men saw themselves as descending from and creating lines of men."[103] Complementarity in this sense, and within the Andean philosophy of existence, sometimes referred to as *yanatin*, was not about biology per se but about relational feminine and masculine forces, and about relational roles—practical, performative, and transbiologic—of being and doing in the spiritual, ritual, political, economic, and everyday realms; roles that created, ordered, produced, reproduced, regenerated, and maintained Andean society, existence, and life.

DOMINATION THROUGH GENDER

If gender complementarity was the fundamental basis for human interaction, cultural regeneration, and Nature's order in Abya Yala, it is no surprise that it also became an essential tool of domination. Such was true in the settler colonialism of North America and for the Spanish Crown and church and its agents in the South: theologians, inquisitors, and criminal authorities who defined and used the categories of the "unnatural" and "sins against nature" (i.e., sodomy and same-sex sexuality) as heteronormative weapons of conquest, civilization, and control, what in essence can be understood as war. Zeb Tortorici's extension of these categories as "against nature" takes us beyond the simple categories of sodomy and homosexuality, opening up broader considerations of how gender, desire, and sexuality operated in the colonial and precolonial past and how this operation constructed and marked divergent conceptions with regard to Nature. Tortorici reminds us that such conceptions in terms of the Spanish regulation "are the work of a long institutional chain of reasoning going back to the early Church Fathers like Saint Augustine and medieval theologians like Thomas Aquinas." In his thirteenth-century *Summa Theologica*, Aquinas wrote, "Just as the order of the right reason is from man, so the order of nature is from God himself. And so in sins against nature, in which the very order of nature is violated, an injury is done to God himself, the orderer of nature."[104]

Aquinas, like the sixteenth-century Acosta, made evident the relation of nature and God, the latter conceived as clearly masculine, male, and one-almighty. God created and ordered nature and, with it, a rationality of the "natural" that endeavored to also define and control the heterosexual, procreative reason of sexual activity and the heteronormative binary-based scheme of gender.

However, the Europeans were not the only ones to use gender as an instrument of domination. Silverblatt maintains that gender was also a central strategy of the Inca imperial conquest. The Incas used the ideology of gender to design and forge ties that would bind the conquered to them, ties that, with time, would also begin to mark asymmetries of class and gender. "As political relations supplanted kinship, gender became the trope through which power was expressed and articulated," Silverblatt explains. "Now more than metaphor, emerging imperial institutions fused the control over women with the control over humankind; gender became a form through which class relations were actualized." Moreover, "the formation of class transformed gender distinctions into gender hierarchy."[105] In this way, the construction of the empire altered the material conditions of life of the once-autonomous Andean peoples in the same way that it transformed the material conditions of life for women and men. The control of one part of humanity over the other had a close relation with the privileges of one sex over the other. By exacerbating the differences between the sexes, class formation left in its wake the hierarchy of gender.[106]

Such processes and perspectives are helpful in complicating notions of gender and patriarchy, and in illuminating colonial difference as not necessarily the beginning of hierarchical gender and patriarchal relations, as was argued earlier in this chapter, but as a historically significant moment and movement promulgated from the outside that radically intervened in what we now term gender, and the interlaced spheres of sexuality, cosmology, and spirituality with their ties to Mother Nature. Thus while Inca imperialism, for example, evolved from an inside understanding of the Andean universe, Spanish colonization worked from a radically distinct and exteriorized rationality. Colonial/modern patriarchy, constructed on the basis of binary gender categories, figured the feminine as a "disturbance of the masculine 'order' and a threat to the 'borders' that the male Spanish subject patrolled in his performance of gender identity."[107] Certainly the Andean same-sex sexuality, androgynous power, and "third-gender" subject threatened these rules and put into question the modern patriarchal system constructed on the basis of the absolute binaries—and/as boundaries—of sex and gender.

Yet, following Horswell as well as various other accounts,[108] including the suggestive drawings of Guamán Poma, we might surmise that culturally sanctioned same-sex sexuality in the Andes was male dominant. While Horswell highlights the cultural connectivity in the Andes of the feminine and androgyne—including in Indigenous narratives from the colonial period—his documentation of the practice of same-sex sexuality seems to suggest that this was primarily among biological males who often took on female-identified traits, participated in cross-dressing, and openly manifested a fluid duality, recognized as a sign of wisdom and spiritual power. The fact that historical studies of same-sex sexuality among Andean women are scarce does not mean that such practices did not exist. Why there is little documentation is a question that possibly has to do with biological dominance beyond absolute categories, including the presence in the Andes of early patriarchal-like structures and subordinations that possibly used gender fluidity and duality to their advantage. It may have to do as well with feminine power, including that present in the female association or relation of and with Pachamama, as I will consider later, and the interest of biological males in experimenting with and sharing this power (thus the fluid duality described earlier). And it may have to do with the fact that the documents, chronicles, and narratives available from precolonial and colonial times were all written by men. Could it be that the male gaze and interpretation produced its own "naturalized" order? And could it be that this interpretation represented another form of gender domination without the absolute binary, dimorphism, boundary, and distinction?

Suggested are narrative accounts from the Caribbean that counter the male-centered gaze. I am thinking of Omise'eke Natasha Tinsley's evocations of the femme queen Ezili and the Ezili pantheon of Voudoun spirits within Black Atlantic sexuality, Audre Lorde's renaming of herself as Zami, a Carriacou name for women who work together as friends and lovers, and Gloria Wekker's rich description of *mati*, a Creole word for same-sex relationships and friendships that have their referents in the Atlantic passage and slave ships but also in the foreground of the sexual subjectivity of Afro-Surinamese women.[109] In her powerful text *Wayward Lives, Beautiful Experiments*, Saidiya Hartman similarly describes the ways Black women have historically refused the gender script, challenged gender norms, and constructed their own ways and practices of sexuality, intimacy, affiliation, and kinship, a reality present, as Betty Ruth Lozano confirms, in the collective memory, past and present, of the Colombian Afro-Pacific.[110] Although all these narratives are of modern times, they suggest ways of being, relating, and loving among women that have prediasporic roots and diasporic continuums.

Gender domination—or, maybe better said, the domination of a male interpretation of the sexual and social worlds—also existed in the premodern West despite the absence of absolute gender and sexual binaries. Here early patriarchy was constructed on a one-sex model. Margaret Greer helps us understand these constructions through her conversation with Thomas Laqueur's text *Making Sex*:

> From the Greeks through the seventeenth century the predominate model of sex was a one-sex model, not the two-sex model of radical dimorphism, of anatomical and physiological incommensurability between males and females that has prevailed since the eighteenth century. The one-sex model saw women as imperfect males, possessing the same organs, but inside rather than outside the body, due to a lack of heat. There was not even a technical term for the vagina or ovaries until the eighteenth century.... The primary authority for this one-sex model over the centuries was Galen "who in the second century A.D. developed the most powerful and resilient model of the structural... identity of the male and female reproductive organs, and demonstrated at length that women were essentially men in whom a lack of vital heat—of perfection—had

resulted in the retention, inside, of structures that in the male are visible without" (Laqueur, 1998, 4).[111]

Greer goes on to show, through the biological determinist Juan Huarte de San Juan's sixteenth-century text *Examen de ingenios para las ciencias* (Examination of genius for the sciences), that the ground and origin of the one-sex model was in the perceptions and power given to Nature (note the use of Huarte's capital *N*): "If Nature, having finished making a perfect man, should want to convert him into a woman, it would require no other work than turning the generative instruments within; and if having made a woman, should wish to change her into a man, after pushing outside the uterus and testicles, Nature would have nothing more to do."[112]

Huarte's "scientifically" misogynistic account of "human nature" related the humoral composition of the body to mental capabilities, arguing, as many did in his time, for the relation among gender, physiological composition, and intellectual potential. Yet as Greer notes, Laqueur believed that such arguments had little to do with biology and the body; "they are about power, legitimacy, and fatherhood, in principle not resolvable by recourse to the senses," Laqueur said.[113] What is evident, then, is that the one-sex model, like the two-sex frame, proceeds from a hierarchically valued gender system to a definition of sexual anatomy, a system and definition that not only inferiorize women but also make us subservient to the model and category of human as man, the basis of patriarchy itself. The resistance to and contestation and subversion of this standard of power, exerted over and with regard to gender and nature, defined a kind of feminism of the time,[114] the reaction against which, of course, was made evident on the European continent in the Spanish Inquisition and witch-hunts that began in the late fifteenth century and extended for more than three hundred years.

The emissaries of the Crown and the church carried these standards established on the continent to the colonies. The dictates of Crown and church came together to constitute the civilizational project and "natural law." As such, the so-called "pagan" adoration of deities—feminine, masculine, androgynous, and fluidly dual—threatened the supremacy of both. Of particular threat in the Andes were the powers attributed to the female deity Pachamama. Her favoring of women and the communal veneration, cult rituals, and sacred relations that women had with her as Nature-Earth were idolatrous practices to be extirpated and condemned on ecclesiastic grounds and, relatedly, on the grounds of patriarchy, gender hierarchy, and civilization.

"Inferior natures" thus became the characteristic and condition associated with female bodies and with Pachamama, a binary division and hierarchy that worked—and works—in both the social and biological spheres to subordinate, exploit, civilize, appropriate, violate, and control. "With the appropriation of the productive and reproductive, bringing together two subjects, women and Pachamama, who provide these subordinate capacities," argues Margarita Aguinaga, "the dominators will obtain not only an expanded and diverse sphere of work, they will not only control economic and reproductive processes and cultural dynamics, but they will also gain dominance over the whole of life."[115]

In this way, the relation of man over woman and over N/nature took hold. Gender, or rather the idea of gender, became an instrument of power, of social classification and identity, but also, and even more crucially, of a simultaneously colonial, civilizational, and masculinized project predicated on marking the (hu)man and, consequently, on dominating and transforming nature and its manifestations in less than (hu)man inferiors. The naturalization of male superiority—that is, the superiority of the white heterosexual male—was the foundation for the structural system of patriarchy and its necessary tie to capitalism; together both established their dominion over all forms of nature and society. As Aguinaga reminds us, "Mother Nature fulfills the double function of producing resources and assimilating space for human cultures on her. Without the domination of nature, the existence of capitalism and its dominant culture is impossible."[116]

Here, the colonial project became solidified on two interrelated fronts: the resignification of and control over Mother Nature as lived cosmology, existence, and life itself, and the resignification of and control over humanity; that is, of who is hu/man. N/nature, in this sense, is at the core of coloniality and the axis from which the intertwinement of gender, race, and knowledge can be more complexly understood.

For the colonizer, only the civilized were human and men or women. "Civilization" was marked by the geopolitics of location (read: Europe), as well as by race, gender, reason, and class. In this sense, it was, as Fanon argued, the European white bourgeois man who made himself into humanity's model: a being of mind and reason.[117] The European white bourgeois woman was the next down on the ladder; she, the one who reproduced race and capital, was human only in her relation to the white bourgeois man.[118] In all of Abya Yala or the Americas, Native peoples were constructed, along with the African-origin peoples forcibly brought to and enslaved on this land, as animal-like, wild, savage, irrational, and pagan beings of nature. In western eyes, they were perceived as nongendered. The colonizing mission was, as Lugones contends, to convert them into males and females in a heteronormative sense; "colonized males became not-human-as-not-men, the human trait, and colonized females became not-human-as-not-women."[119]

The colonial project of civilization was not about humanization; dehumanization was constitutive of its mission. Nonetheless, transforming the colonized into men and women, subservient to the dichotomous gender distinction, was part of the work at hand. For Lugones, this transformation was in nature and not identity, in its repertoire of justifications for abuse, and in its process of the active reduction of the colonized "other"; that is, the dehumanization that fits them for classification and marks them as not quite human. The civilization of N/nature, in this sense, intertwined with, and became an integral part of, the processes of racialization, gendering, and spiritual, cosmological, and existential violences and ruptures. Lugones's explanation is particularly clear and worth quoting at length: "The civilizing transformation justified the colonization of memory and thus of one's sense of self, intersubjective relations, and relation to the spirit world, to land, and to the very fabric of one's conception of reality, identity, social, ecological, and cosmological organization. Thus as Christianity became the most powerful instrument in the transformative mission, the normativity that tied gender and civilization became involved in the erasure of community, of ecological practices, knowledges of planting, weaving, and the cosmos, and not only in changing and controlling reproductive and sexual practices." Here we can begin to appreciate "the tie between the colonial introduction of the instrumental concept of nature central to capitalism and the colonial introduction of the modern concept of gender."[120]

In this way, the modern/colonial use of nature and gender—and the entangled processes of engendering and naturing—worked from an exterior space and place. But it also worked from inside and within, coming to penetrate domestic and community spheres. One such manifestation is regarding Indigenous males who, in response to dehumanization and its order of violence, and in accordance with modernity's scheme, have been continually forced to prove themselves "men." Over time, this has meant the hyperinflation of the role of men within Indigenous communities, including as the public intermediaries with the outside world. This, in turn, has led to the privatization, nuclearization, and depoliticization of the domestic sphere. And it has led to the further "binarization of duality, result of the universalization of one of duality's two terms when constituted as public, in opposition to the other, constituted as private."[121]

In this process, Indigenous women are made supplemental (and subservient) to men, a subservience that uses and exploits the idea of *chachi-warmi*, the complementary Andean man-woman pair. Today, men increasingly recall, simplify, and use the notion of *chachi-warmi* as a way to justify and "sacralize" social relations within the community, naturalize heterosexualism and daily injustices against women and girls, and demonize feminist postures and denunciations of violence and oppression. While debates exist among Indigenous feminists on whether *chachi-warmi* ever marked a real equilibrium (thus challenging the idea that machismo and patriarchy arrived with colonization), its regenerative usage among men nowadays all too often naturalizes discrimination, inequalities, and the exploitation and oppression of women.[122] Segato argues that this situation is made more complex with the visual penetration of modernity in the community sphere. Increasingly, Indigenous men have become inoculated with a western "pornographic eye," she argues; that is, with an exterior-induced objectifying gaze in which sexual access is understood—and practiced—as harm, desecration, and appropriation.[123]

In present-day contexts, gender-based violence is complexly intertwined with the violation of Nature. At the meeting of the Red de Mujeres Defensores de Derechos Sociales y Ambientales (Network of Women Defenders of Social and Environmental Rights) held in Quito in October 2013, the Indigenous and mestiza speakers, representatives of women's community-based, environmental, and social organizations in Bolivia, Guatemala, Peru, and Ecuador, made clear the ways that extractivism (mining, oil and gas extraction, etc.) violates life, Nature, and women. "For us extractivism is rape and invasion," said Lourdes Huanca Atencio from the National Federation of Peasant, Indigenous, Native, Artisan, and Wage-Earning Women in Peru, a violation that takes place on "the territory of our bodies."[124] Here the reference to rape is not metaphorical. Sexual violence is, in fact, one of the principal characteristics and effects of extractivism in this region today, brought on not only by the presence in communities of outsiders tied to extractivist projects and industry but also by the shifts in community dynamics, relations, and structures brought about by this presence, increasing levels of alcoholism, of *machista* behavior, and of other expressions of a male-dominated culture. Women are the ones most affected by extractivism in terms of sexual violence and abuse, but also in terms of health; economic, social, and familial instability; and territorial displacements.

As Huanca Atencio also affirmed, there is an additional problem and element at play here, and that is the way community men are recuperating and reconstituting the Andean ideas of duality and parity (including *chachi-warmi*) as conceptual tools that play into the idea of the superiority of the man, "of the power of testicles," she said, justifying as "natural" the rape of young girls. Cosmology here is distorted to justify men's exertion of force over female bodies as nature, Huanca Atencio argued.[125] As she stated in an interview, "My ancestors, my grandparents taught me to struggle for life, for land and territory; but my ancestors did not teach me to defend the territory that is my body."[126]

Huanca Atencio is not alone in this manifestation and affirmation. Simpson makes a similar claim in the context of Turtle Island and her Nishnaabeg nation. There, as in the Andes, the imposed artificial gender binary has served as a mechanism for controlling Indigenous bodies and making maleness and masculinity superior in power and position. "Gender violence is part of a long history of white men working strategically and persistently to make allies out of straight cisgendered Indigenous men, with clear rewards for those who come into white masculinity imbued with heteropatriarchy and violence, in order to infiltrate our communities and nations."[127]

While gender violence within Indigenous communities and organizations has most often been a silenced subject, Indigenous women are increasingly speaking out, including, as is the case in Ecuador, with respect to the perpetuation of this violence within the practices of the Indigenous system of justice (recognized in this country's 2008 constitution). At an international meeting of feminists in Quito in September 2019 that I attended, the Ecuadorian Collective Runa Feminists, made up of mostly young Otavala Kichwa women, presented the case of a five-year-old Otavala girl raped by an older Indigenous neighbor. The girl's aunt who lives with her gave testimony punctuated by cries and tears. As she detailed, despite repeated attempts by the family and the collective (which includes Kichwa women lawyers) to seek justice from the male-led Indigenous *cabildo*, or community council, and later from the male-led "national" positivist legal system, the perpetrator continues to be without charge. Moreover, he continues to live across the street, producing ongoing nightmares and terror for the girl and her female family members. The men—Indigenous and not—take care of one another, proclaimed a member of the collective; the problem, she said, is when Indigenous women who are supposed to be silent speak out.

In her master's thesis, "Runa Warmikuna Sinchiyarinchik / Fortale(ser) nos siendo mujeres runakuna" (Strengthening us being women persons in existence and with ancestral roots embroidered with Pachamama), Tsaywa

Cañamar—also part of the collective—documents the resistance and re-existence of rural community-based Kichwa women survivors of gender violence. Through an Indigenous methodology based on the traditional activity of embroidery—and literally translated as "the mouth speaking, the hand doing"—six Otavala Kichwa women (including Cañamar herself) weave a conversational dialogue on gender, the lived experiences of gender violence, and the creative capacities of strengthening and healing oneself and others in the everyday and in collective. Against the silences and silencing of Kichwa women that the modern/colonial gender system has—in complicity with Indigenous men—imposed with respect to gender violence in rural communities, and against the continued idealization of gender complementarity in Andean culture, these six women have learned to speak and make freedom together in their own cultural, cosmogonic, and existential terms.[128] Their healing and strengthening are part of the growing insurgent agency among Indigenous women throughout Abya Yala to address internal problems of gender domination and violence through their own pedagogies-as-methodologies, and on their own terms. In so doing, they are cracking coloniality.

At work here are new and emergent critiques on the present-day simplification and recuperation of ancestral cosmologies—including of what Cabnal calls "cosmogonic heteroreality"—and their use by men as mandates to control, order, define, and subordinate women. "The philosophic base of ancestral cosmovisions—and the naming of cosmic elements as feminine and masculine, where one depends on, relates with, and is complementary to the other—has been strengthened," says Cabnal, "in these hegemonic practices of spirituality with which the oppression of women is perpetuated in the heterosexual relation with nature." Thus the importance, she argues, of perspectives that recuperate the "femeology of our female ancestors," perspectives that at the same time challenge perspectives—including those of some feminists—that idealize the gender duality, parity, and complementarity characteristic of Abya Yalean cultures.[129]

Today it is the feminisms of Indigenous, African-descended, and popular sectors that are enabling more complex analyses and articulations of gender, race, sexuality, patriarchy, capitalism, nature, and the continual reconfigurations of the modern/colonial matrices of power. Sometimes with the referent of feminism and frequently without, the majority of these women locate their agency within the long horizon of five-hundred-plus years of resistance and re-existence, and within present-day struggles for the defense and reproduction of nature, territory, land, and life.[130]

For Katy [Betancourt] Machoa, Amazonian leader and director of women's issues in the Confederation of Indigenous Nationalities of Ecuador's governing council from 2014 to 2017, these struggles are part of a historical continuum. They have roots in colonization and its civilizatory project, and in the diverse forms of violence—territorial, ideological, and knowledge and existence based—that this process and project continue to manifest. "Here the relation of *runa*-nature has been particularly impacted, leaving Indigenous women with an overload of disadvantages as compared to men. Numbered are the historical registers that recognize and take up the process of struggle of women. For us [women], they dug a deeper hole," Machoa contends. "They erased us from history, from philosophy, from science and from society, but we never stopped being there. I remit to the present and I listen," says Machoa. "As we take the streets of the capital city, the most felt voices that chant 'the land isn't for sale' are those of women. We know that we were present before because today we are fiercely defying the obstacles of the femicidal society. We continue," she proclaims, "giving birth to Quilago, Dolores Cacuango, Tránsito Amaguaña, Manuela León, to the indomitable Amazonas and so many others that, like us, forged the history of resistance told not from the official sources but from the mobilizations that push us from inherited dignity."[131]

Our force is a female force, Machoa argues. As she explained to one of my classes, "We are the makers of our history. We are Amazonian women warriors fighting for dignity and territory-life, for an-other model, system, way and plan of living and life." Too often the men sell themselves out to the companies and state, enabling extractive industries and interests. As women we are clear about our role today in leading the resistance, she said.[132] These manifestations are complemented by her words spoken elsewhere: "Our territories continue to be threatened, and we continue to defend the inheritance of our children. We have the force, determination, and courage to do so. We women are together in the struggle, we will not be bought, and we will not be sold. We have dignity. So we are the women of the Amazon."[133]

From the south to the north of Abya Yala—including the Amazonian forests, rural deserts, plains, highlands, and coasts and the urban centers—Indigenous, Black, and mestiza women are on the front lines; they are warriors of and for life. Their standpoints and praxis of denunciation and vital relation are both situated and pluriversal, taking form in and on the territories, lands, and contexts of existence and struggle. Here, and in their standpoints-as-actions-as-praxis, these women frequently disrupt and dismantle dimorphic binaries, boundaries, and divisions—including those posed by feminism's original white, western, and bourgeois frame—opening and widening fissures and cracks in modern/colonial rationalities, universalities, and foundations.

I understand this standpoint-as-praxis as decolonial and as feminine-centered. For me, it is demonstrative of an insurgent agency that continues the weaving of present-past, affirms a feminine creative energy that is *the* life-force, and (re)generates a situated praxistic world-sense or world-senses that defy the colonial order and assert insurgent relation. The feminine center here is not meant to suggest gendered exclusion or division, nor is it to mark a sphere of femininity in a patriarchally gendered sense, what Hortense Spillers calls "gendered femaleness."[134] Instead, it denotes and calls forth processes that rethink and reconstruct existence with and from the feminine life-force, transgressing what M. Jacqui Alexander refers to as the sacred and secular divide,[135] and reuniting humanity and Nature. With the feminine-centered come processes that foster and invoke ancestral, spiritual, and existence-based ways of knowing, being, belonging, and becoming in community that re-member correlation and wholeness as a social, political, and existential project.

I am referring to a posture-and/as-practice-and-as-project that is concrete, envisaged, and imagined; a standpoint and praxis that take us beyond biology, bio-reason, and a politics conceived as separatist opposition, rudiments most often maintained in western and westernized feminisms. Here the struggles *against* the heteropatriarchal colonial scheme of gendered, raced, and natured subjugation, classification, separation, capture, control, violation, destruction, and elimination persist. But they persist alongside an offensive insurgence *for* the creation and construction of an otherwise; that is, *for* radically distinct conditions of life, living, articulation, and relation. The fact that women—that is, people who identify as women—are leading many of these struggles is significant. While some feminists, especially in the western academic world, argue that the very use of the term *woman* replicates the binary logic of the colonial/modern gender system, others (including myself) perceive its postured usage in a political, collective, and relationally insurgent sense. That is, as a taken-back term that, not unlike the colonially imposed classificatory naming of "blacks," works to build relation in struggle, making visible our differences (including of race, ethnicity, language, sexuality, territory, ability, and class) and, at the same time, the shared fight against the inferiorization, subalternization, and patriarchal violences that coloniality constructed, reproduces, and maintains. Such was the stance of the letter written in February 2019 by Zapatista women to women in struggle around the world. I share an excerpt:

Compañera, sister:

... Maybe we don't know which feminism is the best one, maybe we don't say "cuerpa" (a feminization of "cuerpo," or body) or however it is you change words around, maybe we don't know what "gender equity" is or any of those other things with too many letters to count. In any case that concept of "gender equity" isn't even well-formulated because it only refers to women and men, and even we, supposedly ignorant and backward, know that there are those who are neither men nor women and who we call "others" (*otroas*) but who call themselves whatever they feel like. It hasn't been easy for them to earn the right to be what they are without having to hide because they are mocked, persecuted, abused, and murdered. Why should they be obligated to be men or women, to choose one side or the other? If they don't want to choose then they shouldn't be disrespected in that choice. How are we going to complain that we aren't respected as women if we don't respect these people? Maybe we think this way because we are just talking about what we have seen in other worlds and we don't know a lot about these things. What we do know is that we fought for our freedom and now we have to fight to defend it so that the painful history that our grandmothers suffered is not relived by our daughters and granddaughters. We have to struggle so that we don't repeat history and return to a world where we only cook food and bear children, only to see them grow up into humiliation, disrespect, and death. We didn't rise up in arms to return to the same thing. We haven't been resisting for 25 years in order to end up serving tourists, bosses, and overseers.... It seems that these new bad governments think that since we're women, we're going to promptly lower our gaze and obey the boss and his new overseers. They think what we're looking for is a good boss and a good wage. That's not what we're looking for. What we want is freedom, a freedom nobody can give us because we have to win it ourselves through struggle, with our own blood.

Compañera, sister:

Don't stop struggling. Even if the bad capitalists and their new bad governments get their way and annihilate us, you must keep struggling in your world. That's what we agreed in the gathering [2018]: that we would all struggle so that no woman in any corner of the world would be scared to be a woman.... Your corner of the world is your corner in which to struggle, just like our struggle is here in Zapatista territory.

Compañera, hermana:

Take care of that little light that we gave you. Don't let it go out. Even if our light here is extinguished by our blood, even if other lights go out in other places, take care of yours because even when times are difficult, we have to keep being what we are, and what we are is women who struggle.[136]

Toward Insurgent Relation

A number of years ago I began to reflect on the political-epistemic insurgency of Indigenous and Afro-descendant movements in Abya Yala's South.[137] To speak of political-epistemic insurgency, I argued, "is to move away from perspectives that only see, study, observe, and describe social movements from the lens of oppositional social action."[138] It is to recognize a shift from reactive resistance *against* toward the construction of political-epistemic actions of intervention *for*; that is, a new social project not just for Indigenous and African-descended peoples but for all. It is "to reveal the political and epistemic 'actionings' that find their ground in and assemble social, collective, and ancestral knowledge, action, and thought, and that work to affect—through this knowledge and thought—the constellations that organize and signify social institutions and structures."[139] For me, this insurgence is decolonial precisely because it puts at the center of debate the lived experiences of coloniality/modernity, but also initiatives, strategies, and practices that fissure and crack colonial power and sow, pose, push, construct, and enable processes of re-existence and liberation. This is the decolonial *for*.

My intention here is to build on this postulate. What are the insurgencies—political, epistemic, *and* existential—present and emergent today that disrupt, traverse, transgress, and take us beyond the colonial/modern binaries of gender and nature? And how do these insurgencies work to (re)create and (re)assemble relation? With these questions as a guide, I close this chapter with four concrete examples that have, in different ways, formed part of my own ongoing learnings in dialogue, shared reflection, and conversation.

BLACKWOMEN INSURGENTS

In her doctoral dissertation—now published as a book and previously cited in this chapter—Betty Ruth Lozano Lerma uses the aforementioned notion of insurgency to describe the cultural, political, social, spiritual, epistemic, and existence-based practices of struggle of Blackwomen in the territory-region of the Colombian-Ecuadorian Pacific.[140] *Insurgency* here, as she develops and documents it, refers to those processes and possibilities of collective analysis, collective theorization, and collective practice—all intertwined—that help engender an otherwise of relational being, thinking, feeling, doing, and living in a place marked by the extremes of violence, racism, and patriarchy in today's matrix of global capitalism/modernity/coloniality.[141]

In this context, "Blackwomen are not just impotent victims, they also exercise power beyond resistance and survival; they are insurgents," Lozano contends.[142] While the strategies and practices of this insurgency are many, the recomposition of the relational ties that enslavement and coloniality/modernity broke is Lozano's principal focus. Her attention is threefold: (1) to the ways that Blackwomen in the Pacific continue to reconstruct the female-centered ties of community and extended family; (2) to the ways that midwives—as part of ancestral philosophies and the cultural capital of Black communities transmitted from generation to generation—continue to knit community, knowledge, and cultural- and existence-based relation; and (3) to the ways that Blackwomen maintain a *cimarron* or maroon habitus, especially at the organizational level. This is what Lozano explains in her dissertation and book as "organizational maroonism."[143]

Here it is midwifery that, in the territory of the Colombian-Ecuadorian Pacific, contributes in a particularly fundamental way to the processes of Blackwomen's insurgence and for the preservation and revindication of life, this understood in an integral and relational sense that, as Lozano explains, is connected to Nature:

> Midwifery is an ancestral practice that expresses a spirituality of dignity, resistance, and insurgency that goes beyond Christian religiosity. A spirituality that does not separate the human being from nature or that conceives the human outside of nature, but poses an interconnection with nature and excludes any feeling of superiority over it. It is a thought that implies articulation with other humans and thinking more as a collective than as individuals. Spirituality is in the link. The world is not an outside to know, therefore, knowledge can only be proffered from intersubjectivity, because everything is connected. From the perspective of the epistemologies of Black communities, there is no separation between bodies, reason, knowledge, emotions, feelings and spirituality. They are conceptions that question the coloniality of knowledge.[144]

Midwives are "the Ananse that weave webs that keep us linked as community and in resistance to the fragmentation imposed by war and modernization,"

Lozano contends.[145] Yet midwives are not the only insurgents, especially if we understand, following Lozano, that Blackwomen's insurgency originated with the kidnappings in Africa, the slave trade, and the multiple ways since that Blackwomen's struggles, resistance, and insurgence took and continue to take form. In this, Lozano locates herself and the various Blackwomen collectives with which she has long worked; she and they are the engaged insurgent participants in this "study." In this sense, Lozano turns on their head the western colonial/modern tenets—that is, the dimorphic binaries—of "research": objectivism, neutrality, distance. "I undertook this research work due to the urgency of thinking and assuming an alternative from our being as Blackwomen in the face of the dynamic, racist and individualistic driving force of the current processes of global accumulation . . . [that] increasingly accentuate the country's dependency, the demand for autonomy as Black communities and social alienation based on a development model that does not fulfill its promises because it can only be transmitted through violence and dispossession."[146]

Moreover, "thinking about epistemic insurgencies from my being as a Blackwoman has implied highlighting a subjectivity that is not the dominant one. A subject that is not that of modernity," she argues. "I am referring to a concrete and living subjectivity that is fed by the ancestral memory of maroonage that sowed the seeds of insurgency that we harvest today and continue to sow to continue this tradition of liberation."[147]

WALKING THE WORD: CHASKI WARMI ABYA YALA

In the Andean-Amazon region of Abya Yala, as is true throughout the Global South and in many Indigenous territories of the North, extractivism—including, and most especially, the industries of oil, mining, gas, hydroelectric plants, logging, monocultivation, and agroindustry—is killing Nature and, with it, the communities and territories of ancestral peoples. Here, as Huanca Atencio described earlier, the violences are multiple: natured, gendered, cosmological, and land, territory, and existence based. Today women are the principal leaders of the struggles against extractivism. And they are the leaders of strategies, struggles, and actions *for* the preservation, maintenance, and regeneration of life. They are the crack makers, the insurgents, and the protagonists of insurgent relation.

It is in this context that the example of Chaski Warmi (Indigenous women messengers of Abya Yala) stands out. At the twenty-second session of the Conference of the Parties on climate change, held in Morocco in

November 2016, this women's network presented the following manifesto or declaration:

> We, Indigenous women of the Amazonian forests, the rivers, the highlands, and the mountains of Abya Yala, have traveled our territories. In these lands we recognize and encounter ourselves. We are part of *Pachamama*; because of the way we relate with her, we feel climate change from the experience and everyday relation of living with our territories.... We feel the crisis caused by extractivist policies and models, of oil and mining, the contamination of water and the atmosphere, and the destruction of forests and of the plant cover of *Pachamama*, all of which has produced grave effects in our lives.[148]

Signed by woman representatives from Guatemala, Chile, Colombia, Bolivia, and Ecuador's highlands and Amazon regions, the declaration is the message of the many women who struggle daily against national and global policies that cause the destruction of Nature. Indigenous women, the declaration sustains, lead the defense of territory today. They experience domestic violence; the social, environmental, and political violence of states; and the violence of the impoverishment of the conditions of life, all constitutive of extractivism and its results. The violence against Pachamama extends in a direct way to Indigenous women, the declaration states, "reflected in the criminalization, imprisonment, assassination, capture, persecution of Pachamama's custodians." Moreover, "from our experience, we can make visible the fact that climate change is not an abstract concept but something palpable in health, in the change of agricultural cycles, in increased work for women, and in the violence against Pachamama or Mother Earth." The problem is with government policies and solutions that, while professing to address climate change, promote extractivism; negate the historical role that Indigenous people, and particularly women, have had with Nature; and disregard "our concrete contributions in the search for solutions that come from knowledge of the territory that we inhabit and our cosmovisions based in ancestral wisdoms."[149]

While the declaration presents a series of proposals to both the region's governments and the United Nations all of which, not surprisingly, have gone unconsidered, it also offers proposals to the women of Abya Yala. These proposals include, among others, the need to organize, join forces, and come together in Chaski Warmi Abya Yala to defend Mother Nature, and walk the word, in order "to be able to reach spaces of community-based, national and international decision making with a more profound knowledge of our realities and our cosmovision as Indigenous women."[150] Without a doubt, they are proposals of insurgent relation.

Chaski Warmi—"Women Messengers" or more broadly "Women Messengers in Defense of Mother Nature"—began in 2015 as a kind of walking methodology/pedagogy among Indigenous women. Chaski Warmi's project—in Ecuador but also in Colombia, Bolivia, Chile, and Guatemala—is to listen to what community-based Indigenous women have to say about their struggles in defense of Nature, about the local effects of extractivism and climate change, and about the traditional practices of women and communities to confront these effects and to create alternatives to survive. Furthermore, it is about carrying these perspectives, knowledges, and experiences—walking the word—from community to community, weaving insurgent relation.

The experiences with which I am most familiar are those of Ecuador.[151] The first was Yaku Chaski Warmikuna (women messengers of the water or river). During eight days in July 2015, a group of Amazonian women from the Kichwa and Waorani Nations traveled the Bobonaza River basin in order to "help make aware and spread the word about extractivist conflicts that affect our communities and our work as women for territorial defense, and promote the strategy to leave oil underground as the only real solution to climate change."[152] They carried messages against oil companies' strategies of aggression and land grabbing, and alerted those they encountered about the co-optation, buying off, and even assassination of community leaders. With these messages they helped construct, articulate, support, and connect resistance and demands for self-governance and self-determination. And they helped make evident the contradictions between Ecuador's radical 2008 constitution (with its recognition of collective rights and Nature's rights and its call for living well, or *buen vivir*) and government-sponsored extractivism. "We categorically reject and denounce all extractivist proposals and actions in our territory, which for us constitutes a unique, indivisible and millennial legacy inherited from our ancestors."[153]

Yamila Gutiérrez Callisaya, an Aymaran Bolivian and part of the May 2017 Chaski Warmi experience in Ecuador's southern Amazon region focused specifically on mining, described how the project has worked in Ecuador to recuperate "from below" the idea and role of the messenger (*chaski*) historically present throughout Abya Yala. "Its objective," Gutiérrez told me, "is to build a process of dialogue among Indigenous women, convened by Indigenous women, about the problematic of extractivism, a problem that affects us as women." The experience of Chaski Warmi makes visible and gives presence to the thought and the political role of Indigenous women; "it is a dialogue among equals, in our own languages, and in and from our own territory, community, and place. Herein lies its value."[154]

As the *chaski*, or messenger, who, before the existence of cell phones and online social media, carried messages from community to community, here women messengers—tied to regional and national Indigenous organizations—listen to, carry, communicate, and walk women's territorially grounded words from river to river, from mountain to mountain, from community to community. Such experience serves to generate reflection, discussion, and debate between and among Indigenous women about the local and lived consequences of mining and oil, agroindustry, and other extractivisms, and about concrete practices and strategies of resistance, existence, and defense of Pachamama. In so doing, it helps plant seeds of awareness and concern, alerting populations about the death that is extractivism, then carrying this message from place to place in order to weave not just communication but, more radically, insurgent relation. But as Gutiérrez argues, it also serves to inform the Indigenous organizations themselves, strengthening the relation between the organization and its community base, and giving concretion, substance, and form to the organization's actions, struggles, and demands with respect to government policy.

While men are not excluded, Chaski Warmi is women centered and women focused. In rural communities and in Indigenous organizations where men continue to be the most visible actors, protagonists, and spokespeople, Chaski Warmi underscores and articulates women's thought, force, and voice. Furthermore, it builds women's own sense of capacity in contexts where women often devalue themselves and other women,[155] thus helping to knit new communal and collective threads and insurgent relations.

Chaski Warmi makes evident what the Amazonian leader Katy [Betancourt] Machoa calls the "flowering of women's rebellion."[156] It reveals how women-led and women-conceived insurgencies are challenging the policies, practice, and project of the extractive-oriented, corporatized, patriarchal state, including Ecuador's "progressive" state (2007–17) that made extractivism the base of the economy and national project. Moreover, it shows how these insurgencies work to construct forms of resistance, re-existence, coexistence, and relation for Nature, territory, and life.

JINEOLOGY

From another region of the globe, Kurdish women offer their epistemic and existence-based insurgence as an example of women's liberation understood as the liberation of society. There is much to learn from this insurgence, including the women-led uprisings that began in 1989 against the colonization of Kurdistan, and with the formation of a women's army (1993), the establishment of a theory/practice of emancipation from the patriarchal system (1996) and a women's liberation ideology (1998), and the construction of a framework and praxis for a democratic, ecological, and gender-egalitarian social order (2000–present), with women's councils, academies, and cooperatives and a women-governed society. Jineology—composed of two words, *jin*, the Kurdish word for "woman," and *logos*, the Greek term for "word" or "lesson," and understood, when put together, as "woman's science"[157]— is a key component of this process, an insurgent strategy and proposition toward overcoming the prevailing, dominant, patriarchal, sexist, and male-centered system of science and thought.[158] Its focus is to call into question not only the ways that the ideas of woman and nature have been manipulated and constructed but also how state, the systems of power, and their institutionalizations form part of this same mentality, which is capitalist patriarchal modernity (see the reflections on undoing nation-state in chapter 4). In this context, "jineology is a radical objection to the prevalent mental structures."[159]

My introduction to jineology has been through ongoing conversations in recent years with members of the Kurdish liberation movement and their sharing of a series of materials, including videos and texts.[160] It is the explicit relation that the movement makes between knowledge-based and existence-based insurgences that, for me, is fundamental. In fact, it is the only example I know of in the world where women are conceiving, constructing, and making a transformative and relational praxis of thought-knowledge-life within the spheres of education, societal organization, politics, economy, ecology, health, ethics, aesthetics, and science. While jineology has its roots in the Middle East, it offers much for rethinking, cracking, and undoing the precepts of positivist social science elsewhere.

The idea of jineology was first articulated by the imprisoned Kurdish liberation leader Abdullah Öclan in *The Sociology of Freedom*: "The masculine discourse has left its mark on the social sciences, like it has on all the sciences. The lines that refer to women are laden with nothing but propaganda that fails to come close to reality. This discourse repeatedly conceals the real status of women, just as the historiographies of civilization conceal class, exploitation, oppression, and torture. Instead of feminism, perhaps the concept of jineolojî (science of women) might better meet the purpose."[161] For Öclan, women are the first colony; nation-state, monotheistic religions, and capitalism all constitute different institutionalized forms of the dominant male.

In the last decades, the Movement of Liberation of the Women of Kurdistan has built jineology from a unity of theory and practice, and through discussions that began in the academies of the mountains and gradually expanded in 2011 to all of society in Kurdistan and among Kurdish women elsewhere. As Necîbe Qeredaxî, founding member of the Center for Jineology in Brussels, explains, "We believe that as a first step we need to ask how mental oppression has been imposed. According to jineology, this oppression has been imposed in three ways: first, women were oppressed sexually and thereby objectified. Second, women became oppressed economically. And third, ideological transformations—such as mythology and religion—have contributed to this oppression." As she goes on to explain, "With the help of jineology we seek to enter into the depths of history and search for the point where women were made to disappear, in order to do things differently."[162] Here women question the influence of the existing system on women's thinking and actions, and research the historical colonization of women and the history of humanity as ways to begin, as Gönül Kaya describes, "to restore the links between knowledge and freedom, which have been torn apart from each other despite there being an inherent relationship between them."[163] Recalled are the words of Alexander that opened this chapter.

Kurdish women make clear that jineology is not an alternative for feminism. While feminism offers some legacies, it often shrouds the differences of lived realities and the importance of a holistic view of social problems. Too often feminism maintains a Eurocentric perspective, Qeredaxî says, and too often feminists "have submitted to the power of the capitalist system and patriarchal mentality. Many feminists don't see the connections between the triangle of patriarchy, capitalism and the nation-state," she says. "Breaking this triangle apart, they break apart their enemy. What then happens is that some men fight against capitalism and the nation-state, but they don't see patriarchy as part of the problem. Or some feminists only see patriarchy as a problem, but don't see how this mentality is linked to the state and to capitalism."[164]

Jineology in this sense is understood, constructed, and practiced as a science, as a communal epistemology grounded in social organization and in re-existence and life itself; a radically distinct social science that aims "to provide women and society direct access within the realm of knowledge and science currently controlled by the rulers."[165] It is precisely because of this radical difference that jineology is postured and practiced not as a specialized area of studies within the social sciences—like women's studies, for instance, has become through much of the world—but instead as an "other" social science, a science that affords a "more adequate method and lens of interpretation and conception of social history, economy, society and politics; a sociology of creation and liberation."[166] "As Kurdish women, we say 'the twenty-first century will be the century of revolution of women and peoples.' We believe that jineology will play a crucial role in the establishment of a liberation mindset, ethical and political structures, and a free society that puts women's liberation at its center. . . . By developing jineology and the sociology of freedom as a new social science, by turning it into the ground base of our societal struggles, it will be possible to unravel the 5,000-year-old Gordian knots and blind spots of history that wait discovery."[167]

———————

"YO SOY MAMA HUACO" / "I AM MAMA HUACO"

A final example of insurgent relation is the intellectual-artistic project "Mama Huaco" developed by the researcher, teacher, and drag queen artist Kosakura/Ángel Burbano. While this project began in the context of Burbano's master's program study and research, its roots were established well before. I remember the first day of my course on feminist theory in Abya Yala; it was the first day as well of the 2017 academic year. When it was Burbano's turn to introduce themself to the class, they spoke of their identity within the lived context of drag, and of their relation with the figure of Mama Huaco. I, for one, was overjoyed; it was the first time I had met someone who shared the attraction I have also had for some years now toward Mama Huaco.[168]

For those readers not familiar, Mama Huaco is a primary figure in the foundational story of Incan civilization. What we know of Mama Huaco comes primarily from Felipe Guamán Poma de Ayala's written and pictorial accounts in his sixteenth-century *Nueva corónica y buen gobierno* and the brief descriptions of Santacruz de Pachakuti in 1613, Inca Garcilaso de la Vega in 1608, and Sarmiento de Gamboa in 1572. The contemporary author Michael Horswell offers a more detailed account, based on a close analysis of these chronicles and narratives, along with other material.[169]

Mama Huaco was the sister of Manco Capac—the mythic father of all Incas—and a *coya*, or Incan queen. Some say she founded the Inca's matriarchal line (pairing with her brother), while others argue that she was infertile, nonreproducing, and "a transgressor of heteronormative patriarchy."[170] Often described as a fierce woman warrior with *supay*, or both good and bad devil-like powers, an idolater, sorcerer, and the keeper or guard of ceremonial seeds (a role typical of neither women nor men), Mama Huaco broke the mold of gendered archetypes. She was an example not only of feminine autonomy and power but also, following Horswell, of gender liminality; thus her aesthetic representation in Guaman Poma as in between woman and man.[171] For me, Mama Huaco embodies freedom, defiance, fluidity, androgyny, and the feminine-centered matrix of insurgent relation that I described earlier, what I have also referred to elsewhere as "gender otherwise."[172]

"What is the significance of Mama Huaco for a travesty body?" asks Burbano in the first line of their master's thesis. "The history of this *coya* and the capacity to tell it, goes beyond what could be considered as text. As the Native women of North America tell us, history ends by us telling it to ourselves." It is in this sense that "to investigate, know, reveal, and ask about Mama Huaco has become a personal exercise... moved by androgynous bodies, like that of Mama Huaco, that have been erased, destroyed, and burnt."[173] As Burbano goes on to explain, "What mobilizes me in this interpretation of Mama Huaco is my desire. This potentiality, movement, and search mobilizes me while I run at night, while I am in transit from one gender to another in this transvestite body that can be read as abnormal, as irrational, perverse, wild, and what some consider senseless."[174]

For Burbano, this thesis is an "interpretative act" in two *tempos*: of Mama Huaco in the historical archives and Mama Huaco in drag, the latter embodied in Burbano themself and in the bodies of a collective feminine "we": eight travesty drag queens who re-represent Mama Huaco in photographs and also in their own identifications.[175] "I am Mama Huaco.... We are Mama Huaco," repeat Kataleya, Bella Montreal, Dakotta Lucifer Delta Magnini, Romina Channel, Dakira Bri, and Larry Cai Freesoul. Her figure and story inspire our imagination, says Dakira; as is the case with me, "she has her masculine part that she shows as an empowered, strong, free, and androgynous woman."[176] It is Burbano—Kosakura (drag name) and Mama Huaco in one—who, with her-his-their creative force, resurrects and re-creates Mama Huaco in body and spirit: "My name is Mama Huaco, I am like you, I have the same masculine force that you have, I have the same beauty that you have, I feel feminine, I feel strong. I feel empowered, with you I feel and am empowered."[177]

With the incorporation throughout the thesis of vignettes of Burbano's own embodied struggles and lived experiences, along with the narratives of drag sisters, Burbano weaves the threads of present-past, creating and revealing insurgencies of relation in which feminine power and androgynous fluidities break binaries and transgress the "live coloniality of the 'gay' community (with its universalized and universalizing identity)"; a coloniality that often negates "our wounds,... our precariousness,... the life expectancy of trans

3.3 Mama Huaco, sixteenth-century drawing by Felipe Guamán Poma de Ayala. In Guamán Poma de Ayala, *Nueva corónica y buen gobierno*, 1615, transcription, prologue, notes, and chronology by Franklin Pease (Caracas: Biblioteca Ayacucho, 1980), 87.

3.4 "I am Mama Huaco." Kosakura's interpretation of Mama Huaco. PHOTO: JUAN CARLOS BAYAS, 2019. IN ÁNGEL BURBANO, "LOS ESPEJOS DE MAMA HUACO: UN ACTO INTERPRETATIVO EN DOS TIEMPOS" (MASTER'S THESIS, UNIVERSIDAD ANDINA SIMÓN BOLÍVAR, QUITO, 2019), 90.

women in Latin America which is 38 years."[178] Moreover, and as Burbano details elsewhere, "after 500 years, we maintain the colonial wound; the only evidence is our body: the feminine body and sexual dissidences—nonbinary, trans, travesties. These bodies that apparently border the archive, can also be reinterpreted from female empowerment. In other words, to recover the same strength of femininity (in the Andes) to re-represent identities or existences still stigmatized even in the twenty-first century (as is the case of trans identities)."[179]

Mama Huaco (figure 3.3), sorceress and idolater, the Andean Eva, the first woman to be accused, according to Guamán Poma, of "adoration of the devil,"[180] reveals the dispossession of an androgynous and female-centered matrix of power present in Incan societies at the time of the colonial invasion. "Mama Huaco represents not only the history of a mythic woman, but also the history of the coloniality of gender incarnated in extirpation."[181] However, and despite this coloniality, "Mama Huaco continues to burst forth with her own presence in the archive and historical record, from liminality, from intelligibility, and from an 'other' matrix of gender." "For the transvestite body, the (drag) show allows us to celebrate. This thesis-story is part of a show-performance, a party in which Mama Huaco is the main drag character. With the much and the little that we have, we have made up her face, we have dressed her, we have adorned her. We are happy to see us in her mirror," says Burbano (figure 3.4), "and now, after the show, we will sleep peacefully. We have a new drag mother."[182]

Closings That Open

I close opening. My questions refuse to cease; they are many and continue to take form. They are questions aimed, most especially, at the praxistic hows: how to more deeply comprehend the ways the colonial/modern matrix of power endures, reconfigures, and works, most especially with regard to gender, race, knowledge, and nature; how to think, sense, act, be-become, and know traversing its boundaries and binaries; and, paraphrasing Alexander, how to reassemble that which belongs together. Is not this reassembly part and parcel of re-existence, of existences otherwise?

I return to my grandmother's stories; that is, to the pieces that still remain in memory and in heart. With this "re-memorying"—making of memory again—and re-membering comes the yearning for that freedom of wholeness and connection that I felt then. It is a yearning anchored not just in childhood but in seven decades of doing life; a desire that, at this older age and in this place of the Andes, I increasingly intuit as possible, doable, and in process.

The intuit and muse are in both a subjective and intersubjective sense. First off, they are about my own becoming. Maybe it is this stage of age in which the dimorphic binaries and boundaries of gender seem less absolute and the sense of being more grounded, whole, and fluid. Maybe it is the intensity of lived experiences and learnings in, with, and from this place that have pushed and enabled me "to be becoming" in existence-based relation, not just with humankind but, relatedly, with the spirits, ancestors, mountains, waters, wind, sky, and all of the living; that is, in and with Nature. Maybe—and most probably—these times of COVID-19 quarantine in which I write have contributed to the acceleration for me of that which was in process. And maybe it is all of this wrapped up together and intertwined that makes my own movements traversing binaries more tangible, heartfelt, and real, fortifying my resolve to fissure and crack the walls that separate and divide the I and we, including what Carrillo Can called the "'other I' at all times in-relation."[183]

The decolonial cracks are there, and so are the crack makers. The examples shared in this chapter are confirmation. Therein lies the intersubjective relation; the cracks (and the crack makers) do not make sense alone; they provoke, convoke, and invoke shared agency and shared sense making toward an otherwise.

I recall María Lugones's use of the I-we and I → we; her idea of the I in company and actively looking for company, and "the enduring not-yet-fulfilled quality of the subject, which also mitigates the 'arrogance' and exemplifies the looking-to-dismantle quality."[184] The I → we works to dismantle the theory/practice and tactic/strategy binaries of the from-above, said Lugones, and it works to rouse interactive intersubjective sense. "I/we I → we see the possibility of resistant, anti-utopian, interactive multiple sense making among *atravesados/atravesadas* who are streetwalker theorists in encounters at the intersections of the local and translocal histories of meaning fashioned in the resisting ⇔ oppressing relation. Sense making in lively cultural modes that take issue with domination in tense inside/outside/in-between conversations, interactions that take in and also disrupt, dismantle, dominant sense."[185]

As I am sure Lugones would agree, "dominant sense" is a constitutive component of the binaries and hierarchies of gender, race, knowledge, and nature that intend to organize, dominate, and control the sense making that is existential relationality and corelational life. The cracks and fissures in this dominance and domination, as I have said, are many. In the fissures and cracks are the manifestations of an "other" sense making and sense doing of re-memberment, reassembly, and re-relation.

Nevertheless, in the present-day reconfigurations of the colonial matrix of power, the binaries, boundaries, and hierarchies are fortified, buttressed, and reinforced. With the rise of a new extreme Right, neofascism—including neofascist neoliberalism[186]—religious fundamentalisms, and religious fundamentalists (most especially in positions of governance and power); systemic racism, along with racist liberalism, (de)humanism, and dehumanities (including in education and with respect to knowledge and thought); ethnogenocides and feminicides; large-scale extractivisms (oil, mining, agroindustry, deforestation, etc.) and accumulation by dispossession; and the overall destruction of Nature as life itself, the cracks are harder to make and more difficult to perceive and maintain.

Certainly the pandemics-virus-violences driven further, as I write, by COVID-19 are facilitating elements and component parts of the reconfigurations. Here the mechanisms of control, division, and separation are clearly intensifying in force, including with respect to social mobilizations and movements. The militarization of many cities and territories throughout the world—including in the United States at the end of Trump's reign—and especially against the massive mobilizations led by Black Lives Matter is visible evidence. Yet the aim of the present-day reconfiguration of the colonial matrix of power is much greater, exemplified by the racialized and territorialized de-existence in course. As I mentioned in chapter 1, the Amazon is one example among many. There the illegal invaders of the land do not quarantine. Deforestation and mining accelerate as quickly as the contagion of the Indigenous inhabitants; in April 2020 alone, deforestation escalated by 64 percent compared with the same month the year before.[187] The intention and promise, expressed publicly by Brazil's president Jair Bolsonaro (but certainly not his or Brazil's alone), are to open the Amazon to profit and business—including agribusiness, transnational mining, logging, hydroelectric plants, and oil companies, among others—which, of course, means the elimination and extermination of all that gets in the way, most especially Indigenous communities.[188] The modern/colonial binary of Man over nature is now more explicitly manifest and comprehended as capital over nature (read: resources, Native peoples, life). Here the COVID-19 pandemic-virus has, without a doubt, been strategically worthwhile.

Nonetheless, and despite all that is in course, the fissures and cracks persist and continue to take form "below." Within them and in their making, people struggle individually and collectively to shape, organize, create, and reinvent senses, processes, and practices of interdependence and corelation, often with the accompaniment of the ancestors, ancients, spirits, and all of the living. It is *this* present that, possibly more than at any other moment in modern times, exhorts intersubjectivity and interconnection, insists on movement that traverses binaries, and implores the making of communities of re-existence.

It seems fitting to finish where I began; that is, with Alexander's poignant words that are a clear call to action: "It took five hundred years, at least in this hemisphere, to solidify the division of things that belong together. But it need not take us another five hundred years to move ourselves out of this existential impasse."[189]

Undoing Nation-State

4

> To rebel against the permanence of...colonial reality
> and not just dream alternative realities but
> to create them, on the ground, in the
> physical world, in spite of being occupied.
> —LEANNE BETASAMOSAKE SIMPSON

Land is at the center of colonial domination, of resistance, and of existence-based struggle, including and especially with respect to nation and state.[1] As Roxanne Dunbar-Ortiz tells us, this is true in the United States, where everything in colonial history is about the land, about "who oversaw it and cultivated it, fished its waters, maintained its wildlife, who invaded it and stole it; how it became a commodity broken into pieces to be bought and sold on the market."[2] And it is true in all of the land-territory that is Abya Yala, from the northernmost tip of what the colonial settlers named Canada to the southern *tierra del fuego* erroneously called Argentina. Of course, it is also true elsewhere.

For peoples throughout the world marked by the legacies and continuation of colonial invasion, kidnapping and enslavement, and forced incorporation into imposed nation-state structures, boundaries, and regimes of domination and control, land and territory remain at/as the heart of ongoing resurgence and insurgence of and for dignity, freedom, existence, and life.[3] I think of the Landless Movement in Brazil and the Land Back movements, including in postapartheid South Africa. And I think of Palestine, a territory occupied by the Israeli colonial state and under Israeli military control since 1967, making it the longest occupation and probably the most continuous landgrab in modern history, beginning in 1947 and continuing until today.[4] There the relation of life, land, and state domination and control could not be clearer: control over who can enter and leave the occupied territories, control over the number of calories that people are permitted to consume in a day, and control of and over life and its dead. Yet, as Ajamu Baraka says, "in the liberal world, Netanyahu is a democrat, and the Palestinians are aggressors."[5]

Juan García Salazar and Abuelo Zenón taught me about the significance of territory for Afro-Pacific communities in what are now Ecuador and Colombia, and the culturally and politically specific historicity of the problem of state. Abuelo Zenón describes it this way: "The configuration of a territory for life was for us always the Great Territorial Comarca of the Pacific,[6] that is the land that the ambition of others brought to us. [It is] where we anchored the love for the land lost, that which remained on the other side of the sea."[7] Existence for us, Abuelo Zenón and maestro-hermano Juan argue, has been molded, signified, and constructed without, despite, and notwithstanding state, in essence to spite state itself. That is, in its margins, blind spots, and "wastelands," and outside the very frames of recognition, rights, citizenship, and borders that state assumes as constitutive and dear. Without a doubt, the nation-state is the imposed referent through which colonial domination, subjugation, regulation, exclusion, and territorial division have been conducted.

Collective memory and oral tradition keep alive the thinking and being that people of African origin have sown and cultivated on lands they were forced to make their own.[8] "We cannot forget that our right to live in these territories is born in the historic reparation of the damage/harm that meant the dispersion of our African blood through America," Abuelo Zenón maintains, "dispersion that through the will of others we had to live these hundreds of years before the configuring of states which now order/regulate us."[9] It took 189 years (after "independence") for the Ecuadorian state to recognize the existence of Afro-Ecuadorians. The state that historically denied existence and rights now confers. With state recognition comes a new set of norms and apparatuses of state control that work to negate, supersede, and disrupt collective memory, existence, and being. Abuelo Zenón says it clearly: "What we are today as people is what we never wanted to be, because what we are today does not depend solely on our will or desire to be. Today we are what the laws of the state direct and dictate that we will be."[10]

While many urban Afro-Ecuadorians applaud this new era of rights, visibility, and inclusionary politics, those who remain rooted to ancestral lands see the contradiction, enigma, and problem at hand, including dis-memory as a recoloniality of sorts, which weakens the very elements on which a collective Black territory, identity, memory, and existence were built. Recalled is Frantz Fanon's assertion in *Black Skin, White Masks* that affirmation within the system depends on the system's denial of ever having illegitimately excluded. How to address this conundrum remains a crucial concern, especially as the contemporary deterritorialization and dispossession of ancestral peoples and lands by the state—the corporate state, paramilitary-state, and narco-state and their allies and agents—become increasingly commonplace throughout the Abya Yala of both the South and North.

Indigenous peoples know this reality well; dispossession of lands, of self-determining authority, and of existence are constitutive of state, its politics, and its practice. The Dene thinker Glen Coulthard makes this especially clear in his description of the Canadian context, a context not dissimilar to other settler-colonial powers, nor totally dissimilar to the external and internal colonial powers present south of the Rio Grande.[11] "Colonial domination continues to be structurally committed to maintain—through force, fraud, and more recently 'negotiations'—ongoing state access to the land and resources that contradictorily provide the material and spiritual sustenance of Indigenous societies on the one hand, and the foundation of colonial-state formation, settlement, and capitalist development on the other."[12]

Building on Coulthard, Leanne Simpson describes this dispossession in an expansive sense; "it is the violent extraction of my body, mind, emotions, and spirit and the relationships they house from Nishnaabewin (Nishnaabeg intelligence), the relational structure that attaches me to Aki (the land)."[13] While refusing dispossession means rebuilding embeddedness, attachments, and interdependence, including with respect to grounded normativity (see the previous chapter), it also means—and at the same time—recognizing state as part of the colonial structure, a structure whose intention is, as Simpson argues, to dispossess.

Dismantling—or at least cracking—the colonial structure in all its still-present forms thus requires considerations of state, including the ways that state, and what Jane Anna Gordon describes as its inseparable counterpart, "statelessness," penetrate existence. Put simply, "the stateless are disproportionately racial, ethnic, and colonized minorities who face ongoing state repression."[14] While the modes and degrees of statelessness are many, as Gordon explains, including imperial colonial endeavors, forced migration,

categories of political membership and citizenship, and contemporary enslavement, the intertwinement of racialized debasement, dispossession, and
the Euro-modern nation-state are always at the center. As Breny Mendoza
reminds us, it is not only the idea and use of race but also gender that marks
this reality. We must not forget how the racialization and gendering of non-
European men and women has been essential to the construction of white
male citizenship and the related western configurations of liberal democracy
and state.[15] Ochy Curiel adds the political regime of heterosexuality to this
mix, a regime that, for Curiel, affects practically all social relations, including the conceptions that have historically defined nations particularly—but
not only—in Latin America and the Caribbean, and these nations' "others."[16]

What are some of the plurinational propositions, I ask, that work to
disrupt, crack, and undo this centricity from the ground up? How do they
conceive, posture, and practice other forms of governance, authority, and
social organization, opening toward plurality, including with regard to the
national and nation(s)?

If, as the Kurdish liberation leader Abdullah Öcalan argues, nation-state
is the spine of capitalist modernity, complexly interlaced with patriarchy
and, I would add, with coloniality, then it is also—as Öcalan maintains, and
at least in its original form—a sort of societal cage that closes in and mo-
nopolizes all social processes. "Diversity and plurality had to be fought, an
approach that led into assimilation and genocide." Not only does the nation-
state "exploit the ideas and the labor potential of the society and colonize
the heads of the people in the name of capitalism. It also assimilates all kinds
of spiritual and intellectual ideas and cultures in order to preserve its own
existence."[17] Öcalan—a political prisoner with a life sentence of solitary con-
finement in a Turkish prison—is thinking from the Middle East and the reality of Kurdistan, a nation without its own state, historically denied identity
and existence, and territorially located in Turkey, Syria, Iraq, and Iran. Yet
his thought opens horizons that cross continents and lands.

I recall Gloria Wekker's reference to the related arguments of Walter
Rodney, Lisa Lowe, and Saidiya Hartman: "State is a colonial artifact that
can't be decolonized." But this doesn't mean we should necessarily leave
state to its own, Wekker said. In fact, and for her, leaving state to its own is
a grave danger. "We need to create new modes of doing and acting together,
decolonially and intersectionally, including with respect to state."[18]

Working both inside and outside the existing state is certainly an option
for some, a way to critically intervene in and to construct other processes of
social organization and governance with, against, or despite state, giving

credence not to the state per se but to the action, agency, and possibility of the people. However, for others, including the women's movement of Kurdistan and the Kurdish Workers' Party founded in Turkey in 1978 and its leader Öcalan, the autonomy and liberation of Kurdish peoples, and especially of women, cannot be achieved in the patriarchal system that is the nation-state, and the mentality in which it is based, including the ties it makes among nationalism, sexism, religious fundamentalisms, and scientificisms in its universities and schools.[19] Freedom and the colonial capitalist modernity that is nation-state cannot coexist, argues Öcalan. Instead of nation-state, he proposes the idea of democratic multi- or plurinational confederalism as the paradigm and project of oppressed peoples. The proposition here is to disrupt the ideological hegemony, centralism, top-down assimilation, and singular, monocultural, militaristic, and market-driven character of state as we know it. And it is to work to create the conditions for a radically distinct organization of society as a whole, one that can also cross nation-state boundaries and borders. "We do not need big theories," Öcalan says. "What we need is the will to lend expression to social needs by strengthening the autonomy of the social actors structurally and by creating the conditions for the organization of the society as a whole."[20] As we will see later in this chapter, this idea and practice of confederalism offers interesting parallels with the plurinational propositions present in the Andes.

———————

I return to the centrality of land, to territory as life, and to the complexities of dispossession in its expansive sense; that is, of existence itself. If nation-states have been, and continue to be—at least for the majority of peoples in the world—a naturalized anchor and conduit of colonial permanence, then should we not turn our thinking and doing toward denaturalizing and undoing them? Here, Simpson's call to action could not be clearer: to "not just dream alternative realities but to create them, on the ground in the physical world in spite of being occupied." So too is her admonishment: "If we accept colonial permanence, then our rebellion can only take place within settler colonial thought and reality."[21]

This chapter takes seriously Simpson's words. Its aim is open reflection on processes, practices, and propositions that disrupt the colonial permanence of nation-state and engender otherwises from the ground up. While there are certainly examples that I could turn to from throughout the globe— particularly the long horizons of First Nations resistance and resurgence—my intention is not to *study about* or simply cite what others have documented.

Instead, it is to *think with and from* the plurinational propositions, contexts, movements, and struggles that I have been in close conversation and engagement with for several decades in both Ecuador and Bolivia.[22]

The aim of the chapter, in this sense, is to open reflection and share considerations on the ways that Indigenous movements, leaders, and intellectuals in both countries have pushed a rethinking and undoing of the "national" and its foundational structures of society, nation, and state. That is, their plurinational propositions that put into play the relation of land-territory and life, issues of self-determining authority and autonomy, and tenets, processes, and prospects for the creation of an "other" social project for society at large, understanding the importance that all this holds for processes of insurgent struggle, action, and thought elsewhere in Abya Yala and the world. Here I share details of these processes little known outside local contexts and the region, not as ethnographic case studies but as political re-existence-based reflection that, while situated, urges cross-territorial—and plurinational—consideration, contemplation, and conversation. In the pages that follow, I invite the reader to accompany me, to *read from* the Indigenous-conceived propositions, to *think with* the otherwise of existence they offer, and to consider what all this means for you, most especially with respect to the undoing of the Euromodern/capitalist/colonial nation-state's naturalization and its universal hegemonic hold.

Before turning to the specifics of the plurinational propositions in Bolivia and Ecuador, let me explore a bit further the lived postulates—as standpoint, existence, and life sense—of plurality, pluralization, and plurinationalization.

Plurality, Pluralization, and Plurinationalization

The plurality of life is a cosmogonic principle central in and to the existence of many Indigenous peoples and nations.[23] Plurality undoes unicity. It challenges the binaries central to western rationality and thought. And, as we saw in the last chapter, it complicates the notion of duality and of complementary pairs that underscores Mesoamerican and Andean cosmologies and tradition, a duality and complementarity in which, as some Indigenous community-based feminists argue, patriarchies (ancestral and western) are engendered, configured, and reconfigured.[24] Moreover, it reminds us of the intimate relation of capitalism, patriarchy, coloniality, and the top-down project of nation-state.

Plurality, in this sense, calls forth a perspective and understanding of life, existence, and relation in which the ideas not only of a singular "universe" but also of the "national"—that is, the "uni-national"—are necessarily denaturalized and contested. The concept, proposition, and prospect of the "plurinational," central to Indigenous movement processes, strategies, and struggles in the Andes, are part, as we will later see, of this denaturalization and contestation.

Of course, both the principle of plurality and the recognition of the plural within the national cross territories and borders. Michaeline Crichlow explains this well with respect to Caribbean contexts where "plural uneven spaces and temporalities constitute nation-states' and subjects' histories." As she aptly contends, creolization, understood as a "historicized process of selective creation and cultural struggle," marks not only the pluralized sociocultural configurations of the Caribbean but also its complex histories and problematic of globalization, nationalization, and regionalization.[25]

In the Andes, it is *mestizaje* that has historically worked to meld the plural into a newly forged union. *Mestizaje* is distinct from creolization in a number of ways. While the latter engages the plurality of sociocultural construction with respect to certain circuits of place, space, "chains of power," and forms of cultural struggle,[26] *mestizaje* negates pluralism and sociocultural dynamism. *Mestizaje* is simultaneously the dominant discourse of power and the unicity of nation; a political-intellectual project forged in the structural and structuring framework of coloniality and the colonial act and established in the ongoing relations of domination. Its base is in the mental category and idea of "race," in the supposed superiority of European-descended whites, and in the physical, cultural, and colonial processes, practices, and project of whitening and racial-ethnic subordination and negation. This is what Silvia Rivera Cusicanqui refers to as *mestizaje*'s colonial matrix.[27] Fundamental to *mestizaje*'s practice and project is the added entanglement of heteropatriarchy, rape, and gendered violence, lest we forget the multiple violations of Native women to enable and further *mestizaje*'s colonial-national project that was the elimination of Indigenous Nations—an elimination not by genocide, as occurred in Argentina, but by ethnocide, cosmocide, and sexual violation, accompanied by and orchestrated through the breakup and takeover of collective territory and land, the dispossession of existence and life. In the Andes, as is true in most of "Latin America" (with Brazil and, to a lesser extent, Colombia and Venezuela the exceptions), *mestizaje*'s project has been "Indian" focused, negating (or only secondarily considering) African-origin peoples. Recalled is Bartolomé de Las Casas's argument made against the enslavement of Indios and for the enslavement of Black Africans; while the former seem to have souls, the latter do not, Las Casas argued in his early work, later retracting this position.[28]

By pushing the transit from Indians to mestizos, the republican and later so-called democratic states did not seek to unite or articulate the pluralities of populations, nor to construct a plural whole. Their project instead was to consolidate *mestizaje* as a discourse of power, shaping and signifying a racist, exclusionary, and homogenizing "national" identity, culture, and state, with an eye toward modernization and westernization. The Ecuadorian thinker Agustín Cueva referred to this as the ambiguous colonial conscience and the inauthenticity that affects all social levels of "national" society.[29] In the same vein, the Bolivian thinker Javier Sanjinés speaks of a reductionist *mestizaje* that made uniform the population and made it impossible for the diverse, the alternative, and the multiple to really come to the surface.[30] Herein lies not only the foundational ambiguity of the nation but also the institution of a permanent and conflictive system of racial and social classification that enabled the universalization of capitalist civilization and the formation of "national" societies.[31]

While the historical problem has been, in a broad sense, with the concept, construction, and project of the (uni)national, it is also relatedly with the supposed consolidation and constitution of nation-state. *The Merriam-Webster Dictionary* defines *nation-state* as "a form of political organization under which a relatively homogeneous people inhabit a sovereign state; especially a state containing one as opposed to several nationalities."[32] This definition, of course, is grounded in western modernity's logic and practice, a logic with German philosophical, cultural, institutional, and ideological roots. It is the West's imposition on and to the rest. Nation-state, from this perspective, requires a centralized form of political power and organization most often tied to forms of capitalist production that configure both internal and international markets. It constitutes a unified coercive structure of authority, territory, and sovereignty. And it demands a notion of unity, inclusion, political identification, and allegiance that transcends the local, ruptures the communal, homogenizes the plural, and makes the individual—that is, the individual recognized and defined by this structure and system—the focal point of state-defined rights.

As I suggested earlier, the hyphenated concoction of nation and national state—that is, nation-state—is in both conception and practice a component part of capitalism/modernity/coloniality, and a strategic element in the construction, consolidation, and reproduction of this model of power.

The Bolivian sociologist René Zavaleta argued—in critical dialogue with Vladimir Lenin—that nation and the national state are paradigmatic forms of unity, organization, and articulation characteristic of capitalism itself.[33] The Kurdish liberation leader Abdullah Öcalan also makes this clear. The national state or nation-state is (hypothetically) what occurs when civil society (a modern concept) is converted into a nation with a sole political power. In this sense, the national state or nation-state is the supposed manifestation and culmination, of sorts, of the nation, of a national society dominated by a national bourgeoisie and with a structure of power configured under these—capitalist, modern, colonial, imperial—conditions of domination.[34]

The underlying principle here is that nationalism produces nations and nation-states in societies, as Aníbal Quijano argues, "configured with relation to the coloniality of power, including in societies with pluricultural and even pluri-national universes."[35] In the second half of the nineteenth century and before the so-called Mexican Revolution, Chile was the only Latin American country, says Quijano, that had these characteristics of national society and nation-state. Of course, the Chilean national oligarchic state was consolidated through strategic political pacts, invited European immigration, and the promise of the genocidal extermination of the Mapuche nation, a promise that—though attempted—was never fully achieved. "The social movements, above all those of the middle classes and the mining proletariat that since 1920 were developing toward a modern nation-state, culminated in the decade of the 1930s with the Popular Front government, a political pact between the Chilean bourgeoisie, the workers' political parties, and the middle classes that served to consolidate the norms and institutions of liberal/bourgeois democracy."[36]

For Quijano, these norms helped bring Salvador Allende to power in 1970.[37] And they also facilitated his fall in the bloody military coup of 1973. The neoliberalization of capitalism that began in the Pinochet dictatorship led to a new adaptation of the Chilean state, "a new capitalist-national society and a new nation-state" directly tied to the necessities and interests of globalization; that is, to the "world-wide re-concentration of the control of labor and the control of the state by global corporations and their global imperial bloc."[38] With the United States taking the lead, Chile became the central Latin American peg in the nation-state ideational regime of market fundamentalism extended not just to the public sphere but to all of social life.[39] Recalled is what Mendoza refers to as the "coloniality of democracy"; that is, how neoliberal democracy, using the artifact of the free market, has been instrumental in the reestablishing of colonial norms within societies and, at the same time, in reconstructing the region's colonial link with the new imperial powers of the Occident or West.[40]

What does this process tell us about the questions of pluralism and problems of nation and the (uni)national state? For Quijano, the global imposition of neoliberalism has led to and drives the continuous erosion of autonomy in Latin America's less democratic and less national states. In Bolivia, for example, neoliberalism worked to dismantle in the late 1980s and the decade of the 1990s, says Luis Tapia, the modalities of populist nationalism and state capitalism established with the 1952 revolution. Neoliberalism undid what there was of the national and opened the way for the bourgeoisie-supported project of transnational sovereignty.[41] Mendoza takes the problematic further: "Market neoliberalism and the democracy of consensus and reconciliation have tried to erase from time and space the memory of violence in Latin America, ... to take us on an exodus outside of historical time and confuse the 'new citizens' with promises of justice, equality, and prosperity in a distant future just as the evangelizers did in the past."[42] Of course, the problem is not just with neoliberalism. As Quijano contends, the problem began well before neoliberalism took hold, "particularly in the Andes where the coloniality of power has historically made unviable the liberal/Eurocentric project of the modern nation-state."[43]

In this sense, the nonviability of the modern nation-state in the Andes is much more complex than an inadequate national bourgeoisie, or an inadequate or interrupted project of nationalization. It is tied to the historical patterns of national/colonial/imperial/global power that have endeavored without total success to displace, erase, eliminate, or supersede the existence of ancestral (sometimes referred to as precapitalist and premodern) civilizations and nations with their own structures of identity, governance, authority, territoriality, spirituality, cosmology, and existence-life. And it is tied to patterns of power that have worked, through the ideas of race, gender, and the modern precept of anthropocentrism, to denigrate, subordinate, and violate the plurality of life, the plurality of bodies, territories and land, identities, knowledges, spiritualities, life practices, and cosmological world-senses of millennial nations and peoples, Indigenous as well as those of African origin whose presence in the region also predates state. This is not to reify, essentialize, or simplify, nor is it to deny the operation of systems, structures, and practices of top-down power within ancestral communities. The ongoing problems and incongruities of heteropatriarchy and gendered violences, corruption, capitalist and extractivist alliances, urbanization, and individualism are only a few examples. Still, while the coloniality of power—and of being, knowledge, and Nature—continues to exert domination and control, it has not had total success. This is because of the ongoing resistance and insurgency of those who have lived the colonial difference, of those peoples who refuse to think from—or solely from—the universalizing paradigms of nation and national state.

In this context, the problem of the national and the questions of state and nation are lived concerns that, as Indigenous movements have argued, demand a conceptual and institutional decolonizing, rethinking, and refounding. Quijano was clear about this demand and its project when he said, "The demand of populations that precisely were victims of non-national and non-democratic states is not for more nationalism or more state. Instead, it is for an 'other' state, that is, to decolonize the state, which is the only way to democratize it." For this process to be successful, Quijano said, "the new state cannot be a nation-state or a national state, but rather it must be pluri- or multi-national, or better yet, inter-national."[44]

Of course, as I have argued throughout this book, the demands of and the struggles waged by peoples who have lived the colonial difference are much broader than state. More profoundly, they are about existence, re-existence, and interexistence, about conditions and relations of life and living in dignity and with others. The struggles and demands, in this sense, are about transforming the modern/colonial matrices of power, and they are about the building of a radically distinct social project and order in which plurality is a necessary principle and a component part.

As we will see in the pages that follow, the idea of the plurinational puts in discussion the logocentric and reductionist way that the national has been thought about. Even more importantly, it puts a limit on the very idea of state itself. Thinking from the contemporary contexts of Bolivia and Ecuador, Salvador Schavelzon describes the Indigenous proposition of a plurinational state "as a pluralism of empowered civilizations, . . . a paradox that proposes the state that at the same time is a non-state, the point where forces of centralization encounter centrifugal forces inspired by difference and opposition to unification, homogeneity, and absolute consensus." In this sense, the plurinational is "not so much a threat for the nation as it is for the state, at least as political modernity understands it."[45] The incommensurability of state is even clearer if we consider "the limits pointed out by Indigenous peoples of the republican form of government, presidentialism, forms of democratic representation, and structural decision-making. The impossibility of these political forms to represent or listen to difference is evident," says Schavelzon, an impossibility pushed further by "the capitalist market that not only impedes expression but also destroys the alternative ways of community."[46]

By disputing and contradicting the monopoly of the national state and its demands of exclusive loyalty, and by bringing into consideration the multiple loyalties of a plural decentered social order, the Indigenous proposition of the plurinational in the Andes marks a radically distinct project and agenda, thought from the subjects historically excluded in the unitary sense of society, nation, and state and supposedly eliminated in the national project of *mestizaje*. But before exploring how these movements have signified, constructed, thought about, and proposed the plurinational, let's look briefly at how the plurinational has been used in other geopolitical contexts.

The Plurinational in Geopolitical Context

The idea of the plurinational is not just an Indigenous proposition and invention. The meaning of the idea and term is heterogeneous and diverse, tied to philosophical and ideological frames, geopolitical context, and the relation—or not—to the global modern/colonial/capitalist order. The idea of the multi- or plurinational was present in the former Soviet Union. It is reflected in recently decolonized countries such as India, Malaysia, Nigeria, and South Africa. And it has been used to describe and define highly industrialized countries such as Canada, Belgium, Switzerland, New Zealand, and Finland.

In a most basic and general sense, a multinational or plurinational state implies the political recognition of the presence and coexistence of two or more ethnically distinct nations or peoples. The term *nation* here refers to a historical community with a determinate natal territory, which shares a distinct language and culture. A country with more than one nation is a plurinational country. Its formation can be voluntary or involuntary and, consequently, it can be plurinational without dismantling racist and colonial structures, without recognizing the equality of its different constituent groups and nations, and without promoting a relationship between them. In Belgium and Switzerland, for example, the multi- or plurinational signifies and represents the voluntary federation of two or more European cultures. Finland and New Zealand are considered multi- or plurinational due to their forced incorporation of Indigenous peoples. And yet others, such as Canada, have been formed through the involuntary incorporation of First Nations peoples as well as through the federation of differing national groups.

These examples make evident that the plurinational itself does not constitute a remedy or reparation that dissolves the historical problems and unequal relations of power, most especially in countries marked by settler colonialism. Nevertheless, these countries have learned that their survival requires a language and politics of recognition. This recognition-based approach (typically associated with liberal pluralism) is reflected in the establishment of Indigenous rights regimes in Asia, northern Europe, the Americas, and Oceania and the Pan-Pacific, regimes that "claim to recognize and accommodate the political autonomy, land rights, and cultural distinctiveness of Indigenous nations within the settler states that now encase them."[47] However, as Coulthard aptly argues, "instead of ushering in an era of peaceful coexistence grounded on the ideal of *reciprocity* or *mutual* recognition, the politics of recognition in its contemporary liberal form promises to reproduce the very configurations of colonialist, racist, patriarchal state power that Indigenous peoples' demands for recognition have historically sought to transcend."[48]

Canada, a well-consolidated democracy and the second-largest territory in the world, is a case in point. Canada recognizes Indigenous peoples—according to official figures about 4 percent of the total Canadian population—as First Nations. This recognition is the result of a long history of Native resistance and struggle, including the Red Power activism that emerged in the 1960s and 1970s and within which pan-Indian assertiveness, political mobilization, and direct confrontation with federal government and state took form. "The effectiveness of our subsequent political struggles," says Coulthard, "once again raised issues of unresolved Native rights and title issues to the fore of Canadian public consciousness." Here Indigenous anticolonial nationalism forced modifications in the colonial power "from a structure that was once primarily reinforced by policies, techniques, and ideologies explicitly oriented around the genocidal exclusion/assimilation double, to one that is now reproduced through a seemingly more conciliatory set of discourses and institutional practices that emphasize our *recognition* and *accommodation*."[49]

This recognition and accommodation extend to the Canadian Constitution, in which Indigenous peoples have a special political status. Constitutional provisions recognize and affirm the existence of "Aboriginal" rights, securing the participation of Indigenous peoples in all future constitutional negotiations. They recognize the different ways of exercising rights, including in urban spaces, and lay the ground for the development of an intercultural juridical practice. Such modifications are part of what Coulthard calls "the now expansive range of recognition-based models of liberal pluralism that seek to 'reconcile' Indigenous assertions of nationhood with settler-state sovereignty via the accommodation of Indigenous identity claims in some form of renewed legal and political relationship with the Canadian state."[50] However, and regardless of the changes or so-called advances established through this politics of recognition, the relationship between Indigenous peoples and the state has "remained *colonial* to its foundation."[51]

What are the lessons here? While there are many, let me emphasize three. First, these examples confirm that the multi- or plurinational state is not a monolithic entity. It takes form from and within particular geopolitical and geocultural contexts. And it is most often the result of the demands and struggles of those peoples and populations historically marginalized by or left out of the "national" project. Second, while the designation of a multi- or plurinational state challenges the homogeneous concept of nation-state, it does not necessarily disrupt or undo the idea and power of state, nor does it necessarily unsettle notions of nation, national unity, nationalism, and state unification. It is the state that accommodates pluralism and diversity within its political and ideological frame, and the state that decides the extent of its modifications. Third, the recognition of the multi- or plurinational, in all of the countries mentioned here, comes from the state itself; in essence, it is a top-down proposition that, as Coulthard argues with respect to Canada, has in no way altered the colonial relations of power.

What is the difference when the idea of the plurinational is proposed from the bottom up, as has occurred in Bolivia and Ecuador, and within the framework of Indigenous movements' struggles of and for decolonization? In what ways do the idea, proposition, and demand of the plurinational in these contexts fissure and crack the dominant precepts of nation and the national state? And in what ways do they reflect and construct a plurinational proposition of thought—a plurinational thinking—that goes beyond state itself, a thinking and thought that are grounded in and give possibility to re-existences and existences otherwise?

These are the questions that began to first occupy my thought in the decade of the 1990s, spurred by dialogue and collaborations with Indigenous intellectuals and leaders, activists, and others in Ecuador and Bolivia. During the Constitutional Assembly processes in 2007–8 in both countries, these questions, their debates, and reflections on them became even more profound as many of us involved grappled together with the idea—as challenge, possibility, and dilemma—of refounding state. For me, this idea began to wane soon after, as the practice and politics of Ecuador's and Bolivia's progressive governments demonstrated in all too many ways the continuation of the problematic project and ills of nation-state and the advance of state corporatization. However, my return to and rethinking of these questions now and in this book have a different aim. I am not concerned with analyzing the constitutions—both of which recognize and name a plurinational state—or the government practice and politics of the named plurinational state in the regimes of Rafael Correa, Evo Morales, and beyond.[52] I am also not interested in considering the viability or applicability of a plurinational state within the same top-down structure. My interest instead is to explore and share reflections on the ways the plurinational has been historically conceived, postured, and thought about on the ground, most especially by Indigenous thinkers, leaders, and movements. Of course, I understand that the designations of top down, bottom up, and on the ground are not fixed, static, or straightforward. Nevertheless, and as I will argue here, it is from the collective base of Indigenous thought, struggle, and praxis that the undoing of nation-state and the weaving of a radically distinct social project can be seen to take form.

Let's look first at Bolivia, where the proposition of the plurinational more visibly began.

The Plurinational in Bolivia: Autonomy, Decolonization, and Self-Determination

In Bolivia, a country with a clear Indigenous majority, the idea and proposition of the plurinational has always been intricately linked to the concepts and practices of autonomy, decolonization, and self-determination.

References to and demands for a plurinational society and state can be traced to the late 1970s in documents associated with the Katarist and Indianist movements. Yet Aymaran critiques of the modern Bolivian nation and state existed way earlier. These critiques were present in the political movement led by Pablo Zárate Willka (in the context of the 1899 civil war), which embraced a program of political autonomy of Indigenous self-government and territorial reconstitution. They were also present in the struggles led by Eduardo Leandro Nina Qhispi in the late 1920s and early 1930s. His proposal for the "Renovation of Bolivia" called for a new constitutional assembly to address the complete omission in the political charter of Indigenous peoples. More critically, his efforts to establish an *ayllu*-based education—that is, a community-based education grounded in kinship and territorial ties and focused on autonomy and the establishment of political and territorial rights—called into question the state itself.[53]

In the 1960s, critical reflections began to take a more organized form. Questions emerged in both urban and rural Aymara communities about the so-called gains of the 1952 Marxist-inspired Nationalist Revolution, a "revolution" based on a supposedly new model and vision of state. As many argued, the use of labor unionism or syndicalism within the structures of nationalism and state power afforded little or nothing for structural change. Moreover, the incorporation of the heretofore excluded population as "citizens" and, as such, as part of the modern Bolivian state and nation only served to strengthen this nation-state, not to transform it.[54] The "new" thus became an oxymoron that perpetuated the colonial condition.

It was also in the 1960s that organizational processes began toward what Aymaran intellectual Esteban Ticona describes as "the recuperation and re-elaboration of the historical knowledge of an indigenous past" and the building of a new generation of ethnic consciousness grounded in the recognition of and the struggle against the ongoing colonial condition, in which a social minority continues to oppress the originally free and autonomous majority society.[55]

The first visible manifestations were among urban Aymara youths. Toward the end of the 1960s, a group of migrant Aymara students organized the November 15th Movement and Cultural Center in a La Paz public high school. With this name they gave homage to the date of execution of the historic figure Tupac Katari (Julian Apaza): November 15, 1781. This movement and center functioned as a kind of study-group space to interrogate and better understand the reality and condition of Aymara migrants and peoples in a country dominated by a white elite. Here, the Indianist intellectual Fausto Reinaga played a fundamental role.

For Reinaga, founder in the late 1960s of the Partido Indio (Indian Political Party), the struggle was not for assimilation into the structures, institutions, and logic of dominant society. Rather it was for the right to existence as an Indian or Indigenous Nation. "The right of Indigenous people, the right to be a NATION, is perennial, inexpressible, and imprescriptible," Reinaga said. "The validity of the Indian Nation throughout four centuries is vital. The Indian Nation is and has been independent of all political contingencies, regimes, and systems of government. It has existed under the government of the Spanish kings and it exists under this Republic.... Bolivia will only be free with the liberation of Indigenous people; the liberation of Indigenous people will be the liberation of Bolivia."[56]

Under the guidance and readings of Reinaga, this youth group began to perceive their problems from the viewpoint of systemic racism, discrimination, and the ongoing colonial condition. They also began to reflect with Reinaga on the significance, meaning, and struggle of nation. Reinaga similarly inspired other collectives of urban Aymara youths, including the cultural-political University-Movement Julian Apaza, which likewise vindicated the anticolonial struggles of Katari.

Other organizations worked in these years to strengthen the ties of culture and politics. The Centro de Promoción y Coordinación Campesina (Center of Peasant Promotion and Coordination) or MINK'A, formed in 1969 by Aymara residents in La Paz and dedicated to the areas of education, organization, and dissemination, strengthened links between urban cultural-political centers and rural agrarian-peasant unions. Other cultural-political organizations—also with the name of Katari—began to take form, including the Centro Campesino Tupac Katari (Tupac Katari Peasant Center), focused on the sociocultural potential of the media (Aymara radio broadcasts and a newspaper) and of an urban agrarian market. Together these urban movements configured one axis or origin of the cultural-ethnic awakening that later became the Katarist movement.[57]

The second axis or origin was in what Silvia Rivera Cusicanqui calls the generational phenomenon of the rural regions. The nationalist transformations brought about by the 1952 revolution, including with relation to agrarian reform, rural schooling, and labor union participation, opened horizons and awakened new expectations. However, they did little to alter the lived conditions of exclusion and marginalization of youths in Aymara highland communities. In fact, the experiences of rural schooling, seasonal migration, cultural and linguistic (Spanish-language) assimilation, labor union manipulation, and promised political participation and citizenship contributed to a growing critical consciousness among these youths. They began to both question and reject servility, paternalism, ethnic discrimination, and ongoing colonial relations of power. And they began to elaborate and defend an ideology grounded in the long memory of cultural difference. From this group of youths emerged the new bases of peasant-Indigenous leadership that in the early 1970s penetrated the official apparatus of labor unionism (the National Confederation of Peasant Workers of Bolivia), processes violently interrupted by the 1971 military coup and the severe repression of the subsequent Banzer dictatorship.[58]

Despite the environment of repression in this period (1971–78), the cultural-political processes of Indigenous-peasant formation and organization continued. During the first years of the Banzer government, the Katarist movement constituted a bridge between urban and rural Aymaras, between leaders functioning clandestinely and community-based highland unions, and between the political postures of cultural reaffirmation and agricultural modernization. By 1973, Katarism was the generic name of a wide ideological movement with multiple institutional and organizational expressions in various cities and in the countryside.[59] In July of this same year, the movement presented its first public document: the *Manifiesto de Tiwanaku* (sometimes written as *Tiahuanaco* and translated as the "Tiwanaku manifesto").

The *Manifiesto*, read during a massive Indigenous-peasant meeting in the pre-Incan Tiwanaku ruins and later widely circulated in Bolivia, Latin America, Europe, and the United States in various languages, established a platform on class, ethnicity, and nation that, as Carlos Macusaya Cruz argues, foresaw the split that was to come within the movement between Indianists and Katarists.[60]

While the *Manifiesto* continued the project of decolonization based on race, class, and nation begun with the University-Movement Julian Apaza, it introduced what Roberto Choque Canqui refers to as a "change in attitude" in which ethnicity and culture were to have a growing role. For Choque, the dissemination of the *Manifiesto* was the "first public historic act that openly rejected the imposition of a rural education alien to our ancestral values and, in so doing, it started up cultural, political, and economic decolonization."[61] It was also the first collective document to establish a broad-based perspective on the problematic of Aymara and Bolivian reality, challenging both the class-based reductionisms of labor unionism and Leftist political parties and the ethnic reductionisms present in some Indigenous sectors. The central argument of the *Manifiesto* was that cultural-ethnic elements and social class are necessarily entwined.[62]

The *Manifiesto* began with the historic phrase pronounced by the Inca Yupanqui to the Spanish courts in 1810: "A people that oppresses another people cannot be free" (Un pueblo que oprime a otro pueblo, no puede ser libre).[63] And it continued, "We, Aymara and Quechua peasants[64] along with the other indigenous cultures of the country, say the same. We feel economically exploited and culturally and politically oppressed. In Bolivia, there has not been an integration of cultures but rather an imposition and domination that has put us in the most bottom and exploited stratum of the social pyramid."[65]

For the collective authors of the *Manifiesto*, the oppression of Indigenous peoples and peasants is not just political and economic, as the traditional (white-mestizo) Left had argued. It is also cultural, ideological, colonial, and existence based. Culture and the historical knowledge and memory of anti-colonial struggle are made subordinate to economic development, the document said. State policies and institutions have not respected "our vision of the world and of life" and have endeavored, especially through education, "to not only convert the Indian into a type of mestizo without personality and definition, but also to equally pursue our assimilation into western and capitalist culture. The result: 'We are foreigners in our own land.'"[66] The *Manifiesto* expressed a lack of trust of political parties of both the Left and the Right, and argued for self-determination and autonomy, including with regard to political organization and liberation (conceived from the combination of ethnic, cultural, and class vindications).[67] The structures of power, nation, and state inherited from the national revolution became, with this document, focal points of conflict, interrogation, and decolonizing struggle. For the subscribers of the *Manifiesto*, the aspiration was "to no longer be a foreigner in our own land."

The very idea that a peasant-Indian movement could emerge in the highlands, question the nationalist-Marxist project of class struggle, and bring to the fore the problem of the ongoing colonial condition—including with regard to nation and state—was unconceivable for the nationalist and Marxist Left. This Left remained blind to racism and to the political significance of processes of cultural, political, sociohistoric, and knowledge-based revaluation; instead they maintained the belief that the "*indio*" was premodern and pre-1952, and, as such, in an advanced state of disintegration. The historical origins of racism of the exploited majorities were similarly outside the purview of the Left, as were the possibilities that Indians could stop being the source of complexes and become a mobilizing lever and force. The very idea of Indian-centered movements in fact brought panic to the traditional Left and its foundational premise: that all forms of exploitation are economic based.[68] Moreover, the idea that there could exist Aymara intellectuals, including within La Paz universities at the time, was inconceivable for the leadership and ranks of both the Left and Right.

For many Aymaran thinkers in the period of the 1960s and 1970s, decolonization was not just racial, cultural, political, and economic; it was also epistemic, grounded in the spheres of thought and in the knowledges that ongoing colonialism has worked to deny. Made evident in this posture was the enduring matrix of modern/colonial power, but also an anticolonial and decolonizing perspective and project that aimed at an "otherwise."

In 1976, three years after the *Manifiesto*, Juan Condori Uruchi wrote, "Although they call us '*campesinos*,' we are Aymaras, workers, miners, professionals, students, and intellectuals; we have been stripped of our personality as Aymara peoples. Who is to blame?... We put up with paternalism and this is exactly what humiliates us, keeps us in poverty, in ignorance and, as a result, mired in subsistence." Moreover, and as Condori argues, "they still say that the Aymara lacks weight in his/her brain... that the *indio* is half animal and half human. [Yet] how could we want to compare the *homo sapiens* of the Andean man/woman with the vain mind of those who, having learned some bookish phrases, try to pass as superior... swelling with egotism and pride?"[69]

THE INDIANIST AND KATARIST DIVIDE, OR KATARISM'S TWO FACES

As alluded to earlier, it was Fausto Reinaga who began and led the ideological construction of Indianism in the 1960s before Katarism as a named movement began to take hold. Indianism's central tenet was the idea of race. That is, on the one hand, the recognition and critique of the practices of racial subordination and discrimination and the system of racialization promulgated and maintained by *q'aras*, or the white-mestizo population, and, on the other, the necessary formation of a specifically Indian consciousness, ideology, and identity.[70] Indianism's demand was for structural—political, epistemic, and existence-based—decolonization. It was also for the recognition of the Indian Nation. With Indianism came the ideas and claims of the plurinational. In the early 1970s, Indianism and Katarism seemed to be two referents that intermeshed without necessary distinction.

It was not until the late 1970s that a clear division within the Indian movement between Indianists and Katarists began to take concrete form as many leaders, forced to go underground during the Banzer dictatorship, reemerged. Some have referred to this divide as Indianist and Katarist, while others speak of Katarism's two factions or faces, one derived from Indianism and the other from a multicultural class-based frame. Evident here are distinct political perspectives of nation-state and of struggle.

The Indian-centered face or faction was predominantly urban based, centered in social, cultural, and civic organizations and, as previously described, in the lived experience of struggle within dominant social structures and institutions (schools, universities, unions, the military, etc.). Led by Constantino Lima, Luciano Tapia, Felipe Quispe, and others—and influenced by Fausto Reinaga and his son Ramiro—this faction took organizational and political form in the Movimiento Indio Tupac Katari (Tupac Katari Indian Movement; MITKA), created in 1978. For MITKA, the struggle was against racism, ethnic discrimination, the colonial state, and the dominant idea of nation: monocultural, homogeneous, and colonial in character and concept. And it was for the decolonization and liberation of the "Indian Nation," understood as inclusive of all Indigenous peoples and their descendants (urban and rural, miners, and workers, regardless of class distinction). Here the political position was clear: "Class struggle will only be resolved in favor of the [Indian] majority when racial discrimination is eliminated."[71]

MITKA identified itself as a movement of national liberation. The "nation" of Bolivia, in MITKA's view, was nothing more than an artifice that fed the disintegration of Indigenous communities, the majority of the Bolivian population. Its proposal, then, grounded in an Indian-centered ideology and a life philosophy of communion with Nature as a civilizational and cultural form, was for "a Bolivian state based in the confederation of its real nations that voluntarily and freely make up a plurinational and pluricultural state."[72] MITKA's goal was for the Indigenous nations to take power. The plan was to reconceptualize the idea and practice of state from the Indigenous majority's plurination. In essence, it was a posture against the modern state and for the construction from the ground up of an Andean otherwise, centered in great part—and as we will see later in this chapter—in the reconstitution of Andean historical structures of authority and governance organized in and through the *ayllu*.

The other face of Katarism, associated with the legendary leader Jenaro Flores, was peasant union based. It found its support in the agrarian contexts and realities of rural communities, and its focal point in the combined struggles of class and culture. The Movimiento Revolucionario Tupac Katari (Tupac Katari Revolutionary Movement; MRTK), organized in 1978, became the counterpoint to MITKA; that is, Katarism's more moderate face. Its difference from the Indianist face was made clear in the 1978 Bolivian Peasant Thesis: "If racism was the first step of our ideology," the thesis said, "we must now overcome it because we are exploited, not only because we are Aymaras, Quechuas, or Cambas [lowland Indigenous], etc., but fundamentally because there is a rich minority that gets richer with our work. We need to change this exploitative society so that our values as Aymaras, Quechuas, Cambas, etc. can be exercised and can develop freely."[73]

For MRTK, the struggles were not just in the sphere of the national but also within labor unionism itself. This faction of Katarism, greater in number and power than MITKA (and more reflective of the posture of the aforementioned *Manifiesto*), succeeded in gradually breaking the military control over peasant communities established in 1952 with the Military-Campesino Pact. And it succeeded in fracturing the hegemony of both the Leftist white bourgeois leadership and the proletariat-based standpoint in the Central Obrera Boliviana (Bolivian Workers' Central Union), a leadership and standpoint that effectively excluded peasant participation and peasant reality. Furthermore, and for the first time in Bolivian history, this face of Katarism pushed a real alliance of Indigenous peasants and workers.

In contrast to MITKA's posture of "outside and against" the colonial nation-state, MRTK vindicated the Bolivian nation through a political strategy of "inside and against," a posture and strategy that challenged the nationalist view of a homogeneous and unidimensional Bolivia.[74] It is this face of Katarism that gave form in 1979 to the Central Sindical Única de Trabajadores Campesinos Bolivianos (CSUTCB), the peasant workers' union that some years later helped bring Evo Morales to power.

In 1983 CSUTCB put forth its "Political Thesis," described in its introduction as "the political and syndical thought of peasants," later approved in a national congress of more than four thousand delegates from throughout Bolivia. "In this document we aim to create the bases of our thought," the thesis's introduction stated. "Throughout these almost five centuries, our enemies of colonial times and of the republican era have tried to make us think what they wanted us to think, to say only what they were interested in us saying, to live imitating them, and, finally, to accept our situation of oppression, exploitation, racism, to despise our own cultures, to accept abuses and being supplanted. This Thesis is a response to our history of subjection and submission. It is a response that rejects all forms of subjugation and seeks the construction of a new society without hunger, free and just, where we can live as human beings."[75]

For CSUTCB, the fundamental ideas of the thesis were rooted in the "centenarian struggles of our peoples and leaders," including Julian Apaza (Tupac Katari), Bartolina Sisa, José Gabriel Condorcanqui (Tupak Amaru), Micaela

Bastides, Pablo Willka Zarate, and many others. And they were rooted in the construction of a new and more recent syndicalism, free of all forms of political imposition. The thesis rejected outright classist reductionisms that "intend to convert us into only *'campesinos'* or peasants," as well as "ethnic reductionisms that convert the struggle into one of *'indios'* against *'whites.'*" In this sense, it seemed to echo the Tiwanaku *Manifiesto* of ten years before, and to take further its decolonializing proposition and demand. Who are we? the thesis asked.

> We are the inheritors of great civilizations. We are also the inheritors of a permanent struggle against all forms of exploitation and oppression. We want to be free in a society without exploitation and oppression and organized in a plurinational State that develops our cultures and our authentic forms of self-government.... We Campesinos Aymaras, Qhechwas, Cambas, Chapacos, Chiquitanos, Canichanas, Itenamas, Cayubabas, Ayoreodes, Tupiwaranies, and others, are the legitimate owners of this land. We are the seed from which Bolivia was born, but until today they treat us as outcasts in our own land. [Despite] ... our different languages, organizational systems, world visions, and historical traditions, we are joined in a permanent struggle ... to reaffirm our own historical identity, to develop our own culture and to be subjects, not objects, of history.... Liberation is our shared cause.[76]

Liberation is clearly understood here as part and parcel of a decolonizing project, grounded in identity, history, culture, knowledge, cosmology, and land, and in the radical transformation of the institutions and structures of power, including nation-state.

These five hundred years of struggle against different forms of oppression and exploitation offer valuable experiences and lessons for the future, the thesis contended. First off, these centuries of struggle teach us about resistance and about the liberation struggles to maintain with dignity national and cultural identities. Second, they help us understand our shared cultural roots in the struggles against the ongoing colonial system; our shared objective, "to eradicate all forms of racial discrimination and exile in our own land"; and our brotherhood as workers fighting against capitalist exploitation and the capitalist colonial system. "Our thought does not permit a unilateral reduction of our history to a struggle that is purely class-based or purely ethnic in character," the thesis contends. "In the practice of these two dimensions, we recognize not only our unity with workers but also our own culturally differentiated personality." Third, our history shows a capacity to adapt and renew the methods of struggle without losing the continuity of our historical roots. Fourth, it reminds us of our social organizational capacities (*ayllus*) and of our knowledges (scientific, technological, agro-productive) that maintained societies without hunger and governments without exploitation. Fifth, it has taught us who our enemies are, including the state that "channels its neocolonial and imperial interests by means of multiple mechanisms of domination." "It is the structure of power that has to be changed," the thesis maintains, "and not just the governments that direct this structure."[77]

> Finally, our history teaches us that we can develop a united struggle of the oppressed, respecting the diversity of languages, cultures, historical traditions, and forms of organization and labor. Our struggle is for the expression of this diversity in all spheres of national life. We do not want patches or partial reforms; we want a definitive liberation and the construction of a plurinational and pluricultural society that maintains the unity of a State, combining and developing the diversity of the Aymara, Qhechua, Tupiguarani, Ayoreode nations and all the nations that integrate it. There cannot be a true liberation without respecting the plurinational diversity of our country and the diverse forms of self-governance of our peoples.[78]

Clearly evident here is a signification of the plurinational as fundamental to liberation, decolonization, and the building of an existence and coexistence otherwise. Of course, this takes us back to the problematic of the national and to the two-pronged question of nation and state.

ONGOING QUESTIONS OF THE NATION AND THE NATIONAL STATE

In the early 1980s (and before the CSUTCB political thesis), sociologist René Zavaleta argued that the character of the nation, or the way in which the nation is revealed in the state, is a problem around which all political and ideological struggles are fought. "For us Bolivians, the formation of the national state and the nation itself are inconclusive processes."[79] While Zavaleta mentions the pluri- or multinational—"the multinational nation is an ersatz of what could not be converted into nation"—it is just that, a mention without further consideration or development.[80] Moreover, in his subsequent statement that "the millennial vindication of Bolivia's Katarist movement should be taken up in its concrete democratic content and not in its incongruence with the apparent criterion of modernity,"[81] Zavaleta seems to suggest the continued existence in the Andean world of other organizational forms beyond and despite state and modernity's hold, and in their cracks. However, he does not develop this idea, nor does he take into consideration the depth of Indianist and Katarist thought (contemporaneous with his own thinking).

From their birth in urban and rural communities in the 1960s to their more organized development in the 1970s and 1980s, Indianism and Katarism placed at the center of debate in Bolivia the problem of the modern/colonial structures and matrices of power, including the hegemonic constructs of state and nation, but also the continued presence of an otherwise of identity, organization, authority, existence, and thought. Of course, this analysis did not just begin in the 1960s; its foundational roots are in the long horizon of lived rebellion, insurgence, and struggle, and in the varied spaces of collective reflection, including the first Indigenous Congress in 1945, where diverse leaders from both highland and lowland nations came together.[82]

For Javier Sanjinés, "katarism's core is located in the possibility of recuperating a powerful contrahegemonic tradition that opposes both the liberal project of national construction, and the Western ideas of cultural homogeneity and a citizenry of cultural mestizaje." In its political praxis, Katarism has questioned the deficient and incomplete reading of Bolivia as a homogeneous and unidimensional reality.[83] It impelled the articulation—without definitive synthesis or fusion—of class and racial-ethnic struggle. And it brought to the fore the problem of state, opening a level of debate, analysis, and critical discussion that far surpassed that of the white-mestizo Left.

In the 1990s, Katarism took on more complex and problematic dimensions. With the naming of Gonzalo Sánchez de Lozada (Goni) to the presidency in 1993 in an alliance between the National Revolutionary Movement (Sánchez de Lozada's party) and the MRTK,[84] then led by Victor Hugo Cárdenas, a new political era was ushered in. For the first time in Bolivian history, an Aymara and Katarist, Cárdenas, came to assume the vice presidency. With Cárdenas, Katarism, in its more moderate version, entered the sphere of state. Here, and as we will later see in the case of Ecuador, a new problematic emerged.

Because of Cárdenas, Goni introduced the idea of a plurinational state at the close of his presidential campaign.[85] However, its concretion never came to fruition. Nevertheless, in the period of the Goni government (1993–97), Cárdenas was able to push legislative and constitutional reforms that acknowledged Bolivia's multiethnic and pluricultural character. He enabled the legalization of some communal lands, established Indigenous bilingual education programs, decentralized government, recognized three hundred local governments, and promoted local participation through the Law of Popular Participation (1994), a law that gave relative autonomy to rural municipal governments and legal recognition and rights to local participation, while at the same time consolidating the territorial fragmentation of the *ayllus*.[86] He was also central in the reform of national education, a reform that, for the first time in history, took into account the multiculturalism and plurilingualism of the population.

Seen from the lens of internal colonialism and historical exclusion, such reforms represented an important change, a new "politics of recognition," to recall Coulthard's critique and phrase.[87] However, regardless of the modifications, the uninational structure of state remained, as did the colonial relationship of state-Indigenous peoples, now further exacerbated by the multicultural logic of global capitalism and its neoliberal project. During Goni's first and second terms, economic reforms and policies put more than 50 percent of national capital in private hands.

Some have referred to this period and experience as Katarism's pluri-multi face; a Katarism co-opted, captured, and watered down. However, a different reading puts the Katarist Cárdenas, and not the movement, at the center. From this perspective, the inclusion of Cárdenas was both individual and representative. That is to say, it activated a politics of individual inclusion based on ethnic difference, and, at the same time, it orchestrated what I have described elsewhere as a "representative inclusion" in which Cárdenas was assumed to represent the Katarist movement and all Aymaras and Indigenous peoples.[88] Here the strategies of multicultural co-optation, capture, and capital were clear: use Cárdenas to bring Indigenous peoples into global capitalism and its neoliberal project and, at the same time, pacify movement-based opposition. These strategies were component parts of the World Bank's policy on Indigenous peoples begun in 1990 shortly after the massive uprising of Ecuador's Indigenous movement, as I will later explain. Cárdenas was useful in this sense not only in Bolivia but also more broadly in the Andean region. I recall his frequent visits to Ecuador in this period sponsored by both government and multilateral institutions, in which he also met with leaders of the Confederation of Indigenous Nationalities of Ecuador (CONAIE) and other Indigenous organizations. As an Aymara intellectual, Cárdenas was well respected; his role in a neoliberal government, however, was part of the larger debate among Indigenous leaders about participation in the state and about the ties between state and growing transnational interests.

There is much that could be said about the Katarist Cárdenas in the Bolivian state. Suffice it to say that this period resurrected the problem debated by Katarist factions in the late 1970s; that is, the vindication of a political strategy of "inside and against" versus the Indianist-centered posture of "outside and against" the colonial nation and state. Cárdenas represented the strategy of "inside." The posture of the "outside" in the decade of the 1990s and into the twenty-first century did not disappear; its agency and critique grew.

THE RECONSTITUTION OF AUTONOMY AND SELF-DETERMINATION

While neoliberalism was taking hold in government, movements, mobilizations, actions, and alliances against the neoliberal project and for an otherwise of existence were taking form "below." The 1990 March for Territory and Dignity and subsequent marches throughout the 1990s brought together Native peoples in the struggle for autonomy and self-determination, laying the ground for subsequent alliances between the highland-based National Council of Ayllus and Markas of Qullasuyu and the Confederation of Indigenous Peoples of Eastern Bolivia, the organization of lowland Indigenous peoples.

With the national council's formation in 1997, the project of reconstitution of the *ayllu* begun at the local level now had an institutional base. One of its aims was to transform the uninational state into a radically distinct proposition and project of state—a plurinational state—thought not from the modern colonial state but from the knowledge and ancestral experience of Andean community-based governance and organization.

In broad terms, the reconstitution of the *ayllu* meant a repositioning of Native authorities; a rebuilding of organizational, political, and social forms of communal relation and governance; a reconstruction of Indigenous thought; and the "renovation of Bolivia."[89] As Marcelo Fernández Osco, one of the founding members of the Aymara Oral History Workshop, argues, the reconstitution and strengthening of the *ayllu* were "part of the process of the organizational decolonization of Bolivian society, for the construction of new types of social subjects, more organic and effective in their appeal with the Bolivian State; it was a 'return to our own,' in order 'to be ourselves again.'"[90] The Aymara Oral History Workshop played an important role in this process.

Ayllu has no equivalent word in English, or in any other western language. This is precisely because its concept and practice come from a distinct logic, cosmology, and ancestral-cultural-existence-based world-sense. For Fernández Osco, "the *ayllu* devised as a 'great cosmic house' in the reading of Pachacuti Yamqui Salcamaygua ([1613] 1995), could be read as poiesis, while reciprocally reconciling thought with matter and time, and the social person, the *jaqi*, with the world. It is a sum of forces and vitalities, the *pachakuti* that contemporary social movements so much wield, whose purpose is not precisely politics in the Aristotelian sense but rather *suma jaqana*, *buen vivir*, or life in plentitude."[91]

In this sense, the process of reconstitution is both productive and propositional. It is a proposal for structural change in governance and in the very notion of state; structural change of the still-colonial society, and structural change in the spheres of territory, life, and existence. It implies the recuperation of the identity of Aymara and Quechua peoples—in essence, their dignity-based re-existence—this as a principal element for the construction of political participation, something the modern/colonial state has never been able, or never wanted, to understand.

For the Aymaran intellectual Yamila Gutiérrez Callisaya, reconstitution signifies an intentional process of recuperation: recuperation of knowledges and production—of textiles, agriculture, seeds, and so on—in which is implied the nexus, connections, and relationality[92] of humans, the cosmos, and other-worlds. It is the recuperation of structures of authority, of governance, education, production, and community, all part of this relationality, and the recuperation of harmony and the interrelationality of life. Together this recuperation "calls up ancestral continuity, but also calls for a more critical look at the structures and practices of relationality, complementarity, and parity, particularly with regards to the agency and role of women in all aspects of the *ayllu* and its reconstitution."[93] Recalled are the discussions of chapter 3.

In the political, epistemic, and existence-based project and practice to reconstitute the *ayllu*, state is not the central referent. The plurinational is signified in and through autonomy in action, including within the structures of authority and the connections they posture and make with other instances of government, including—but not limited to—says Gutiérrez, state government. State not only loses its centrality here; it also loses its top-down agency of authority, control, and structural-institutional organization.

Although the processes (most especially in the 1990s) to reconstitute the *ayllu* were highland based, alliances were fostered with other land- and territory-based struggles and organizations, including in the lowlands. Within these Indigenous alliances, the central concern was how to strengthen Indigenous self-government as democratic, collective, and communal. It was not about political recognition or inclusion within the modern colonial state.

ALLIANCES AGAINST CAPITAL-STATE AND FOR AN OTHERWISE

These alliances, along with others, could be witnessed in the massive popular protests in Cochabamba against the privatization of water in 2000, protests that expanded the critique of state, including to popular sectors. They also took form in the protests led by Felipe Quispe in La Paz that, among other concerns, targeted the anti-Indigenous racism and the conditions of marginalization propagated by the state. With the 2003 "war of gas," triggered by the planned exportation of natural gas to the United States and Mexico via Chile in Goni's second term of government (2001–3), came another set of protests led by El Alto's urban Aymara majority and involving a broad base that included both Indigenous and non-Indigenous middle-class sectors.

The gas and water wars made evident the complicity as well as the transnationalization of capital and state. Goni was forced to resign and, soon after, fled to the United States. Neoliberalism's hegemony began to fissure, opening a radically different social, cultural, and political moment, anti-imperialist and anticolonial in posture, and decolonizing in agenda. It was a moment that took shape and form on the ground, from the peoples, communities, and organizations both urban and rural whose agency, subjectivity, and other-modes of existence and life sense had been historically subalternized, manipulated, or denied.

This moment is significant in and of itself for the shift it marked and the collective processes it engendered in rethinking and remaking Bolivia, the idea of nation, and the structure and practice of state. The otherwise here became not just a focus of struggle but, more importantly, a locus of possibility. Felipe Quispe (popularly referred to as *el Mallku*) came to represent the more radical Indian-centered perspective, and Evo Morales and the Movimiento al Socialismo (Movement for Socialism) became the central actors of a broader-based coalition of rural and urban Indigenous peoples, peasants, coca growers, miners, youths, and activist intellectuals. However, the postures, while different, moved beyond the simple binary opposition of inside and outside. Rather, they seemed to construct—at least at the outset—a more fluid and relational tension and dialectic of "outside-inside-against," a construction that denotes a continuous flow, filtration, and articulation of agency and subject positions.

Recalled is my discussion in chapter 2 of work outside and inside educational institutions, which at times implies using the system against the system.

In 2006 the Pacto de Unidad (Pact of Unity), a national alliance of grassroots organizations, gave thought and substance to the idea and possibility of the refounding of the Bolivian state.[94] The pact was an important player in the beginning years of the Morales government and a central actor in the Constitutional Assembly (2006–8) and the drafting of the new political charter (later weakened and "watered down" by the political party–based Congress). While the details of the collective and alliance-based processes of rethinking/refounding Bolivia are much too complex to present here,[95] a brief mention of the ways the plurinational was conceived in these processes of making the new constitution is useful, particularly for understanding its nexus with autonomy, decolonization, and self-determination, as well as its proposition of an otherwise.

Raúl Prada, one of the assembly members, described in 2007 three important contributions toward the idea and practice of the plurinational. First, the plurinational is a conception of the emergence of nations from a decolonizing perspective. Second, it is communitarian in the sense that it brings together certain collective communitarian institutions and gives credence to these other-institutional forms. Third, it positions autonomy and autonomous forms as an advanced modality of political administrative decentralization.[96]

For Fernando Garcés, Ecuadorian intellectual-activist and then Bolivian resident involved with the Pact of Unity, plurality and articulation were the pact's central postulates and strategic aims. In this sense, the term *plurinational state* refers both to the plurality of nations and the plurality of the nation, he explained. On the one hand, the plurinational permits an articulation and a legality of distinct nations within the state, and, on the other, it permits channels of expression of cultural diversity within the Bolivian nation; hence, Indigenous autonomies and intercultural autonomies.[97]

In its collective conceptualization, the plurinational questioned the structural bases of domination, advocated for an integral transformation of the colonial model of nation-state, and called for the construction of an intercultural society as a necessary component of the work toward plurinationalization and decolonization, understanding all three as intertwined. State itself was not the aim. With the officialization of the Constitution, however, it necessarily became the project; here within, the problem so began. Suffice it to say that in the almost twelve-year reign of the Morales government, the problem of state remained. Although the recognition and naming of the "Plurinational State of Bolivia" had a strong discursive adhesion among the Indigenous majority and progressive sectors, including in the international sphere, government policy and practice did little—or at least not enough—to undo the structural foundations of the nation-state and the racism that plagued it from its beginnings. The undoing was, rather, on the ground; there the historical reality and ongoing proposition and praxis of the plurinational—in terms of social organization, self-determining authority and autonomy, and communal practice—continued its advance, pushing decolonization from below, this time from nations, communities, and peoples who, for the first time in over five hundred years, saw their agency and project as integral to the shared intercultural making of the plurination.[98]

Let's now turn to Ecuador, where plurinationality, interculturality, and decolonization are also intimately woven.

Ecuador: Plurinationality, Interculturality, and the Project of the Plurinational State

From the four *suyus*—the four directions that make up Andean social and cosmological organization (understood in western terms as east, west, north, and south), the *churros* (ancestral conch shells) and *cachos* (bulls' horns) sounded. Their resonance roused and convoked. Thousands of Kichwa women, men, and children responded to the call, emerging from the highland communities, from the peaks, valleys, and foothills of Ecuador's countryside. With the echo of the *churros* and *cachos*, and the accompaniment of the force of Pachamama, they began the long march to Quito, blocking highways and all access to the capital city.

This was the June 1990 Inti Raymi (Sun Festival–Summer Solstice) uprising, a contemporary emergence, resurgence, and insurgence of Indigenous peoples that shook this country, turned the imaginary of a white-mestizo nation on its head, and forever changed the contemporary political landscape of Ecuador, the Andean region, and the Abya Yala of the South. From then on, "Indians" could no longer be categorized as simply rural peasants or peon laborers in haciendas, towns, and urban centers. They were political actors and a powerful social movement with which government, national society, and state had to contend.

From the cathedral in Quito's historic center, the logistic epicenter of the uprising, CONAIE presented its sixteen-point document of demands to the then government. It defined a program for Indigenous control over Indigenous affairs and summarized an agenda for redefining the role of Indigenous peoples in society. Included were issues of culture and knowledge (bilingual education, traditional medicine), economic concerns (debts, credit, development), and political demands (community governance and control, and the constitutional recognition of a plurinational and intercultural state). This last demand became, from then on, a central organizing component of Ecuador's Indigenous movement, a demand finally met with the 2008 constitution.[99]

Of course, Indigenous agency and struggle in Ecuador did not begin with this uprising or list of demands. It traversed centuries, including the centuries before so-called independence and colonial Spanish rule, a struggle also waged against Incan imperialism and imposition. The contemporary formation of a countrywide movement is, however, more recent. Its roots can be traced to the last half of the twentieth century, to the first highland Indigenous organization (the Ecuadorian Indigenous Federation), formed in the 1940s and led by Dolores Cacuango, and most especially to the conjunction of voices and forces that came together in 1984 to form the first national organization: the Coordinadora de Nacionalidades Indígenas del Ecuador (Coordinating Council of Indigenous Nationalities of Ecuador; CONACNIE). In 1986 CONACNIE became CONAIE. As the historic Kichwa leader, lawyer, and intellectual Luis Macas recalls, "From the beginning, the insurgency of thought was rebelling.... Part of the birth of unity of voice and force, came from our identification as nationalities, our demand to break the liberal state, and our making of the plurinational option into a great *minga*, a collective work effort."[100]

(PLURI)NATIONALITY AS SELF-RECOGNITION

In Ecuador, the proposition of the plurinational began in the Amazon. The Confederación de Nacionalidades Indígenas de la Amazonia Ecuatoriana (Confederation of Indigenous Nationalities of the Ecuadorian Amazon; CONFENAIE), formed in 1980, was the first organization to reference Indigenous nationalities (i.e., nations). With a focus on territorial autonomy and self-government, the defense of languages and cultural traditions, and the political articulation of the diverse Indigenous nationalities of the Amazonian region, CONFENAIE gave both practice and base to the idea of the plurinational and, relatedly, to the political urgency of unity and intercultural relation among Indigenous nationalities or nations. The project here had no direct relation to state. On the contrary, it was for self-determining authority and autonomy, against the state that for decades had enabled the invasion of and the incursion into the Amazon for national and transnational profit. Here, oil exploration and extraction, lumber-based deforestation, and missionary "civilization and salvation" were allies with and of state in the shared endeavors of extermination and dispossession.[101] While the Shuar Federation in the Amazon and the highland Indigenous organization of Kichwa peoples, ECUARUNARI (Ecuador Runacunapac Riccharimui), had, since 1963 and 1972 respectively, opened debates on the importance of Indigenous identities within the construct of "national" society, it was CONFENAIE's conceptualization and identification of Indigenous nationalities that served as the milestone.

Shortly after CONFENAIE introduced the idea of nationalities, CONAC-NIE took form as a countrywide articulator of Native peoples self-recognized as nationalities. The council's president, Ampam Karakas (an Amazonian Shuar), described it this way: "We, the Indian organizations, the Indian peoples, want to give ourselves our own names, maintain our identity, our personality. And to the extent that we want to encompass the different Indian peoples, whatever their historical development, and in the face of this dilemma, we have opted for the term 'Indigenous nationalities.' This resolution is not due to an outside suggestion, it is because we understand that the category 'nationality' expresses the economic, political, cultural, linguistic aspects of our peoples. It places us in national and international life."[102]

In 1986 CONACNIE convoked its first nationwide assembly, in which CONAIE was formed. Here the movement toward a "confederation of nationalities" was key, a sign, says the Kichwa leader Humberto Cholango, "that Indigenous peoples and nationalities are different from the rest of the population, constituted by an organic political structure, territory, language, community systems of organization, and [millennial] uses and customs that remain in force."[103]

While the plurinational continued to define both the territory-based processes of organization and life in the Amazon (where ten nationalities coexist) and the praxis of CONAIE's confederation, it became—with the 1990 uprising—the center of CONAIE's political project and transformational proposition with regard to nation and state. Fundamental here was the relation that CONAIE constructed between plurinationality and interculturality.

_____

THE PLURINATIONAL-INTERCULTURAL CONNECTION

In the mid-1980s, the idea of interculturality began to take form as an organizing component of CONAIE's emergent sociopolitical project. While the term *intercultural* was not new—its use in Latin American began in 1982 as a referent and descriptor of education programs for Indigenous students—interculturality as conceived, postured, and constructed by the Indigenous movement was new in that it surpassed the sole idea of cultural relation. For horizontal cultural relations to exist, it is necessary to first create conditions of equality and equity from difference, the movement said, which requires the building of a radically distinct economic, social, political, and cultural order. Interculturality, in this sense, was understood as a political process, practice, and project aimed at structural and institutional transformation. As an Ecuadorian social activist once said, "Interculturality is simply the possibility of life, of an alternative life-project that profoundly questions the instrumental irrational logic of capitalism in these times."[104]

In CONAIE's historical political project disseminated and published in different versions throughout the 1990s, the sense of interculturality as a decolonizing proposition began to take form. This political project named interculturality as one of nine ideological and organizing principles directly tied to the idea of a plurinational state: "The principle of interculturality respects the diversity of Indigenous nationalities and peoples as well as Ecuadorians from other social sectors. But, at the same time, it demands the unity of these in the economic, social, cultural, and political fields, with eyes towards transforming the present structures and building a new plurinational state, in the frame of equality of rights, mutual respect, peace, and harmony among nationalities and peoples."[105]

Throughout the 1990s and up until the Ecuadorian Constitutional Assembly of 2007–8, the principle of interculturality guided the demands, actions, and proposals of the Indigenous movement directed, in large part, and as we will see later, at rethinking, undoing, and refounding state. These demands, actions, and proposals established the sociopolitical significance and foundation of interculturality. The argument was clear: the difference of Indigenous peoples is not just cultural but also historical, political, economic, and knowledge and existence based; that is, at the same time colonial. The struggles and transformations as such had to be structural, the movement said, decolonizing in project and nature, and aimed at the creation and construction of a social project of political authority and of life, a project with justice, equity, dignity, and solidarity. The demands and proposals called for profound changes in the economic, social, judicial, political, and educational spheres aimed at the construction of a plurinational and intercultural society in which Indigenous and other historically excluded cultures, peoples, and knowledges would be considered constitutive. "The proposal of interculturality for us is profound," argued Macas in 2004, "in that it touches the essence of dominant power and the economic system in force."[106]

As a concept situated in and thought from an Indigenous movement and from the prospective perspective of transformation-based struggle, interculturality's significance is often difficult to grasp in the Global North and in the "Latin" America that continues to think from a western-centric, white, and whitening paradigm. In part, this is because interculturality transgresses the domain of academia that presumes to hold the patent on concepts and the ownership over the theoretical activity of conceptualization. Recalled here is the argument of Leanne Betasamosake Simpson about the generation of concepts and theory from the ground up. The embodied thought, practice, and struggle of Indigenous communities, organizations, and movements counters the tenets of academia in which theory is by nature decontextualized knowledge and the activity of "academics."[107]

Moreover, the idea that an Indigenous movement can put forth concepts, guiding principles, and political projects for society in its totality challenges the very precepts of modernity/coloniality. In this sense, both interculturality and plurinationality defy the political-intellectual project of the white-mestizo nation. But they also defy the hegemonic authority of much of the so-called Left that, in Latin America specifically and the world in general, continues to critique the postures and processes of social movements that it cannot control, co-opt, or capture.

Furthermore, the interculturality postured by CONAIE disobeys multiculturalism's logic. Neither the liberal precepts of diversity, equality, and individual rights nor the neoliberal project of inclusion is at its core. Its base instead is in the sensing and constructing of a different philosophical, civilizational, and life-based project grounded in the collectively conceived principles of interdependence, complementarity, and relation, principles ever more relevant in a world reigned by stark individualism, global capitalism, and the elimination of all that gets in its way.

This concept, of course, differs from that employed by multilateral institutions, international nongovernmental organizations, and Latin American states. The fact that the term *interculturality* entered into the vocabulary and politics of these institutions in the early 1990s is, of course, not coincidental. At the same time that Ecuador's Indigenous movement emerged as a plurinational and regional force with a serious critique of the structures and institutions of society and state, the multilateral development banks began to take interest in Indigenous peoples and in the concept of interculturality.

The World Bank's 1991 operational policy directive 4.20, "Indigenous Peoples," is one of the clearest examples. This policy served as a model and guide for the creation of regional policies that would promote the participation of Indigenous peoples in plans, projects, and programs of state members, thus ensuring neoliberalism's advance. By offering "concrete opportunities for the interaction between Indigenous peoples and World Bank and government officials,"[108] the policy aimed to quash Indigenous resistance, weaken organizations, and foster a functional version of interculturality that would bring the "Natives" into the fold. In this and other World Bank–guided public policies—including those that supported the multiculturalist constitutional reforms of the 1990s in the region—interculturality was neither transformative nor critical of the established social, political, and economic order. Instead, it was functional to this order.

"Functional interculturality" recognizes ethnic and cultural diversity in order to include this diversity within the established social structure. Interculturality here does not touch the causes of asymmetry and social and cultural inequality or question the state, its institutions, and its structures; it plays by and to the "rules of the game." In this sense, it is perfectly compatible with the neoliberal model and the multicultural logic of global capitalism, a model-logic that, while recognizing difference, sustains its production and administration within the national order. Difference is thus neutralized, emptied of all effective meaning, and made to be functional to this order, to the dictates of the capitalist and modern/colonial matrix of power, and to the expansion of neoliberalism and the market.

This "functional interculturality" draws from what Raimon Panikkar describes as multiculturalism's still-colonialist syndrome of cultural superiority and benign and condescending hospitality, and it extends its project.[109] Through individual inclusion, the facade of dialogue, and the discourse of citizenship, functional interculturality constitutes a more complex mode of domination that captures, co-opts, pacifies, demobilizes, and divides movements,

collectives, and leaders; impels individualism, complacency, and indifference; and shrouds the structural and increasingly compound convolution of
capitalism and coloniality. The fact that this utilitarian signification, practice, and use of interculturality followed, and in some cases paralleled, the
Indigenous-defined principle, project, and proposition is, of course, by no
means fortuitous; it is part and parcel of the prevailing and modernizing
politics of capture, catchment, and co-optation[110] that has characterized the
region since the decade of the 1990s and the emergence with force in contemporary times of Indigenous peoples' political, epistemic, and existence-
based insurgency and struggle.

The decolonizing interculturality postured by CONAIE is a component
part of this political, epistemic, and existence-based insurgency and struggle. Its conceptualization makes visible lived legacies and long horizons of
domination, oppression, exclusion, and colonial difference, and the manifestations of these legacies in social structures and institutions.[111] Its project
calls for radical change in the dominant order and in its foundational base of
capitalism, western modernity, and ongoing colonial power, while its practice
works to create and construct radically distinct possibilities and conditions
of coexistence and correlation within, between, and among logics, frameworks,
and senses of being, thinking, knowing, and living. Included here is the work to
undo the singular, universal, and universalizing notions and projects of nation,
society, and state, as well as of western-centric knowledge. In this sense, the
idea of the national, as Indigenous leaders and movements argue, must also be
transformed in ways that enable and stress the plurinational, this understood
not as division but as a more adequate pluriversal or interversal form of articulation and integration. It is in this way that the projects and processes of
interculturality and plurinationality are integrally related.

THE INDIGENOUS PROPOSITION OF A PLURINATIONAL STATE

The movement's idea of a plurinational state evolved in meaning and form
over several decades, during which CONAIE publicly presented the proposal
four times. These four political moments help reveal the context of Indigenous insurgence in Ecuador, and the developing strategy and substance of
the Indigenous-conceived plurinational and intercultural project.

The first political moment was in the massive 1990 Indigenous uprising
mentioned earlier, in which CONAIE included plurinationality (*plurinacionalidad*) in its list of sixteen demands to the Ecuadorian government.[112]
Among these demands was that of the recognition of Indigenous peoples

in conditions equal to those given to the nation or "nationality" of white-mestizos. Here CONAIE made clear the meaning of *nationality*: historical and political entities that have a common identity, history, language, and culture, and a common territory in which they have exercised traditional forms of social, economic, judicial, and political organization and authority. In 1990 CONAIE identified twelve different Indigenous nationalities in Ecuador; today it names fourteen Indigenous nationalities and eighteen Indigenous peoples.[113] The demand of recognition of the plurinational character of the country, state, and nation logically followed. While government did not formally accept the demand, it marked an important milestone in the heretofore colonial history of the society and nation; from this moment on, the Indigenous presence, organization, and sociopolitical agency could be neither negated nor denied.

The second moment of public discussion about the plurinational occurred in the context of the 1997–98 National Constitutional Assembly and the popular assemblies that preceded it. In contrast to almost ten years before when the demand had its base in a posture of resistance, insurgence, and opposition to the dominant frames of nation and state, here the plurinational arose in the context of local and national politics. In 1996, after much internal debate, the movement decided to enter the political-legislative sphere. With the formation of Pachakutik, conceived not as a political party but as an alliance between the Indigenous movement and other historically oppressed sectors—a rainbow coalition of sorts—the political arm of CONAIE took form.

After only several weeks of campaign, Pachakutik won seventy-five seats in the 1996 local and legislative elections, a majority of which went to Indigenous men and women. Pachakutik's then agenda was transformation from the bottom up; that is, change at the local levels of municipal governments with eyes toward constitutional reforms and the building on the ground and step by step of a radically different state institution and structure. In the debates opened by Pachakutik and CONAIE at the local level, in communities, and with other social and cultural sectors, and in the emergent experiences of local government practice, the idea of a plurinational state began to take hold. The central argument: that the building of this new state required a broad-based collaboration and communication between diverse groups, organizations, and social sectors from the ground up in order to re-form, interculturalize, and plurinationalize government structures and institutions. The aim and project were the building and articulation of a social, political, and ethical decolonizing project thought not just for Indigenous peoples but, more broadly, for society at large. In the early 2000s and during a period of approximately five years, I had the experience of being part of this process in the canton of Cotacachi. At the invitation of the Indigenous mayor's office, we—myself and a group of my graduate students organized into what we referred to as the Intercultural Workshop—worked collaboratively with the local government and local Indigenous, Afro, and mestizo urban and rural communities in a project aimed to build interculturality in and through participatory policy and practice.

This second moment was distinct from that of 1990. Now the initiative, while primarily Indian led, was no longer just Indian centered. It was made up of historically oppressed groups in a rainbow coalition of sorts including, in addition to the Indigenous movement, Afro-Ecuadorians, women's movements, and environmental activists, among others. It was directed at all of society with the aim of contributing to "the construction of an alternative civilizatory proposal, a new type of state, and a deepening of democracy."[114]

Together, plurinationality and interculturality were central axes, processes, and projects of both the social and political movements and their shared insurgent struggle. In the proposal to the 1997–98 National Constitutional Assembly, CONAIE made clear its posture of interculturality as a central principle in the construction of all aspects of a plurinational state: "In order for the new Constitution to be a real and faithful reflection of the country's reality and for it to truly respond to the principles of a real democracy, it is essential to lay the groundwork of a pluricultural society. As such, the principle of interculturality needs to constitute the backbone of structural and super-structural reforms, that is, in both their form and content. To not do this, each reform will continue to exclude and disavow diversity, our own existence as Indigenous nationalities and peoples, and our coexistence with others."[115]

Despite the arguments presented, the National Assembly voted down the plurinational proposal with the argument that it would divide and fragment *the nation*. Still, there were advances in terms of the reforms achieved, including the formal recognition of Indigenous peoples self-identified as nationalities, and the formal recognition (for the first time in Ecuador's history) of Black or Afro-Ecuadorian peoples. Also recognized were fifteen collective rights. The recognitions and reforms, however, left the monocultural and uninational state intact.

"Although we lost in the proposal to decolonize the state and name the state as plurinational," said Luis Macas, "what we did attain was the recognition of the distance between Ecuadorian citizenship and the pre-existence of Indigenous nationalities."[116] Such recognition was central in that it marked the difference between citizenship as a status and right of all Ecuadorians, and nationality as Native-origin peoples with collective forms of identity that predate state. As Macas explained, "Citizenship is not what we are struggling for or defending.... To think that we are not Indigenous peoples but citizens, is to individualize communities and peoples, to ignore the concepts of reciprocity, complementarity, and solidarity, ignoring as well the internal rights of each people." Moreover, as he argued, "in our communities, we resolve things collectively and this is what we should continue to do. Citizenship is the relation of the state with the individual. It does not consider nationalities, collective peoples, or future generations. This relation deepens individualism."[117]

For Macas, difference is what gives ground to the prospect, debate, and entwinement of plurinationality and interculturality. "The struggle for plurinationality means recognizing us first as Indigenous nations," Macas contends, "and it means recognizing the other and crossing cultural borders. Plurinationality is our contribution—an Indigenous contribution—for the emancipation of our countries of Abya Yala, of our plural and diverse America."[118] The recognition here is not just of cultural diversity but, more critically, of the diversity of nations, a diversity that acknowledges and admits lived difference (historical, cultural, and colonial). Interculturality, as a linked and complementary Indigenous proposal and contribution, departs from, engages, and respects this difference, including the difference that underlines collective identities and communal and community-based systems of living, systems incompatible with the capitalist system that drives the dominant structure and project of state. Although the 1998 constitution did not take seriously the demand for a plurinational state, it did begin to take into account the difference of ancestral nations and peoples, as well as the collective rights that such ancestral difference marks. For Macas, this was an advance in the struggle.

However, the problem is that this constitutional recognition also represented and advanced the multicultural logic of neoliberalism and transnational capitalism, including the multicultural constitutionalism of which this logic is part. With this constitution, policies and politics of privatization began to take hold, and the exploitation of natural resources—located primarily in Indigenous and Afro-Ecuadorian communities' lands—grew in leaps and bounds. The bottom-up proposal of plurinationality lost to neoliberalism's top-down regional and global project, and interculturality (in the hands of state) began to lose its critical edge, becoming functional to the national/transnational agenda and project.

The third moment of public discussion and debate was in 2003, in the context of the so-called Indigenous-military alliance government of Lucio

Gutiérrez. In the short eight months of this alliance, during which historical Indigenous leaders held high posts (including Macas as minister of agriculture and the Kichwa intellectual and lawyer Nina Pacari as minister of foreign relations), CONAIE and Pachakutik once again put on the table their shared mission to construct a more just society and an intercultural and plurinational state. "A new alliance cannot be simply of electoral character; it must consolidate itself in and through both work and a political vision," said CONAIE in its "Political Mandate for a Plan of National Government." "The actions presented in this mandate are not about quotas, favors, or royalties for Indigenous peoples and nationalities. They constitute legitimately achieved rights of Ecuadorian peoples. The construction of a plurinational state and society is a socio-historic necessity."[119]

In this document, CONAIE developed further its conceptualization of a plurinational state, including the priorities and areas of action of this state in the political, economic, and social spheres. It argued that the plurinational state guards essential principles such as self-determination, interculturality, and plurinational democracy, the last understood as a bottom-up process with the participation of all peoples and grounded in different levels of administration, planning, and decision-making. Interculturality is described here as a process based in the rights of peaceful coexistence and of recognition and mutual respect among all nationalities, peoples, and social sectors. It is a process in which the state becomes a social, political, and judicial guarantor of a different social project that seeks a coexistence in an equality of rights, social justice, and conditions of peace and harmony.

If we compare this proposal with the former ones, we can begin to see how Indigenous leaders were trying to push a process of transition. In CONAIE's 1997 version of its own internal "Political Project," the organization described interculturality as one of nine central ideological principles that constitute and drive this organization's political project and the construction of "a new democracy, . . . anti-colonial, anti-capitalist, anti-imperialist, and anti-segregationist," that guarantees the "maximum and permanent participation of Indigenous peoples and nationalities in decision-making and the exercise of political power in the plurinational state."[120] In 2003 the proposal was to move toward an alternative paradigm of state: "From the capitalist, bourgeois and exclusive state, toward an inclusive Plurinational State that socially, economically, politically, judicially, and culturally integrates all sectors of the country. This is a step," said CONAIE, "from dominant power's classist and elitist State, toward a Plurinational State constituted by all the social sectors that exist in Ecuador, and with representation and power. The maximum goal of the Plurinational State is to gradually resolve the inherited social ills, such as: illiteracy, poverty, unemployment, racism, incipient production, etc., until satisfying the basic material, spiritual, and cultural necessities ... guaranteeing the exercise of individual and collective rights."[121]

However, and as occurred in other moments of public proposal, the idea of the plurinational state was once again rejected. This was because the so-called alliance government lasted only eight months. But it was also because the majority society still considered it a divisionary Indian-centered project. In the short time that members of the Indigenous movement occupied high-up government posts, racism reached new realms. Dominant white-mestizo society refused to accept the Indigenous presence, questioned the capacity of Indigenous men and women to govern, and negated their ability (as Indians and members of a social-political-ethnic movement) to represent the interests of the dominant, white-mestizo nation. The fact that these leaders-intellectuals publicly defined and described their presence not as individuals or citizens but as part of a historical collectivity of community, nation/nationality, and movement was understood by dominant sectors as a signal in and of itself that their presence, interest, and action could only have as their goals retaliation and revenge against whites and white-mestizos.

The racialization of society in these months became more intense, spurred on by the press and by the publication of the results of an obviously manipulated national census that identified 85 percent of the country as mestizo and only 7 percent Indigenous (in contrast to previous estimates of up to 40 percent). Intellectuals and journalists of both the Right and Left began to refer to "our mestizo nation." A daily tabloid put in gigantic letters on its front page, "*Indios* Go Home." Newspaper editorials and television and radio commentaries began to once again cite the country's foundational thinkers and name the political and epistemic project of *mestizaje* as the core of *the* nation, the state, and national unification.

Of course, it was not the proposed project of plurinationality in and of itself that sparked racism and racial division. More precisely, it was the fear intentionally planted in the non-Indigenous populace, a fear that Indigenous leaders would seek ethnic retribution.[122] In the mind of this populace, the plurinational state signaled the reckoning and was part of the payback.

Suffice it to say that 2003 was a devastating year for the movement. The so-called alliance government led to serious divisions within the movement itself, most especially between urban and rural organizations, the latter of which had questioned from the outset the movement's presence "inside" state. Pachakutik's collective decision to leave government in August 2003 happened too late. The movement had already lost its previous insurgent agency and force.[123]

In 2007 CONAIE launched for the fourth time the proposal of a plurinational state, this time in the days when the National Constitutional Assembly was about to begin. In contrast to the 1997–98 assembly, which was conceived within the frame of neoliberal government and made up of politicians and traditional political parties, this assembly brought together representatives from all social sectors. It was conceived as a refounding of state, in then-president Rafael Correa's words "an ending of the long neoliberal night," and the building .of inclusive and participatory processes toward a new society and twenty-first century socialism.

The press release that accompanied CONAIE's proposal entitled "The Constitution of the Plurinational State of Ecuador's Republic" maintained that "this is the precise historical moment for Indigenous nationalities and peoples and other social sectors of the country to make a structural, political, and judicial change in the Ecuadorian State. From 1830 to the present, 19 Constitutions have been drawn up without the full participation of Indigenous nationalities and peoples; they have constituted the powers of the state as a result of and within the frame of a dominant colonial regime." It went on to argue, "We need to build a different state, a Plurinational State in order to eradicate the regionalism and exclusion to which we have been subject by an imposed pyramidal state and its form of exclusive, authoritarian, and repressive government. . . . A Plurinational State, pluricultural and of direct, participatory democracy, as a new model of political organization for the decolonization of our nations and peoples and to make reality the principle of a country with unity in diversity and social equality."[124]

CONAIE's proposal of principles and guidelines to the 2007–8 Constitutional Assembly described the plurinational state as "a model of political organization for the decolonization of our nations and peoples, a model that seeks to cast away forever the colonial and monocultural shadows that have accompanied us for the last more than 200 years."[125] Here the idea of plurinationality went beyond state. More broadly, it pointed to and called forth the project of decolonization, that which, as we previously saw, also oriented Bolivian processes and perspectives.

Distinct from the uninational state that only represents dominant sectors, the plurinational state, as conceived in the 2007 proposal, "recognizes, respects, and promotes the unity, equality, and solidarity among all of Ecuador's nationalities and peoples, regardless of their historical, political, and cultural differences, and in order to guarantee a dignified life, economically just and balanced, and socially intercultural and inclusive."[126] The proposal called for a reordering of political, administrative, economic, and legal structures, and for recognition of the legitimate claim and right of Indigenous and ancestral peoples to determine their own processes of economic, social, cultural, scientific, and technological development. It referenced an organization that could represent the union of the political, economic, and social power of all peoples and nationalities under the same government and directed by a constitution. And it highlighted the necessity of a "plurinational system of state, ... for the well-being of the populace and not the economic profitability of the market."[127]

This proposal, clearly more developed than the others previously mentioned, emphasized five areas of intervention synthesized as follows:

- POLITICS: The declaration of the plurinational character of the state, the recognition of community-based governments as a form of historical-legal-political organization, and the renaming of the National Congress as the Plurinational Legislative Assembly, with direct representation of Indigenous and Afro-Ecuadorian peoples

- ECONOMICS: The establishment of a socially responsible, ecological, equitable, and communitarian economic model that protects and guarantees collective and communitarian property and food sovereignty; propitiates the nationalization of natural resources; affords legislation with relation to water, lands, and territories; and emphasizes collective well-being: *sumak kawsay* (in Kichwa) or *buen vivir* (in Spanish), roughly translated as "life in plentitude"

- SOCIAL INSTITUTIONS: The guarantee of access to a national system of intercultural and bilingual education for all and, as an ancestral right, a system of Indigenous-centered bilingual intercultural education; a system of traditional medicine (Indigenous and Afro-Ecuadorian) and intercultural health; and the democratization of the media

- INTERNATIONAL RELATIONS: The guarantee of no involvement in international war plans and in government agreements that imply the concession of political-legal sovereignty and of national territory to foreign powers; the protection of migrants in their countries of residence; and the promotion of regional unity in the Andes and South America

- COLLECTIVE RIGHTS: The expansion of collective rights in ways that are compatible with the 2007 UN Declaration on the Rights of

Indigenous Peoples, and the application of these rights with respect to autonomy, self-determination, territory, health, education, and the administration of justice

As can be observed, CONAIE's 2007 proposal offers a series of crucial elements for state undoing, reordering, and rethinking. However, despite its claim that it considers the proposals of other social sectors including women, environmentalists, Black peoples, migrant organizations, LGBTI-identified people, workers, intellectuals, academics, and children and youths, the proposal remained primarily Indigenous centered and Kichwa and highland focused. It glossed over not only the diversity of regions within the country (i.e., the Amazon and coast) but also the diversity of peoples, realities, and struggles. In this sense, the focus on interculturality as plurinationality's complementary pair was, in this proposal, noticeably weakened.

Still, as fundamental axes of Ecuador's Indigenous movement during practically two decades, interculturality and plurinationality have a cumulative conceptualization that remains interwoven. Together they constitute the only articulated framework in Ecuador for undoing the colonial tare and thinking and making a radically distinct society, state, and nation, something that the Left has never been able to accomplish. This is the only case in Abya Yala, and possibly in the world, where an Indigenous-conceived project has filtered into the social psyche and consciousness of other social sectors, enabling the formulation of a constitution considered by many the most radical in the world. Here it was not just the content but also the process that was unique. Instead of political parties (as was the Bolivian case), the Constitutional Assembly was made up of civil society representatives from all social sectors who, over the course of nine months, contemplated, studied, and critically debated the issues at hand. As an adviser to the assembly on the conceptualization of the intercultural and plurinational state and on Afro-Ecuadorian collective rights, I witnessed firsthand the depth of the sociopolitical and pedagogical process led by the assembly's president, Alberto Acosta, and the otherwise of thought it enabled with respect to society, state, and nation. While I entered the process with serious doubts about the possibility of undoing nation-state, the assembly experience suggested that this undoing had already begun. As I wrote in my 2009 book *Interculturalidad, estado, sociedad: Luchas (de)coloniales de nuestra época* (Interculturality, state, society: (De)colonial struggles of our times)—a text that documented the processes that led to, enabled, and made the Ecuadorian and Bolivian constitutions—the very precepts of society, state, and nation seemed to be experiencing decolonializing movement and an otherwise of proposition and thought.[128] The examples within the Ecuadorian political charter are many, including the recognition of Pachamama and the social struggles of liberation against all forms of colonialism and domination; the *thinking with* nonwestern knowledges and systems of life/living including within the educational system and institutions; the recognition and building of the plurality within the nation and the plurality and distinctiveness of nations within the nation; the recognition of the rights of Nature; and the identification of the transversal axis of *buen vivir, sumak kawsay,* or life and living in plentitude, which questions the previous foundational models and practices of state, modernist visions of development, and neoliberal policies focused on individual welfare and consumption.[129]

The Constitution is noteworthy for the "other" conceptualizations, cosmogonies, and philosophies of being, knowledge, existence, and life it makes present, a result of the political, epistemic, and existence-based insurgencies of the Indigenous movement and its actions and agency impelled from the ground up that, since 1990, have worked to denaturalize canonical ways of apprehending-constructing-being in the world and of understanding-constructing-articulating society and state. Yet, as we all know, constitutions in and of themselves are not enough. Moreover, as political charters of state (dependent on state institutions and state interpretation, adoption, and application), constitutions remain in character, proposition, and practice top down. While in the Ecuadorian case (not dissimilar to Bolivia's), the Constitution's content may unsettle unicity, western modernity's singular frame, and neoliberalism's hold—opening the possibility of other-logics and other-paths of coexistence and re-existence—experience shows that it is not the Constitution, laws, or legal rights per se that plurinationalize and interculturalize. Plurinationality and interculturality cannot be mandated; they must be constructed. Neither is a point of arrival. Rather, they suppose ongoing processes and practices of political, epistemic, and existence-based action and actionings that work to confront on a daily basis the continuous regeneration and the constant rearrangement of the colonial matrices of power.

Paths to Ponder
and Questions to Walk

Almost half a century after the debates on plurinationality began in Ecuador, and even more in Bolivia, the questions and problems of society, state, and nation remain. Moreover, and with more than fifteen years of progressive governments in Bolivia (Evo Morales [2006–19] and Luis Arce [2020–present]) and ten years in Ecuador (Rafael Correa in Ecuador [2007–17]) and radically distinct constitutions that recognize the plural character of the nation (the plurination), acknowledge the need to plurinationalize and interculturalize society, and name plurinational and intercultural states, it is ever clearer that state government and governance are not and cannot be the primary aim and principal motor of social transformation. This was evident during Morales's government, and it was even more true during Correa's reign, which outrightly rejected plurinational precepts and processes, functionalized interculturality, and actively worked to dismantle and criminalize social movements. As we have learned in both these contexts, decolonization, plurinationalization, and, in a related sense, interculturalization cannot be legislated, conceived, and practiced as top-down initiatives and, worse yet, coexist with and be supported and funded by capitalist-extractivist economies based not only on the extraction of natural resources but also on the extraction and dispossession of life itself.[130] When they are—as we have learned in both countries—they become part and parcel of the same matrix of power that, despite progressive or Leftist identifications, enables global capitalism, patriarchy, and coloniality to flourish and continue.

While the struggles against extractivism and for land-territory as life persist, they have been complicated further by the interrelated processes of state denationalization and corporatization, all tied (including in the Morales and Correa governments) to the interests, control, and accumulation of global capital. While the partners may change (China instead of the United States, for instance), the impact and project still stand. Of course, in this context we can ask whether the otherwise is not about the ongoing resurgence and insurgence to resist and persist, to negate the mode of existence and the practice-project-pandemic of de-existence that the coloniality of power in its present-day reconfigurations fosters, sanctions, and enables.

As I have endeavored to show here, the propositions of and for the plurinational as conceived and constructed by Indigenous movements in the Andes have not been about reforming state, expanding the politics of recognition, or offering state to the stateless. Nor have they been about pluralizations of the existent state and nation, although some Indigenous leaders continue to defend this route through electoral political-party politics. They have been about undoing nation-state in concept, principle, practice, and foundation.

While the questions present in decades past of inside or outside, despite or against state, or, as some contend, maybe all at the same time, have not disappeared, today there is a growing sentiment among many, not only in Abya Yala but around the world, of the need to disrupt the centricity of state as the marker, controller, and determinant of existence and life. I think of the practices of the Kurdish women's movement to build radically distinct— and women-led—forms of social organization, education, health, governance, and community life in Rojava, Syria, to create a women-centered society without state; what Alessia Dro, activist of the Kurdish women's movement, describes as a plurinational women-led confederal Kurdistan, against capitalism, patriarchy, and state and for the liberation of women as the social and societal liberation of all.[131] Moreover, and as another activist of the movement, Dilar Dirik, contends, this struggle is not just about Kurds. "Kurdish people and in particular Kurdish women embody the multi-layered oppression of many peoples who have been subjected to various forms of colonialism. Not only have the Kurds expressed their solidarity and support for many other stateless struggles in the world, but their own extreme oppression and resistance appeals to colonized and oppressed people all over the world in an almost universal sense." The Rojava revolution is unique in many aspects, Dirik argues. "It already had a solid ideological base, . . . was built on the ideas of democratic confederalism, self-sustainability, self-governance, autonomy, true independence: not through the state, but in the sense of living without approval; . . . of establishing something in spite of the oppressive dominant system and its attacks."[132] Is this "living without approval" and creation "in spite of" the system not evidence of the cracks, I ask, and of the undoing of nation-state in motion?

I think as well of the autonomy-based experiences of hundreds of Zapatista communities in Chiapas, Mexico, against, in spite of, despite, and outside what they refer to as the "bad government" that is state. While this lived autonomy of and among diverse Indigenous peoples has not been without intense struggle and continual creative invention and reinvention, it too is evidence of stateless praxis and coloniality's cracks.

And I think of the community-based social reorganizations taking place today in urban and rural territories throughout the globe, including—but not only—in response to the endemic statelessness and contemporary enslavement that Jane Anna Gordon describes, and the blatant manifestations of state abandonment and neglect during these present times of COVID-19. As Gordon states, "Contemporary enslavement and statelessness remain uniquely valuable for thinking clearly about the aims of political life, including how we might conceive the relationship between laboring and public standing or belonging."[133]

The questions about how to undo the specter of nation-states—including why, where, with whom, how, and with what practices of fissure, dismantlement, and deconstruction—continue even though, as we know, it is the corporatized, and not the national, state that now occupies and rules. So also continue the questions about the plurinational and its propositions, possibilities, and praxis not just in the Andes but in rural and urban territories-lands throughout the globe where Indigenous, African-origin, and other ancestral nations and peoples struggle against the ongoing and growing dispossession that is colonial permanence-in/as-state.

I recall the six weeks I spent in South Africa in 2018, an experience that dispelled any utopian visions that I may have held of a postapartheid state. As a fellow at the Stellenbosch Institute of Advanced Study, I witnessed the white power of this economically rich wine region and its stark contrast with the surrounding townships, the "residence" of the Black workers who cleaned white houses, businesses, and streets; who labored on white-owned land; and who continued to serve white owner-masters. Although I understand that dismantling apartheid is a long, complex process, the racism and racialized organization that I witnessed each day confirmed that, at least in this region, white supremacy and apartheid still stood. It was Steve Biko's *I Write What I Like* that guided my sensations, learnings, questionings, and thought day after day. And it was Biko's analysis of white racism, unfreedom, and freedom of self-determination that pushed a reading beyond state. One phrase particularly stands out: "The myth of integration as propounded under the banner of liberal ideology must be cracked and killed because it makes people believe that something is being done," Biko said. "Because it is difficult to bring people from different races together in this country, achievement of this is in itself a step forward towards the total liberation of the blacks. Nothing could be more irrelevant and therefore misleading. Those who believe in it are living a fools' paradise," he argued.[134] While Biko's words were published in 1978, they seemed to continue to ring true in 2018, reminding me that while the South African state is a necessary player in apartheid's dismantling, liberation from this structure and its colonial permanence requires an undoing of the nation-state, which, despite the "postapartheid" label, remains in many ways entrenched. The massive student protests of Rhodes Must Fall and Fees Must Fall, along with the land-based and Land Back movements, were evidence, as I learned from conversations with activists and critical intellectuals, of state entrenchment, but also of the force of the disrupting, cracking, and undoing taking place on the ground.

I don't pretend to suggest that the nation-state as we know it can or will simply disappear. I also don't negate the possibilities of using the system against the system, or even working toward transformation from within. The 2021–22 debates in Chile's Constitutional Assembly on the naming and building of a plurinational society and state are one example. Yet, as I believe I have made clear here, my interest and energy, particularly in these current times, are with and toward that which is taking place "below." The plurinational propositions described here are a few examples among many. What are the new or emergent propositions, insurgencies, and resurgencies taking form today in other regions of the world? How are they working to undo nation-state? With what sense, practice, and horizon of dignity, self-determining authority, and existence, re-existence, and inter- and coexistence? And in what ways do these plurinational propositions connect and cross?

The paths to ponder and the questions to walk multiply as I close; they multiply for me and, I suspect, they multiply for you as well. I once again recall the words of Leanne Betasamosake Simpson that opened this chapter, words that seem to echo and manifest the resurgences and insurgences that I have detailed here. Yet, after all these pages, I now read-hear the gist of her words more broadly and clearly as simultaneous rebuke, urgency, and invitation: to "not just dream alternative realities but to create them, on the ground, in the physical world, in spite of being occupied."[135] Is this not what undoing nation-state—in concept, specter, and practice—and summoning plurinational propositions from the land and on the ground are about? That is, creating alternatives that transgress colonial thought and reality, crack coloniality's permanence and hold, and build re-existences and existences otherwise.

Sowing Re-Existences 5

The people have forgotten,
but the seed remembers.
—ROBIN WALL KIMMERER

Sow in order to BE again...
sowings and re-sowings of life.
—ABUELO ZENÓN

I begin this last chapter with the words of Robin Wall Kimmerer, member of the Citizen Potawatomi Nation,[1] and those of Abuelo (Grandfather) Zenón,[2] wise elder and sage of the Afro-Pacific. From their diverse territories and ancestral roots, both teach us about seeds and sowings of existence and re-existences; that is, as Kimmerer says, "if we are willing to learn."[3]

For Kimmerer, the seeds and sowing are of corn, of maize, or *mahiz*, understood as "the bringer of life," the "sacred life giver," the "Mother of All Things," the "Wonderful Seed." This seed is at the center of origin stories of Maya and Potawatomi peoples. It is also part, Kimmerer tells us, of the history of colonization—of invaders who seek to replace original lifeways with their own, taking what they want and attempting to erase the rest—and of slavery, in which "sacred maize is forced to carry genes not their own and enslaved to an industrial purpose."[4]

How we think about seeds, plants, and sowings matters. In the western worldview, says Kimmerer, seeds and plants are thought of as objects, without perception, will, or personhood, and sowing is most often the work of machines. Indigenous ways of knowing are quite different. The seeds are the memory of my ancestors, Kimmerer says. They are a "tangible link to history and identity and cultural continuity in the face of all the forces that sought to erase them." Kimmerer celebrates the life inside each kernel with a song, singing to them while they are in her hand and before putting them in the soil. "Plants are respected as bearers of gifts, as persons, indeed often times as teachers. Who else has the capacity to transform light, air, and water into food and medicine—and then share it?" Kimmerer asks. "Who cares for the people as generously as plants? Creative, wise, and powerful, plants are imbued with spirit in a way that the western worldview reserves only for humans.... The nature of these two ways of understanding the world is written in vivid green ink in our respective cornfields."[5]

Kimmerer's rooted words speak to, from, and with the maize and the seed savers, seed stewards, seed sowers, and seedkeepers. They remind me of the practices that surround the planting of corn in the Andes and the herstorical relation between agricultural productivity and female power. While men traditionally open the ground, women sow the seeds. Yet it is the special autonomous power passed down among some women from generation to generation and related to the spheres of ritual and work— understood as a spirit, androgynous, and *supay* force (see chapter 3)—that evokes a particular relation with respect to cultivation, planting, and seeds. It is this female power that transgresses the gender binary and divide, a female strength, spirit, and sense that is both and neither woman-man and that, in Andean cultural tradition, held the responsibility and role of seedkeeper.[6]

Kimmerer tells us that in the Native traditions she is involved with in upstate New York, the seedkeepers there refer to the process of bringing back the seeds and the respect for them as *rematriation*. She cites seedkeeper Rowen White's explanation: "The word 'rematriation' reflects the restoration of the feminine seeds back into the communities of origin. The Indigenous concept of Rematriation refers to reclaiming of ancestral remains, spirituality, culture, knowledge and resources, instead of the more Patriarchally associated Repatriation. It simply means back to Mother Earth, a return to our origins, to life and co-creation, rather than Patriarchal destruction and colonization, a reclamation of germination, of the life giving force of the Divine Female." They are replanting the sacred, Kimmerer says, and here "they remember the Corn Mother's name." For Kimmerer, "the invitation to decolonize, rematriate, and renew the honorable harvest extends beyond Indigenous nations to everyone who eats. Mother Corn claims us all as corn-children under the husk; her teachings of reciprocity are for all."[7] I remember the similar words that end the video entitled "Semillita: Canto en defensa de la vida" (Little seed: Song in defense of life) made by Indigenous women in Ecuador after the October 2019 rebellion mentioned in chapter 1:

"We are all grains or kernels of the same corn."[8] Moreover, in the ear of the corn or corncob we are united.

Abuelo Zenón is another guardian of the seeds and sower of and for existence, re-existence, and life. As the real and symbolic grandparent-ancestor of the women and men of African origin born in the territory-region of the Colombo-Ecuadorian Pacific, it is Zenón who is said to restore the seeds and plant and cultivate collective memory, ancestral thought, and life. This vital memory-thought is a component part of a praxis of long horizon, without individual owners, and planted in territory as a philosophy, as a principle of faith, as a collective proposal to sustain dignity, being, existence, and life. Here sowing is constitutive, and it is enabling. It is related, says Abuelo Zenón, to the historical struggle to once again *be* after the dehumanization of enslavement and the dehumanizing politics of racialization, negation, and exclusion that have continued since. The seeds planted then and the seeds sown now are seeds that "permit us to be where we have not been, to become where we were not, where our being and existence were and are disavowed."[9] They are seeds of re-existence, and they are seeds of life.

For me, these seeds and this sowing can't be separated from the cries that opened this book and the cracks made, postured, revealed, and widened throughout. Together they interweave in attitude, complicity, and creative zealous movement and struggle to redefine, resignify, and affirm life in conditions of dignity and self-determination, and to make present and walk an otherwise of thinking, knowing, feeling, sensing, being-becoming, existing, and living in the margins and fissures of coloniality's logic, structure, and matrix of power. The practice of sowing is the praxis of cracks. Both are conscious acts and actions of cultivation that open, nurture, tend, and enable germinations, roots, and the rise up of existence, re-existence, hope, and pluriversal possibility in territories, places, and spaces, and for peoples throughout the globe.

How are we to think about the work of sowing re-existence in these present times of violence-dispossession-war-death, and of dehumanizations and de-existences spreading and swelling? How is such sowing taking place, and with what pedagogies-methodologies, practice, and praxis in material, symbolic, epistemic, spiritual, and existential terms? And what are the seeds that birth, propagate, prosper, and breathe life, cracking coloniality and its totalizing semblance and sense? These are the questions that guide my situated reflections here, questions that I ask readers to also consider from their own territories and embodied and situated places and spaces of struggle and life.

Planting Life
Where There Is Death

To plant life where there is death. This is just a starting point, argues René Olvera Salinas.[10] It is a strategy of struggle rooted not in doctrines, creeds, or dogmas but in the organization with others of everyday agendas for bread, dignity, and being-becoming in ways that begin to reconstitute—symbolically, socially, politically, epistemically, spiritually, existentially, and materially—a sense, hope, and possibility of living.

To plant life where there is death has been and is the route and horizon of millions of people, organizations, collectives, communities, and peoples on Planet Earth to not disappear, says the collective weave and transterritorial crack that is Pueblos en Camino (Peoples in Route), a weave-crack of which I consider myself part. "Ours are times of Horror, where dying is daily: we die without a roof, without land, without work, without health, without education, without freedom, without democracy, with impunity. Professional politicians and businessmen kill us to gain money and power, they make us kill ourselves or react with their same violence.... And for that reason, ours are times to Resist by sowing life."[11]

Here resistance is re-existence in and with the "We." "We resist bad governments trying to create our own; We resist the capitalist desire for profit with economies from the people; We resist patriarchy by creating community between women and men; We resist coloniality by declassifying ourselves; We resist death by sowing life."[12]

It is precisely this act to resist re-existing that challenges the system of violence-dispossession-war-death and de-existence that I detailed at the outset of this book. It is a challenge, that, as Pueblos en Camino manifests, "demands that we break the defeat, the impotence, the manipulation, the fragmentation, the co-option and the wear and tear." However, the challenge becomes greater with coloniality's present-day mutations and reconfigurations, and the unscrupulous atrocities it announces and births. "This time it comes for everything, it proclaims that there is no one who can stop it. That we must fear it, resign ourselves and get used to it.... It insults us and tramples on us to see if we can resist and stop it. To see if we are capable of recognizing its message of terror and death, its decision to kill, hunt down, crush, disappear, rape, promise, buy, cheat, recruit, entertain, and drive us crazy, to cause much, much pain and rage, to make us drown in the gesture, the cry, and the oblivion. All this makes us try to do a lot, but [for the system] what we do is irrelevant and useless. It assumes then that we are not capable of doing more than what it permits."[13]

Pueblos en Camino circulated these words in 2016. Today, the assumption that we can't do more than what the system permits is solidified and pushed further by the pandemic of COVID-19. The limits and restrictions are part not just of state policy but, more broadly, of the new global order taking form. They instill terror, incite silence and division, foster obedience, and debilitate collective action. Likewise, they announce death. While death due to COVID-19 is the public broadcast, many urban and rural communities of color know well the broader project of violence-dispossession-war-death and de-existence occurring and the complicities of government in its construction, manifestation, and implementation; that is, in the selective administration of life. In 2021 COVID-19 vaccines are one more visible manifestation and orchestration of this administration. As the so-called first world rushes to guarantee its survival, the so-called third world—outside and within the borders of the first—pleads for the first's benevolence and goodwill. In the meantime, third-world governments ensure that the limited doses available go to those in power and their allies, family, and friends. At play is not only COVID-19 but more crucially the molding of a global order in which de-existence is a necessary and instrumental cog.

Up against this reality, the act of planting is an insurgent act. It is insurgent for its intentionality and revolt; for its making, sprouting, reviving, resurging, constructing, and creating possibilities, hopes, and practices of life and living that not only defy and disobey the dominant logic-system and global order but also contribute to its fissures and cracks. The sowing here is about the prospect of growing an otherwise, a something else within and making cracks.

I think about the sowing, occurring as I write, of seeds of education, community, existence, and life in the midst of the ongoing war occurring in the regions of Cauca and Chocó in Colombia, and particularly in the urban and rural humanitarian zones of Buenaventura. As community members and their allies recently explained to me, the sowing is a necessary part of land-based and human-based survival. Moreover, and for many of those in Buenaventura, the sowing is constitutive of processes of territorial return after more than two decades of forced exile and displacement.[14] With this physical return has come the need to reactivate our own systems of education-culture and economy-society, they argue, and to fight for the right to community-based autonomy, defense, territorial permanence, and nonrepetition of the violence lived. All this is about sowing and resowing life where there is death, a sowing that, as they maintain, requires the cultivation of "transformative memory" and its ties with justice.

In an action never seen in this region or probably elsewhere, community members have sent more than a hundred letters to those who in the late 1990s perpetrated horrific acts of violence, including the dismemberment of leaders as the community of adults and children were forced to watch. The letters sent to ex-military perpetrators—some imprisoned and some not— call for recognition of that which occurred, the naming of those who gave the orders, and face-to-face meetings as spaces not of pardon but of learning, reconciliation, and nonrepetition. These meetings—constitutive of what the communities describe as festivals of memories, encounters of truth and justice, and restorative education—are working to "teach" the agents of violence about how their assassinations of leaders, adults, youths, and children destroyed both lives and community. And they are working to re-member, pushing forth the life-force of memory over oblivion, and building truth, justice, and peace as necessary steps toward community re-existence. Here the cries of that lived open fissures and cracks of re-membrance, self-determination, and life despite death, planting seeds that continue to germinate and to grow narratives of hope for a communal present and future of nonviolence and nonrepetition, and of social, territorial, and environmental justice. The developing educational project of what they name the University of Peace is part and parcel of this endeavor. With its three-pronged emphasis on memory-justice, environment-territory, and democracy-participation, the "university"— without campus, academic structure, or state approval—is a space of sowing through dialogue, thinking, reflection, and action. All this occurred at the same time that the militarization of the region during 2020–21 increased more than tenfold. The Colombian government publicly announces protection against the forces that dispute land, drugs, and control, while further enabling and inciting violence-dispossession-war-death and its reconfigurations. The words of two women leaders from two different communities continue to resonate in my mind and heart. They remind me of the special feminine power and force with respect to the seeds and sowing.

The first woman told me with much pride about how her river-basin community was the only in the region that had been able, through territorial defense, to keep mining companies out. "Despite assassinations, they [the companies and their narco-para-state allies and forces] have not been able to displace us, yet with the new strategy to attack our food sovereignty through fumigation, we wonder if and how we can survive."[15] For her and her community, how to plant seeds and sow life are crucial questions and vital challenges. The second woman, self-described as *campesina* (a rural peasant or countrywoman dedicated to working the land), recounted the assassination of her seventeen-year-old daughter in 2006, part of the continual assassination of youths in what are called "false positives."[16] "In the face of this violence, we have made a seedbed of sorts, what we call the 'House of Memory' and the 'Refuge of Knowledge,' spaces where those affected by the violences, and most especially women, youth, and children come together to raise our voices, our knowledge and thought. We are seeds that continue to germinate," she said.[17]

To resist re-existing, as these Colombian communities and many other communities in the world argue, is a mandate of and for life that refuses death.

Seedbeds of Doing-Thinking

I think about the seedbeds present in different territories of the globe and what Michele Lobo refers to as "the vitality of human and more-than-human power that struggles but emerges from the cracks, fissures and margins to seed plural becomings."[18] Lobo is thinking of her worlds of India, Australia, and beyond, and of her feeling of this vitality, a feeling that connects with mine. Although seedings are always situated, they weave pluriversal associations and relations, as well as what Morgan Ndlovu calls planetary coalitions.[19]

Seedbeds, of course, take on different meaning, reasons for being, and forms depending on the needs, aims, and urgency of the sowers. Brought to mind are what the Zapatistas referred to in 2015 as "seedbeds of critical thought." "We see that in some places meetings of thought are called 'seminars,' we believe this is because 'seminar' means 'seedbed'; seeds are made there that sometimes grow quickly and sometimes take time. So we said let's make a seedbed of ideas, of analysis, of critical thought about how the capitalist system is at present," Subcomandante Insurgente Galeano explained.[20] The proposition—as Galeano and other subcomandantes and comandantes contend in the first of three volumes that document this May 2015 seedbed of thought—was for a collective meeting, an alliance of critical thought, struggle, and action where "thought speaks its word" about how to resist the "capitalist hydra," with its multiple, growing, changing, and regenerating heads.[21] The call here was not just for a planting of new seeds and seedbeds within the Zapatista communities and ranks but also for reflections on seeds and seedbeds elsewhere in other struggles; in essence, shared reflections on the strategies and praxis of sowing in order to grow new methods—new pedagogies—of struggle.

"The seed . . . that questions, provokes, encourages, and urges us to keep analyzing and thinking. A seed so that other seeds listen that they have to grow and so that they do so in their own way, following their own calendar and geography."[22] This means carefully selecting the seeds to sow. "Look to see what seed is good," says SupMoisés, "and which seed you think is not good, or can't be put in practice."[23] It's about choosing which seeds serve us, he argues. And, in this sense, it is about what and how: what and how to sow, and how to make the seeds, the sowing, and the cultivation part of the fight and struggle, part of the breaking not just of ground but also of capitalism and coloniality's supposed impenetrability and totality.

While the Zapatista notion of the seedbed derives from *seminar*, it references and constructs a practice that in many ways diverges from that of seminars in the academic world. If, as all too often occurs, the practice of the latter is a meeting of speaking heads—a meeting of theory-as-thought and thought-as-theory—the practice of the first has the motor of inquiry and questioning, the reflexivity and reflectivity of theorization in/as praxis, and, above all, the aim of transforming a lived reality. Furthermore, and as SupMoisés explains, "it is not the analysis of one person that determines, but the interchange of analyses, of reflections, of thoughts"; a sharing that is collective, without owners, and obliges a together-thinking.[24] The "critical" is all of this: a redefining distanced from paradigms, "paradogmas," and genealogies defined in and by the West.

The Zapatistas' convocation and provocation here was not just for their meeting or event. Rather it was a convocation and provocation without the limits and restrictions of calendars and geographies, of place, time, and date. Seedbeds take time to sprout and grow and, even more, their whereabouts are pluriversal; seedbeds are all over. As such, I ask about the seeds that make up the seedbeds in what Katerina Teaiwa refers to as the many landscapes, seascapes, and skyscapes of the Global South, including, and for Teaiwa, Oceania and the Pan-Pacific.[25] I wonder about the seeds and seedbeds present in the farmers' struggles in India, which are growing in force as I write, and about the seeds and seedbeds of Palestinians that defy Israel's intended capture and control of land and life. I think of the seeds and seedbeds planted by Kurdish women in Rojava and the communal re-existences, autonomy, democracy, and revolution they sprout, as well as the seedbed of critical thought that is jineology, their women-conceived social science (see chapter 3).[26] I also think about the pluriversality of seeds and seedbeds of decolonial praxis that work to reclaim Indigenous education and knowledge production throughout the globe, including—but not only—in the Americas, South Africa, and Australia.[27] And I think of the seedbeds of thought-action that are Black Lives Matter in its situated and global creations and manifestations. All of this to name just a few of the many seedbeds that sow existences and re-existences cracking the dominant matrix or matrices of power.

The seeds, of course, are not the same worldwide. Their selection, their protection, their preservation, and the memory and knowledge that they contain and retain are situated, this despite attempts to universalize and globalize, including through epistemic and genetic homogenizations and modifications. The seeds that I refer to here challenge the global-colonial plan-structure-order and defy monocultivation and market-based controls. They are diverse, resurgent, and regenerative; they embody, signify, assemble, and re-member the continuation of the living and of life. Do not the seeds beget re-existence, I ask, and at the same time enable cross-fertilizations, "planetary coalitions" and exchanges, including of thinking and doing, and resurgent and insurgent struggle?

I ask about the seeds carried by and with the wind; the seeds that need other seeds to propagate, grow, and give fruit; and those that flower words, thought, memory, and rebellion. The seeds that each, in their own way, seek sustenance, liberation, and life's breath. "We are seeds," say some, "cracking concrete," as Climbing PoeTree's Alixa García and Naima Penniman sing-say; that negate dis-memory and death, as the Nasa peoples and Indigenous guard in Cauca, Colombia, proclaim; and that break city asphalt and make present the force to live, as the Rio de Janeiro city councilor, favela resident, and feminist lesbian Marielle Franco made evident before she was brutally shot down;[28] seeds that sprout and grow re-existence, I maintain, in places and spaces that the capitalist-colonial system cannot even begin to fathom. I cannot help but recall the words written on the wall of the Museo de la Ciudad (City Museum) in Quito in October 2020, words that remember and call forth Ecuador's great October 2019 rebellion: "The seed is the starting point for change. From its eruption, the small seed germinates and transforms into something new. It re-creates life."[29] The seedbeds, in this sense, are not always visible to the eye nor necessarily part of an intentional plan; they are a consequence of the seeds and the possibilities of sowing and growing.

I return to the Zapatista proposition of seedbeds of critical thought, and its suggestion that criticalness in and of thought is grown in the shared search, analysis, reflection, and thinking of what to do and how to do it, which of course necessitates not just criticizing the system but deepening understandings of how it works, how it mutates, reconfigures, and takes form locally and in other territories. Struggle and survival, in this sense, require not one but a series of lenses: "the microscope, the long-distance lens, the inverted periscope, and the orbital telescope. This is what provokes theory."[30]

Practices of Sowing

Since I can remember, I have always sowed. Sowing not only provides sustenance for my body, spirit, and soul, but it also proffers relation, accompaniment, and reciprocity in the continual making and cultivating of existence, re-existence, and life.

I lived for several years during the 1970s on a seventy-five-acre farm in central Massachusetts. The initial lure was the possibility to be part of a communal project of farming and living. For better or worse, the communal project broke up after a few months, primarily due to the patriarchal authority of its mastermind-leader. My then partner and I decided to stay after he left. For three years I dedicated myself to learning the art and practice of organic farming. The first year was the hardest because the learning was primarily alone. I prepared the acre-and-a-half garden by hand, carefully considering what to plant and how to plant it. As I made the furrows in the earth, I wondered about the peoples who inhabited these lands hundreds of years before, peoples who I now know were of the Nipmuc Nation. I made them offerings and I asked their permission to sow seeds. The work was arduous. I struggled with groundhogs, with making compost and natural pesticides, and with the everyday labor of cultivation. One day I observed an older man—the father of the man I paid the rent to—watching me from afar. He began to appear each day during the summer months. He never approached me nor I him. The harvest was plentiful. I exchanged vegetables for other foodstuffs and necessities at the local store, sold at a farmers' market, and preserved for the long winter months ahead.

As fall began to take hold, the man appeared one day at my door. His name was Elmer. Elmer told me that he had farmed this land years before, just as his ancestors had done and had taught him. I recall well his words: "I have watched you plant, cultivate, and harvest, and have seen your determination, diligence, and care. You did well for a beginner but you still have much to learn. The practice of sowing takes time to master, and it requires knowledges that are passed down. I will show you some of what I know, that is if you are willing to learn." It was apple season, and Elmer said that we were to start there. "We will make cider and let one bottle go hard and then drink it together. This will begin the teaching and learning." With Elmer as elder-teacher-guide, I learned much in a together-doing. What is more, I began to understand sowing as lived practice tied up with existence itself, as both an act and activity that is situated, conscious, grounded, generative, interdependent, relational, reciprocal, and persistent.

Brought to mind are Kimmerer's reflections on the circle of reciprocity that links sowing with people and seeds: "We cannot live without them and they cannot live without us.... We care for the seeds, and the seeds care for us...nourishing people and culture at the same time." Seeds that are only handled by machine are without these links of life and care, she says, without history, identity, and cultural continuity. For Kimmerer, the practice of sowing is about this, about history, identity, and cultural continuity, about heritage and memory, about asking permission of Mother Nature or Mother Earth to receive the seeds, and about "celebrating the life inside each kernel with a song."[31]

I think again of Abuelo Zenón's practice of sowing "in order to be." For this grandfather-elder, the sowing "to be" is a cultural and historical practice that occurs "where our being and existence were," and, as Juan García Salazar adds, "are *still* disavowed."[32] With Abuelo Zenón, others involved in this same sowing are called forth. I think most especially of the ancestor-guide Frantz Fanon.

In a colonial anti-Black world, life for Black peoples is most often perceived "not as a flowering...but as a permanent struggle against an omnipresent,...ever-menacing, and...incomplete death," said Fanon.[33] This persistent death, as he made clear in *A Dying Colonialism* as well as in *Black Skin, White Masks* and *Wretched of the Earth*, is both reflection and product of the racialized colonial project. Here the systematic negation of Black peoples' humanity justifies dehumanizing violences, naturalizes structural racism, and forces the "colonized" to constantly ask themselves, "In reality, who am I?"[34] Such questioning, as Fanon explains, is not individual. It goes beyond ontology and identity, and is wrapped up in lived existence itself, in being Black in a white-dominated world. The colonial endeavor is to instill a lived sense of nonexistence and "a zone of nonbeing."[35]

Existence and being require what Fanon referred to as a sociogenic perspective. Lewis Gordon explains it well: "The sociogenic pertains to what emerges from the social world, the intersubjective world of history, culture, language, and economics. In that world, he [Fanon] reminds us, it is the human being who brings such forces into existence."[36] Fanon's aim with sociogeny was not simply that of a socio-diagnostic, as I argued in chapter 1. More crucially, it was actional, directed toward de-alienation and the affirming and rebuilding—in essence a sowing and flowering—of being, humanity, Black consciousness, and life. That is, of re-existence; in Fanon's words, "introducing invention into existence."[37] In a similar vein, this is what he referred to at the end of *Wretched of the Earth* as "a change of skin."[38] Fanon was not referring to a change of skin color but instead to a radical alteration that, as Nelson Maldonado-Torres explains, points toward "the formation of a decolonial attitude as part of the movement of colonized subjectivity in its quest for re-humanization and decolonization" and, relatedly, for re-existence.[39]

For Fanon and Abuelo Zenón, as well as for other philosopher-sages of Africana existence, the problem of humanity denied reveals and gives presence to efforts and struggles to reconstruct humanity and/as new forms of living and life, including—following Sylvia Wynter—beyond western humanism and "after Man."[40] In this reconstruction, I find affinity with Gordon's conceptualization and posturing of Africana or Black existential thought as that which "builds upon the problems of existence generated by the complex history of black peoples" and rooted in the struggles "to live and to be."[41] Here Gordon is drawing from a long legacy of thinkers concerned with freedom, being, agency, and liberation, many of whom emerged from strong oral traditions. Frederick Douglass, Anna Julia Cooper, Marcus Garvey, Martin Luther King Jr., Malcolm X, and Angela Davis are just a few. But the affinity does not stop with his conceptualization and construction of existence-based philosophy or thought. It is also with Gordon's pedagogical-methodological linking of thought and praxis, and most especially in the ways that he makes present and gives credence to the ancestors and elders. That is, to "the need for values premised upon ancestral obligation as a fight against nihilism—that is against human denigration through understanding how the ancestors struggled against worse odds," and the "sense of ancestral obligation (respecting the elders) in black communities," both of which are crucial to collective being, belonging, and living on.[42] While Gordon is in continual conversation with many of the decolonial philosophers of existence known in the English-speaking world, particularly with Fanon, he also seems to be in conversation, as I have argued elsewhere, with the Afro-Pacific decolonial thinker-philosopher-sages, Abuelo Zenón and his grandson—guardian of Afro-Ecuadorian collective memory and now also ancestor—García.[43] While I will return later to Gordon, let's explore now how García and Abuelo Zenón understand and describe the concept and practice of cultural and existence-based sowing.

"The idea of planting or sowing has much to do with the world of communities and ancestral territory, with the traditions of peoples of African origin who live in these territories," García explains. "The concept of sowing within territory is vital. In order to live in and on territory or land one must sow, to make mother earth produce in order to live. This is the same concept that is used when we talk about cultural sowing. To speak of cultural plantings then, is to speak of cultivation, of production, of perpetuating cultural seeds that the elders planted in the space of territory and that continue on until today." Yet in these times, and especially among the younger generations, "the sowing and the cultural seeds are increasingly thought of less. To return to the sowings is important not only to strengthen ourselves as collective peoples of African origin, but also to recognize and comprehend why territory has been and continues to be a vital space, a space where we have sown and where all—life, knowledges, existences—are planted, including acts of resistance and of ancestral tradition."[44] In this sense, and as Abuelo Zenón contends, the reference to yesterday is important. "Yesterday has to be seen as the time when our ancestors with their ways of life and their philosophies to use the gifts of mother earth, anchored the ancestral right that we now claim," an ancestral right of territory and collective existence. Yesterday was also the time when the elders planted resistance as seeds of collective memory that can be dug up, recovered, used, and reused today.[45] The evocation here is not to tradition per se, understood in an essentialist, fundamentalist, and antimodern sense. Nor is it to philosophy as a discipline or disciplinary thought. Instead, it is to a decolonizing conception of existence that comes out of experience and living, a conception, experience, and living that are continually thought and rethought, reconstituted and re-created.[46]

The sowing and seeds, in this sense, are necessarily related to ongoing struggles: "struggles to once again be persons after the dehumanization of enslavement and the politics of negation and exclusion that continued in the Republics and later the states. The seeds sown were—and still are—seeds of life.... Sowing is how we came to be and become where we were not," García says in concert with Abuelo Zenón.[47] And sowing is how we have planted and cultivated the long horizon of life and loss, says Zenón. "The mandate to sow each of these territorial spaces with the cultural seed of origin gave us back our love for the land, the new land that the ambition of others brought us to. Sowing the new land with the culture of origin helped us heal the pain caused by the loss of the motherland that remained on the other side of the sea." He continues, "It is one of the many acts of reparation of the damage that slavery caused us."[48]

For peoples whose humanity has been denied, sowing is tied to existence itself, to physical, symbolic, ontological, social, cultural, territorial, and cosmogonic-spiritual-sacred re-existences, and to the continuation of knowledges, wisdoms, dignity, and life. In essence, sowing is a component and constitutive part of living pedagogies-methodologies in continuous regeneration, of the praxistic and ongoing work of germinating, cultivating, and growing a shared and collective sense of existing, of being, becoming, and belonging, and of life living on. Here, the sower has a particularly crucial role, argue the Africana philosophers Abuelo Zenón and García, including in making contemporary the words of the ancestors for the continued existence of current and future generations. "When one works with stories and riddles turning them into knowledge—including within schools—so that children can encounter ancestral knowledges, one is sowing," García says. "It may be that one has to change some of the sowing methods, but this too is part of the charge the elders have left us: to pass the seed that they left sown." In this action of returning, recuperating, and re-creating this existence-based knowledge for the new generations, we are sowing, and we are sowers, affirms García.[49]

In two decades of shared work and existence-based conversation, maestro-hermano Juan taught me about the significance of sowing for African-origin peoples in the Great Comarca of the Afro-Pacific. He and Abuelo Zenón together spoke of the seeds that the women kidnapped from African soil carried in the *zumbo* of their heads; "not in the hair because their hair was cut off, but in the inside part of the head that no one could touch, destroy, or see." These were the seeds of a memory of long horizon, of long life, that remained well stored until they could be planted on this territory—now our ancestral territory—maestro-hermano Juan said, that is the Great Comarca of the Afro-Pacific. "It was a nude territory without roots, a territory ruled by the other, empty of our inheritance, our being. But sometime—none of us know exactly when—the elders began to sow magical-spiritual figures, legends, knowledges, words, and laws about the use of water, the earth, and new forms of life in the hills, mountains, rivers, and trees."[50] And they sowed the placentas and umbilical cords of those born in this territory. With this cultural sowing, we began to be, argue maestro-hermano Juan and Abuelo Zenón.[51] Sowing was and is an act of collective self-reparation and of resistance, they contend; it is a becoming, making, and doing of, in, and for life.

In his many texts, Juan García gives centrality to the voice-seed of the elders transmitted orally over the generations. However, he has also emphasized the importance of the word-as-seed, which, against the threat of dis-memory today among younger generations, gives reason to writing oral memory, oral traditions, and the oral word. "It is a reason that works to challenge the history and coloniality of power: this subjugation that schooling signifies for our youth and children," he once explained.[52] The word-seeds become another form of planting, acting, and enacting collective memory, a doing that in writing—and "riting"—can position words as humanizing forces of collective re-creation and re-existence up against the present-day politics of individual inclusion that works to whiten, culturally dis-member, individualize, and divide, and against the present-day reality of dispossession and deterritorialization.

During the last couple of years of his life, and in the intense and intensive conversations that gave form to the book *Pensar sembrando/sembrar pensando con el Abuelo Zenón* (To think sowing/to sow thinking with Grandfather Zenón), written in three voices (García's, Zenón's, and mine),[53] maestro-hermano Juan helped me understand not only the deep significance of sowing for him and for African-origin communities forced to create being, belonging, and territory-as-existence-as-life in a land that was not but now is theirs, but also the significance of sowing for me; that is, my praxis, role, and responsibility as a sower.

He made me see how in various spaces and places, including in the doctoral program briefly described in chapter 2, I have scattered seeds over fertile minds and lands, seeds that have taken root, sprouted, matured, and flourished, taking on their own essence, presence, and life well beyond me, my intentionality, my actions, and my gaze. This, he told me, was part of the critical decolonizing work of sowing. It is to create in community the fecund conditions for planting. Then it is to sow the seeds and nurture their germination and growth, while at the same time positing possibilities for both their harvest and propagation here and elsewhere. Your sowing, he said, is of a community that traverses geographical boundaries and borders. It is different, in this sense, from the sowing of collective memory of and on ancestral territories, he explained, different from the generational responsibility that he himself assumed as life project. Yet you too have a role and responsibility here, this teacher-brother-friend-grandfather guide said to me as his time to depart was coming near. It is to continue to sow, grow, nurture, cultivate, and disseminate the seeds I am leaving you with, including those present in the Fondo Documental Afro-Andino (Afro-Andean Documentary Fund) that we built together and in its archive of readings, legends, stories, life histories, and testimonial narratives that await circulation, the seeds that you too—but in a different way—will protect and carry, he said, in the *zumbo* of your heart-head.

Rising Up
and Living On

Sowing is situated and it's pluriversal; so too is the rising up. The seeds are many, diverse in substance and form, and in all that they retain, sustain, enable, and carry. Resounding in my mind is the phrase that I first heard among the Nasa Indigenous Guard in Cauca, Colombia, and more recently among Indigenous women in Ecuador's Amazon: "They wanted to bury (entomb) us, but they didn't know that we are seeds." Throughout this region and in many other territories of the globe, the seeds are both the literal and metaphorical signifier of resistance, resurgence, re-existence, and life. "We are seeds" sustains hope, posits active subjectivity, evokes decolonial attitudes, conjures collectivity, and summons the possibility of living on.

In the first chapter of *Existencia Africana*, Lewis Gordon reminds us that the question and decision of living on is directly connected to existence itself, to the recognition of one's racial situation, to the meaning of one's birth, and of course to the very significance of life given the continual forces of nihilism and conditions of human denigration.[54] Gordon's reflections are in relation to how Africana thought not only theorizes this existential reality but also gives substance, impetus, possibility, and hope by affirming the peoplehood, existential thinking, and epistemic contributions of dehumanized people. Africana thought in this sense, and for Gordon, is living on, a living on that, in essence, also engenders and verifies the notion of re-existence present throughout this book.

Re-existence and living on are, of course, not only the purview of Africana thought. As I have argued throughout this book, they are constitutive of the decolonizing life struggles of the many who refuse to succumb to coloniality's patterns of power and project of violence-dispossession-war-death and dehumanization-dehumanity-de-existence all combined; the many who make coloniality crack; and the many who sow and grow in the fissures and margins otherwises of knowing, thinking, sensing, loving, being-becoming, and belonging-living. The praxis of re-existence is the praxis of cracking and of sowing, and it is the praxis of decoloniality rising up. It is the vitality, in

Lobo's words, of human and more-than-human power; the reassembling and re-membering of that which coloniality has torn apart and that which, following M. Jacqui Alexander, belongs together; and the creative capacity, in Adolfo Albán Achinte's terms, to resignify and redefine life in conditions of both individual and collective dignity, affirmation, and self-determination.[55]

The significance and sense of re-existence, re-existences, and what I have referred to throughout this book as existences otherwise cannot be encapsulated in a single definition; confined to theory as separate from social subjectivity, movement, and practice; restricted to a particular territory or region; or rooted in the racial, gendered, and natured essentialisms that coloniality has produced and reproduced. The significance and sense are crafted in the concrete actions, practices, pedagogies, processes, and praxis of decolonial doing in which knowledge, subjectivity, spirituality, life philosophies and cosmologies, and social struggles are necessarily part.

Re-existence's significance and sense are made in connecting cries and cracks, asking and walking, traversing binaries and boundaries, undoing nation-state, and sowing and resowing, as each chapter suggests. The rising up and living on are just that: the plurality and pluriversality of re-existences burgeoning from the earth and in spaces and places little fathomed and least expected, sprouting hope, flowering rebellion, breathing life, offering sustenance, and giving us seeds that remember.

I close with the poem of my former student and longtime friend Samyr Salgado:

As if the horizon decided to come close
a few steps ahead
—that is to say towards us—
as if it dared to come.
Hope, which through the cracks,
insists on being reborn,
goes out to the meeting of tomorrow,
below
one can feel the warmth of the grandmother stones, one can hear the
    voices of time
that speak and sing,
below,
the collective work of hands and hearts / persist in nurturing and
    weaving life . . .
the seeds of corn,

the spirit of water,
of fire
of the mountain . . .
of the word that we are,
beat within us.
As if hope rebels
to wait for tomorrow
as if she were something,
that she lived now.[56]

EPILOGUE

As I place the finishing touches on this book, the world around me is in a state of commotion. I feel it would be remiss to let this book go without sharing with all of you a bit about these lived moments that, despite being temporally and geographically situated, make evident once again the long horizons of rising up, living on, that are never outdated.

It is June 21, 2022, the beginning of what peoples north of the equator recognize as the summer solstice, the winter solstice for those in the equator's souths. Among Indigenous peoples in the Andes, the celebration is Inti Raymi, the dawning of a new cycle, a new year. Today is also the thirty-second anniversary of Ecuador's 1990 massive Indigenous uprising (described in chapter 4), and it is the ninth day of the countrywide strike organized by the Confederación de Nacionalidades Indígenas de Ecuador (CONAIE) against the economic, political, social, and existence-related policies of Ecuador's national government and state.

In these nine days, the mobilizations in the countryside, provinces, and cities have grown. Highways and roads are blocked with burning tires, piled-high dirt, logs, branches, and debris, and by the bodies of Indigenous men and women—the latter in the first line of defense—all who say enough with the politics of impoverishment that, for the majority in this plurination, threaten life itself. While government forces have, in some areas, been able to temporarily open highways and roads, the resistance and persistence of community members far outweigh government's efforts. As the days increase, so too does state authorized violence and repression. Last week ended with the signing of a presidential decree putting three provinces—including the province of Pichincha, which includes the capital city of Quito—in a state of exception or emergency; yesterday a new decree was signed extending the state of exception to three additional provinces, putting a great part of the country in the control of state, military, and police forces.

Since dawn today, the helicopters and surveillance planes have not stopped their roar overhead. The national mobilization continues, but the force of the uprising and strike are now concentrated in Quito, the seat of state government. Yesterday, thousands of Indigenous community members began arriving to Quito in caravans of trucks and on foot, breaking police barricades, defying mechanisms of control, and exercising their collective right to resist, rise up, and live on. As a CONAIE tweet yesterday stated: "We aren't arriving to Kito, here we have always been, we only come by thousands for a just cause against the bad government. We do not come to destroy, we want answers and benefits for all. Reject hate, racism and vandalism." And another tweet: "We are not here to take over Quito. The capitol is already besieged and militarized, and taken over by delinquency, unemployment, poverty, and the bad government. We feed the cities, we come to demand answers and benefits for all." Many in the capitol came out to welcome the caravans and express their solidarity, alliance, and agreement with CONAIE's ten-point list of demands conceived for the society at large: (1) reduction of and control over the rising cost of gasoline, with special attention to agricultural based sectors; (2) economic relief for over 4 million families; (3) fair prices for agricultural products; (4) attention to employment and labor laws; (5) moratoriums on the expansion of mining and oil fields; (6) respect for the twenty-one collective rights (of Indigenous and Afro-descendant peoples); (7) a halt to the privatization of strategic sectors and of the heritage of Ecuadorians; (8) policies to control prices and market speculation of basic need products; (9) access to and funding of health and education; and (10) security, protection, and the generation of effective public policies to stop the wave of violence, delinquency, narcotrafficking, and organized crime.

The government, of course, had already begun, several days before, to prepare its offensive against the survivors of 530 years of colonial violence and repression. Several thousand police and military were already installed around the presidential palace, in the entrance roads to the city, and strategically in the national Casa de Cultura (House of Culture)—now converted (since June 19, 2022) into a police barracks—and the nearby Arbolito Park, the central gathering places in recent decades of social movement protests, mobilization, and organization, including the 2019 October rebellion (see chapter 1). Close to both are the universities that opened their doors to house thousands of Indigenous women, children, and elder community members in October 2019, constituting humanitarian peace zones against the violence and repression.

In contrast to several years past, these same universities began to circulate communiques at the end of last week, stating that this time they would not receive the Indigenous protestors. However, two—the public Central University of Ecuador and the Salesian Polytechnical University—decided yesterday to open their campuses on humanitarian grounds. My university—the Universidad Andina Simón Bolívar (UASB)—once considered the most progressive in the country, among other reasons, for its close relationship and alignment with social movements, and for the spaces and/as cracks of decolonial reflection and debate made within by students and a few professors, refused to open its doors. Despite the numerous efforts—including manifestos, public pronouncements and communiques, and letters to the rector—of students and many of us faculty members to turn this decision around, university officials refused, closing the installations and ordering faculty and students to *teletrabajar* (telecommute). A tweet that circulated today in the media and with the hashtag UASBAbranLasPuertas (UASBOpenYourDoors) says much: "Don't drop the discourse! The most decolonial process is to open the doors now!"

This morning police threw tear bombs into the installations of the Salesian Polytechnical University and this afternoon into the Central University. The surrounding areas of both are now heavily militarized. Throughout the city, ongoing reports in the alternative social media document the use by police of gases, bullets, and motorcycles to mow down protestors and inhibit marches and mobilization. An alert has also begun to circulate about the supposed authorization by the head of police operations of the use of stinger rubber ball grenades, forty thousand of which were said to arrive today on a flight from Colombia. Helicopters and drones seem to multiply with the hours, as does the tension, conflict, indignation, and desperation; so too multiplying are the number of wounded. In the meantime, the country's president calls for dialogue on the government's terms. I can't help but think of the continuing problem of nation-state and the transnational and corporate interests involved. Will we—all of us fed up with these structures of capitalist, racist, heteropatriarcal, modern/colonial power—ever find a way out of this conundrum? I think of the euphoria of the masses in Colombia right now after the historic win of Gustavo Petro, the Leftist presidential candidate, and Francia Márquez, Afro-Colombian lawyer, activist, and community-based leader, as vice president. I wonder if the hope now sown in Colombia will grow to be the concrete possibility of systemic transformation, or at least a widening crack in the longtime structures of violence-dispossession-war-death. And I wonder, as may some of you, if changes in national government—while certainly important and necessary—are ever enough.

The days have passed since I began these notes; it is now day 15 in the national strike. In the last days, the Indigenous movement won back the Casa de Cultura and Arbolito Park, pushed the revocation of the state of exception, and secured two presidential decrees that respond, in lukewarm terms, to a few of the demands. The movement remains steadfast in its mobilization and the completion of its demands, now joined by many other sectors of the population, some of which are calling for the overthrow of the country's president. As has occurred multiple times during the last several decades, it is the Indigenous movement that once again has brought to the fore the structural problems facing this plurination; structural problems that, without a doubt, are present throughout the globe. In this sense, and as movement leaders make clear, an overthrow will not address the deeper structural concerns that, for the vast majorities, deny the possibility of a dignified life.

In the meantime, the white and whitened elite continue to organize what they call "marches for peace." Dressed in white—some showing the guns they have tucked in their belts—they call for an end to the mobilizations, a normalizing of everyday life, and the elimination of the Indigenous protestors and people from their city streets. If government does not respond, they say, they will take things into their own hands. Racism reigns, as is true in so many territories of the world; whiteness continues its colonial mark pretending to determine who is more and who is less human, and who deserves—in essence, has and retains the privilege of—existence itself.

Yet, here in Ecuador, as is true in much of Abya Yala and the Global South, coloniality has never been able to totally consolidate its project or hold. While the Indigenous movement leads the current protests, mobilizations, and demands, it has also, in the last several decades, pushed and enabled processes of learning, unlearning, and relearning among many other sectors of society, processes that continue to fracture and fissure the colonial matrices of power and ask and walk possibilities of otherwises, elsewheres, and a plural something else.

So, I close these final notes to you, my dear readers, not knowing the outcomes of this uprising and strike, how it will continue to take form, and how it will end, at least for now. While the result certainly matters, it is not the reason for my words, my *escrevivência* or writing-living, shared here. With these ending words I hope to open reflection once again on the realities of these times, on present-past intertwinements, on territorial interconnections, and on relations of corporalities, subjectivities, and struggles for dignity and life in the lands that I, you, and we call home. Corporalities, subjectivities, and struggles that refuse, transgress, disrupt, un-suture, and unsettle the capitalist, colonial, racist, gendered, and heteropatriachal structures, systems, and practices that attempt to define and determine existence; corporalities, subjectivities, and struggles that seed, sow, and grow re-existences in the decolonial cracks, and life where there is death. This is the necessary and urgent work at hand, central, without a doubt, to what I understand, describe in this book, and offer for shared reflection with all of you as rising up, living on.

NOTES

BEGINNINGS

Unless otherwise noted, all translations in this book are my own.

1 Chapter epigraph is from Corinne Kumar, "The One Central Mountain: Universalisms in Political Discourse," in *Asking We Walk: The South as New Political Imaginary, Book One: In the Time of the Earth*, 2nd ed., ed. Corinne Kumar (Bangalore: Streelekha, 2011), 284.

2 The Nipmuc, or "fresh water people," occupied the interior portion of what is now Massachusetts and parts of Rhode Island and Connecticut. The original homelands included all of present-day central Massachusetts from the New Hampshire–Vermont borders and south of the Merrimac Valley to include Tolland and Windham Counties in Connecticut and the northwest portion of Rhode Island. To the east, the homelands included the Natick/Sudbury area going west to include the Connecticut River valley. See "A Brief Look at Our History," Nipmuc Nation, accessed April 20, 2021, https://www.nipmucnation.org/our-history.

3 Bill Shaner, "A Hidden History Uncovered in Ashland," *MetroWest Daily News* (Framingham, MA), June 26, 2016, https://www.metrowestdailynews.com/news /20160626/hidden-history-uncovered-in-ashland; Stephen A. Mrozowski et al., "Magunkaquog Materiality, Federal Recognition, and the Search for a Deeper History," *International Journal of Historical Archeology* 13, no. 4 (2009): 430–63.

4 Nipmuc Nation, "Brief Look."

5 Mrozowski et al., "Magunkaquog Materiality," 441.

6 Mrozowski et al., "Magunkaquog Materiality," 441.

7 "Superfund Site: Nyanza Chemical Waste Dump Ashland, MA," US Environmental Protection Agency, accessed January 24, 2022, https://cumulis.epa.gov /supercpad/SiteProfiles/index.cfm?fuseaction=second.Cleanup&id=0100948.

8 See Bill Shaner, "Nipmuc Healing Ceremony to Usher in Ashland-Nyanza Memorial Garden," Wicked Local Ashland, June 12, 2016, https://ashland .wickedlocal.com/news/20160612/nipmuc-healing-ceremony-to-usher-in -ashland-nyanza-memorial-garden. Also see the project's website: http://www .ashlandnyanzaproject.com/.

9　Eve Tuck and K. Wayne Yang, "Decolonization Is Not a Metaphor," *Decoloni-zation: Indigeneity, Education, and Society* 1, no. 1 (2012): 1–40.

10　My reference to *western* in lowercase letters here and throughout this book is intentional, meant to wrest power from its capitalization.

11　Tuck and Yang, "Decolonization."

12　As Yancy explains, "Being un-sutured is a powerful concept as it implies, especially for whites, the capacity to tarry with the multiple ways in which their whiteness is a problem and to remain with the weight of that reality and the pain of that realization." George Yancy, "White Suturing, Black Bodies, and the Myth of a Post-racial America," Society for the Arts in Religious and Theological Studies, 2018, https://www.societyarts.org/white-suturing-black -bodies-and-the-myth-of-a-post-racial-america.html.

13　See Aníbal Quijano, "Coloniality of Power, Eurocentrism, and Latin Amer-ica," *Nepantla Views from South* 1, no. 3 (2000): 533–80.

14　See my arguments in Catherine E. Walsh, "Decoloniality in/as Praxis," in *On Decoloniality: Concepts, Analytics, Praxis*, by Walter D. Mignolo and Catherine E. Walsh (Durham, NC: Duke University Press, 2018), 16.

15　See Walter D. Mignolo, *Local Histories/Global Designs: Coloniality, Subaltern Knowledges, and Border Thinking* (Princeton, NJ: Princeton University Press, 2000).

16　Richard Gott, "The 2006 SLAS Lecture: Latin America as a White Settler Society," *Bulletin of Latin American Research* 26, no. 2 (2007): 269–89.

17　Emil Keme, "For Abiayala to Live, the Americas Must Die: Toward a Trans-hemispheric Indigeneity," *Native American and Indigenous Studies* 5, no. 1 (Spring 2018): 43.

18　Tuck and Yang, "Decolonization," 2.

19　Laura E. Pérez, *Eros Ideologies: Writings on Art, Spirituality, and the Decolonial* (Durham, NC: Duke University Press, 2019), 79.

20　M. Jacqui Alexander, *Pedagogies of Crossing: Meditations on Feminism, Sexual Politics, Memory, and the Sacred* (Durham, NC: Duke University Press, 2005), 5.

21　Lewis R. Gordon, *Existentia Africana: Understanding Africana Existential Thought* (New York: Routledge, 2000), 10, 14, 164.

22　Frantz Fanon, *Black Skin, White Masks*, trans. from the French by Charles Lam Markmann (New York: Grove, 1967), 11.

23　Emmanuel Chukwudi Eze, *On Reason: Rationality in a World of Cultural Conflict and Racism* (Durham, NC: Duke University Press, 2008), 222.

24　Adolfo Albán Achinte, "Pedagogías de la re-existencia: Artístas indígenas y afrocolombianos," in *Pedagogías decoloniales: Prácticas insurgentes de resistir, (re) existir y (re)vivir*, ed. Catherine Walsh (Quito: Abya-Yala, 2013), 1:455.

25　Adolfo Albán Achinte, *Sabor, poder y saber: Comida y tiempo en los valles afroan-dinos de Patía y Chota-Mira* (Popayán, Colombia: Universidad del Cauca, 2015), 39–40n27. Recalled here as well is Stephan Nathan Haymes's powerful text "Pedagogy and the Philosophical Anthropology of African-American Slave Culture," in *Not Only the Masters' Tools: African-American Studies in Theory and*

Practice, ed. Lewis R. Gordon and Jane Anna Gordon, (Boulder, CO: Paradigm, 2006), 173–203.

26 Albán, *Sabor*, 40n27.

27 Adolfo Albán Achinte, "Epistemes 'otras': Epistemes disruptivas?" *Revista Kula* 6 (2012): 30. Also see my citing of and thinking with Albán in Walsh, "Decoloniality in/as Praxis," 18, 95.

28 Carlos Walter Porto-Gonçalves, "Lucha por la Tierra: Ruptura metabólica y reapropiación social de la naturaleza," *Polis: Revista Latinoamericana* 45 (2016), http://journals.openedition.org/polis/12168

29 Lexico, s.v. "re-existence," accessed May 17, 2022, https://www.lexico.com/definition/re-existence.

30 Conceição Evaristo, "Conceição Evaristo: Imortalidade além de um título," interview by Ivana Dorali, in *Mestre das Periferias: O encontro de Ailton Krenal, Conceição Evaristo, Nêgo Bispo e Marielle Franco (in memorian)*, ed. Jailson de Souza e Silva (Rio de Janeiro: Eduniperferias, 2020), 153–54. Also see Conceição Evaristo, *Becos da memória* (Belo Horizonte, Brazil: Massa, 2006).

31 Alexander, *Pedagogies of Crossing*, 283.

32 Abdullah Öcalan, *Democratic Confederalism* (London: Transmedia, 2011), 13.

CHAPTER ONE: CRIES AND CRACKS

1 Chapter epigraph is from Alixa García and Naima Penniman, "Who Decides?," track 6 on *Intrinsic*, by Climbing PoeTree (2017), https://climbingpoetree.bandcamp.com/track/who-decides. Also see mediasanctuary, "Climbing Poetree 'Who Decides?,'" YouTube, August 1, 2019, video, 5:55, https://www.youtube.com/watch?v=eDJneLFbORc.

2 "Bio," Climbing PoeTree, accessed May 17, 2022, http://www.climbingpoetree.com/bio/.

3 María Lugones, *Pilgrimages/Peregrinajes: Theorizing Coalition against Multiple Oppressions* (New York: Rowman and Littlefield, 2003), 228.

4 Lugones, *Pilgrimages/Peregrinajes*, 6.

5 José Elizondo and Karla Ávila, "Pienso, luego me desaparecen," *El Fardadio*, September 26, 2015, http://www.elfaradio.com/2015/09/26/pienso-luego-me-desaparecen/.

6 The 2020 film *The Trial of the Chicago 7*, written and directed by Aaron Sorkin, affords a glimpse into some of the revolutionary postures and struggles of the late 1960s and early 1970s and their tensions and contradictions.

7 Catherine Walsh, "(Des)humanidad(es)," *Alter/nativas*, no. 3 (2014): 2.

8 Arturo Villavicencio, "Hacia dónde va el proyecto universitario de la Revolución Ciudadana?," in *El correismo desnudo*, various authors (Quito: Montecristi vive, 2013), 217.

9 Here I recall the cries that Mayra Estévez describes as sonorous acts of rebellion against the colonial context and its dominant sonorities: "a vibration in defense." Mayra Estévez, "Estudios sonoros en y desde Latinoamérica: Del régimen colonial de la sonoridad a las sonoridades de la sanación" (PhD diss.,

Universidad Andina Simón Bolívar, 2016), 84, http://repositorio.uasb.edu.ec
/handle/10644/4956.

10 Subcomandante Insurgente Galeano, in Comisión de la Sexta del Ejercito
Zapatista de Liberación Nacional (EZLN), *El pensamiento crítico frente a la hidra
capitalista, I* (Chiapas: EZLN and the Sexta, 2015), 318.

11 Nelson Maldonado-Torres, *Against War: Views from the Underside of Modernity*
(Durham, NC: Duke University Press, 2008), 4.

12 Maldonado-Torres, *Against War*, 5.

13 Leanne Betasamosake Simpson, *As We Have Always Done: Indigenous Freedom
through Radical Resistance* (Minneapolis: University of Minnesota Press,
2017), 46.

14 I recognize Achille Mbembe's concepts of necropolitics and necropower,
which, as he states, "account for the various ways in which, in our contemporary world, weapons are deployed in the interest of maximum destruction of persons and the creation of *death-worlds*, new and unique forms of
social existence in which vast populations are subjected to conditions of life
conferring upon them the status of *living dead*." Achille Mbembe, "Necropolitics," *Public Culture* 15, no. 1 (2003): 40. However, my arguments here are
somewhat distinct. First, I am thinking with and from the ways that people
who live this violence-dispossession-war-death name and describe it, as well
as how they not only resist but, more significantly, re-exist despite it. Second,
my thinking and analysis find ground in coloniality's long horizon, which,
while suffering continual mutations and reconfigurations, reveals the ongoing
nature of this matrix of power and the ongoing presence of decolonial resurgences, insurgences, creations, and inventions. Here the past and present
are not distinct moments but coconstitutive. And third, my concern is not
so much with the fatalism of these times but with the creative sowing of re-
existence and life where there is violence and death; that is, with the creative
actional force of existence.

15 Vilma Almendra, *Entre la emancipación y la captura: Memorias y caminos desde la
lucha Nasa en Colombia* (Quito: Abya-Yala, 2017), 210.

16 Almendra, *Entre la emancipación y la captura*, 210.

17 "Entre 2016 y 2020 han sido asesinados casi mil líderes sociales en Colombia,"
Noticias de América Latina y el Caribe, July 17, 2020, https://www.nodal
.am/2020/07/colombia-971-lideres-sociales-y-218-excombatientes-asesinados
-desde-la-firma-de-los-acuerdos-de-paz/.

18 Almendra, *Entre la emancipación y la captura*, 214.

19 Manuel Rozental, comments made at the session on Colombia's national
strike, "Feria del Libro Insurgente," Quito, October 16, 2021.

20 Maribel Hernández, "Asesinan a Berta Cáceres, líder hondureña contra la explotación medioambiental de las transnacionales," *elDiario.es*, March 4, 2016,
http://www.eldiario.es/desalambre/Asesinan-Berta-Caceres-medioambiental
-Honduras_0_490651434.html.

21 Comisión de la Sexta del EZLN, *El pensamiento crítico*.

22   See Yamile Alvira, "El lugar del canto y la oralidad como prácticas estético-pedagogías para la reafirmación de la vida y su existencia en los andes caja-marquinos," in *Pedagogías decoloniales: Prácticas insurgentes de resistir, (re)existir y (re)vivir*, ed. Catherine Walsh (Quito: Abya-Yala, 2017), 2:245–72.

23   See María Eugenia Borsani and Relmu Ñamku, "Encarnization político-judicial, neocolonialismo y expropiación territorial," in Walsh, *Pedagogías decoloniales*, 2:315–36.

24   On June 19, 2022, Francia Márquez became the new vice president of Colombia. See her biography in "Francia Márquez," Wikipedia, last updated July 9, 2022, https://es.wikipedia.org/wiki/Francia_M%C3%AIrquez.

25   "Asesinan en Colombia a la defensora medioambiental Yolanda Maturana," *El Mundo Internacional*, February 2, 2018, http://www.elmundo.es/internacional /2018/02/02/5a74962046163f4e1b8b4676.html.

26   Red Mariposas de Alas Nuevas Construyendo Futuro, *La muerte de Sandra Patricia Angulo no es un asesinato más, es un feminicidio* (Buenaventura, Colombia, April 2015), manifesto circulated by email.

27   Betty Ruth Lozano, email communication accompanying her daughter's public denunciation, October 12, 2020.

28   Verónica Gago, "Treinta años de espera, dos siglos de condena," *Página 12*, March 4, 2016, https://www.pagina12.com.ar/diario/suplementos/las12/13 -10424-2016-03-04.html.

29   Segato, quoted in Gago, "Treinta años de espera."

30   Gago, "Treinta años de espera."

31   Segato, quoted in Gago, "Treinta años de espera."

32   Paulo Freire, *Pedagogy of Indignation* (Boulder, CO: Paradigm, 2004), 61.

33   Enrique Dussel, *Ética de la liberación en la edad de la globalización y de la exclusión* (Madrid: Trotta, 2002), 436.

34   Freire, *Pedagogy of Indignation*, 98.

35   Adolfo Albán Achinte, "¿Interculturalidad sin decolonialidad? Colonialidades circulantes y prácticas de re-existencia," in *Diversidad, interculturalidad y construcción de ciudad*, ed. Wilmer Villa and Arturo Grueso (Bogotá: Universidad Pedagógica Nacional-Alcaldía Mayor, 2008), 64–96.

36   María Teresa Garzón, "Proyectos corporales: Errores subversivos: Hacia una performatividad decolonial del silencio," in *Tejiendo de otro modo: Feminismo, epistemología y apuestas descoloniales en Abya Yala*, ed. Yuderkys Espinosa, Diana Gómez, and Karina Ochoa (Popayán, Colombia: Universidad de Cauca, 2014), 223–36.

37   Maldonado-Torres, *Against War*.

38   Estévez, "Estudios sonoros en y desde Latinoamérica," 82.

39   Edouard Glissant, *El discurso antillano* (1981; Havana: Casa de las Américas, 2010), 16.

40   Comisión de la Sexta del EZLN, *El pensamiento crítico*.

41   Lluvia Cervantes, intervention in the panel "Sembrar vida donde está la muerte," Universidad Central, Bogotá, Colombia, February 5, 2019.

42 SupGaleano quoted in Comisión de la Sexta del EZLN, *El pensamiento crítico*, 326.

43 L. Hevia, "El feminicidio tiene relación con la devaluación de los cuerpos que ahora no valen nada: Entrevista con María Lugones," *Diario La Mañana Neuquen*, November 5, 2012.

44 Sofía Zaragocín et al., "Mapeando la criminalización del aborto en el Ecuador," *Revista de Bioética y Derecho* 43 (2018): 109–25. Also see Marcela Lagarde, "Del femicidio al feminicidio," *Desde el jardín de Freud*, no. 6 (2006): 216–26.

45 "The Women Killed on One Day around the World," BBC News, November 25, 2018, https://www.bbc.com/news/world-46292919.

46 Nidia Bautista, "Femicide Is a Growing Issue in the United States," *Teen Vogue*, August 28, 2020, https://www.teenvogue.com/story/femicide-is-a -growing-issue-in-the-united-states.

47 Isabel Kennon and Grace Valdevitt, "Women Protest for Their Lives: Fighting Femicide in Latin America," Atlantic Council, February 20, 2020, https:// www.atlanticcouncil.org/blogs/new-atlanticist/women-protest-for-their-lives -fighting-femicide-in-latin-america/.

48 Kennon and Valdevitt, "Women Protest"; "Femincidio en América Latina," Telesur, July 4, 2016, https://www.telesurtv.net/news/Crimenes-impunes-el -rastro-del-feminicidio-en-America-Latina-20160704-0009.html#; "Fueron asesinadas 2,240 mujeres en México en los primeros siete meses de 2020, de acuerdo con cifras oficiales," Infobae, August 26, 2020, https://www.infobae .com/america/mexico/2020/08/26/fueron-asesinadas-2240-mujeres-en-mexico -en-los-primeros-siete-meses-de-2020-de-acuerdo-con-cifras-oficiales/; Catherine Walsh, "Gritos, grietas y siembras de vida: Entretejeres de lo pedagógico y lo decolonial," in Walsh, *Pedagogías decoloniales*, 2:17–45.

49 See, for instance, Naomi García Cabezas, "COVID-19: Femicidios en América Latina," Ayuda en acción, October 26, 2020, https://ayudaenaccion.org/ong /blog/mujer/violencia-genero-cifras/.

50 Nidia Bautista, "Femicide Is a Growing Issue."

51 See Pueblos en Camino, "Pronunciamiento/Posicionamiento de Movilización 24 de abril de 2016: Mujeres habitantes del Estado de México," in "El feminicidio es una herramienta del capital-patriarcado: 'Vivas y organizadas hasta derrotar el monstruo machista,'" Pueblos en Camino, May 2, 2016, http:// pueblosencamino.org/?p=2759.

52 Javier Corrales, "Un matrimonio perfecto: Evangélicos y conservadores en América Latina," *New York Times*, Spanish edition, January 19, 2018, https:// www.nytimes.com/es/2018/01/19/opinion-evangelicos-conservadores-america -latina-corrales/.

53 Walsh, "Gritos, grietas y siembras"; Sonia Corrêa, "Gender Ideology: Tracking Its Origins and Meanings in Current Gender Politics," *Engenderings* (blog), London School of Economics and Political Science, December 11, 2017, https://blogs.lse.ac.uk/gender/2017/12/11/gender-ideology-tracking-its-origins -and-meanings-in-current-gender-politics/; Claudia Vianna and Alexandre

Bortolinni, "Anti-gender Discourse and LGBT and Feminist Agendas in State-Level Education Plans: Tensions and Disputes," *Educação e Pesquisa* 46 (2020): e221756, https://doi.org/10.1590/s1678-4634202046221756.

54 See María Paula Granda Vega, *El macho sabio: Racismo y sexismo en el discurso del president Rafael Correa* (Quito: La Tierra, 2017).

55 Patricia del Río, "Nada más queda," *El Comercio* (Lima), February 8, 2018, https://elcomercio.pe/opinion/rincon-del-autor/violacion-ninos-menor-edad -violadores-miedo-queda-patricia-rio-noticia-495575.

56 See "Anti-LGBT Curriculum Laws in the United States," Wikipedia, last updated May 13, 2022, https://en.wikipedia.org/wiki/Anti-LGBT_curriculum _laws_in_the_United_States.

57 See Roman Kuhar and Aleš Zobec, "The Anti-gender Movement in Europe and the Educational Process in Public Schools," *Center for Educational Policy Studies Journal* 7, no. 2 (2016): 29–46; Roman Kuhar and David Paternotte, *Anti-gender Campaigns in Europe: Mobilizing against Equality* (New York: Rowman and Littlefield International, 2017); Borbála Juhász and Enikő Pap, *Backlash in Gender Equality and Women's and Girls' Rights* (Brussels: European Union, Policy Department for Citizens' Rights and Constitutional Affairs, June 2018), https://www.europarl.europa.eu/RegData/etudes/STUD/2018/604955/IPOL _STU(2018)604955_EN.pdf.

58 Cited in Sonia Corrêa, "Interview: The Anti-gender Offensive as State Policy," Conectas: Human Rights, March 7, 2020, https://www.conectas.org /en/noticias/interview-the-anti-gender-offensive-as-state-policy/. Also see Jesús Casquete, "Un nuevo fascismo en Europa?," *Democracia Siglo XXI* (blog), February 16, 2021, https://teodulolopezmelendez.wordpress.com/2021/02/16 /un-nuevo-fascismo-en-europa/.

59 Piro Rexhepi, "From Orientalism to Homonationalism: Queer Politics, Islamophobia and Europeanization in Kosovo," *Southeastern Europe* 40 (2016): 34.

60 See Puar (2007) and Schulman (2011), cited in Rexhepi, "From Orientalism to Homonationalism," 33.

61 See Piro Rexhepi, Samira Musleh, and Romana Mirza, "Bandung Before and After: Islam, the Islamicate and the De/colonial," *ReOrient* (2020), https:// www.criticalmuslimstudies.co.uk/bandung-before-and-after/; Sirin Adlbi Sibai, *La cárcel del feminismo: Hacia un pensamiento islámico decolonial* (Madrid: Akal, 2016).

62 Corrales, "Un matrimonio perfecto."

63 Radar Sarkar, "The Alliances of Leftists and Evangelicals in Latin America," NACLA, October 2021, https://nacla.org/alliances-leftists-and-evangelicals -latin-america.

64 This letter was originally read at the International Conference-Homage to Aníbal Quijano and the Decoloniality of Power Today, Lima, Peru, May 7–9, 2019, and subsequently published as Catherine Walsh, "Reflexiones en torno a la colonialidad/descolonialidad del poder en América Latina hoy: Una carta

a Aníbal Quijano," *Otros Logos* 10, no. 10 (December 2019): 12–19, http://www
.ceapedi.com.ar/otroslogos/Revistas/0010/02%202019%20Catherine%20
Walsh.pdf.

65 José Ángel Quintero Weir, "La emergencia de Nosotros I," Pueblos en
Camino, January 18, 2019, https://pueblosencamino.org/?p=6988.

66 I refer the reader to the incredibly well-documented book by Gerard Colby,
*Thy Will Be Done: The Conquest of the Amazon: Nelson Rockefeller and Evange-
lism in the Age of Oil*, with Charlotte Dennett (New York: HarperCollins,
1995).

67 See my dialogue with Borsani in Walsh, "(Des)humanidad(es)."

68 Quintero Weir, "La emergencia de Nosotros I."

69 "Ministerio de Defensa asegura que el uso de la fuerza en las manifestaciones
fue necesario," *El Comercio*, November 29, 2019, https://www.elcomercio.com
/actualidad/ministerio-defensa-fuerza-manifestaciones-paro.html.

70 "'No tenemos nada que ocultar': Lenin Moreno," *La Hora*, November 9, 2019,
https://www.lahora.com.ec/quito/noticia/1102285057/no-tenemos-nada-que
-ocultar-lenin-moreno.

71 Milagros Aguirre, "Las medias verdades de una rebelión de 11 días," *Rebelión*,
October 2019, http://www.rebelion.org/docs/262149.pdf.

72 Alianza de Organizaciones para los Derechos Humanos, *Verdad, justicia y
reparación: Informe de verificación sobre Derechos Humanos en el paro nacional y
levantamiento indígena* (Quito: Alianza de Organizaciones para los Derechos
Humanos, October 2019), https://www.inredh.org/archivos/pdf/informe_final
alianza%202019_oct.pdf.

73 Kevin Gosztola, "Trump Applauds Bolivia's Military Coup as US Establishment Media Blame Morales for Turmoil," Common Dreams, November 12,
2019, https://www.commondreams.org/views/2019/11/12/trump-applauds
-bolivias-military-coup-us-establishment-media-blame-morales-turmoil.

74 These notes, originally written in Spanish and finished on November 12, 2019,
appeared in Catherine Walsh, "El despertar de octubre y el cóndor: Notas
desde Ecuador y la región," *Sobre 1991: Revista de Estudios Internacionales* 2,
no. 1 (December 2019): 84–90. An English translation appeared in Catherine
Walsh, "On the October Awakening(s) and the Condor: Notes from Ecuador
and the Region," *Black Issues in Philosophy*, November 28, 2019, https://blog
.apaonline.org/2019/11/28/on-the-october-awakenings-and-the-condor-notes
-from-ecuador-and-the-region/.

75 Xavier Ramos, "Más de 150 comunidades indígenas en el Oriente del Ecuador
siguen afectadas por el derrame de petróleo," *El Universo* (Ecuador), April 30,
2020, https://www.eluniverso.com/noticias/2020/04/30/nota/7827513/derrame
-petroleo-afecta-mas-150-comunidades-indigenas-oriente.

76 See "Organizaciones indígenas, religiosas y de derechos humanos presen-
taron acción de protección y medidas cautelares contra el Estado y empresas
petroleras por derrame de petróleo," INREDH, April 29, 2020, https://www
.inredh.org/index.php/noticias-inredh/covid-19/1356-organizaciones

-indigenas-religiosas-y-de-derechos-humanos-presentan-accion-de-proteccion
-y-medidas-cautelares.

77 "Alerta 47," Alianza por los Derechos Humanos, June 3, 2020, https://
ddhhecuador.org/sites/default/files/documentos/2020-06/Alerta%2047.pdf.

78 "La OPS advierte que ya hay 20 mil indígenas de la Amazonía con COVID-19,"
Noticias de América Latina y Caribe, May 20, 2020, https://www.nodal.am
/2020/05/la-ops-advierte-que-ya-hay-20-mil-indigenas-de-la-amazonia-con
-covid-19/.

79 "Mortes por covid-19 entre indígenas precisam virar assunto para a CIDH,"
Conselho Indigenista Missionario, April 6, 2020, https://cimi.org.br/2020/06
/mortes-por-covid-19-entre-indigenas-precisam-virar-assunto-para-a-comissao
-interamericana-de-direitos-humanos/.

80 "Amazonía: Exterminio y ecocidio, políticas de Estado," Pueblos en Camino,
May 31, 2020, https://pueblosencamino.org/?p=8475.

81 "COVID-19 and Indigenous Peoples," Socioambiental.org, accessed May 17,
2022, https://covid19.socioambiental.org/. This page offered the following
statistics on the levels of COVID-19 among Amazonian Indigenous peoples
in Brazil in February 2021: 48,071 affected, 957 deaths, and 161 Indigenous nations and groups affected.

82 Catherine Walsh, "(Des)existir: Mi segunda carta a Aníbal Quijano,"
Revista Descolonialdad y Autogobierno, no. 3 (October 2020): 26–31 (my
translation).

83 Comments by Veronica Grefa, representative of one of the affected communities, at the roundtable discussion on resistance to extractivism, "Feria del
Libro Insurgente," Quito, October 15, 2021.

84 For an excellent analysis of the significance of the social uprising and strike in
the ethnicized and racialized city of Cali, see Betty Ruth Lozano Lerma, "Social Uprising, Racism, and Resistance in Cali's National Strike," South Atlantic
Quarterly 121, no. 2 (2022): 425–34.

85 Ronald Soria, "El país latinoamericano donde la policía mata a más negros
que en Estados Unidos," El Expreso, June 4, 2020, https://www.expreso.ec
/actualidad/mundo/latinoamerica-pais-policia-mata-negros-ee-uu-12882.html.

86 César Muñoz, "Brazil Suffers Its Own Scourge of Police Brutality," Americas Quarterly, June 3, 2020, https://www.americasquarterly.org/article/brazil
-suffers-its-own-scourge-of-police-brutality/.

87 Roberta Gondim de Oliveira et al., "Racial Inequalities and Death on the
Horizon: COVID-19 and Structural Racism," Cadernos Saúde Pública 36, no. 9
(2020): 2.

88 Saidiya V. Hartman and Frank B. Wilderson III, "The Position of the Unthought," Qui Parle 13, no. 2 (Spring/Summer 2003): 187.

89 Luz Argentina Chiriboga, Jonatás y Manuela (Quito: Campaña Nacional
Eugenio Espejo por el Libro y la Lectura, 2010).

90 Glissant, El discurso antillano, 16.

91 Edouard Glissant, Tratado del todo-mundo (Barcelona: El Cobre, 2006), 30.

92 Leonard Cohen, "Anthem," track 5 on *The Future* (Columbia Records, 1992).

93 Gloria E. Anzaldúa, *Light in the Dark/Luz en lo Oscuro: Rewriting Identity, Spirituality, and Reality*, ed. AnaLouise Keating (Durham, NC: Duke University Press, 2015), 8.

94 Anzaldúa, *Light in the Dark*, 1, 82.

95 In a short piece entitled "The Future of the World Social Forum: To Be or Not to Be?" published online on *Other News* in February 2018, a month before the scheduled World Social Forum in Salvador da Bahia, Brazil, Francine Mestrum wrote, "As for the WSF itself, the hope of the first years for really sharing alternatives for the neoliberal and capitalist world order is also dwindling." Furthermore, and as Fernando Coronil once argued, while the World Social Forum sought to articulate activists and activist organizations in a common alliance against neoliberalism and for social justice and democracy, "it has been easier for them to criticize neoliberalism than to articulate a viable alternative to it." Fernando Coronil, "The Future in Question: History and Utopia in Latin America, 1989–2010," in *Business as Usual: The Roots of the Global Financial Meltdown*, ed. Craig Calhoun and Georgi Derluguian (New York: New York University Press, 2011), 238.

96 Comisión de la Sexta del EZLN, *El pensamiento crítico*, 121.

97 Comisión de la Sexta del EZLN, *El pensamiento crítico*, 221.

98 Catherine Walsh, "Pedagogical Notes from the Decolonial Cracks," *Emisférica* 11, no. 1 (2014), https://hemisphericinstitute.org/en/emisferica-11 -1-decolonial-gesture/11-1-dossier/pedagogical-notes-from-the-decolonial -cracks.html.

99 Colectivo Grietas, "Editorial," *Grietas* 1, no. 1 (July 2012): 6.

100 Colectivo Grietas, "Editorial," 4.

101 Catherine Walsh, "Las estrategias de la(s) insurgencia(s): Entrevista a Catherine Walsh," interview by René Olvera Salinas and Germania Fernández, *Grietas* 1, no. 1 (July 2012): 11–19.

102 Dilar Dirik, "Living without Approval," interview by Jonas Stall, in *Stateless Democracy: New World Academy Reader #5*, with the Kurdish Women's Movement, ed. Renée In der Maur and Jonas Staal (Utrecht, Netherlands: BAK, 2015), 43.

103 Rafael Bautista, "Bolivia: Del Estado colonial a estado plurinacional" (unpublished manuscript, La Paz, 2009).

104 Gustavo Esteva, *Nuevas formas de revolución: Notas para aprender de las luchas del EZLN y de la APRO* (Oaxaca: El Rebozo, 2014), 40–41.

105 Esteva, *Nuevas formas de revolución*, 41.

106 Esteva, *Nuevas formas de revolución*, 65, 7.

107 Paulo Freire, *El grito manso* (Buenos Aires: Siglo XXI, 2003), 55.

108 Freire, *El grito manso*, 59.

109 For a discussion of this "seedbed," see chapter 5.

110 Comisión de la Sexta del EZLN, *El pensamiento crítico*, 355.

111 Comisión de la Sexta del EZLN, *El pensamiento crítico*, 198, 201.

112 Subcomandante Insurgente Marcos, 2003, quoted in Colectivo Grietas, "Editorial," 7–8.

113 John Holloway, *Agrietar el capitalismo: El hacer contra el trabajo* (Buenos Aires: Herramienta, 2011), 22–23, 28–29. In English, see John Holloway, *Crack Capitalism* (London: Pluto, 2010).

114 Holloway, *Agrietar el capitalismo*, 8–9.

115 Anzaldua, *Light in the Dark*, 45–46.

116 See W. E. B. Dubois, *The Souls of Black Folk* (1903; New York: Millennial Publications, 2014); Frantz Fanon, *Black Skin, White Masks*, trans. from the French by Charles Lam Markmann (New York: Grove, 1967); Aimé Cesaire, *Discourse on Colonialism* (1972; New York: Monthly Review, 2000).

117 Steve Biko, *I Write What I Like*, 40th anniversary ed. (Johannesburg: Picador Africa, 2017), 149–50. It was this book of Biko's that became my guiding light during my six-week stay in Stellenbosch, South Africa, in 2018. While the experience of being a fellow at the Stellenbosch Institute for Advanced Study was certainly enriching, the still-visible reality of apartheid in the small city of Stellenbosch not only ruptured the imaginary of postapartheid that I held before this visit—my first to South Africa—but also made real the still-present white cocoon of which Biko writes, of racism and of the monopolization of privilege and wealth.

118 Sylvia Wynter, "'No Humans Involved': An Open Letter to My Colleagues," *Forum NHI Knowledge for the 21st Century* 1, no. 1 (Fall 1994): 42.

119 Wynter, "'No Humans Involved,'" 55.

120 Wynter, "'No Humans Involved,'" 70.

121 Such interconnectedness, of course, does not suggest a collapse or equation of perspectives and subject positions. As a Fanonian philosopher and a Black woman of Jamaican origin, Wynter lives race and racialization and its intersections with gender. Anzaldúa's thought, on the other hand, is grounded in a creative mestiza consciousness and in the lived folds of ethnicity, class, gender, and sexuality.

122 Anzaldúa, *Light in the Dark*, 79.

123 Anzaldúa, *Light in the Dark*, 82.

124 Anzaldúa, *Light in the Dark*, 73.

125 Tupac Shakur, "The Rose That Grew from Concrete," AllPoetry, accessed May 16, 2022, https://allpoetry.com/The-Rose-That-Grew-From-Concrete.

126 Of course, this is not the only way to understand the fissures or cracks. As Juan García Salazar, the grandfather of Ecuador's Black movement, once explained to me, in the Black communities of the Afro-Pacific territory-region (Colombia-Ecuador), people sometimes speak of fissures or cracks in terms of threats and dangers. The cracks are the spaces, García said, in which that which is foreign and from outside the community can get in, where the real or symbolic *bicho* (insect) eats away and destroys from within. Personal conversation, Quito, April 2016. Certainly, the use of such practices of fissure are not limited to the Afro-Pacific but have been long present in many contexts

of community-based struggle. Biko's documentation of the practices used by South Africa's apartheid regime to disenable the collective enunciations of Black people, boost intertribal competition, and separate shared struggles serves as an additional example. See Biko, *I Write What I Like*.

127 Luz Ribeiro, Facebook post, August 20, 2017, https://pt-br.facebook.com /luzribeiropoesia/posts/1799439980085719/.

128 Manuel Toledo, "La grieta en la Tate: Entrevista a Doris Salcedo," *Esfera pública*, October 10, 2007, https://esferapublica.org/nfblog/la-grieta-en-la-tate -entrevista-con-doris-salcedo/.

129 See "Movement Space," Decolonize This Place, accessed May 17, 2022, https://decolonizethisplace.org/movement-space.

130 Yinka Elujoba, "Jacob Lawrence, Peering through History's Cracks," *New York Times*, September 17, 2020, https://www.nytimes.com/2020/09/17/arts/design /jacob-lawrence-metropolitan-museum.html.

131 Elujoba, "Jacob Lawrence."

132 Bobby Seale, foreword to *Black Panther: The Revolutionary Art of Emory Douglas*, by Emory Douglas (New York: Rizzoli, 2007), 13–14.

133 In her poem entitled "definition for blk/children," Sonia Sanchez says it like it is: "A policeman is a pig and he shd be in a zoo with all the other piggy animals / and until he stops killing blk / people cracking open their heads remember / the policeman is a pig (oink/oink)." Quoted in Douglas, *Black Panther*, 27.

134 Danny Glover, preface to Douglas, *Black Panther*, 10.

135 Quoted in Daliri Oropeza, "Sensibilidad Zapatista: ¿Arte para qué y para quién?," *Grieta*, December 10, 2019, http://www.grieta.org.mx/index.php/2019 /12/10/sensibilidad-zapatista-arte-para-que-y-para-quien/.

136 In Oropeza, "Sensibilidad Zapatista."

137 Radio Pozol, "(Español) EZLN: 'Son las artes la semilla en la que la humani- dad renacerá,'" Radio Zapatista, December 15, 2019, https://radiozapatista.org /?p=32716&lang=en.

138 Oropeza, "Sensibilidad Zapatista."

139 Caleb Duarte, "EDELO (En Donde Era la ONU) Where the United Nations Used to Be," Calebduarte.org, accessed May 17, 2022, http:// www.calebduarte .org/edelo.

140 Daniel B. Coleman, "My Praxis," personal website, accessed May 17, 2022, https://www.danielbcoleman.com/biodbc.

141 Daniel B. Coleman, "Scholarship & Teaching," personal website, accessed May 17, 2022, https://www.danielbcoleman.com/scholarship.

142 See Raúl Moarquech Ferrera Balanquet, "Writing Mariposa Ancestral Memory," *Caribbean In Transit Arts Journal* 1, no. 4 (Spring 2013): 38–42. Also see his performance "Mariposa Ancestral Memory" in Art Labour Archives, "Raúl Moarquech Ferrera Balanquet @ Decolonizing the 'Cold' War. Be.Bop 2013," YouTube, January 5, 2014, video, 38:13, https://www.youtube.com/watch ?v=n95bMl-A4Nw.

143 Lukas Avendaño and Edgar Cartas Orozco, "Where Is Bruno?," Hemispheric Institute, 2019, https://hemisphericinstitute.org/en/encuentro-2019 -performances/item/2821-performances-007.html.

144 Violeta Kiwe Rozental Almendra and Vilma Almendra Quiguanás, *Cristina Bautista: This Land's Bleeding Flight* (Cauca, Colombia: Pueblos en Camino, 2020). The book can be downloaded at https://pueblosencamino.org/?p =9109.

145 Nelson Maldonado-Torres, "Hashtag Lessons from the US and South Africa about Racism and Antiblackness," *Mail and Guardian*, June 29, 2020, https://mg.co.za/opinion/2020-06-29-hashtag-lessons-from-the-us-and-south -africa-about-racism-and-antiblackness/.

146 Felipe Araujo, "Brazil Must Address Its Own Police Violence," *Foreign Policy*, July 27, 2020, https://foreignpolicy.com/2020/07/07/brazil-must-address-its -own-racist-police-violence/.

147 Araujo, "Brazil Must Address."

148 See chapter 3 for a discussion of jineology. Also see my discussion in chapter 4 of the Kurdish liberation movement's critique of state and proposal of and for democratic confederalism.

149 Audre Lorde, *Sister Outsider*, rev. ed. (1984; Berkeley: Crossing, 2007), 110.

150 Lewis R. Gordon, "Shifting the Geography of Reason," talk given at the Caribbean Philosophical Association Summer School, May 24, 2021.

151 Paulo Freire, *Pedagogy of the Oppressed* (New York: Continuum, 1974).

152 See Sandy Grande, "Red Pedagogy: The Un-methodology," in *Handbook of Critical and Indigenous Methodologies*, ed. Norma Denzin, Yvonne Lincoln, and Linda Tuhiwai Smith (London: Sage, 2008), 233–54; Linda Tuhiwai Smith, *Decolonizing Methodologies: Research and Indigenous Peoples* (London: Zed Books, 1999), esp. 167.

153 See chapter 3 in this book. Also see Catherine E. Walsh, "(Decolonial) Notes to Paulo Freire: Walking and Asking," in *Educational Alternatives in Latin America: New Modes of Counter-hegemonic Learning*, ed. Robert Aman and Timothy Ireland (London: Palgrave Macmillan, 2019), 207–30.

154 See my texts "Not Just Philosophers of Existence, but Pedagogues of Existence: A Letter to Lewis Gordon and to Frantz Fanon," in *Fanon and the Crisis of European Man*, 2nd ed., by Lewis R. Gordon (New York: Routledge, in press); "On Justice, Pedagogy, and Decolonial(izing) Praxis," *Educational Theory* (in press); "Decoloniality, Pedagogy and Praxis," in *Encyclopedia of Educational Philosophy and Theory*, ed. Michael Adrian Peters (Singapore: Springer, 2017), 366–70; "Fanon y la pedagogía de-colonial," *Revista Nuevamérica/Novamérica*, no. 122 (2009): 60–63; and "Introducción: Lo pedagógico y lo decolonial: Entretejiendo caminos," in *Pedagogías decoloniales: Prácticas insurgentes de resistir, (re)existir y (re)vivir*, ed. Catherine Walsh (Quito: Abya-Yala, 2013), 1:23–68.

155 See Fanon, *Black Skin, White Masks*. Also see Nelson Maldonado-Torres, "Frantz Fanon and CLR James on Intellectualism and Enlightened

Rationality," *Caribbean Studies* 33, no. 2 (July–December 2005): 149–94; and Sylvia Wynter, "Towards the Sociogenic Principle: Fanon, the Puzzle of Conscious Experience, of 'Identity' and What It's Like to Be 'Black,'" in *National Identity and Sociopolitical Changes in Latin America,* ed. Mercedes Durán-Cogan and Antonio Gómez-Moriano (New York: Routledge, 2001), 30–66.

156 M. Jacqui Alexander, *Pedagogies of Crossing: Meditations on Feminism, Sexual Politics, Memory, and the Sacred* (Durham, NC: Duke University Press, 2005), 7.

157 Alexander, *Pedagogies of Crossing,* 281, 282.

158 Alexander, *Pedagogies of Crossing,* 298.

159 Frantz Fanon, *Los condenados de la tierra,* 3rd Spanish ed. (Mexico City: Fondo de Cultura Económica, 2001), 288, 292.

CHAPTER TWO: ASKING AND WALKING

1 Chapter epigraph is from Corinne Kumar, introduction to *Asking We Walk: The South as New Political Imaginary, Book One: In the Time of the Earth,* 2nd ed., ed. Corinne Kumar (Bangalore: Streelekha, 2011), xxii.

2 Kumar, introduction, xxi–xxii.

3 Iván Illich, *La sociedad desescolarizada* (1971; Querétaro, Mexico: El Rebozo, 2013), 17.

4 M. Jacqui Alexander, *Pedagogies of Crossing: Meditations on Feminism, Sexual Politics, Memory, and the Sacred* (Durham, NC: Duke University Press, 2005), 7.

5 Illich's arguments in *Deschooling Society* and other texts (along with his practice in the Cuernavaca-based Intercultural Center for Documentation) were toward relational and what he termed "convidial" forms of existing, learning, and living outside, against, and without school, and, in essence, without education.

6 Iván Illich quoted in David Cayley, "Illich, Goodman, Freire: Encuentros y desencuentros: De las conversaciones entre Iván Illich y David Cayley," *Opciones,* supplement of *El Nacional* 29 (February 19, 1993): 8, translated from David Cayley, *Iván Illich in Conversation* (Toronto: Anansi, 1992), 206.

7 See Gustavo Esteva, Madhu Prakash and Dana Stuchul, "From a Pedagogy for Liberation to Liberation from Pedagogy," in *Rethinking Freire: Globalization and the Environmental Crisis,* ed. C. A. Bowers and Frederique Apffel-Marglin (Mahwah, NJ: Lawrence Erlbaum, 2004), 13–30.

8 Sylvia Wynter, "Unsettling the Coloniality of Being/Power/Truth/Freedom: Towards the Human, after Man, Its Overrepresentation—an Argument," *New Centennial Review* 3, no. 3 (Fall 2003): 257–337.

9 Katherine McKittrick, "Yours in the Intellectual Struggle: Sylvia Wynter and the Realization of Living," in *Sylvia Wynter: On Being Human as Praxis,* ed. Katherine McKittrick (Durham, NC: Duke University Press, 2015), 1–8.

10 Brought to mind now is María Lugones's emphasis on coalition as necessary in the work of resistance against oppression. See María Lugones, *Pilgramages/Peregrinajes: Theorizing Coalition against Multiple Oppressions* (New York: Rowman and Littlefield, 2003).

11 I take the title of this section from bell hooks, *Teaching to Transgress: Education as the Practice of Freedom* (New York: Routledge, 1994).

12 Children make the best theorists because they have not yet been schooled into accepting as natural routine social practices, Terry Eagleton once argued. Children "insist on posing to those practices the most embarrassingly general and fundamental questions, regarding them with a wondering estrangement which we adults have long forgotten. Since they do not yet grasp our social practices as inevitable, they do not see why we might not do things differently," said Eagleton in *The Significance of Theory*. Quoted in bell hooks, *Teaching to Transgress*, 59. Yet what Eagleton failed to see (or mention) is how children absorb, from a young age, the practices of systemic racism and sexism.

13 J. Nozipo Maraire, *Zenzele* (New York: Delta, 1996), 26.

14 George Yancy, "White Suturing, Black Bodies, and the Myth of a Post-racial America," Society for the Arts in Religious and Theological Studies, 2018, https://www.societyarts.org/white-suturing-black-bodies-and-the-myth-of-a -post-racial-america.html.

15 Dance has always been one of my interests, aptitudes, and pleasures. As a child, my parents enrolled me in ballet. However, their hope was not that I would become a dancer but that ballet would help discipline and "school" me. After several years, the dance teacher convinced my mother that my talent was in less structured and more fluid movement; the teacher moved me to jazz. My mother never told my father. Yet one day, he announced that my dance classes were to end. The reason was my body; with my thick legs and round buttocks, I would never be a ballerina, he said, and so why should he continue to waste his money. I learned to hate my body. During my two-year undergraduate stay at UMass–Amherst, and as part of my corporal taking back, I returned to dance. Yet it was after leaving the university that I began to more seriously study jazz, African, and contemporary dance, and even, for a period, participate in a dance troupe.

16 For my brief description of this privilege written some years later, see my preface to *Education Reform and Social Change: Multicultural Voices, Struggles, and Visions*, ed. Catherine E. Walsh (Mahwah, NJ: Lawrence Erlbaum, 1996), xi.

17 Kelvin A. Santiago-Valles, *"Subject People" and Colonial Discourses: Economic Transformation and Social Disorders in Puerto Rico, 1898–1947* (Albany: State University of New York Press, 1994).

18 The lawyer in this case, Gabe Kaimowitz, had argued and won a case some years before on Black English in Ann Arbor, Michigan.

19 See Catherine E. Walsh, *Pedagogy and the Struggle for Voice: Issues of Language, Power, and Schooling for Puerto Ricans* (New York: Bergin and Garvey, 1991).

20 Walsh, *Education Reform and Social Change*.

21 Paulo Freire, *Pedagogy of the Oppressed* (New York: Continuum, 1974), 183.

22 As Freire once told me, his encounter with bell hooks was an important force in pushing his unlearning and relearning.

23 Quoted in Catherine E. Walsh, "Making a Difference: Social Vision, Pedagogy, and Real Life," in Walsh, *Education Reform and Social Change*, 228.

24 Quoted in Walsh, "Making a Difference," 237.

25 SCaLD, "Reclaiming Our Voices," in Walsh, *Education Reform and Social Change*, 129.

26 SCaLD, "Reclaiming Our Voices," 144–45. Also see Adriana Jasso and Rosalba Jasso, "Critical Pedagogy: Not a Method but a Way of Life," in *Reclaiming Our Voices: Bilingual Education, Critical Pedagogy and Praxis*, ed. Jean Frederickson (Ontario, CA: California Association for Bilingual Education, 1995), 253–59; and Bill Terrazas and Students for Cultural and Linguistic Democracy (SCaLD), "Struggling for Power and Voice: A High School Experience," in Frederickson, *Reclaiming Our Voices*, 279–309.

27 Among these cases were *Hispanic Parent Advisory Council v. Lynn, Hispanic Parent Advisory Council v. Holyoke, Vecinos del Barrio v. Holyoke* (voting rights case), and the case filed by the Lawyers' Committee for Civil Rights and META, Inc. on behalf of the Boston Bilingual Master Parents Advisory Council. In addition, I served as an educational expert in the metropolitan three-way desegregation case in Hartford, Connecticut, *Sheff v. O'Neil*. For a comprehensive account of the ongoing nature of this case, see Patricia O'Rourke, "Roots of Radical Love in Education: Theorizing in a Concrete Struggle for Justice" (PhD diss., University of Connecticut, 2022). For documentation of some of my work with respect to these cases, see Catherine E. Walsh, "'Staging Encounters': The Educational Decline of US Puerto Ricans in [Post]-colonial Perspective," *Harvard Educational Review* 68, no. 2 (1998): 218–43; Catherine E. Walsh, "Engaging Students in Their Own Learning: Literacy, Language, and Knowledge Production with Latino Adolescents," in *Adult Biliteracy in the United States*, ed. David Spener (Washington, DC: Center for Applied Linguistics and Delta Systems, 1994), 211–42; Catherine E. Walsh, *Enabling Academic Success for Secondary Students with Limited Formal Schooling: A Study of the Haitian Literacy Program at Hyde Park High School in Boston* (Providence, RI: Northeast and Islands Regional Educational Laboratory at Brown University, 1999); and Walsh, *Pedagogy and the Struggle*.

28 This program later became the sustenance and model for an amendment to the 1992 US federal court consent order on improved and equal educational access for students with limited English proficiency in the Boston Public Schools. With the 1994 amendment, the system was required to establish literacy programs at high schools and middle schools for students with limited formal schooling. However, this requirement was never totally implemented.

29 The teachers I am referring to here are Lionel Hogu and Gary Daphnis. For a description of this program and a participatory evaluation of its first ten years, see Walsh, *Enabling Academic Success*. Among our findings was that despite several years at the most of formal schooling, more than half of the students graduated and 39 percent went on to college.

30 Presentation at the opening panel of the IV Latin American Colloquia on Coloniality/Decoloniality of Power, Knowledge, Being in Salvador da Bahia, Brazil, March 9, 2018.

31 Catherine E. Walsh, "Decoloniality in/as Praxis," in *On Decoloniality: Concepts, Analytics, Praxis*, by Walter D. Mignolo and Catherine E. Walsh (Durham, NC: Duke University Press, 2018), 74.

32 Illich, *La sociedad desescolarizada*, 16.

33 Illich, *La sociedad desescolarizada*, 139.

34 Illich quoted in Cayley, "Illich, Goodman, Freire," 8.

35 Illich quoted in Cayley, "Illich, Goodman, Freire," 8.

36 Lewis R. Gordon, "A Pedagogical Imperative of Pedagogical Imperatives," *Thresholds* 36, nos. 1–2 (2010): 27–35.

37 Myles Horton and Paulo Freire, *We Make the Road by Walking: Conversations on Education and Social Change*, ed. Brenda Bell, John Gaventa, and John Peters (Philadelphia: Temple University Press, 1990).

38 See Paulo Freire and Antonio Faundez, *Por una pedagogía de la pregunta*, 2nd ed. (Mexico City: Siglo XXI, 2014).

39 At dawn on May 25, 2014, Subcomandante Insurgente Marcos, Zapatista spokesperson and military chief, died a symbolic death. The collective decision by the Ejercito Zapatista de Liberación Nacional (Zapatista National Liberation Army; EZLN) to end SupMarcos's existence, an existence created by the EZLN in 1994, was strategic. "We realized that there was already a generation that could look at us face to face, that could listen to us and talk to us without seeking a guide or a leader, without intending to be submissive or become followers. Marcos, the character, was no longer necessary.... This figure was created and now its creators, the Zapatistas, are destroying it. If anyone understands this lesson from our *compañeros* and *compañeras*, they will have understood one of the foundations of zapatismo." See, in English, Subcomandante Insurgente Galeano, "Between Light and Shadow," EZLN, May 27, 2014, https://enlacezapatista.ezln.org.mx/2014/05/27/between-light -and-shadow/.

40 Subcomandante Insurgente Marcos, "La historia de las preguntas," *La Jornada*, December 13, 1994.

41 Kumar, introduction to *Asking We Walk*, xxii.

42 For the results of this study, see Catherine Walsh, "El desarrollo sociopolítico de la educación intercultural bilingüe en el Ecuador: Un análisis de perspectivas y posiciones," *Pueblos Indígenas y Educación* 31–32 (July–December 1994): 99–164.

43 These notes, published in part elsewhere, are expanded here as part of my still-ongoing dialogic reflection with Paulo. See, for example, Catherine E. Walsh, "Decolonial Pedagogies Walking and Asking. Notes to Paulo Freire from AbyaYala," *International Journal of Lifelong Education* 34, no. 1 (2015): 9–21; and Catherine E. Walsh, "(Decolonial) Notes to Paulo Freire: Walking and Asking," in *Educational Alternatives in Latin America: New Modes of*

Counter-hegemonic Learning, ed. Robert Aman and Timothy Ireland (London: Palgrave Macmillan, 2019), 207–30.

44 Freire, *Pedagogy of the Oppressed,* 53.

45 Peter McLaren, *Revolutionary Multiculturalism: Pedagogies of Dissent for the New Millennium* (Boulder, CO: Westview, 1997).

46 See chapter 4 of this book.

47 Sandy Grande, "Red Pedagogy: The Un-methodology," in *Handbook of Critical and Indigenous Methodologies,* ed. Norma Denzin, Yvonne Lincoln, and Linda Tuhiwai Smith (London: Sage, 2008), 238.

48 Alexander, *Pedagogies of Crossing,* 7.

49 Alexander, *Pedagogies of Crossing,* 7.

50 *Palenque* refers to the ancestral communities of the Afro-Pacific that conserve a maroon heritage, while *comarca* names the broader territory or land made up of *palenques.*

51 "*Maestro-hermano* [teacher-brother] Juan" is the way that, over the years, I came to refer to and address Juan García Salazar.

52 See Catherine Walsh and Juan García Salazar, "(W)riting Collective Memory (De)spite State: Decolonial Practices of Existence in Ecuador," in *Black Writing, Culture, and the State in Latin America,* ed. Jerome C. Branche (Nashville: Vanderbilt University Press, 2015), 253–66.

53 Juan García Salazar and Catherine Walsh, *Pensar sembrando/sembrar pensando con el Abuelo Zenón* (Quito: Universidad Andina Simón Bolívar/Abya-Yala, 2017).

54 hooks, *Teaching to Transgress,* 56, 12.

55 Nelson Maldonado-Torres, "Interrogating Systematic Racism and the White Academic Field," Frantz Fanon Foundation, 2020, https://fondation -frantzfanon.com/interrogating-systemic-racism-and-the-white-academic -field/.

56 See Catherine Walsh, "Political-Epistemic Insurgency, Social Movements, and the Refounding of State," in *Rethinking Intellectuals in Latin America,* ed. Mabel Moraña and Bret Gustafson (Madrid: Iberoamericana Vervuert, 2010), 199–212.

57 Walsh, "Decoloniality in/as Praxis," 34.

58 There are exceptions of course. I recall the summer institute organized by María Lugones in 2007 at the University of Binghamton's Center of Philosophy, Interpretation and Culture, a center that María cofounded in 2006 and directed for many years, and which was tied to the interdisciplinary master's and doctoral program with the same name, where María also taught. At the summer institute, María talked to me about her efforts within the center to build a praxical space for action and thought, a coalition and community of learning and living in which graduate students were the foundation. During my time at the institute, I witnessed these insurgent efforts in/as decolonizing praxis and learned, through conversations with students, about how this praxis extended to the doctoral program, then under María's direction (2005–7). We were allies. While this program stopped receiving students in

2017, the description on the 2010 webpage evidences María's decolonial and decolonizing influence: "Among the developments important to the PIC [Philosophy, Interpretation and Culture] program is the recurrent claim that the Western tradition—philosophic, scientific, artistic, ethical and political, cultural, humanistic and so forth—has in profound respects come to an end." As such, the program posed then a series of crucial questions: "How do concerns with gender and race, colonialism and culture, bear upon relations to the Western canon and the need to supplement or discard it? How do issues of oppression and injustice bear upon challenges to Western rationality from within and without? In what ways does feminist theory interact with the history of Western philosophy and with post-modern and post-colonial studies? What challenges have emerged from worldwide developments in feminism to much of contemporary philosophy, social theory and literary theory? What kinds of responses are emerging from recent writings on aesthetics, colonization and decolonization, hybridity and cultural survival, to the claims that Western philosophy is Eurocentric? What are the implications of global developments—economic, political and cultural—for philosophy's future?" "Philosophy, Interpretation and Culture (PIC)—Graduate," Binghamton University, State University of New York, accessed May 18, 2022, http://www.binghamton.edu:8080/exist/rest/bulletin/2010-2011/ collegesAndSchools/harpur/departments/58harpurOU.xml?_xsl=/bulle tin/2010-2011/xsl/compose.xsl.

59 Stuart Hall, "Cultural Studies and Its Theoretical Legacies," in *Stuart Hall: Critical Dialogues in Cultural Studies*, ed. David Morley and Kuan-Hsing Chen (New York: Routledge, 1996), 263.

60 For reflections on these processes, see Catherine Walsh, "Shifting the Geopolitics of Critical Knowledge: Decolonial Thought and Cultural Studies 'Others' in the Andes," in *Globalization and the Decolonial Option*, ed. Walter D. Mignolo and Arturo Escobar (New York: Routledge, 2010), 78–93; Catherine Walsh, "The Politics of Naming: (Inter)cultural Studies in De-colonial Code," *Cultural Studies* 26, no. 1 (2012): 108–25; Catherine Walsh, "Qué saber, qué hacer y cómo ver? Los desafíos y predicamentos disciplinares, políticos y éticos de los estudios (inter)culturales desde América Andina," in *Estudios culturales latinoamericanos: Retos desde y sobre la región andina*, ed. Catherine Walsh (Quito: Universidad Andina Simón Bolívar/Abya Yala, 2003), 11–28; and the collection of essays in this last volume.

61 Joaquin Barriendos, "La colonialidad del ver: Hacia un nuevo diálogo visual interepistémico," *Nómadas* 35 (2011): 13–29.

62 Wilmer Miranda, "Existencias/re-existencias desde la sensorialidad: más allá del imperio de la mirada," essay presented in the Latin American Cultural Studies Doctoral Program, Universidad Andina Simón Bolívar, Quito, Ecuador, July 2020.

63 Linda Tuhiwai Smith, *Decolonizing Methodologies: Research and Indigenous Peoples* (London: Zed Books, 1999), 69.

64 Tendayi Sithole explains especially well the significance of Fanon's call for the disruption of method: "a means of introducing black subjects as subjects proper as opposed to objects. This means that black subjects are in charge of method, and this is the crux of Fanon's philosophy in which antagonisms are created within method by those objectified by method." Tendayi Sithole, "Frantz Fanon: Africana Existentialist Philosopher," *African Identities* 14, no. 2 (2016): 179.

65 I am thinking here with Gordon's assertion that "Fanon advocated the position of embodied interrogatives, of human being re-entering a relationship of questioning." Lewis R. Gordon, "Theory in Black: Teleological Suspensions in Philosophy of Culture," *Qui Parle* 18 (2010): 202.

66 Lugones, *Pilgrimages/Peregrinajes*, 28.

67 Lugones, *Pilgrimages/Peregrinajes*, 15.

68 Bagele Chilisa, *Indigenous Research Methodologies* (Los Angeles: Sage, 2012), 14.

69 Chilisa, *Indigenous Research Methodologies*, 14, with reference to Mohanty (1991).

70 Chela Sandoval, *Methodology of the Oppressed* (Minneapolis: University of Minnesota, 2000), 1.

71 I am reminded of Nelson Maldonado-Torres's words: "The benevolent white and liberal academic establishment approaches deviation from the existing trends and tracks of study by faculty members whose work draws from traditions of research that critically engage racism, not as innovation and relevant critique of established research practices, but as lack of sophistication and training. Scholars in general, and particularly scholars of color, whose work draws from a long tradition of identifying and critiquing systemic racism are expected to assimilate into established standards of research, even though these standards have failed to identify and address systemic racism or have been an active part of systemic racism." Maldonado-Torres, "Interrogating Systemic Racism."

72 So too ends my formal relation with the university, commencing (in January 2023) and celebrating my deinstitutionalization; in essence, my new status as "deinstitutionalized."

73 Alexander, *Pedagogies of Crossing*, 16.

74 Lugones, *Pilgrimages/Peregrinajes*, 6, 228.

75 For another description of my experience in the Escuelita, see Walsh, "Decoloniality in/as Praxis," 86–88.

76 Subcomandante Galeano, in Comisión de la Sexta del EZLN, *Pensamiento crítico frente a la hidra capitalista, I* (Chiapas: EZLN, 2015), 14.

77 I am reminded of Glen Coulthard's description of the Dechinta Centre for Research and Learning, a community-based intergenerational experience in Denendeh in the Northwest Territories of Canada, an experience that Coulthard describes as land-based decolonial education. For Coulthard, Dene scholar and center cofounder, this experience works to generate political, autonomous, and decolonial theory on the land, building on noncapitalist bush economies, strengthening Indigenous knowledges, and challenging

western education's model of dispossession and genocide. Glen Coulthard et al., "The Decolonial Everyday: Reflections on Indigenous Education and Land-Centered Praxis," presentation in the plenary panel at the conference Imagined Borders, Epistemic Freedoms: The Challenge of Social Imaginaries in Media, Art, Religion and Decoloniality, University of Colorado, Boulder, January 9, 2020. Also see the center's webpage, https://www.dechinta.ca/.

78 See Alexander, *Pedagogies of Crossing*; and Lugones, *Pilgrimages/Peregrinajes*.

79 Cora Coralina (1889–1985) is the pseudonym of the Brazilian writer, poet, and educator Anna Lins dos Guimarães Peixoto Bretas. This poem was initially published in *Poemas dos Becos de Goiás e estórias mais* (Sao Paulo: Editora José Olympio, 1965) and is widely available on the internet. My translation is of the Spanish version taken from Cora Coralina, "Estoy hecha de retazos," 8sorbosdeinspiracion.com, August 20, 2019, http://www.8sorbosdeinspiracion .com/estoy-hecha-de-retazos/.

CHAPTER THREE: TRAVERSING BINARIES AND BOUNDARIES

1 Chapter epigraph is from M. Jacqui Alexander, *Pedagogies of Crossing: Meditations on Feminism, Sexual Politics, Memory, and the Sacred* (Durham, NC: Duke University Press, 2015), 283.

2 Laura E. Pérez, "Spirit Glyphs: Reimagining Art and Artist in the Work of Chicana Tlamatinime," *Rhetorics of the Americas*, ed. Damian Baca and Víctor Villanueva (New York: Palgrave Macmillan, 2010), 198.

3 Sandra Harding, "Latin American Decolonial Social Studies of Scientific Knowledge: Alliances and Tensions," *Science, Technology, and Human Values* 41, no. 6 (2016): 1076.

4 Harding, "Latin American," 1077.

5 Oyèrónké Oyewùmi, *The Invention of Women: Making an African Sense of Western Gender Discourses* (Minneapolis: University of Minnesota Press, 1997), 152.

6 Oyewùmi, *Invention of Women*, ix.

7 See Aníbal Quijano, "Coloniality of Power, Eurocentrism, and Latin America," *Nepantla: Views from South* 1, no. 3 (2000): 533–80.

8 My use of both the past and present tenses here (e.g., *was* and *is*) is intentional. It is to make evident my belief that Quijano's thought and spirit live on, particularly for those of us who were close to him.

9 María Lugones, "The Coloniality of Gender," *Worlds and Knowledges Otherwise* 2 (Spring 2008): 4.

10 María Lugones, "Pasos hacia un feminismo decolonial," in *Feminismo descolonial: Nuevos aportes teórico-metodológicos a más de una década*, ed. Yuderkys Espinosa Miñosa (Quito: Abya-Yala, 2019), 25.

11 Breny Mendoza, "Coloniality of Gender and Power: From Postcoloniality to Decoloniality," in *Oxford Handbook of Feminist Theory*, ed. Lisa Disch and Mary Hawkesworth (Oxford Handbooks Online, 2016), https://www .oxfordhandbooks.com/view/10.1093/oxfordhb/9780199328581.001.0001 /oxfordhb-9780199328581-e-6.

12 Lugones, "Coloniality of Gender," 3, 12.

13 I thank Pedro DiPietro for pointing this out.

14 Gloria Wekker, *White Innocence: Paradoxes of Colonialism and Race* (Durham, NC: Duke University Press, 2016), 101.

15 Oyewùmi, *Invention of Women*, 2.

16 Sander Gillman, quoted in Stuart Hall, "The Spectacle of the Other," in *Representation. Cultural Representations and Signifying Practices*, ed. Stuart Hall (London: Sage, 1997), 265.

17 Hall, "Spectacle of the Other," 267.

18 Wekker, *White Innocence*, 107.

19 Personal conversations with Romana Mirza, January 7, 2020, Boulder, Colorado, and continued in later email exchanges. Also see Mirza's paper "Women Undercover: Exploring the Intersectional Identities of Muslim Women through Modest Fashion and Digital Storytelling," presented at the conference Imagined Borders, Epistemic Freedoms: The Challenge of Social Imaginaries in Media, Art, Religion and Decoloniality, University of Colorado, Boulder, January 8, 2020.

20 See Mirza's own digital story on YouTube, April 19, 2018, video, 4:35, https://youtu.be/c7adl48pkOk. For other stories from her "Women Undercover" research project, see Romana Mirza, "Underneath This Hijab," YouTube, February 11, 2019, video, 4:38, https://youtu.be/8J-dTCRCyYY; and Romana Mirza, "Beyond the Cover," YouTube, April 28, 2019, video, 4:03, https://youtu.be/emUFC-SSYAI.

21 Betty Ruth Lozano Lerma, *Aportes a un feminismo negro decolonial: Insurgencias epistémicas de mujeresnegras-afrocolombianas tejidas con retazos de memorias* (Quito: Universidad Andina Simón Bolívar and Abya-Yala, 2019).

22 Lugones, "Coloniality of Gender," 4.

23 Lugones, "Coloniality of Gender," 2.

24 Lugones, "Coloniality of Gender," 13.

25 As Quijano reminds us, dichotomy is, in fact, a cornerstone of western rationality, naturalized and accepted without question. See Aníbal Quijano, "Colonialidad del poder y clasificación social," *Journal of World-Systems Research* 6, no. 2 (Summer/Fall 2000): 342–86.

26 Pedro DiPietro, "Ni humanos ni animals," paper presented at the Universidad Andina Simón Bolívar, Quito, Ecuador, February 18, 2020. For a critical discussion on African American ungenderings and genderings, see Hortense J. Spillers's provocative text "Mama's Baby, Papa's Maybe: An American Grammar Book," *Diacritics* 17, no. 2 (Summer 1987): 64–81.

27 Betty Ruth Lozano Lerma, "El feminismo no puede ser uno porque las mujeres somos diversos: Aportes a un feminism negro decolonial desde la experiencia de las mujeres negras del Pacifico colombiano," *La manzana de la discordia* 5, no. 2 (July–December 2010): 7–24.

28 Lozano Lerma, "El feminismo," 13.

29 Lozano Lerma, "El feminismo," 8. Here Lozano is thinking with Audre Lorde's well-known phrase and argument, "The master's tools will never

dismantle the master's house." Audre Lorde, *Sister Outsider*, rev. ed. (1984; Berkeley: Crossing, 2007), 110.

30 See Saidiya V. Hartman, *Wayward Lives, Beautiful Experiments: Intimate Histories of Riotous Black Girls, Troublesome Women, and Queer Radicals* (New York: Norton, 2019); and Spillers, "Mama's Baby, Papa's Maybe."

31 See Catherine E. Walsh, "Decoloniality in/as Praxis," in *On Decoloniality: Concepts, Analytics, Praxis*, by Walter D. Mignolo and Catherine E. Walsh (Durham, NC: Duke University Press, 2018), 40–41.

32 Lorena Cabnal, "Acercamiento a la construcción de la propuesta de pensamiento epistémico de las mujeres indígenas feministas comunitarias de Abya Yala," in *Feminismos diversos: El feminismo comunitario* (Madrid: Acsur/Las Segovias, 2010), 14.

33 Cabnal, "Acercamiento," 15.

34 Rita Laura Segato, "El sexo y la norma: Frente estatal, patriarcado, desposesión, colonialidad," *Estudos Feministas* 22, no. 2 (May–August 2014): 603.

35 Rita Laura Segato, "Género y colonialidad: En busca de claves de lectura y de un vocabulario estratégico descolonial," in *La cuestión descolonial*, ed. Aníbal Quijano and Julio Mejía Navarrete (Lima: Universidad Ricardo Palma, 2010).

36 Aura Cumes, "Patriarcado, dominación colonial y epistemologías mayas," Museu d'Art Contemporani de Barcelona, 2019, https://img.macba.cat/public /uploads/20190611/Patriarcado_dominacinin_colonial_y_epistemologn_as _mayas.4.pdf.

37 Yamila Gutiérrez Callisaya, personal conversation, February 2020.

38 See Oyewùmi, *Invention of Women*, 16; Alexander, *Pedagogies of Crossing*, 283; and Irene Silverblatt, *Moon, Sun and Witches: Gender Ideologies and Class in Inca and Colonial Peru* (Princeton, NJ: Princeton University Press, 1987), xix, xxviii.

39 See, in particular, two of my previous texts: "Life and Nature 'Otherwise': Challenges from the Abya-Yalean Andes," in *The Anomie of the Earth: Philosophy, Politics, and Autonomy in Europe and the Americas*, ed. Federico Luisetti, John Pickles, and Wilson Kaiser (Durham, NC: Duke University Press, 2015), 93–118; and "Afro and Indigenous Life-Visions in/and Politics: (De)colonial Perspectives in Bolivia and Ecuador," *Bolivian Studies Journal*, no. 18 (2011): 49–69.

40 Silverblatt, *Moon, Sun, and Witches*, xxvi.

41 Oyewùmi, *Invention of Women*, 7.

42 Cumes, "Patriarcado," 10.

43 Manuel Zapata-Olivella, *La rebelión de los genes: El mestizaje americano en la sociedad futura* (Bogotá: Altamir, 1997), 362.

44 Juan García Salazar and Catherine Walsh, *Pensar sembrando/sembrar pensando con el Abuelo Zenón* (Quito: Universidad Andina Simón Bolívar/Abya-Yala, 2017), 252.

45 For an excellent critique of posthumanism from a decolonial perspective, see Zimitri Erasmus, "Sylvia Wynter's Theory of the Human: Counter-, Not Post-humanist," *Theory, Culture and Society* 37, no. 6 (2020): 47–65.

46 Marisol de la Cadena, *Earth Beings: Ecologies of Practice across Andean Worlds* (Durham, NC: Duke University Press, 2015), 24–25.

47 Juan de Santa Cruz Pachacuti, *Relación de antigüedades deste reyno de Pirú*, 1613, ed. Pierre Duviols and César Itier (Cuzco: Centro de Estudios Regionales Andinos Bartolomé de las Casas, 1993).

48 Declaration of Community Feminism at the World Conference of Peoples on Climate Change (Cochabamba, Bolivia, April 2010), cited in Margarita Aguinaga et al., "Pensar desde el feminism: Críticas y alternativas al desarrollo," in *Alternativas descoloniales al capitalism colonial/moderno*, comp. Pablo Quintero (Buenos Aires: Ediciones del Signo, 2016), 131.

49 This notion of denaturalization and desacralization comes from Carlos Cullen, cited in Grimaldo Rengifo Vasquez, "Education in the Modern West and Andean Culture," in *The Spirit of Regeneration: Andean Culture Confronting Western Notions of Development*, ed. Frederique Apffel-Marglin (London: Zed, 1998), 172–92.

50 Walter D. Mignolo. "Introduction to José de Acosta's *Historia Natural y Moral de las Indias*," in *Natural and Moral History of the Indies*, by José de Acosta, trans. Frances López-Morillas (Durham, NC: Duke University Press, 2002), xviii.

51 Rengifo Vasquez, "Education in the Modern West," 173.

52 Walter D. Mignolo, *The Darker Side of Western Modernity: Global Futures, Decolonial Options* (Durham, NC: Duke University Press, 2011), 11.

53 Rengifo Vasquez, "Education in the Modern West," 183.

54 Eduardo Gudynas, "Imágenes, ideas y conceptos sobre la naturaleza en América Latina," in *Cultura y naturaleza: Aproximaciones a propósito del bicentenario de la Independencia de Colombia*, ed. Leonardo Montenegro (Bogotá: Jardín Botánico José Celestín Mutis, 2011), 267–92.

55 Gudynas, "Imágenes, ideas y conceptos," 271.

56 Gudynas, "Imágenes, ideas y conceptos," 272.

57 Mignolo, *Darker Side of Western Modernity*, 13.

58 See Arturo Escobar, "Epistemologías de la naturaleza y colonialidad de la naturaleza. Variedades del realismo y constructivismo," in Montenegro, *Cultura y naturaleza*, 49–74; Enrique Leff, *Saber ambiental* (Mexico City: Siglo XXI, 1998); Vandana Shiva, *Monocultures of the Mind* (London: Zed, 1993); and Vandana Shiva, *Biopiracy: The Plunder of Nature and Knowledge* (Cambridge, MA: South End, 1997).

59 Santiago Castro-Gómez, *La hybris del punto cero: Ciencia, raza e ilustración en la Nueva Granada (1750-1816)* (Bogotá: Pontificia Universidad Javeriana, 2005), 48.

60 See Castro-Gómez, *La hybris*; Santiago Castro-Gómez, "La historia natural en el orden clásico y geopolítica del saber," in Montenegro, *Cultura y naturaleza*, 337–54; Leonardo Montenegro, "Cultura y naturaleza: Aproximaciones a propósito del bicentenario de la independencia de Colombia," in Montenegro, *Cultura y naturaleza*, 9–19; Mauricio Nieto, "Historia natural y la apropiación del nuevo mundo en la ilustración española," *Bulletin de l'Institut français d'études andines* 32, no. 3 (2003): 417–29; and Mary Louise Pratt, *Imperial Eyes:*

Travel Writing and Transculturation (New York: Routledge, 1992). Such expeditions, of course, were not limited to the Andes. The accounts of the German naturalists Johann von Spix and Car von Martius in Brazil (1817–20) speak of the simultaneous magnificence, beauty, richness, savageness, and danger of the landscape and of the need for western culture, as the superior force, to domesticate, civilize, and dominate Nature, including the Indians. See Gudynas, "Imágenes, ideas y conceptos," 270–71.

61 Pratt, *Imperial Eyes*, 15.

62 Alberto Acosta, "Toward the Universal Declaration of Rights of Nature, Thoughts for Action," *America Latina en Movimiento*, September 26, 2010.

63 Mignolo, *Darker Side of Western Modernity*, 11.

64 See Carl Schmitt, *The Nomos of the Earth in International Law of the Jus Publicum Europaeum*, trans. and annotated by G. L. Ulmen (New York: Telos, 2003).

65 Erasmus, "Sylvia Wynter's Theory," 49; Walter Mignolo, "Sylvia Wynter: What Does It Mean to Be Human?," in *Sylvia Wynter: On Being Human as Praxis*, ed. Katherine McKittrick (Durham, NC: Duke University Press, 2015), 109. Also see Sylvia Wynter, "1492: A New World View," in *Race, Discourse, and the Origin of the Americas: A New World View*, ed. Vera Lawrence Hyatt and Rex Nettleford (Washington, DC: Smithsonian Institution Press, 1995), 6–57.

66 Mignolo, "Sylvia Wynter," 110.

67 Gönül Kaya, "Why Jineology? Re-constructing the Sciences towards a Communal and Free Life," in *Stateless Democracy: New World Academy Reader #5*, with the Kurdish Women's Movement, ed. Renée In der Maur and Jonas Staal (Utrecht, Netherlands: BAK, 2015), 89.

68 Comité de Jineolojî Europa, *Jineoloji* (Neuss, Germany: Mezopotamien Verlag und Vertriebs, 2018).

69 Wekker, *White Innocence*, 100–101.

70 Sylvia Marcos, *Taken from the Lips: Gender and Eros in Mesoamerican Religions* (Boston: Brill, 2006), 14.

71 See Marcos, *Taken from the Lips*.

72 Oyewùmi, *Invention of Women*, 29.

73 Ifi Amadiume, *Male Daughters, Female Husbands: Gender and Sex in an African Society*, 2nd ed. (1987; London: Zed Books, 2015).

74 Cumes, "Patriarcado," 6.

75 See Manuela L. Picq and Josi Tikuna, "Indigenous Sexualities: Resisting Conquest and Translation," E-International Relations, August 20, 2019, https://www.e-ir.info/2019/08/20/indigenous-sexualities-resisting-conquest -and-translation/; and their citing of Ivan Olita's short film *Third Gender: An Entrancing Look at Mexico's Muxes* (2017).

76 Isaac Esau Carrillo Can, "Androgynous Eroticism in the Yucatec Maya Cosmology and Language," translated by Raúl Moarquech Ferrera Balanquet and Daniel Chávez, in "Erotic Sovereignty at the Decolonial Crossroads," ed. Raúl Moarquech Ferrera Balanquet (unpublished manuscript, 2017), 67.

77 Marcos, *Taken from the Lips*.

78 See Pete Sigal, *The Flower and the Scorpion: Sexuality and Ritual in Early Nahua Culture* (Durham, NC: Duke University Press, 2011).

79 Briceño Chel and Reyes Ramirez, quoted in Carrillo Can, "Androgynous Eroticism," 67.

80 Quoted in Silverblatt, *Moon, Sun, and Witches*, 41.

81 Carrillo Can, "Androgynous Eroticism," 68.

82 Carrillo Can, "Androgynous Eroticism," 66. Also see Carrillo Can's award-winning novel *U yóok'otilo'ob áak'ab/Danzas de la noche* (Mexico City: Conacultura, 2011).

83 Carrillo Can, "Androgynous Eroticism," 67.

84 Isaac Esau Carrillo Can, personal conversation, Duke University, February 2014.

85 Pedro DiPietro, "Neither Humans, Nor Animals, Nor Monsters: On the Coloniality of Transgender" (unpublished manuscript, 2020).

86 See, for example, among other English-language references, Ruth Palacios, "Lukas Avendaño: Reflections from Muxeidad," *Siwarmayu* (blog), accessed May 16, 2022, https://siwarmayu.com/lukas-avendano-reflections-from-muxeidad/; and Lukas Avendaño, "Lukas Avendaño Muxes, muxe performance artist teaser 2016," Facebook, June 30, 2019, https://es-la.facebook.com/815823491862168/videos/lukas-avenda%C3%B1omuxes-muxe-performance-artistteaser-2016/2341678702739605/.

87 Sylvia Marcos, "Otroa Compañeroa—La fluidez de género: Una emergencia contemporánea con raices ancestrales," Camino al andar, June 20, 2021, https://sylviamarcos.wordpress.com/2021/06/15/otroa-companeroa-la-fluidez-de-genero-una-emergencia-contemporanea-con-raices-ancestrales/.

88 Leanne Betasamosake Simpson, *As We Have Always Done: Indigenous Freedom through Radical Resistance* (Minneapolis: University of Minnesota Press, 2017), 123. Also see Will Roscoe's comprehensive linguistic index of the ways to refer to "alternative genders" in more than 150 North American Indian nations. Roscoe, *Changing Ones: Third and Fourth Genders in Native North America* (Basingstoke, UK: Palgrave, 1998).

89 See Ellen Goldberg, *The Lord Who Is Half Woman: Ardhanārīśvara in Indian and Feminist Perspective* (New York: State University of New York Press, 2002).

90 "India Recognizes Transgender People as Third Gender," *Guardian*, April 15, 2014, https://www.theguardian.com/world/2014/apr/15/india-recognises-transgender-people-third-gender. While the term *third gender* is seeing increasing use in different contexts throughout the world, we can ask about whether it shrouds cosmological millennial roots and serves to support the modern/colonial western gendered framework.

91 See Jaime Arocha, *Ombligados de Ananse: Hilos ancestrales y modernos en el Pacífico colombiano* (Bogotá: Universidad Nacional de Colombia, Facultad de Ciencias Humanas, 1999); and Lozano Lerma, *Aportes*.

92 Arocha, *Ombligados de Ananse*, 13.

93 Lozano Lerma, *Aportes*, 293.

94 Oyewùmi, *Invention of Women*, 140.

95 See Manuel Zapata Olivella, *Changó, the Biggest Badass*, trans. Jonathan Tittler (Lubbock: Texas Tech University Press, 2010).

96 See Simpson, *As We Have Always Done*; Alex Wilson, "How We Find Ourselves: Identity Development and Two-Spirit People," *Harvard Educational Review* 66, no. 2 (1996): 303–18; Qwo-Li Driskill, "Doubleweaving Two Spirit: Building Alliances between Native and Queer Studies, Sexuality, Nationality, and Indigeneity," *GLQ: A Journal of Lesbian and Gay Studies* 16, nos. 1–2 (2010): 69–92; and Qwo-Li Driskill et al., eds., *Queer Indigenous Studies: Critical Interventions in Theory, Politics, and Literature* (Tucson: Arizona University Press, 2011).

97 Michael Horswell, *Decolonizing the Sodomite: Queer Tropes of Sexuality in Colonial Andean Culture* (Austin: University of Texas Press, 2005), 2.

98 Horswell, *Decolonizing the Sodomite*, 23.

99 Horswell, *Decolonizing the Sodomite*, 19. Curiously enough, and in a different sense, for Pratt the naturalist-collector figure also had a "certain androgyny about it; its production of knowledge has some decidedly non-phallic aspects." Pratt, *Imperial Eyes*, 33. As such, and following Pratt, we can ask how it figures into the "natural" order.

100 Gloria Anzaldúa, *Borderlands = La Frontera: The New Mestiza* (San Francisco: Aunt Lute Books, 1987), 46.

101 Anzaldúa, *Borderlands*, 47.

102 Anzaldúa, *Borderlands*, 47.

103 Silverblatt, *Moon, Sun, and Witches*, xxviii.

104 Zeb Tortorici, "Against Nature: Sodomy and Homosexuality in Colonial Latin America," *History Compass* 10, no. 2 (2012): 170.

105 Silverblatt, *Moon, Sun, and Witches*, xxiv.

106 Silverblatt, *Moon, Sun, and Witches*, 15.

107 Horswell, *Decolonizing the Sodomite*, 4.

108 See, for example, Tortorici, "Against Nature"; and Sigal, *Flower and the Scorpion*.

109 See Omise'eke Natasha Tinsley, *Ezili's Mirrors: Imagining Black Queer Genders* (Durham, NC: Duke University Press, 2018); Audre Lorde, *Zami: A New Spelling of My Name: A Biomythography* (Berkeley, CA: Crossing, 1982); and Gloria Wekker, *The Politics of Passion: Women's Sexual Culture in the Afro-Surinamese Diaspora* (New York: Colombia University Press, 2006).

110 Hartman, *Wayward Lives, Beautiful Experiments*; personal conversations with Betty Ruth Lozano Lerma, Quito, April 2016.

111 Margaret R. Greer, *María de Zayas Tells Baroque Tales of Love and the Cruelty of Men* (University Park: Pennsylvania State University Press, 2000), 68.

112 Huarte de San Juan, quoted in Greer, *María de Zayas*, 68.

113 Laqueur quoted in Greer, *María de Zayas*, 70.

114 Greer's analysis of feminism in the seventeenth-century writings of María de Zayas in Spain is particularly enlightening in this regard.

115 Margarita Aguinaga Barragán, "Ecofeminismo: Mujer y Pachamama, no solo es possible una crítica al capitalism y patriarcado," *Flor del Guanto* 4 (December 2012): 10.

116 Aguinaga Barragán, "Ecofeminismo," 11.

117 Frantz Fanon, *Black Skin, White Masks*, trans. from the French by Charles Lam Markmann (New York: Grove, 1967).

118 María Lugones, "Methodological Notes toward a Decolonial Feminism," in *Decolonizing Epistemologies: Latina/o Theology and Philosophy*, ed. Ada María Isasi-Díaz and Eduardo Mendieta (New York: Fordham, 2012), 73.

119 Lugones, "Methodological Notes," 73.

120 Lugones, "Methodological Notes," 74–75.

121 Segato, "Género y colonialidad," 15.

122 Julieta Paredes, *Hilando fino desde el feminismo comunitario* (Querétaro, Mexico: Grietas, 2012).

123 Segato, "El sexo y la norma," 17.

124 Lourdes Huanca Atencio, intervention at the meeting of the Red de Mujeres Defensores de Derechos Sociales y Ambientales, Quito, October 2013.

125 Huanca Atencio, intervention.

126 Lucy Santacruz and Judith Flores, "Entrevista a Lourdes Huanca Atencio, de la Federación Nacional de Mujeres Campesinas, Artesanas, Indígenas, Nativas y Asalariadas de Perú," *Flor de Guanto* 4 (December 2012): 46.

127 Simpson, *As We Have Always Done*, 52.

128 Tsaywa Cañamar, "Runa Warmikuna Sinchiyarinchik/Fortale(ser)nos siendo mujeres runakuna" (master's thesis, Universidad Andina Simón Bolívar, Quito, 2020), https://repositorio.uasb.edu.ec/handle/10644/7411. As Tsaywa's thesis director, I had the opportunity to listen to her detailed accounts of the methodology, the dialogic conversations, the horrors of violences lived, and the multiple ways these women resisted and re-existed, weaving together a strength and a sense of freedom. With Tsaywa, I learned, listening, reading, and conversing *with* this female force-energy-power woven with Pachamama.

129 Cabnal, "Acercamiento," 16, 24.

130 The Aymara Bolivian Yamila Gutiérrez explains why, for her, the label of feminism is not adequate: "For me, feminism remains a western, anthropocentric, and individualist posture or position. It seems to suggest a disassociation or an unlinking from something, a setting off from the integral whole, from the activity of existence, of life, which is shared among all beings, including with the ancestors. The person is not just a person, the person is not a person alone, nor is her thought separate from the integral sphere of territory, beings, the cosmos, etc. As Indigenous women we have, feel, and create a connection and relation. We also know, recognize, and struggle against the machismo and male privilege present in our families, communities, and *ayllus*. *Feminism* is not the word we use, nor does its concept and standpoint—born and constructed outside of our contexts—adequately reflect our project." Personal conversation, Quito, June 2, 2017.

131 While Betancourt is her legal last name, Machoa is her name of use. Katy [Betancourt] Machoa, "El florecimiento de la rebeldía," text presented in the photographic exhibit *Mujeres en la lucha social ecuatoriana*, organized by the Collective Desde el Margen, Universidad Andina Simón Bolívar, Quito, November 21–25, 2017.

132 Comments by Machoa as an invited speaker in my course Contemporary Feminist Theory and Interculturality in Abya Yala, November 28, 2017.

133 Machoa, quoted in James Giménez, "Mujeres indígenas contra petroleras chinas en Ecuador: 'Estamos dispuestas a morir por nuestra selva,'" *elDiario.es*, March 25, 2016, https://www.eldiario.es/desalambre/amazonicas-ecuador-defienden-territorio-supervivencia_1_5863501.html. See also Catherine E. Walsh, "Resisting, Re-existing, and Co-existing (De)spite State: Women's Insurgencies for Territory and Life in Ecuador," in *Decolonial Feminism in Abya Yala: Caribbean, Meso, and South American Contributions and Challenges*, ed. Yuderkys Espinosa Miñoso, María Lugones, and Nelson Maldonado-Torres (New York: Rowman and Littlefield, 2022), 217–44.

134 Spillers, "Mama's Baby, Papa's Maybe," 80.

135 Alexander, *Pedagogies of Crossing*.

136 Zapatista Women, "Letter from the Zapatista Women to Women in Struggle around the World," Enlace Zapatista, February 2019, https://enlacezapatista.ezln.org.mx/2019/02/13/letter-from-the-zapatista-women-to-women-in-struggle-around-the-world/.

137 See, for example, Catherine Walsh, "Political-Epistemic Insurgency, Social Movements and the Refounding of the State," in *Rethinking Intellectuals in Latin America*, ed. Mabel Moraña and Bret Gustafson (Madrid: Iberoamericana Vervuert, 2010), 199–212.

138 Walsh, "Political-Epistemic Insurgency," 202.

139 Walsh, "Political-Epistemic Insurgency," 203.

140 Lozano Lerma, *Aportes*.

141 While I directed Betty Ruth's dissertation, our dialogue and conversation are not limited to this context but have included, over a number of years, ongoing shared collaborations, exchanges, and reflections. Among these, and directly related to aspects of her doctoral project described here, was her engaged conversation with Juan García Salazar and me, both in the context of our dialogic text *Pensar sembrando/sembrar pensando* and the oral testimonies and narratives and print materials that form part of the Fondo Documental Afro-Andino mentioned in the previous chapter, most especially those of midwives from the Esmeraldas Pacific region.

142 Betty Ruth Lozano Lerma, "Pedagogías para la vida, la alegria y la re-existencia: Pedagogías de mujeres negras que curan y vinculan," in *Pedagogías decoloniales: Prácticas insurgentes de resistir, (re)existir y (re)vivir*, ed. Catherine Walsh (Quito: Abya-Yala, 2017), 2:288–89.

143 Lozano Lerma, *Aportes*, 175–76.

144 Lozano Lerma, *Aportes*, 128.

145   Lozano Lerma, *Aportes*, 128.

146   Lozano Lerma, *Aportes*, 293.

147   Lozano Lerma, *Aportes*, 293. Recalled here are Hortense J. Spillers's words: "We are less interested in joinging the ranks of gendered femaleness than gaining the insurgent ground as female social subject." Spillers, "Mama's Baby, Papa's Maybe," 80.

148   B. Chancosa et al., "Mujeres indígenas de latinoamerica enfrentan el cambio climático desde sus procesos de adaptabilidad cultural: Chasaqui warmikuna del Abya Yala frente al cambio climático 'Haciendo caminar la palabra,'" document prepared for the twenty-second session of the Conference of the Parties, Morocco (Quito: Ecuarunari, 2016).

149   Chancosa et al., "Mujeres indígenas."

150   Chancosa et al., "Mujeres indígenas."

151   This familiarity comes not only from following the web, social media, and public presentations but most especially from ongoing conversations with some of the participants, particularly Yamila Gutiérrez Callisaya, a graduate student of mine who was part of one of the women-messenger journeys in the Ecuadorian Amazon.

152   Braulio HyC, "Yaku Chaski Warmi Kuna: Mujeres mensajeras por el petróleo baja la tierra" (Tegantai: Agencia de Noticias Ecologistas, July 27, 2015). Also see Braulio's video "Yakuchaski Warmikuna: Mensajeras del Río Curaray," Saramanta Warmikuna, May 23, 2016, http://www.saramanta.org/video-yakuchaski-warmikuna-mensajeras-del-rio-curaray/.

153   "Yaku Chaski Warmi Kuna finaliza primera etapa," press release circulated on social media, Puyo, Pastaza Province, Ecuador, July 27, 2015.

154   Yamila Gutiérrez, personal conversation, Quito, June 2, 2017.

155   Gutiérrez, personal conversation.

156   Words taken from Machoa, "El florecimiento de la rebeldía."

157   Interview with Necîbe Qeredaxî, in Brecht Neven and Marlene Shäfers, "Jineology: From Women's Struggles to Social Liberation," *Roar*, November 26, 2017, https://roarmag.org/essays/jineology-kurdish-women-movement/.

158   Kaya, "Why Jineology?"

159   Comité de Jineologî, *Jineologî*, 12.

160   See Jineology's English-language website, accessed May 20, 2022, https://jineoloji.org/en/.

161   Abdullah Öclan, *The Sociology of Freedom: Manifesto of the Democratic Civilization* (2008; Oakland, CA: PM Press, 2020), 3:294.

162   Qeredaxî, in Neven and Shäfers, "Jineology."

163   Kaya, "Why Jineology?," 92–93.

164   Qeredaxî, quoted in Neven and Shäfers, "Jineology."

165   Kaya, "Why Jineology?," 91.

166   Comité de Jineologî Europa, *Jineologî*, 61.

167   Kaya, "Why Jineology?," 93.

168 While this was our first shared encounter with Mama Huaco, it certainly was not the last. In fact, it was just the beginning. Over the next several years (and continuing into the present), we discussed her figure, potential, and power at length, in the context of the master's thesis (which I had the honor to direct), in seminars and public events, and in everyday struggles to crack the coloniality of gender and enable the power, possibility, and dynamism of an otherwise.

169 Horswell, *Decolonizing the Sodomite*.

170 Horswell, *Decolonizing the Sodomite*, 223, in discussion with Sarmiento.

171 Horswell, *Decolonizing the Sodomite*, 158–59.

172 Catherine Walsh, "On Gender and Its Otherwise," in *The Palgrave Handbook of Gender and Development*, ed. Wendy Harcourt (London: Palgrave Macmillan, 2016), 34–47.

173 Ángel Burbano, "Los espejos de Mama Huaco: Un acto interpretivo en dos tiempos" (master's thesis, Universidad Andina Simón Bolívar, Quito, 2019), 7, https://repositorio.uasb.edu.ec/handle/10644/7591?mode=full.

174 Ángel Burbano, "El espejo de Ipa Mama Huaco," personal website of Ángel Burbano, August 21, 2017, https://angelburbanos22.wixsite.com /angelitox100pre/post/el-espejo-de-ipa-mama-huaco.

175 These photographs also formed part of the exhibit *Archivxs: Exposición Orgullo LGBTIQ+*, held in Quito in 2019.

176 Dakira Bri, cited in Burbano, "Los espejos de Mama Huaco," 81.

177 Burbano, "Los espejos de Mama Huaco," 69.

178 Burbano, "Los espejos de Mama Huaco," 9.

179 Ángel Burbano, "Mama Huaco," in the exhibit *Archivxs: Exposición Orgullo LGBTIQ+*, Quito, 2019, 30.

180 See Felipe Guamán Poma de Ayala, *Nueva corónica y buen gobierno*, 1615, transcription, prologue, notes, and chronology by Franklin Pease (Caracas: Biblioteca Ayacucho, 1980), 82, 86.

181 Burbano, "Los espejos de Mama Huaco," 82.

182 Burbano, "Los espejos de Mama Huaco," 9.

183 Carrillo Can, "Androgynous Eroticism," 65.

184 María Lugones, *Pilgrimages/Peregrinajes: Theorizing Coalition against Multiple Oppressions* (New York: Rowman and Littlefield, 2003), 227.

185 Lugones, *Pilgrimages/Peregrinajes*, 228–29.

186 See Adrián Neubauer and Angel Méndez-Núñez, "New Educational Horizons Following the Rise of the 'New Far Right' in Europe: A Documentary Analysis," *Education Policy Analysis Archives* 30, no. 23 (February 22, 2022): 1–23, https://epaa.asu.edu/index.php/epaa/article/view/5486.

187 Raimundo Paccó and Alba Santandreu, "La deforestación de la Amazonía se extiende tan rápido como la COVID-19," *La Vanguardia*, May 28, 2020, https:// www.lavanguardia.com/natural/20200528/481433474349/la-deforestacion-de -la-amazonia-se-extiende-tan-rapido-como-la-covid-19.html.

188 Camilo Hernández, "La deforestación y el COVID-19, las amenazas a la vida en el Amazonas brasileño," AA, June 21, 2020, https://www.aa.com.tr/es /mundo/la-deforestaci%C3%B3n-y-el-covid-19-las-amenazas-a-la-vida-en-el -amazonas-brasile%C3%B1o/1885092.

189 Alexander, *Pedagogies of Crossing*, 283.

CHAPTER FOUR: UNDOING NATION-STATE

1 Chapter epigraph is from Leanne Betasamosake Simpson, *As We Have Always Done: Indigenous Freedom through Radical Resistance* (Minneapolis: University of Minnesota Press, 2017), 153.

2 Roxanne Dunbar-Ortiz, *An Indigenous Peoples' History of the United States* (Boston: Beacon, 2014), 1.

3 Jane Anna Gordon reminds us that this forced incorporation was of distinct regional groups that had long lived semiautonomously. "Such groups became, in their own view, *nations without states*, or *nations occupied by illegitimate states*, even when they possessed formal citizenship within First or Second World powers." Jane Anna Gordon, *Statelessness and Contemporary Enslavement* (New York: Routledge, 2020), 19.

4 See "Palestine and Israel: Mapping an Annexation," *Aljazeera*, June 26, 2020, https://www.aljazeera.com/news/2020/6/26/palestine-and-israel-mapping-an -annexation#historyannex.

5 Ajamu Baraka, "From Palestine to Colombia: The End of the White World Colonial/Capitalist Project?," Black Agenda Report, May 12, 2021, https:// mronline.org/2021/05/15/from-palestine-to-colombia-the-end-of-the-white -world-colonial-capitalist-project/.

6 The Great Comarca is the historical Black territory that extends from what is now Panama to the north of Ecuador. It united the territorial *palenques,* or free Black communities, and afforded a model of territorial, political, ethnic-communitarian organization in which land tenure, ancestral forms of territorial administration, and the sustainable use of natural resources were key. While state divisions and practices have worked to dismantle the Great Comarca, *palenques* continue to persist and resist today.

7 Quoted in Catherine Walsh and Juan García Salazar, "(W)riting Collective Memory (De)spite State: Decolonial Practices of Existence in Ecuador," in *Black Writing, Culture, and the State in Latin America*, ed. Jerome C. Branche (Nashville: Vanderbilt University Press, 2015), 261.

8 Walsh and García, "(W)riting Collective Memory."

9 Quoted in Walsh and García, "(W)riting Collective Memory," 259.

10 Quoted in Walsh and García, "(W)riting Collective Memory," 259.

11 Of course, the histories, herstories, and theirstories of settler-colonial power in eighteenth-century North America are distinct from the coloniality constructed, developed, and imposed beginning in 1492 in what is now known as Latin America. The differential ways the latter established and consolidated

the ideas of race and gender, Euro-modernity, and capitalism entwined, and the ways the former founded state on ideologies of white supremacy, practices of enslavement, and policies of genocide and land theft, certainly matter. Nonetheless, the parallels between both are increasingly apparent today, most especially with respect to corporate state practices and projects of dispossession. See Dunbar-Ortiz, *Indigenous Peoples' History*. Also see Glen Coulthard's description of the structural/objective and recognitive/subjective features of colonialism following Fanon, in Glen Coulthard, *Red Skin, White Masks: Rejecting the Colonial Politics of Recognition* (Minneapolis: University of Minnesota Press, 2014), 32–33.

12 Coulthard, *Red Skin, White Masks*, 7.

13 Simpson, *As We Have Always Done*, 43.

14 Jane Anna Gordon, *Statelessness and Contemporary Enslavement*, 4.

15 See Breny Mendoza, "La epistemología del sur: La colonialidad del género y el feminismo latinoamericano," in *Aproximaciones críticas a las prácticas teórico-políticas del feminismo latinoamericano*, coord. Yuderkys Espinosa Miñoso (Buenos Aires: En la frontera, 2010), 19–36; and Breny Mendoza, "Coloniality of Gender and Power: From Postcoloniality to Decoloniality," in *The Oxford Handbook of Feminist Theory*, ed. Lisa Disch and Mary Hawkesworth (Oxford Handbooks Online, 2016), https://www.oxfordhandbooks.com/view/10.1093/oxfordhb/9780199328581.001.0001/oxfordhb-9780199328581-e-6.

16 Ochy Curiel, *La nación heterosexual* (Bogotá: Brecha lésbica and En la frontera, 2013).

17 Abdullah Öcalan, *Democratic Confederalism* (London: Transmedia, 2011), 13.

18 Remarks by Gloria Wekker at the María Lugones Decolonial Summer School, online from the Netherlands, July 2, 2021.

19 Melike Yasar and Ana Maria Morales, "El facismo no es un estado que no reconoce a la sociedad, es la ideología de la guerra," *Revista Amazonas*, no. 1 (October 2019): 21–33.

20 Öcalan, *Democratic Confederalism*, 26.

21 Simpson, *As We Have Always Done*, 153.

22 It is important to note that my references to the processes in Kurdistan are not totally dissimilar. They are rooted in and part of ongoing conversations with members of the movement begun much more recently (2018) and oriented toward thinking and building relation between Kurdistan and Latin America, their territories, and their existence-based struggles beyond and despite nation-state.

23 Lorena Cabnal, talk given in the offices of Acción Ecológica, Quito, March 20, 2017.

24 See Lorena Cabnal, "Acercamiento a la construción de la propuesta de pensamiento epistémico de las mujeres indígenas feministas comunitarias de Abya Yala," in *Feminismos diversos: El feminismo comunitario* (Madrid: Acsur/Las Segovias, 2010), 11–25; and Tsaywa Cañamar, "Runa Warmikuna Sinchiyarinchik/Fortale(ser)nos siendo mujeres runakuna" (master's thesis, Universidad

Andina Simón Bolívar, Quito, 2020), https://repositorio.uasb.edu.ec/handle
/10644/7411.

25 Michaeline Crichlow, *Globalization and the Post-Creole Imagination: Notes on
Fleeing the Plantation* (Durham, NC: Duke University Press, 2009), 1, 15.

26 Crichlow, *Globalization*, 16.

27 Silvia Rivera Cusicanqui, "La raíz: Colonizadores y colonizados," in *Violencias encubiertas en Bolivia*, ed. Xavier Albó and Raúl Barrios (La Paz: CIPCA-
Aruwiyiri, 1993), 1:27–139. Also see Javier Sanjinés, *Mestizaje Upside Down:
Aesthetic Politics in Modern Bolivia* (Pittsburgh: University of Pittsburgh Press,
2004).

28 See Bartolomé de Las Casas, *Short Account of the Destruction of the Indies* (London: Penguin, 1999); and Lawrence Clayton, "Bartolomé de Las Casas and the
African Slave Trade," *History Compass* 7, no. 6 (2009): 1526–41.

29 Agustín Cueva, *Sobre nuestra ambigüedad cultural* (Quito: Editora Universitaria,
1974).

30 Sanjinés, *Mestizaje Upside Down*.

31 Aníbal Quijano, "Colonialidad del poder, cultura y conocimiento en América
Latina," *Dispositio/n* 24, no. 51 (1999–2000): 137–48.

32 *Merriam-Webster*, s.v. "nation-state," accessed May 23, 2022, http://www
.merriam-webster.com/dictionary/nation%E2%80%93state.

33 Zavaleta, *El Estado en América Latina* (Cochabamba, Bolivia: Los amigos del
libro, 1990), 45, 57–58.

34 Zavaleta, *El Estado en América Latina*. Also see Aníbal Quijano, "Estado-nación
y movimientos indígenas en la región andina: Cuestiones abiertas," *Revista del
Observatorio Social de América Latina: Movimientos sociales y gobiernos en la region
andina: Resistencias y alternativas* 8, no. 19 (2006), 15–24; and Jane Anna Gordon,
Statelessness and Contemporary Enslavement.

35 Quijano, "Estado-nación," 22.

36 Quijano, "Estado-nación," 20.

37 As Quijano reminds us, it is important to recall the strong presence throughout the twentieth century of the idea and discourse of nationalism on the
Latin American Left. This idea and discourse were rooted in the Third
International's call for strategic alliances between the dominated/exploited
and the national bourgeoisie against imperial domination in the struggles for
socialism and the control of the nation-state.

38 Quijano, "Estado-nación," 21.

39 For a discussion of this ideational regime, see Margaret R. Somers cited in
Jane Anna Gordon, *Statelessness and Contemporary Enslavement*, 29–30. Until
recently Chile remained an example in this regard. Yet in October 2019 this
example and legacy began to crumble with the massive protests against
neoliberalism (including its base in the Pinochet constitution) begun by
students and subsequently expanding to include almost all sectors of the
population (except the ruling class). The state response then was extreme
violence, a violence directed at urban youths as well at the Mapuche nation.

The 2021–22 Constitutional Assembly and the election in December 2021 of Leftist Gabriel Boric as president offer promises of change. However, as of today (June 2022), Mapuche communities and land continue to be militarized.

40 Breny Mendoza, *Ensayos de crítica feminista en Nuestra América* (Mexico City: Herder, 2014), 246.

41 Bolivian state capitalism, according to Tapia, is what gave base and form to the political construction of a modern Bolivian nation. Nation, in this case, was not the project of a national bourgeoisie. It was a modern project begun and defended by workers and middle-class sectors, nationalist and populist in proposition and vision. See Luis Tapia, *Una reflexión sobre la idea de un estado plurinational* (La Paz: Oxfam, 2008).

42 Mendoza, *Ensayos*, 249.

43 Quijano, "Estado-nación," 22.

44 Quijano, "Estado-nación," 21.

45 Salvador Schavelzon, *Plurinacionalidad y Vivir Bien/Buen Vivir: Dos conceptos leídos desde Bolivia y Ecuador post-constituyentes* (Buenos Aires: CLACSO, 2015), 167.

46 Schavelzon, *Plurinacionalidad*, 167.

47 Coulthard, *Red Skin, White Masks*, 2.

48 Coulthard, *Red Skin, White Masks*, 3.

49 Coulthard, *Red Skin, White Masks*, 6.

50 Coulthard, *Red Skin, White Masks*, 3.

51 Coulthard, *Red Skin, White Masks*, 6.

52 See, for example, Catherine Walsh, *Interculturalidad, estado, sociedad: Luchas (de)coloniales de nuestra época* (Quito: Universidad Andina Simón Bolívar, 2009).

53 See Marcelo Fernández Osco, *La ley del ayllu* (La Paz: Programa de Investigación Estratégica en Bolivia, 2000); Esteban Ticona, "Eduardo Nina Quispe: El emancipador, educador y político Aymara," in *Pedagogías decoloniales: Prácticas insurgentes de resistir, (re)existir y (re)vivir*, ed. Catherine Walsh (Quito: Abya-Yala, 2013), 1:331–56. Personal conversations over a number of years with both these Aymaran intellectuals, along with others, have been crucial in guiding my reflections and understandings.

54 Tapia, *Una reflexión*, 62–63. Also see Marcelo Fernández Osco, "El ayllu y la reconstitución del pensamiento Aymara" (PhD diss., Duke University, 2009). As this latter author explains, the condition of citizenship offered by the state is distinct from—and works to fragment and disable—the identity of a collective people; citizenship does not express the political rights sought and claimed in history (137).

55 Esteban Ticona, *Organización y liderazgo aymara, 1979–1996* (Cochabamba, Bolivia: Agroecología Universidad de Cochabamba, 2000), 144.

56 Fausto Reinaga, *Manifiesto Partido Indio de Bolivia* (La Paz: Fausto Reinaga, 1970), 63, 64.

57 See Javier Hurtado, *El Katarismo* (La Paz: Hisbol, 1986); Silvia Rivera Cusi-
    canqui, *Oprimidos pero no vencidos: Luchas del campesinado aymara y qhechwa,
    1900–1980* (La Paz: Hisbol, 1986); and Ticona, *Organización y liderazgo aymara.*

58 Rivera Cusicanqui, *Oprimidos pero no vencidos*, 128–29.

59 Katarism takes as its principal reference the anticolonial uprising of Tupac
    Katari and Bartolina Sisa in 1781. However, according to Ticona, it also has
    a symbolic connotation related to the *katari*, or snake, which constitutes a
    totem for the Aymara peoples and symbolizes the earthquake and revolution
    from below. Ticona, *Organización y liderazgo aymara.*

60 Carlos Macusaya Cruz, "Autoría y significado político del Manifiesto de
    Tiahuanaco," *Pukara*, no. 95 (July 2014): 6–8. Among the critical reflections
    of Macusaya is one on the authorship of the manifesto. "It was the priest
    Gregorio Iriarte who drafted the Manifesto," says Macusaya (7). While the
    Katarists Jenaro Flores and Teodomiro Rengel were behind the initiative, the
    document's language and thought are those of Iriarte, Macusaya maintains.

61 Roberto Choque Canqui, "El Manifiesto de Tiwanaku (1973) y el inicio de la
    descolonización," *Revistas bolivianas* 4, no. 11 (2010): 11, http://www.revistasbo
    livianas.ciencia.bo/pdf/fdc/v4n11/a04.pdf.

62 Ticona, *Organización y liderazgo aymara.*

63 "Primer Manifiesto de Tiahuanaco," in Hurtado, *El Katarismo*, 303. This
    phrase is also cited in Fausto Reinaga's texts *La Revolución India* (1970) and
    Tesis India (1971), both published a couple of years before the *Manifiesto de
    Tiwanaku.*

64 The term *campesino*, or peasant, has a history in the Andes tied to class strug-
    gle and the traditional Left. In Bolivia, it was introduced in the 1952 revolu-
    tion by the National Revolutionary Movement as an integrative mechanism,
    conceived as a way to connect all Native peoples in a common identity
    and surpass the negative hacienda-based connotations of *indio*, a colonially
    imposed and classificatory term. In the context of Katarism, *indio* was part of
    a new sociocultural and historical consciousness that, as I will later explain,
    had two political manifestations: one ethnic and Indian-centered (i.e., Indian-
    ist), and the other simultaneously culture and class based, often expressed by
    the dual expression of *indio-campesino.*

65 "Primer Manifiesto," in Hurtado, *El Katarismo*, 303.

66 "Primer Manifiesto," in Hurtado, *El Katarismo*, 304.

67 See Hurtado, *El Katarismo*, 59–60, 303–7.

68 Hurtado, *El Katarismo*, 246–47.

69 Juan Conori Uruchi, "Quiénes somos en Qullasuyo," cited in Choque Canqui,
    "El Manifiesto de Tiwanaku," 14.

70 *Indianism*—or *indianismo* in Spanish—is the term most often used to refer to
    this political consciousness and ideology. While Indianism began in Bolivia,
    it is now widely recognized throughout Abya Yala as an Indian-based po-
    litical stance grounded in the lived colonial experience and in anticolonial
    and decolonizing struggles of liberation. Indianism is radically distinct from

indigenismo, a non-Indigenous sociocultural and sociopolitical posture or tendency typically of folkloric, assimilationist, integrationist, and recolonizing nature.

71 MITKA's Clandestine Manifesto, cited in Macusaya, "Autoría y significado politico," 7.

72 MITKA, 1978, cited in Marie-Chantal Barre, *Ideologías indigenistas y movimientos indios* (Mexico City: Siglo XXI, 1983), 108. Recalled here is the Kurdish liberation leader Abdullah Öcalan's proposal of plurinational confederalism rooted in the millennial history of a peoples and not in state. See Öcalan, *Democratic Confederalism*.

73 "Tesis del Campesinado Boliviano," in Hurtado, *El Katarismo*, 322.

74 Sanjinés, *Mestizaje Upside Down*, 175.

75 CSUTCB, "Tesis Política," in Rivera Cusicanqui, *Oprimidos pero no vencidos*, 185–86.

76 CSUTCB, in Rivera Cusicanqui, *Oprimidos pero no vencidos*, 187–88.

77 CSUTCB, in Rivera Cusicanqui, *Oprimidos pero no vencidos*, 196–98.

78 CSUTCB, in Rivera Cusicanqui, *Oprimidos pero no vencidos*, 198.

79 René Zavaleta, *El estado en América Latina* (Cochabamba, Bolivia: Los amigos del libro, 1990), 45.

80 Zavaleta, *El estado en América Latina*, 53.

81 Zavaleta, *El estado en América Latina*, 57.

82 I thank the Indianist intellectual Elizabeth Huanca for pointing this out to me.

83 Sanjinés, *Mestizaje Upside Down*, 174–75.

84 In 1985, Jenaro Flores founded the Tupac Katari Revolutionary Movement of Liberation (MRTKL; the result of a preelectoral division within the MRTK) and ran as its presidential candidate. The MRTKL participated in elections again in 1989, this time with Víctor Hugo Cárdenas as presidential candidate. The National Revolutionary Movement and MRTKL alliance came later, in 1993, with the win of Sánchez de Lozada as president and Cárdenas as vice president. Also included in the National Revolutionary Movement–MRTKL alliance was the Leftist Movimiento Bolivia Libre and the populist party Unión Cívica Solidaridad.

85 Salvador Schavelzon, *El nacimiento de Estado Plurinacional de Bolivia: Etnografía de una Asamblea Constituyente* (Buenos Aires: CLACSO/Plural, 2012), 90n63.

86 Fernández Osco, "El Ayllu," 138.

87 Coulthard, *Red Skin, White Masks*.

88 See Catherine Walsh, "Afro In/Exclusion, Resistance, and the 'Progressive' State: (De)colonial Struggles, Questions, and Reflections," in *Black Social Movements in Latin America: From Monocultural Mestizaje to Multiculturalism*, ed. Jean Muteba Rahier (New York: Palgrave, 2012), 15–34.

89 Fernández Osco, "El Ayllu," 4.

90 Fernández Osco, "El Ayllu," 136.

91 Fernández Osco, "El Ayllu," 5.

92 As explained in the previous chapter, relationality is one of the central concepts (along with complementarity, correspondence, and reciprocity) of an Andean philosophy. In a basic sense, it refers to the interconnection (axiological and lived) among all elements; that is, an integral coexistence—in balance and harmony—with the cosmos and with all its affective, ecological, ethical, aesthetic, productive, spiritual, and intellectual variables. See Josef Estermann, *Filosofía andina* (Quito: Abya-Yala, 1998). For Simón Yampara, it is the emulative energy of conversation between the members of the biotic community; the lived experience with the world, people in space-time with ancestral deities and the natural biotic community. See Simón Yampara, "Cosmovisión, Uruq-Oacha, desarrollo y/o qamaña andino," in *Educación intra e intercultural: Alternativas a la reforma educativa neocolonizadora*, ed. Freddy Delgado and Juan Carlos Mariscal (La Paz: Plural, 2006), 23–36.

93 Part of personal and ongoing conversations with Yamila Gutiérrez Callisaya, Quito, June 2017.

94 Included in this initial alliance were the National Council of Ayllus and Markas of Qullasuyu, the Confederation of Indigenous Peoples of Bolivia, CSUTCB, the National Confederation of Peasant Indigenous Originary Women of Bolivia (Bartolina Sisa), and the Syndicalist Confederation of Intercultural Communities of Bolivia.

95 For a detailed discussion, see Schavelzon, *El nacimiento*.

96 Raúl Prada, "Entrevista a Raúl Prada Alcoreza," in *Asamblea Constituyente Bolivia: Información oficial de recursos naturales renovables, tierra-territorio y medio ambiente*, by Asamblea Constituyente (Sucre: Asamblea Constituyente de Bolivia, 2007), 3–4.

97 Personal conversations with Fernando Garcés via email, January–April 2008.

98 During the 2019–20 political coup in which Evo Morales was forced out of government, the subsequent imposition of a "de facto" ultraright government, and the ongoing waves of racialized violence against Indigenous and popular sectors, the "plurinational" became even more conflictive, banished from state discourse and documents. Not only was the constitutional base of the Plurinational State disavowed, but its referent—considered synonymous with the Indigenous-led project of decolonization—was publicly renounced as a detriment, determent, and danger to the "Nation"; that is, to the comeback of the white-mestizo nation. While the 2020 presidential election of Luis Arce halted this comeback, racial tensions remain high, as do the sociopolitical conflicts inside and outside the political party of the Movement for Socialism. In this present context, the plurinational is increasingly at the center of debate, particularly among Indianist and Indigenous intellectuals who see the need to strengthen its concept and praxis from society and in the social, political, and economic spheres, rather than (or in addition to) the still-predominant focus of state.

99 For a detailed description in English of the uprising, see Marc Becker, "The Children of 1990," *Alternatives* 35 (2010): 291–316.

100 Luis Macas, "Construyendo desde la historia, Resistencia del movimiento indígena en el Ecuador," in *Plurinacionalidad: Democracia en la diversidad*, ed. Alberto Acosta and Esperanza Martínez (Quito: Abya-Yala, 2009), 83.

101 See the comprehensive study by Gerard Colby, *Thy Will Be Done: The Conquest of the Amazon: Nelson Rockefeller and Evangelism in the Age of Oil*, with Charlotte Dennett (New York: HarperCollins, 1995).

102 Quoted in Hernán Ibarra, "Intelectuales indígenas, neoindigenismo e india-nismos en el Ecuador," *Revista Ecuador Debate: Etnicidades e Identificaciones* 48 (1999): 83.

103 Quoted in Katy Betancourt Machoa, "La plurinacionalidad: Una praxis social en Pastaza" (master's thesis, Universidad Andina Simón Bolívar, Quito, 2020), 33. The description and use of "confederation" here once again recall the arguments of Öcalan.

104 Virgilio Hernández, in Catherine Walsh, *Interculturalidad crítica y (de)coloniali-dad: Ensayos desde Abya Yala* (Quito: Abya-Yala, 2012), 52.

105 CONAIE, *Proyecto político* (Quito: CONAIE, 1997), 12.

106 Luis Macas, "Diversidad y plurinacionalidad," *Boletín ICCI-ARY Rimay* 6, no. 64 (2004): 2.

107 Simpson, *As We Have Always Done*.

108 Cindy Buhl, *A Citizen's Guide to the Multilateral Development Banks and Indig-enous Peoples* (Washington, DC: Bank Information Center, 1994), 29.

109 Raimon Panikkar, "La interpelación intercultural," in *El discurso intercultural: Prologómenos a una filosofía intercultural*, ed. Graciano González R. Arnaiz (Madrid: Biblioteca Nueva, 2002), 23–76.

110 See Vilma Almendra, "Palabrando: Entre el despojo y la dignidad," in *Pedagogías decoloniales: Prácticas insurgentes de resistir, (re)existir y (re)vivir*, ed. Catherine Walsh (Quito: Abya-Yala, 2017), 2:209–44.

111 This is what I have referred to, in conversation with Fidel Tubino, as "criti-cal" interculturality, thus making a clear distinction with the "functional" interculturality previously described. See Walsh, *Interculturalidad crítica y (de) colonialidad*; and Fidel Tubino, "La interculturalidad crítica como proyecto ético-político," Encuentro continental de educadores agustinos, Lima, Janu-ary 24–28, 2005, https://oala.villanova.edu/congresos/educacion/lima-ponen -02.html.

112 As should be clear by now, nationalism is not the referent or signifier in either Bolivia or Ecuador. The proposition and struggle are not for a separat-ist or a pluralized nationalism, but rather for the building of a radically distinct social project that challenges the hegemonic ideology and precept of nation and nation-state.

113 For CONAIE, *people* is understood as "a collectivity cohered by a set of factors, including the occupation of a defined territory, the use of a com-mon language, the sharing of a common culture, common history, and common aspirations, factors that not only differentiate them from other peoples, but that have also made possible their development of social

institutions and of relatively autonomous forms of organization. An indigenous people is defined as such in relation to a society that is not native or indigenous." CONAIE, *Proyecto político*, 47. Within the Kichwa nationality (the largest nationality), for example, there are fourteen distinct peoples, each with their own specific form of identification, dress, traditional custom, geographical locations, and economic activity, but with a language and a broader history and identity in common. Afro-Ecuadorians also constitute a "peoples."

114 CONAIE, *Las nacionalidades indígenas y el Estado plurinacional* (Quito: CONAIE, 1998), 15.

115 CONAIE, *Las nacionalidades indígenas*, 12.

116 Macas, "Construyendo desde la historia," 93.

117 Macas, "Construyendo desde la historia," 96.

118 Macas, "Construyendo desde la historia," 94.

119 CONAIE, *Políticas para el Plan de Gobierno Nacional: El mandato de la CONAIE* (Quito: CONAIE 2003), 2.

120 CONAIE, *Proyecto político*, 11.

121 CONAIE, *Políticas para el Plan de Gobierno Nacional*, 2.

122 The orchestration of "white fear" is certainly not limited to Ecuador; especially recalled are similar processes in South Africa and colonial Rhodesia (now Zimbabwe).

123 In fact, the insurgent force of the movement was not to be publicly witnessed again until the multitudinous Indigenous-led uprising of October 2019 against the increasing neoliberalization of government and its socioeconomic policy. This uprising, the largest in Ecuadorian history, was met by levels of state violence never before seen. See Catherine Walsh, "On the October Awakening(s) and the Condor: Notes from Ecuador and the Region," *Black Issues in Philosophy*, November 28, 2019, https://blog.apaonline.org /2019/11/28/on-the-october-awakenings-and-the-condor-notes-from-ecuador -and-the-region/. Also see the epilogue in this book.

124 CONAIE, "Propuesta del Estado Plurinacional de la República del Ecuador" (mimeograph, Quito, 2007).

125 CONAIE, "Propuesta de la CONAIE frente a la Asamblea Constituyente: Principios y lineamientos para la nueva constitution del Ecuador" (mimeograph, Quito, 2007), 5–6.

126 CONAIE, "Propuesta del Estado Plurinacional," 3.

127 CONAIE, "Propuesta de la CONAIE frente a la Asamblea," 9–10.

128 See Walsh, *Interculturalidad, estado, sociedad*.

129 See Catherine Walsh, "Political-Epistemic Insurgency, Social Movements and the Refounding of the State," in *Rethinking Intellectuals in Latin America*, ed. Mabel Moraña and Bret Gustafson (Madrid: Iberoamericana Vervuert, 2010), 199–212. Also see my descriptions in Walter D. Mignolo and Catherine E. Walsh, *On Decoloniality: Concepts, Analytics, Praxis* (Durham, NC: Duke University Press, 2018), 65–66.

130 I am referring to economies based almost entirely on oil, gas, mining, lumbering and massive deforestation, hydroelectric plants, agroindustry, palm oil production, and megatourism, among other capital-oriented practices that extract and exploit land and the very bases of life itself. Today extractivism and its interests, logics, policies, businesses, and practices are the major causes of violence, contamination, disease, displacement, dispossesion, deterritorialization, destruction, and death in Indigenous, peasant, and African-descendant communities throughout the Americas, with women the most affected.

131 Alessia Dro, representative of the Kurdish women's movement, comments in untitled panel presentation at the international online event Revolución en construcción: Mujeres tejiendo futuro, August 30, 2020.

132 Dilar Dirik, "Living without Approval," interview by Jonas Staal, in *Stateless Democracy: New World Academy Reader #5*, with the Kurdish Women's Movement, ed. Renée In der Maur and Jonas Staal (Utrecht, Netherlands: BAK, 2015), 50.

133 Jane Anna Gordon, *Statelessness and Contemporary Enslavement*, 130.

134 Steve Biko, *I Write What I Like*, 40th anniversary ed. (Johannesburg: Picador Africa, 2017), 23.

135 Simpson, *As We Have Always Done*, 153.

CHAPTER FIVE: SOWING RE-EXISTENCES

1 First chapter epigraph is from Robin Wall Kimmerer, "Corn Tastes Better on the Honor System," *Emergence Magazine*, October 31, 2018, https://emergencemagazine.org/story/corn-tastes-better/. I thank my friend Nina Tepper for sharing this text and its podcast with me.

2 Second chapter epigraph is from Abuelo Zenón, in Juan García Salazar and Catherine Walsh, *Pensar sembrando/sembrar pensando con el Abuelo Zenón* (Quito: Universidad Andina Simón Bolívar/Abya-Yala, 2017), 38.

3 Kimmerer, "Corn Tastes Better."

4 Kimmerer, "Corn Tastes Better."

5 Kimmerer, "Corn Tastes Better."

6 See Regina Harrison, *Signs, Song, and Memory in the Andes: Translating Quechua Language and Culture* (Austin: University of Texas Press, 1989); and Michael Horswell, *Decolonizing the Sodomite: Queer Tropes of Sexuality in Colonial Andean Culture* (Austin: University of Texas Press, 2005).

7 Kimmerer, "Corn Tastes Better."

8 See the video with English subtitles in Semillita Canto, "Semillita—Canto en defensa de la vida," YouTube, November 2, 2019, video, 4:59, https://youtu.be/3E8FhZXMhyA.

9 García Salazar and Walsh, *Pensar sembrando*, 247.

10 René Olvera Salinas, "Pedagogías de resistencia: De los *cómo* sembrar vida donde está la muerte," in *Pedagogías decoloniales: Prácticas insurgentes de resistir, (re)existir, y (re)vivir*, ed. Catherine Walsh (Quito: Abya-Yala, 2017), 2:205.

11 "Encuentros para sembrar vida: Más allá de lo que permite el sistema," Pueblos en Camino, April 3, 2016, http://pueblosencamino.org/?cat=54.

12 "Encuentros para sembrar vida."

13 "Encuentros para sembrar vida."

14 Personal conversations on February 6 and February 26, 2021, with the human rights activist Santiago Mera, part of the coordinating team of the University of Peace, and dialogue on February 27, 2021, with the community members who form part of this project.

15 Words of Zaida (pseudonym) in the online dialogue with community members from the project of the University of Peace, February 26, 2021.

16 In Colombia *false positives* refers to the innocent people extrajudicially killed by members of the Colombian army and then falsely labeled as enemy combatants of either the National Liberation Army or the Revolutionary Armed Forces of Colombia.

17 Words of Cristina (pseudonym) in the online dialogue with community members from the project of the University of Peace, February 26, 2021.

18 Michele Lobo, "Decoloniality: Seeding Pluriversal Imaginaries," *Postcolonial Studies* 23, no. 4 (2020), 575.

19 Morgan Ndlovu, "Well-Intentioned but Vulnerable to Abuse," *Postcolonial Studies* 23, no. 4 (2020): 579–83.

20 Subcomandante Insurgente Galeano, in Comisión de la Sexta del Ejército Zapatista de Liberación Nacional (EZLN), *El pensamiento crítico frente a la hidra capitalista, I* (Chiapas: EZLN, 2015), 30.

21 SupGaleano, in Comisión de la Sexta del EZLN, *El pensamiento crítico*, 30.

22 SupGaleano, in Comisión de la Sexta del EZLN, *El pensamiento crítico*, 33.

23 SupMoisés, in Comisión de la Sexta del EZLN, *El pensamiento crítico*, 179.

24 SupMoisés, in Comisión de la Sexta del EZLN, *El pensamiento crítico*, 214–15.

25 Katerina Teaiwa, "On Decoloniality: A View from Oceania," *Postcolonial Studies* 23, no. 4 (2020): 601–3.

26 See Michael Knapp, Ercan Ayboga, and Anja Flach, *Revolution in Rojava: Democratic Autonomy and Women's Liberation in the Syrian Kurdistan* (London: Pluto, 2016).

27 This proposition of decolonial praxis was made clear in the plenary panel "The Decolonial Everyday: Reflections on Indigenous Education and Land-Centered Praxis" with Glen Coulthard, Leanne Betasamosake Simpson, Lindsey Schneider, and Clint Carroll at the conference Imagined Borders, Epistemic Freedoms: The Challenge of Social Imaginaries in Media, Art, Religion and Decoloniality, University of Colorado, Boulder, January 9, 2020, as well as the talks at this same conference by the University of the Free State (Bloemfontein, South Africa) professors Matau Setshase and Motsaathebe Serekoane, who, each in their own way, poignantly elucidated the decolonial relations and work of the spiritual, epistemic, and existential. Also see the book by the Torres Strait Islander Martin Nakata, *Disciplining the Savages, Savaging the Disciplines* (Canberra: Aboriginal Studies Press, 2007).

28 See Marinete Franco et al., "Marielle Franco: Una flor que rompe o asfalto," in *Mestre das Periferias: O encontro de Ailton Krenal, Conceição Evaristo, Négo Bispo*

e Marielle Franco (in memorian), ed. Jailson de Souza e Silva (Rio de Janeiro: Eduniperferias, 2020), 71–78.

29 Exposition "Memoria del estadillo social," Museo de la Ciudad, Quito, October 2020.

30 SupGaleano, in Comisión de la Sexta del EZLN, *El pensamiento crítico*, 361.

31 Kimmerer, "Corn Tastes Better."

32 In García Salazar and Walsh, *Pensar sembrando*, 41.

33 Frantz Fanon, *A Dying Colonialism*, trans. from the French by Haakon Chevalier, with an introduction by Adolfo Gilly (New York: Grove, 1965), 128.

34 Frantz Fanon, *Wretched of the Earth*, trans. from the French by Constance Farrington (New York: Grove, 1963), 250.

35 Frantz Fanon, *Black Skin, White Masks*, trans. from the French by Charles Lam Markmann (New York: Grove, 1967), 8. For a discussion of the zone of nonbeing, also see Lewis R. Gordon, "Through the Zone of Nonbeing: A Reading of *Black Skin, White Masks* in Celebration of Fanon's Eightieth Birthday," *CLR James Journal* 11, no. 1 (2005): 1–43; Sylvia Wynter, "Unsettling the Coloniality of Being/Power/Truth/Freedom: Towards the Human, after Man, Its Overrepresentation—an Argument," *New Centennial Review* 3, no. 3 (Fall 2003): 257–337; Nelson Maldonado-Torres, "On the Coloniality of Being: Contributions to the Development of a Concept," in *Globalization and the Decolonial Option*, ed. Walter D. Mignolo and Arturo Escobar (New York: Routledge, 2010), 94–124; Walter D. Mignolo, *The Darker Side of Western Modernity: Global Futures, Decolonial Options* (Durham, NC: Duke University Press, 2011); and Walter D. Mignolo, *The Darker Side of the Renaissance: Literacy, Territoriality, and Colonization*, 2nd ed. (Ann Arbor: University of Michigan Press, 2003).

36 Lewis R. Gordon, *What Fanon Said: A Philosophical Introduction to His Life and Thought* (New York: Fordham University Press, 2015), 22.

37 Fanon, *Black Skin, White Masks*, 229.

38 While Constance Farrington's English translation of *Wretched of the Earth* uses the phrase "turn over a new leaf" (316), both the original French text and Julieta Campo's Spanish translation refer to a change of skin.

39 Nelson Maldonado-Torres, "En la búsqueda de la madurez decolonial: Una carta a Catherine Walsh," in *Gritos, grietas y siembras de nuestros territories del Sur: Catherine Walsh y el pensamiento crítico-decolonial en América Latina*, ed. Alicia Ortega-Caicedo and Miriam Lang (Quito: Universidad Andina Simón Bolívar/Abya-Yala, 2020), 203.

40 Wynter, "Unsettling the Coloniality."

41 Lewis R. Gordon, "African-American Philosophy, Race, and the Geography of Reason," in *Not Only the Masters' Tools*, ed. Lewis R. Gordon and Jane Anna Gordon (Boulder, CO: Paradigm, 2006), 20.

42 Lewis R. Gordon, "African-American Philosophy," 26; Lewis R. Gordon, *Existentia Africana: Understanding Africana Existential Thought* (New York: Routledge, 2000), 144.

43 See Catherine Walsh, "Lewis R. Gordon: Existential Incantations That Cross Borders and Move Us Forward," in *Black Existentialism: Essays on the Transformative Thought of Lewis R. Gordon*, ed. danielle davis (New York: Rowman and Littlefield International, 2019), 121–34.

44 In García Salazar and Walsh, *Pensar sembrando*, 35–36.

45 Abuelo Zenón, in García Salazar and Walsh, *Pensar sembrando*, 44.

46 Recalled is Paget Henry's assertion of the life-affirming character of African attitudes toward existence, and Maldonado-Torres's avowal of a decolonial attitude linked to the creation of practices and ways of thinking that undermine coloniality. See Paget Henry, *Caliban's Reason: Introducing Afro-Caribbean Philosophy* (New York: Routledge, 2000), 37; and Nelson Maldonado-Torres, "Outline of Ten Theses on Coloniality and Decoloniality," Frantz Fanon Foundation, 2016, http://fondation-frantzfanon.com/outline-of-ten-theses-on -coloniality-and-decoloniality/.

47 In García Salazar and Walsh, *Pensar sembrando*, 38.

48 Abuelo Zenón, in García Salazar and Walsh, *Pensar sembrando*, 245, 247.

49 In García Salazar and Walsh, *Pensar sembrando*, 39.

50 In García Salazar and Walsh, *Pensar sembrando*, 38–39.

51 In García Salazar and Walsh, *Pensar sembrando*, 225.

52 Catherine Walsh and Juan García Salazar, "(W)riting Collective Memory (De)spite State: Decolonial Practices of Existence in Ecuador," in *Black Writing, Culture, and the State in Latin America*, ed. Jerome C. Branche (Nashville: Vanderbilt University Press, 2015), 256.

53 In a form not usual for published texts, this book is written in three fonts representing three distinct voices. The problem came not only with this writing and narrative style—which we were able to negotiate with the publisher—but also, and more critically, with the issue of authorship since Abuelo Zenón was initially included as first author. Given the norms of copyright laws, we were asked to provide Zenón's identification, address, and telephone number. As the reader can imagine, our explanation that although Zenón could not be seen or physically located, he existed, was neither accepted nor understood. The only alternative offered was to eliminate his name from the list of authors. Thus the last part of the title: "Thinking with Grandfather Zenón."

54 Lewis R. Gordon, *Existencia Africana*, 14–16.

55 Lobo, "Decoloniality"; M. Jacqui Alexander, *Pedagogies of Crossing: Meditations on Feminism, Sexual Politics, Memory, and the Sacred* (Durham, NC: Duke University Press, 2005); Adolfo Albán Achinte, *Prácticas creativas de re-existencia: Más allá del arte . . . el mundo de lo sensible* (Buenos Aires: Ediciones del Signo, 2017).

56 Samyr Salgado, "Utopía del Ahora," in Walsh, *Pedagogías decoloniales*, 2:53–54.

BIBLIOGRAPHY

Acosta, Alberto. "Toward the Universal Declaration of Rights of Nature,
Thoughts for Action." *América Latina en Movimiento*, September 26, 2010.

Adlbi Sibai, Sirin. *La cárcel del feminismo: Hacia un pensamiento islámico decolonial.*
Madrid: Akal, 2016.

Aguinaga, Margarita, Miriam Lang, Dunia Mokrani, and Alejandra Santillana.
"Pensar desde el feminism: Críticas y alternativas al desarrollo." In *Alternativas descoloniales al capitalism colonial/moderno*, compiled by Pablo Quintero,
113–35. Buenos Aires: Ediciones del Signo, 2016.

Aguinaga Barragán, Margarita. "Ecofeminismo: Mujer y Pachamama, no solo es
posible una crítica al capitalismo y patriarcado." *Flor del Guanto* 4 (December 2012): 10–11.

Aguirre, Milagros. "Las medias verdades de una rebelión de 11 días." Rebelión,
October 2019. http://www.rebelion.org/docs/262149.pdf.

Albán Achinte, Adolfo. "Epistemes 'otras': Epistemes disruptivas?" *Revista Kula* 6
(2012): 22–34.

Albán Achinte, Adolfo. "¿Interculturalidad sin decolonialidad? Colonialidades
circulantes y prácticas de re-existencia." In *Diversidad, interculturalidad y
construcción de ciudad*, edited by Wilmer Villa and Arturo Grueso, 64–96.
Bogotá: Universidad Pedagógica Nacional-Alcaldía Mayor, 2008.

Albán Achinte, Adolfo. "Pedagogías de la re-existencia: Artístas indígenas y
afrocolombianos." In *Pedagogías decoloniales: Prácticas insurgentes de resistir, (re)
existir y (re)vivir*, edited by Catherine Walsh, 1:443–68. Quito: Abya-Yala, 2013.

Albán Achinte, Adolfo. *Prácticas creativas de re-existencia: Más allá del arte . . . el mundo
de lo sensible*. Buenos Aires: Ediciones del Signo, 2017.

Albán Achinte, Adolfo. *Sabor, poder y saber: Comida y tiempo en los valles afroandinos
de Patía y Chota-Mira*. Popayán, Colombia: Universidad del Cauca, 2015.

Alexander, M. Jacqui. *Pedagogies of Crossing: Meditations on Feminism, Sexual Politics,
Memory, and the Sacred*. Durham, NC: Duke University Press, 2005.

Alianza por los Derechos Humanos Ecuador. "Alerta 47." June 3, 2020. https://
ddhhecuador.org/sites/default/files/documentos/2020-06/Alerta%2047.pdf.

Alianza de Organizaciones para los Derechos Humanos. *Verdad, justicia y reparación: Informe de verificación sobre Derechos Humanos en el paro nacional y levantamiento indígena*. Quito: Alianza de Organizaciones para los Derechos Humanos, October 2019. https://www.inredh.org/archivos/pdf/informe _final_alianza_%202019_oct.pdf.

Almendra, Vilma. *Entre la emancipación y la captura: Memorias y caminos desde la lucha Nasa en Colombia*. Quito: Abya-Yala, 2017.

Almendra, Vilma. "Palabrando: Entre el despojo y la dignidad." In *Pedagogías decoloniales: Prácticas insurgentes de resistir, (re)existir y (re)vivir*, edited by Catherine Walsh, 2:209–44. Quito: Abya-Yala, 2017.

Alvira, Yamile. "El lugar del canto y la oralidad como prácticas estético-pedagógías para la reafirmación de la vida y su existencia en los Andes cajamarquinos." In *Pedagogías decoloniales: Prácticas insurgentes de resistir, (re)existir y (re)vivir*, edited by Catherine Walsh, 2:245–72. Quito: Abya-Yala, 2017.

Amadiume, Ifi. *Male Daughters, Female Husbands: Gender and Sex in an African Society*. 1987. 2nd ed. London: Zed Books, 2015.

Anzaldúa, Gloria. *Borderlands = La Frontera: The New Mestiza*. San Francisco: Aunt Lute Books, 1987.

Anzaldúa, Gloria. *Light in the Dark/Luz en lo Oscuro: Rewriting Identity, Spirituality, and Reality*. Edited by AnaLouise Keating. Durham, NC: Duke University Press, 2015.

Araujo, Felipe. "Brazil Must Address Its Own Police Violence." *Foreign Policy*, July 27, 2020. https://foreignpolicy.com/2020/07/07/brazil-must-address-its -own-racist-police-violence/.

Arocha, Jaime. *Ombligados de Ananse: Hilos ancestrales y modernos en el Pacífico colombiano*. Bogotá: Universidad Nacional de Colombia, Facultad de Ciencias Humanas, 1999.

Avendaño, Lukas, and Edgar Cartas Orozco. "Where Is Bruno?" Hemispheric Institute, 2019. https://hemisphericinstitute.org/en/encuentro-2019 -performances/item/2821-performances-007.html.

Baraka, Ajamu. "From Palestine to Colombia: The End of the White World Colonial/Capitalist Project?" Monthly Review Online, May 15, 2021. https:// mronline.org/2021/05/15/from-palestine-to-colombia-the-end-of-the-white -world-colonial-capitalist-project/.

Barre, Marie-Chantal. *Ideologías indigenistas y movimientos indios*. Mexico City: Siglo XXI, 1983.

Barriendos, Joaquín. "La colonialidad del ver: Hacia un nuevo diálogo visual interepistémico." *Nómadas* 35 (2011): 13–29.

Bautista, Nidia. "Femicide Is a Growing Issue in the United States." *Teen Vogue*, August 28, 2020. https://www.teenvogue.com/story/femicide-is-a-growing -issue-in-the-united-states.

Bautista, Rafael. "Bolivia: Del Estado colonial al estado plurinacional." Unpublished manuscript, La Paz, 2009.

BBC News. "The Women Killed on One Day around the World." November 25, 2018. https://www.bbc.com/news/world-46292919.

Becker, Marc. "The Children of 1990." *Alternatives* 35 (2010): 291–316.

Betancourt Machoa, Katy. "La plurinacionalidad: Una praxis social en Pastaza." Master's thesis, Universidad Andina Simón Bolívar, Quito, 2020.

[Betancourt] Machoa, Katy. "El florecimiento de la rebeldía." Text presented in the photographic exhibit *Mujeres en la lucha social ecuatoriana*, organized by the Collective Desde el Margen, Universidad Andina Simón Bolívar, Quito, November 21–25, 2017.

Biko, Steve. *I Write What I Like*. 40th anniversary ed. Johannesburg: Picador Africa, 2017.

Borsani, María Eugenia, and Relmu Ñamku. "Encarnización político-judicial, neocolonialismo y expropiación territorial." In *Pedagogías decoloniales: Prácticas insurgentes de resistir, (re)existir y (re)vivir*, edited by Catherine Walsh, 2:315–36. Quito: Abya-Yala, 2017.

Buhl, Cindy. *A Citizen's Guide to the Multilateral Development Banks and Indigenous Peoples*. Washington, DC: Bank Information Center, 1994.

Burbano, Ángel. "El espejo de Ipa Mama Huaco." Personal website of Ángel Burbano, August 21, 2017. https://angelburbanos22.wixsite.com/angelitoxioopre /post/el-espejo-de-ipa-mama-huaco.

Burbano, Ángel. "Los espejos de Mama Huaco: Un acto interpretativo en dos tiempos." Master's thesis, Universidad Andina Simón Bolívar, Quito, 2019. https://repositorio.uasb.edu.ec/handle/10644/7591?mode=full.

Burbano, Ángel. "Mama Huaco." In the exhibit *Archivxs: Exposición Orgullo LGBTIQ+*, Quito, 2019.

Cabnal, Lorena. "Acercamiento a la construcción de la propuesta de pensamiento epistémico de las mujeres indígenas feministas comunitarias de Abya Yala." In *Feminismos diversos: El feminismo comunitario*, 11–25. Madrid: Acsur/Las Segovias, 2010.

Cabnal, Lorena. Talk given in the offices of Acción Ecológica, Quito, March 20, 2017.

Cañamar, Tsaywa. "Runa Warmikuna Sinchiyarinchik/Fortale(ser)nos siendo mujeres runakuna." Master's thesis, Universidad Andina Simón Bolívar, Quito, 2020. https://repositorio.uasb.edu.ec/handle/10644/7411.

Carrillo Can, Isaac Esau. "Androgynous Eroticism in the Yucatec Maya Cosmology and Language." Translated by Raúl Moarquech Ferrera-Balanquet and Daniel Chávez. In "Erotic Sovereignty at the Decolonial Crossroads," edited by Raúl Moarquech Ferrera-Balanquet, 66–81. Unpublished manuscript, 2017.

Carrillo Can, Isaac Esau. *U yóok'otilo'ob áak'ab/Danzas de la noche*. Mexico City: Conaculta, 2011.

Casquete, Jesús. "Un nuevo fascismo en Europa?" *Democracia Siglo XXI* (blog), February 16, 2021. https://teodulolopezmelendez.wordpress.com/2021/02/16 /un-nuevo-fascismo-en-europa/.

Castro-Gómez, Santiago. "La historia natural en el orden clásico y geopolítica del saber." In *Cultura y naturaleza: Aproximaciones a propósito del bicentenario de la Independencia de Colombia*, edited by Leonardo Montenegro, 337–54. Bogotá: Jardín Botánico José Celestín Mutis, 2011.

Castro-Gómez, Santiago. *La hybris del punto cero: Ciencia, raza e ilustración en la Nueva Granada (1750–1816)*. Bogotá: Pontificia Universidad Javeriana, 2005.

Cayley, David. *Iván Illich in Conversation*. Toronto: Anansi, 1992.

Cayley, David. "Illich, Goodman, Freire: Encuentros y desencuentros: De las conversaciones entre Iván Illich y David Cayley." *Opciones,* supplement of *El Nacional* 29 (February 19, 1993): 8–9. Translated from *Iván Illich in Conversation,* by David Cayley. Toronto: Anansi, 1992, 206–7.

Cervantes, Lluvia. "Sembrar vida donde está la muerte." Presentation at the Universidad Central, Bogotá, Colombia, February 5, 2019.

Cesaire, Aimé. *Discourse on Colonialism*. 1972. New York: Monthly Review, 2000.

Chancosa, Blanca, N. Santi, M. C. Ventura, C. Flores, G. Panchi, S. Lupa, A. Cahuiya, C. Lozano, and I. Ramos. "Mujeres indígenas de latinoamérica enfrentan el cambio climático desde sus procesos de adaptabilidad cultural: Chasaqui warmikuna del Abya Yala frente al cambio climático 'Haciendo caminar la palabra.'" Document prepared for the twenty-second session of the Conference of the Parties, Morocco. Quito: Ecuarunari, 2016.

Chilisa, Bagele. *Indigenous Research Methodologies*. Los Angeles: Sage, 2012.

Chiriboga, Luz Argentina. *Jonatás y Manuela*. Quito: Campaña Nacional Eugenio Espejo por el Libro y la Lectura, 2010.

Choque Canqui, Roberto. "El Manifiesto de Tiwanaku (1973) y el inicio de la descolonización." *Revistas bolivianas* 4, no. 11 (2010): 11–15. http://www.revistas-bolivianas.ciencia.bo/pdf/fdc/v4n11/a04.pdf.

Clayton, Lawrence. "Bartolomé de Las Casas and the African Slave Trade." *History Compass* 7, no. 6 (2009): 1526–41.

Cohen, Leonard. "Anthem." Track 5 on *The Future*. Columbia Records, 1992.

Colby, Gerard. *Thy Will Be Done: The Conquest of the Amazon: Nelson Rockefeller and Evangelism in the Age of Oil*. With Charlotte Dennett. New York: HarperCollins, 1995.

Colectivo Grietas. "Editorial." *Grietas* 1, no. 1 (July 2012): 4–6.

Coleman, Daniel B. "My Praxis." Personal website. Accessed May 17, 2022. https://www.danielbcoleman.com/biodbc.

Coleman, Daniel B. "Scholarship & Teaching." Personal website. Accessed May 17, 2022. https://www.danielbcoleman.com/scholarship.

Comisión de la Sexta del EZLN (Ejercito Zapatista de Liberación Nacional). *El pensamiento crítico frente a la hidra capitalista, I*. Chiapas: EZLN, 2015.

Comité de Jineolojî Europa. *Jineolojî*. Neuss, Germany: Mezopotamien Verlag und Vertriebs, 2018.

CONAIE (Confederación de Nacionalidades Indígenas del Ecuador). *Las nacionalidades indígenas y el Estado plurinacional*. Quito: CONAIE, 1998.

CONAIE (Confederación de Nacionalidades Indígenas del Ecuador). *Políticas para el Plan de Gobierno Nacional: El mandato de la CONAIE*. Quito: CONAIE, 2003.

CONAIE (Confederación de Nacionalidades Indígenas del Ecuador). "Propuesta de la CONAIE frente a la Asamblea Constituyente: Principios y lineamientos para la nueva Constitución del Ecuador." Mimeograph, Quito, 2007.

CONAIE (Confederación de Nacionalidades Indígenas del Ecuador). "Propuesta del Estado Plurinacional de la República del Ecuador." Mimeograph, Quito, 2007.

CONAIE (Confederación de Nacionalidades Indígenas del Ecuador). *Proyecto político*. Quito: CONAIE, 1997.

Conselho Indigenista Missionario. "Mortes por covid-19 entre indígenas precisam virar assunto para a CIDH." April 6, 2020. https://cimi.org.br/2020 /06/mortes-por-covid-19-entre-indigenas-precisam-virar-assunto-para-a -comissao-interamericana-de-direitos-humanos/.

Coronil, Fernando. "The Future in Question: History and Utopia in Latin America, 1989–2010." In *Business as Usual: The Roots of the Global Financial Meltdown*, edited by Craig Calhoun and Georgi Derluguian, 213–92. New York: New York University Press, 2011.

Corrales, Javier. "Un matrimonio perfecto: Evangélicos y conservadores en América Latina." *New York Times*, Spanish edition, January 19, 2018. https:// www.nytimes.com/es/2018/01/19/opinion-evangelicos-conservadores -america-latina-corrales/.

Corrêa, Sonia. "Gender Ideology: Tracking Its Origins and Meanings in Current Gender Politics." *Engenderings* (blog), London School of Economics and Political Science, December 11, 2017. https://blogs.lse.ac.uk/gender/2017/12 /11/gender-ideology-tracking-its-origins-and-meanings-in-current-gender -politics/.

Corrêa, Sonia. "Interview: The Anti-gender Offensive as State Policy." *Conectas: Human Rights*, March 7, 2020. https://www.conectas.org/en/noticias /interview-the-anti-gender-offensive-as-state-policy/.

Coulthard, Glen. *Red Skin, White Masks: Rejecting the Colonial Politics of Recognition*. Minneapolis: University of Minnesota Press, 2014.

Coulthard, Glen, Leanne Betasamosake Simpson, Lindsey Schneider, and Clint Carroll. "The Decolonial Everyday: Reflections on Indigenous Education and Land-Centered Praxis." Presentation in the plenary panel at the conference Imagined Borders, Epistemic Freedoms: The Challenge of Social Imaginaries in Media, Art, Religion and Decoloniality, University of Colorado, Boulder, January 9, 2020.

Crichlow, Michaeline. *Globalization and the Post-Creole Imagination: Notes on Fleeing the Plantation*. Durham, NC: Duke University Press, 2009.

Cueva, Agustín. *Sobre nuestra ambigüedad cultural*. Quito: Editora Universitaria, 1974.

Cumes, Aura. "Patriarcado, dominación colonial y epistemologías mayas." Museu d'Art Contemporani de Barcelona, 2019. https://img.macba.cat/public /uploads/20190611/Patriarcado_dominacinin_colonial_y_epistemologn_as _mayas.4.pdf.

Curiel, Ochy. *La nación heterosexual*. Bogotá: Brecha lésbica and en la frontera, 2013.

de la Cadena, Marisol. *Earth Beings: Ecologies of Practice across Andean Worlds*. Durham, NC: Duke University Press, 2015.

DiPietro, Pedro. "Neither Humans, Nor Animals, Nor Monsters: On the Coloniality of Transgender." Unpublished manuscript, 2020.

DiPietro, Pedro. "Ni humanos ni animales." Paper presented at the Universidad Andina Simón Bolívar, Quito, February 18, 2020.

Dirik, Dilar. "Living without Approval." Interview by Jonas Stall. In *Stateless Democracy: New World Academy Reader #5*, with the Kurdish Women's Movement, edited by Renée In der Maur and Jonas Staal, 27–56. Utrecht, Netherlands: BAK, 2015.

Driskill, Qwo-Li. "Doubleweaving Two Spirit: Building Alliances between Native and Queer Studies, Sexuality, Nationality, and Indigeneity." *GLQ: A Journal of Lesbian and Gay Studies* 16, no. 1–2 (2010): 69–92.

Driskill, Qwo-Li, Chris Finely, Brian Joseph Gilley, and Scott Lauria Morgensen, eds. *Queer Indigenous Studies: Critical Interventions in Theory, Politics, and Literature*. Tucson: Arizona University Press, 2011.

Dro, Alessia. Comments in untitled panel presentation at the international online event Revolución en construcción: Mujeres tejiendo futuro, August 30, 2020.

Duarte, Caleb. "EDELO (En Donde Era la ONU) Where the United Nations Used to Be." Calebduarte.org. Accessed May 17, 2022. http:// www.calebduarte.org /edelo.

Dubois, W. E. B. *The Souls of Black Folk*. 1903. New York: Millennial Publications, 2014.

Dunbar-Ortiz, Roxanne. *An Indigenous Peoples' History of the United States*. Boston: Beacon, 2014.

Dussel, Enrique. *Ética de la liberación en la edad de la globalización y de la exclusión*. Madrid: Trotta, 2002.

El Comercio. "Ministerio de Defensa asegura que el uso de la fuerza en las manifestaciones fue necesario." November 29, 2019. https://www.elcomercio .com/actualidad/ministerio-defensa-fuerza-manifestaciones-paro.html.

Elizondo, José, and Karla Ávila. "Pienso, luego me desaparecen." *El Fardado*, September 26, 2015. http://www.elfaradio.com/2015/09/26/pienso-luego-me -desaparecen/.

El Mundo Internacional. "Asesinan en Colombia a la defensora medioambiental Yolanda Maturana." February 2, 2018. http://www.elmundo.es/internacional /2018/02/02/5a74962046163f4e1b8b4676.html.

Elujoba, Yinka. "Jacob Lawrence, Peering through History's Cracks." *New York Times*, September 17, 2020. https://www.nytimes.com/2020/09/17/arts/design /jacob-lawrence-metropolitan-museum.html.

Erasmus, Zimitri. "Sylvia Wynter's Theory of the Human: Counter-, Not Post-humanist." *Theory, Culture and Society* 37, no. 6 (2020): 47–65.

Escobar, Arturo. "Epistemologías de la naturaleza y colonialidad de la naturaleza: Variedades del realismo y constructivismo." In *Cultura y naturaleza: Aproxi-*

maciones a propósito del bicentenario de la independencia de Colombia, edited by Leonardo Montenegro, 49–74. Bogotá: Jardín Botánico José Celestino Mutis, December 2011.

Estermann, Josef. *Filosofía andina*. Quito: Abya-Yala, 1998.

Esteva, Gustavo. *Nuevas formas de revolución: Notas para aprender de las luchas del EZLN y de la APRO*. Oaxaca: El Rebozo, 2014.

Esteva, Gustavo, Madhu Prakash, and Dana Stuchul. "From a Pedagogy for Liberation to Liberation from Pedagogy." In *Rethinking Freire: Globalization and the Environmental Crisis*, edited by C. A. Bowers and Frederique Apffel-Marglin, 13–30. Mahwah, NJ: Lawrence Erlbaum, 2004.

Estévez, Mayra. "Estudios sonoros en y desde Latinoamérica: Del régimen colonial de la sonoridad a las sonoridades de la sanación." PhD diss., Universidad Andina Simón Bolívar, Quito, 2016. http://repositorio.uasb.edu.ec/handle /10644/4956.

Evaristo, Conceição. *Becos da memória*. Belo Horizonte, Brazil: Massa, 2006.

Evaristo, Conceição. "Conceição Evaristo: Imortalidade além de um título." Interview by Ivana Dorali, in *Mestre das Periferias: O encontro de Ailton Krenal, Conceição Evaristo, Nêgo Bispo e Marielle Franco (in memorian)*, edited by Jailson de Souza e Silva, 131–63. Rio de Janeiro: Eduniperferias, 2020.

Eze, Emmanuel Chukwudi. *On Reason: Rationality in a World of Cultural Conflict and Racism*. Durham, NC: Duke University Press, 2008.

Fanon, Frantz. *Black Skin, White Masks*. Translated from the French by Charles Lam Markmann. New York: Grove, 1967.

Fanon, Frantz. *Los condenados de la tierra*. 3rd Spanish ed. Mexico City: Fondo de Cultura Ecónomica, 2001.

Fanon, Frantz. *A Dying Colonialism*. Translated from the French by Haakon Chevalier, with an introduction by Adolfo Gilly. New York: Grove, 1965.

Fanon, Frantz. *Wretched of the Earth*. Translated from the French by Constance Farrington. New York: Grove, 1963.

Fernández Osco, Marcelo. "El ayllu y la reconstitución del pensamiento Aymara." PhD diss., Duke University, 2009.

Fernández Osco, Marcelo. *La ley del ayllu*. La Paz, Bolivia: Programa de Investigación Estratégica en Bolivia, 2000.

Ferrera Balanquet, Raúl Moarquech. "Writing Mariposa Ancestral Memory." *Caribbean InTransit Arts Journal* 1, no. 4 (Spring 2013): 38–42.

Ferrera Balanquet, Raúl Moarquech. "Mariposa Ancestral Memory." Art Labour Archives: "Raúl Moarquech Ferrera Balanquet @ Decolonizing the 'Cold' War. Be.Bop 2013." YouTube, January 5, 2014. https://www.youtube.com /watch?v=n95bMl-A4Nw.

Franco, Marinete, Antônio Franco, Anielle Franco, Luyara Franco, and Eduardo Alves. "Marielle Franco: Una flor que rompe o asfalto." In *Mestre das Periferias: O encontro de Ailton Krenal, Conceição Evaristo, Nêgo Bispo e Marielle Franco (in memorian)*, edited by Jailson de Souza e Silva, 71–78. Rio de Janeiro: Eduniperferias, 2020.

Freire, Paulo. *El grito manso*. Buenos Aires: Siglo XXI, 2003.

Freire, Paulo. *Pedagogy of Indignation*. Boulder, CO: Paradigm, 2004.

Freire, Paulo. *Pedagogy of the Oppressed*. New York: Continuum, 1974.

Freire, Paulo, and Antonio Faundez. *Por una pedagogía de la pregunta*. 2nd ed. Mexico City: Siglo XXI, 2014.

Gago, Verónica. "Treinta años de espera, dos siglos de condena." *Página 12*, March 4, 2016. https://www.pagina12.com.ar/diario/suplementos/las12/13 -10424-2016-03-04.html.

García, Alixa, and Naima Penniman. "Who Decides?" Track 6 on *Intrinsic*, by Climbing PoeTree. 2017. https://climbingpoetree.bandcamp.com/track/who -decides.

García Cabezas, Naomi. "COVID-19: Femicidios en América Latina." Ayuda en Acción, October 26, 2020. https://ayudaenaccion.org/ong/blog/mujer /violencia-genero-cifras/.

García Salazar, Juan, and Catherine Walsh. *Pensar sembrando/sembrar pensando con el Abuelo Zenón*. Quito: Universidad Andina Simón Bolívar/Abya-Yala, 2017.

Garzón, María Teresa. "Proyectos corporales: Errores subversivos: Hacia una performatividad decolonial del silencio." In *Tejiendo de otro modo: Feminismo, epistemología y apuestas descoloniales en Abya Yala*, edited by Yuderkys Espinosa, Diana Gómez, and Karina Ochoa, 223–36. Popayán, Colombia: Universidad de Cauca, 2014.

Giménez, James. "Mujeres indígenas contra petroleras chinas en Ecuador: 'Estamos dispuestas a morir por nuestra selva.'" *elDiario.es*, March 25, 2016. https://www.eldiario.es/desalambre/amazonicas-ecuador-defienden -territorio-supervivencia_1_5863501.html.

Glissant, Edouard. *El discurso antillano*. 1981. Havana: Casa de las Américas, 2010.

Glissant, Edouard. *Tratado del todo-mundo*. Barcelona: El Cobre, 2006.

Glover, Danny. Preface to *Black Panther: The Revolutionary Art of Emory Douglas*, by Emory Douglas, 10–11. New York: Rizzoli, 2007.

Goldberg, Ellen. *The Lord Who Is Half Woman: Ardhanārīśvara in Indian and Feminist Perspective*. New York: State University of New York Press, 2002.

Gondim de Oliveira, Roberta, Ana Paula da Cunha, Ana Giselle Dos Santos Gadelha, Christiane Goulart Carpio, Rachel Barros de Oliveira, and Roseane Maria Corrêa. "Racial Inequalities and Death on the Horizon: COVID-19 and Structural Racism." *Cadernos Saúde Pública* 36, no. 9 (2020): 1–14.

Gordon, Jane Anna. *Statelessness and Contemporary Enslavement*. New York: Routledge, 2020.

Gordon, Lewis R. "African-American Philosophy, Race, and the Geography of Reason." In *Not Only the Masters' Tools*, edited by Lewis R. Gordon and Jane Anna Gordon, 3–50. Boulder, CO: Paradigm, 2006.

Gordon, Lewis R. *Existentia Africana: Understanding Africana Existential Thought*. New York: Routledge, 2000.

Gordon, Lewis R. "A Pedagogical Imperative of Pedagogical Imperatives." *Thresholds* 36, nos. 1–2 (2010): 27–35.

Gordon, Lewis R. "Shifting the Geography of Reason." Talk given at the Caribbean Philosophical Association Summer School, May 24, 2021.

Gordon, Lewis R. "Theory in Black: Teleological Suspensions in Philosophy of Culture." *Qui Parle* 18 (2010): 193–214.

Gordon, Lewis R. "Through the Zone of Nonbeing: A Reading of *Black Skin, White Masks* in Celebration of Fanon's Eightieth Birthday." *CLR James Journal* 11, no. 1 (2005): 1–43.

Gordon, Lewis R. *What Fanon Said: A Philosophical Introduction to His Life and Thought*. New York: Fordham University Press, 2015.

Gosztola, Kevin. "Trump Applauds Bolivia's Military Coup as US Establishment Media Blame Morales for Turmoil." Common Dreams, November 12, 2019. https://www.commondreams.org/views/2019/11/12/trump-applauds-bolivias -military-coup-us-establishment-media-blame-morales-turmoil.

Gott, Richard. "The 2006 SLAS Lecture: Latin America as a White Settler Society." *Bulletin of Latin American Research* 26, no. 2 (2007): 269–89.

Granda Vega, María Paula. *El macho sabio: Racismo y sexismo en el discurso del presidente Rafael Correa*. Quito: La Tierra, 2017.

Grande, Sandy. "Red Pedagogy: The Un-methodology." In *Handbook of Critical and Indigenous Methodologies*, edited by Norma Denzin, Yvonne Lincoln, and Linda Tuhiwai Smith, 233–54. London: Sage, 2008.

Greer, Margaret R. *María de Zayas Tells Baroque Tales of Love and the Cruelty of Men*. University Park: Pennsylvania State University Press, 2000.

Guamán Poma de Ayala, Felipe. *Nueva corónica y buen gobierno*. 1615. Transcription, prologue, notes, and chronology by Franklin Pease. Caracas: Biblioteca Ayacucho, 1980.

Guardian. "India Recognizes Transgender People as Third Gender." April 15, 2014. https://www.theguardian.com/world/2014/apr/15/india-recognises -transgender-people-third-gender.

Gudynas, Eduardo. "Imágenes, ideas y conceptos sobre la naturaleza en América Latina." In *Cultura y naturaleza: Aproximaciones a propósito del bicentenario de la independencia de Colombia*, edited by Leonardo Montenegro, 267–92. Bogotá: Jardín Botánico José Celestín Mutis, 2011.

Haddad, Mohammed. "Palestine and Israel: Mapping an Annexation." *Aljazeera*, June 26, 2020. https://www.aljazeera.com/news/2020/6/26/palestine-and -israel-mapping-an-annexation#historyannex.

Hall, Stuart. "Cultural Studies and Its Theoretical Legacies." In *Stuart Hall: Critical Dialogues in Cultural Studies*, edited by David Morley and Kuan-Hsing Chen, 262–75. New York: Routledge, 1996.

Hall, Stuart. "The Spectacle of the Other." In *Representation: Cultural Representations and Signifying Practices*, edited by Stuart Hall, 223–90. London: Sage, 1997.

Harding, Sandra. "Latin American Decolonial Social Studies of Scientific Knowledge: Alliances and Tensions." *Science, Technology, and Human Values* 41, no. 6 (2016): 1063–87.

Harrison, Regina. *Signs, Song, and Memory in the Andes: Translating Quechua Language and Culture*. Austin: University of Texas Press, 1989.

Hartman, Saidiya V. *Wayward Lives, Beautiful Experiments: Intimate Histories of Riotous Black Girls, Troublesome Women, and Queer Radicals*. New York: Norton, 2019.

Hartman, Saidiya V., and Frank B. Wilderson III. "The Position of the Unthought." *Qui Parle* 13, no. 2 (Spring/Summer 2003): 183–201.

Haymes, Stephan Nathan. "Pedagogy and the Philosophical Anthropology of African-American Slave Culture." In *Not Only the Masters' Tools: African-American Studies in Theory and Practice*, edited by Lewis R. Gordon and Jane Anna Gordon, 173–203. Boulder, CO: Paradigm, 2006.

Henry, Paget. *Caliban's Reason: Introducing Afro-Caribbean Philosophy*. New York: Routledge, 2000.

Hernández, Camilo. "La deforestación y el COVID-19, las amenazas a la vida en el Amazonas brasileño." *AA*, June 21, 2020. https://www.aa.com.tr/es/mundo/ladeforestaci%C3%B3n-y-el-covid-19-las-amenazas-a-la-vida-en-el-amazonas-brasile%C3%B1o/1885092.

Hernández, Maribel. "Asesinan a Berta Cáceres, líder hondureña contra la explotación medioambiental de las transnacionales." *elDiario.es*, March 4, 2016. http://www.eldiario.es/desalambre/Asesinan-Berta-Caceres-medioambiental-Honduras_0_490651434.html.

Hevia, L. "El feminicidio tiene relación con la devaluación de los cuerpos que ahora no valen nada: Entrevista con María Lugones." *Diario La Mañana Neuquen*, November 5, 2012.

Holloway, John. *Agrietar el capitalismo: El hacer contra el trabajo*. Buenos Aires: Herramienta, 2011.

Holloway, John. *Crack Capitalism*. London: Pluto, 2010.

hooks, bell. *Teaching to Transgress: Education as the Practice of Freedom*. New York: Routledge, 1994.

Horswell, Michael. *Decolonizing the Sodomite: Queer Tropes of Sexuality in Colonial Andean Culture*. Austin: University of Texas Press, 2005.

Horton, Myles, and Paulo Freire. *We Make the Road by Walking: Conversations on Education and Social Change*. Edited by Brenda Bell, John Gaventa, and John Peters. Philadelphia: Temple University Press, 1990.

Huanca Atencio, Lourdes. Intervention at the meeting of the Red de Mujeres Defensores de Derechos Sociales y Ambientales. Quito, October 2013.

Hurtado, Javier. *El Katarismo*. La Paz: Hisbol, 1986.

HyC, Braulio. "Yaku Chaski Warmi Kuna: Mujeres mensajeras por el petróleo baja la tierra." *Tegantai: Agencia de Noticias Ecologistas*, July 27, 2015.

HyC, Braulio. "Yakuchaski Warmikuna: Mensajeras del Río Curaray," *Saramanta Warmikuna*, May 23, 2016. Accesed June 17, 2022. http://www.saramanta.org/video-yakuchaski-warmikuna-mensajeras-del-rio-curaray/.

Ibarra, Hernán. "Intelectuales indígenas, neoindigenismo e indianismos en el Ecuador." *Revista Ecuador Debate: Etnicidades e Identificaciones* 48 (1999): 71–94.

Illich, Iván. *La sociedad desescolarizada*. 1971. Querétaro, Mexico: El Rebozo, 2013.

Infobae. "Fueron asesinadas 2,240 mujeres en México en los primeros siete meses de 2020, de acuerdo con cifras oficiales." August 26, 2020. https://www .infobae.com/america/mexico/2020/08/26/fueron-asesinadas-2240-mujeres -en-mexico-en-los-primeros-siete-meses-de-2020-de-acuerdo-con-cifras -oficiales/.

INREDH. "Organizaciones indígenas, religiosas y de derechos humanos presen- taron acción de protección y medidas cautelares contra el Estado y empre- sas petroleras por derrame de petróleo." April 29, 2020. https://inredh.org /organizaciones-indigenas-religiosas-y-de-derechos-humanos-presentan -accion-de-proteccion-y-medidas-cautelares/.

Jasso, Adriana, and Rosalba Jasso. "Critical Pedagogy: Not a Method but a Way of Life." In *Reclaiming Our Voices: Bilingual Education, Critical Pedagogy and Praxis*, ed. Jean Frederickson, 253–59. Ontario, CA: California Association for Bilingual Education, 1995.

Juhász, Borbála, and Enikő Pap. *Backlash in Gender Equality and Women's and Girls' Rights*. Brussels: European Union, Policy Department for Citizens' Rights and Constitutional Affairs, June 2018. https://www.europarl.europa.eu /RegData/etudes/STUD/2018/604955/IPOL_STU(2018)604955_EN.pdf.

Kaya, Gönül. "Why Jineology? Re-constructing the Sciences towards a Commu- nal and Free Life." In *Stateless Democracy: New World Academy Reader #5*, with the Kurdish Women's Movement, edited by Renée In der Maur and Jonas Staal, 83–96. Utrecht, Netherlands: BAK, 2015.

Keme, Emil. "For Abiayala to Live, the Americas Must Die: Toward a Transhemi- spheric Indigeneity." *Native American and Indigenous Studies* 5, no. 1 (Spring 2018): 42–68.

Kennon, Isabel, and Grace Valdevitt. "Women Protest for Their Lives: Fighting Femicide in Latin America." Atlantic Council, February 20, 2020. https:// www.atlanticcouncil.org/blogs/new-atlanticist/women-protest-for-their -lives-fighting-femicide-in-latin-america/.

Kimmerer, Robin Wall. "Corn Tastes Better on the Honor System." *Emergence Magazine*, October 31, 2018. https://emergencemagazine.org/story/corn-tastes -better/.

Knapp, Michael, Ercan Ayboga, and Anja Flach. *Revolution in Rojava: Democratic Autonomy and Women's Liberation in the Syrian Kurdistan*. London: Pluto, 2016.

Kuhar, Roman, and David Paternotte. *Anti-gender Campaigns in Europe: Mobilizing against Equality*. New York: Rowman and Littlefield International, 2017.

Kuhar, Roman, and Aleš Zobec. "The Anti-gender Movement in Europe and the Educational Process in Public Schools." *Center for Educational Policy Studies Journal* 7, no. 2 (2016): 29–46.

Kumar, Corinne. Introduction to *Asking We Walk: The South as New Political Imagi- nary, Book One: In the Time of the Earth*, 2nd ed., edited by Corinne Kumar, xiii–xxii. Bangalore: Streelekha, 2011.

Kumar, Corinne. "The One Central Mountain: Universalisms in Political Discourse." In *Asking We Walk: The South as New Political Imaginary, Book One: In the Time of the Earth*, 2nd ed., edited by Corinne Kumar, 266–86. Bangalore: Streelekha, 2011.

Lagarde, Marcela. "Del femicidio al feminicidio." *Desde el jardín de Freud*, no. 6 (2006): 216–26.

La Hora. "'No tenemos nada que ocultar': Lenin Moreno." November 9, 2019. https://lahora.com.ec/quito/noticia/1102285057/no-tenemos-nada-que -ocultar-lenin-moreno.

Las Casas, Bartolomé de. *Short Account of the Destruction of the Indies*. London: Penguin, 1999.

Leff, Enrique. *Saber ambiental*. Mexico City: Siglo XXI, 1998.

Lobo, Michele. "Decoloniality: Seeding Pluriversal Imaginaries." *Postcolonial Studies* 23, no. 4 (2020): 575–78.

Lorde, Audre. *Sister Outsider*. 1984. Rev. ed. Berkeley: Crossing, 2007.

Lorde, Audre. *Zami: A New Spelling of My Name: A Biomythography*. Berkeley: Crossing, 1982.

Lozano Lerma, Betty Ruth. *Aportes a un feminismo negro decolonial: Insurgencias epistémicas de mujeresnegras-afrocolombianas tejidas con retazos de memorias*. Quito: Universidad Andina Simón Bolívar and Abya-Yala, 2019.

Lozano Lerma, Betty Ruth. "El feminismo no puede ser uno porque las mujeres somos diversos: Aportes a un feminismo negro decolonial desde la experiencia de las mujeres negras del Pacifico colombiano." *La manzana de la discordia* 5, no. 2 (July–December 2010): 7–24.

Lozano Lerma, Betty Ruth. "Pedagogías para la vida, la alegría y la re-existencia: Pedagogías de mujeres negras que curan y vinculan." In *Pedagogías decoloniales: Prácticas insurgentes de resistir, (re)existir y (re)vivir*, edited by Catherine Walsh, 2:273–90. Quito: Abya-Yala, 2017.

Lozano Lerma, Betty Ruth. "Social Uprising, Racism, and Resistance in Cali's National Strike." *South Atlantic Quarterly* 121, no. 2 (2022): 425–34.

Lugones, María. "The Coloniality of Gender." *Worlds and Knowledges Otherwise* 2 (Spring 2008): 1–17.

Lugones, María. "Methodological Notes toward a Decolonial Feminism." In *Decolonizing Epistemologies: Latina/o Theology and Philosophy*, edited by Ada María Isasi-Díaz and Eduardo Mendieta, 68–86. New York: Fordham, 2012.

Lugones, María. "Pasos hacia un feminismo decolonial." In *Feminismo descolonial: Nuevos aportes teórico-metodológicos a más de una década*, edited by Yuderkys Espinosa Miñosa, 25–37. Quito: Abya-Yala, 2019.

Lugones, María. *Pilgrimages/Peregrinajes: Theorizing Coalition against Multiple Oppressions*. New York: Rowman and Littlefield, 2003.

Macas, Luis. "Construyendo desde la historia: Resistencia del movimiento indígena en el Ecuador." In *Plurinacionalidad: Democracia en la diversidad*, edited by Alberto Acosta and Esperanza Martínez, 81–98. Quito: Abya-Yala, 2009.

Macas, Luis. "Diversidad y plurinacionalidad." *Boletín ICCI-ARY Rimay* 6, no. 64 (2004): 2.

Macusaya Cruz, Carlos. "Autoría y significado político del Manifiesto de Tiahuanaco." *Pukara*, no. 95 (July 2014): 6–8.

Maldonado-Torres, Nelson. *Against War: Views from the Underside of Modernity.* Durham, NC: Duke University Press, 2008.

Maldonado-Torres, Nelson. "En la búsqueda de la madurez decolonial: Una carta a Catherine Walsh." In *Gritos, grietas y siembras de nuestros territories del Sur: Catherine Walsh y el pensamiento crítico-decolonial en América Latina*, edited by Alicia Ortega-Caicedo and Miriam Lang, 189–208. Quito: Universidad Andina Simón Bolívar/Abya-Yala, 2020.

Maldonado-Torres, Nelson. "Frantz Fanon and CLR James on Intellectualism and Enlightened Rationality." *Caribbean Studies* 33, no. 2 (July–December 2005): 149–94.

Maldonado-Torres, Nelson. "Hashtag Lessons from the US and South Africa about Racism and Antiblackness." *Mail and Guardian*, June 29, 2020. https://mg.co.za/opinion/2020-06-29-hashtag-lessons-from-the-us-and -south-africa-about-racism-and-antiblackness/.

Maldonado-Torres, Nelson. "Interrogating Systematic Racism and the White Academic Field." Frantz Fanon Foundation, 2020. https://fondation -frantzfanon.com/interrogating-systemic-racism-and-the-white-academic -field/.

Maldonado-Torres, Nelson. "On the Coloniality of Being: Contributions to the Development of a Concept." In *Globalization and the Decolonial Option*, edited by Walter D. Mignolo and Arturo Escobar, 94–124. New York: Routledge, 2010.

Maldonado-Torres, Nelson. "Outline of Ten Theses on Coloniality and Decoloniality." Frantz Fanon Foundation, 2016. http://fondation-frantzfanon.com /outline-of-ten-theses-on-coloniality-and-decoloniality/.

Maraire, J. Nozipo. *Zenzele.* New York: Delta, 1996.

Marcos, Sylvia. "Otroa Compañeroa—La fluidez de género: Una emergencia contemporánea con raices ancestrales." Camino al andar, June 20, 2021. https://sylviamarcos.wordpress.com/2021/06/15/otroa-companeroa -la-fluidez-de-genero-una-emergencia-contemporanea-con-raices -ancestrales/.

Marcos, Sylvia. *Taken from the Lips: Gender and Eros in Mesoamerican Religions.* Boston: Brill, 2006.

Mbembe, Achille. "Necropolitics." *Public Culture* 15, no. 1 (2003): 11–40.

McKittrick, Katherine. "Yours in the Intellectual Struggle: Sylvia Wynter and the Realization of Living." In *Sylvia Wynter: On Being Human as Praxis*, edited by Katherine McKittrick, 1–8. Durham, NC: Duke University Press, 2015.

McLaren, Peter. *Revolutionary Multiculturalism: Pedagogies of Dissent for the New Millennium.* Boulder, CO: Westview, 1997.

Mendoza, Breny. "Coloniality of Gender and Power: From Postcoloniality to Decoloniality." In *The Oxford Handbook of Feminist Theory*, edited by Lisa Disch and Mary Hawkesworth. Oxford Handbooks Online, 2016. https://www.oxfordhandbooks.com/view/10.1093/oxfordhb/9780199328581.001.0001/oxfordhb-9780199328581-e-6.

Mendoza, Breny. *Ensayos de crítica feminista en Nuestra América*. Mexico City: Herder, 2014.

Mendoza, Breny. "La epistemología del sur: La colonialidad del género y el feminism latinoamericano." In *Aproximaciones críticas a las prácticas teórico-políticas del feminismo latinoamericano*, coordinated by Yuderkys Espinosa Miñoso, 19–36. Buenos Aires: En la frontera, 2010.

Mestrum, Francine. "The Future of the World Social Forum: To Be or Not to Be?" *Other News*, February 2018.

Mignolo, Walter D. *The Darker Side of the Renaissance: Literacy, Territoriality, and Colonization*. 2nd ed. Ann Arbor: University of Michigan Press, 2003.

Mignolo, Walter D. *The Darker Side of Western Modernity: Global Futures, Decolonial Options*. Durham, NC: Duke University Press, 2011.

Mignolo, Walter D. "Introduction to José de Acosta's *Historia Natural y Moral de las Indias*." In *Natural and Moral History of the Indies*, by José de Acosta, xvii–xxviii. Translated by Frances López-Morillas. Durham, NC: Duke University Press, 2002.

Mignolo, Walter D. *Local Histories/Global Designs: Coloniality, Subaltern Knowledges, and Border Thinking*. Princeton, NJ: Princeton University Press, 2000.

Mignolo, Walter D. "Sylvia Wynter: What Does It Mean to Be Human?" In *Sylvia Wynter: On Being Human as Praxis*, edited by Katherine McKittrick, 106–23. Durham, NC: Duke University Press, 2015.

Mignolo, Walter D., and Catherine E. Walsh. *On Decoloniality: Concepts, Analytics, Praxis*. Durham, NC: Duke University Press, 2018.

Miranda, Wilmer. "Existencias/re-existencias desde la sensorialidad: Más allá del imperio de la mirada." Essay presented in the Latin American Cultural Studies Doctoral Program, Universidad Andina Simón Bolívar, Quito, Ecuador, July 2020.

Mirza, Romana. "Digital Story." YouTube, April 19, 2018, video, 4:35. https://youtu.be/c7adl48pkOk.

Mirza, Romana. "Women Undercover: Exploring the Intersectional Identities of Muslim Women through Modest Fashion and Digital Storytelling." Paper presented at the conference Imagined Borders, Epistemic Freedoms: The Challenge of Social Imaginaries in Media, Art, Religion and Decoloniality, University of Colorado, Boulder, January 8, 2020.

Mirza, Romana, and Women Undercover research project. "Beyond the Cover." YouTube, April 28, 2019, video, 4:03. https://youtu.be/emUFC-SSYAI.

Mirza, Romana, and Women Undercover research project. "Underneath This Hijab." YouTube, February 11, 2019, video, 4:38. https://youtu.be/8J-dTCRCyYY.

Montenegro, Leonardo. "Cultura y naturaleza: Aproximaciones a propósito del bicentenario de la independencia de Colombia." In *Cultura y naturaleza: Aproximaciones a propósito del bicentenario de la independencia de Colombia*, edited by Leonardo Montenegro, 9–19. Bogotá: Jardín Botánico José Celestín Mutis, 2011.

Mrozowski, Stephen A., Holly Herbster, David Brown, and Katherine L. Priddy. "Magunkaquog Materiality, Federal Recognition, and the Search for a Deeper History." *International Journal of Historical Archeology* 13, no. 4 (2009): 430–63.

Muñoz, César. "Brazil Suffers Its Own Scourge of Police Brutality." *Americas Quarterly*, June 3, 2020. https://www.americasquarterly.org/article/brazil-suffers -its-own-scourge-of-police-brutality/.

Nakata, Martin. *Disciplining the Savages, Savaging the Disciplines*. Canberra: Aboriginal Studies Press, 2007.

Ndlovu, Morgan. "Well-Intentioned but Vulnerable to Abuse." *Postcolonial Studies* 23, no. 4 (2020): 579–83.

Neubauer, Adrián, and Angel Méndez-Núñez. "New Educational Horizons Following the Rise of the 'New Far Right' in Europe: A Documentary Analysis." *Education Policy Analysis Archives* 30, no. 23 (February 22, 2022): 1–23. https:// epaa.asu.edu/index.php/epaa/article/view/5486.

Neven, Brecht, and Marlene Shäfers. "Jineology: From Women's Struggles to Social Liberation." *Roar*, November 26, 2017. https://roarmag.org/essays /jineology-kurdish-women-movement/.

Nieto, Mauricio. "Historia natural y la apropiación del nuevo mundo en la ilustración española." *Bulletin de l'Institut français d'études andines* 32, no. 3 (2003): 417–29.

Nipmuc Nation. "A Brief Look at Our History." Accessed April 20, 2021. https:// www.nipmucnation.org/history.

Noticias de América Latina y Caribe. "Entre 2016 y 2020 han sido asesinados casi mil líderes sociales en Colombia." July 17, 2020. https://www.nodal.am/2020 /07/colombia-971-lideres-sociales-y-218-excombatientes-asesinados-desde-la -firma-de-los-acuerdos-de-paz/.

Noticias de América Latina y Caribe. "La OPS advierte que ya hay 20 mil indígenas de la Amazonía con COVID-19." May 20, 2020. https://www.nodal.am /2020/05/la-ops-advierte-que-ya-hay-20-mil-indigenas-de-la-amazonia-con -covid-19/.

Öcalan, Abdullah. *Democratic Confederalism*. London: Transmedia, 2011.

Öcalan, Abdullah. *The Sociology of Freedom: Manifesto of the Democratic Civilization*. Vol. 3. 2008. Oakland, CA: PM Press, 2020.

Olvera Salinas, René. "Pedagogías de resistencia: De los *cómo* sembrar vida donde está la muerte." In *Pedagogías decoloniales: Prácticas insurgentes de resistir, (re)existir, y (re)vivir*, edited by Catherine Walsh, 2:195–208. Quito: Abya-Yala, 2017.

Oropeza, Daliri. "Sensibilidad Zapatista: ¿Arte para qué y para quién?" *Grieta*, December 10, 2019. http://www.grieta.org.mx/index.php/2019/12/10/sensibilidad -zapatista-arte-para-que-y-para-quien/.

O'Rourke, Patricia. "Roots of Radical Love in Education: Theorizing in a Concrete Struggle for Justice." PhD diss., University of Connecticut, 2022.

Oyewùmi, Oyèrónké. *The Invention of Women: Making an African Sense of Western Gender Discourses*. Minneapolis: University of Minnesota Press, 1997.

Paccó, Raimundo, and Alba Santandreu. "La deforestación de la Amazonía se extiende tan rápido como la COVID-19." *La Vanguardia*, May 28, 2020. https://www.lavanguardia.com/natural/20200528/481433474349/la-deforestacion-de-la-amazonia-se-extiende-tan-rapido-como-la-covid-19.html.

Palacios, Ruth. "Lukas Avendaño: Reflections from Muxeidad." *Siwarmayu* (blog). Accessed May 16, 2022. https://siwarmayu.com/lukas-avendano-reflections-from-muxeidad/.

Panikkar, Raimon. "La interpelación intercultural." In *El discurso intercultural: Prologómenos a una filosofía intercultural*, edited by Graciano González R. Arnaiz, 23–76. Madrid: Biblioteca Nueva, 2002.

Paredes, Julieta. *Hilando fino desde el feminismo comunitario*. Querétaro, Mexico: Grietas, 2012.

Pérez, Laura E. *Eros Ideologies: Writings on Art, Spirituality, and the Decolonial*. Durham, NC: Duke University Press, 2019.

Pérez, Laura E. "Spirit Glyphs: Reimagining Art and Artist in the Work of Chicana Tlamatinime." In *Rhetorics of the Americas*, edited by Damian Baca and Víctor Villanueva, 197–226. New York: Palgrave Macmillan, 2010.

Picq, Manuela L., and Josi Tikuna. "Indigenous Sexualities: Resisting Conquest and Translation." E-International Relations, August 20, 2019. https://www.e-ir.info/2019/08/20/indigenous-sexualities-resisting-conquest-and-translation/.

Porto-Gonçalves, Carlos Walter. "Lucha por la Tierra: Ruptura metabólica y reapropiación social de la naturaleza." *Polis: Revista Latinoamericana* 45 (2016). http://journals.openedition.org/polis/12168.

Prada, Raúl. "Entrevista a Raúl Prada Alcoreza." In *Asamblea Constituyente Bolivia: Información oficial de recursos naturales renovables, tierra-territorio y medio ambiente*, by Asamblea Constituyente, 3–4. Sucre: Asamblea Constituyente de Bolivia, 2007.

Pratt, Mary Louise. *Imperial Eyes: Travel Writing and Transculturation*. New York: Routledge, 1992.

Pueblos en Camino. "Amazonía: Exterminio y ecocidio, políticas de Estado." May 31, 2020. https://pueblosencamino.org/?p=8475.

Pueblos en Camino. "Encuentros para sembrar vida: Más allá de lo que permite el sistema." April 3, 2016. http://pueblosencamino.org/?cat=54.

Pueblos en Camino. "Pronunciamiento/Posicionamiento de Movilización 24 de abril de 2016: Mujeres habitantes del Estado de México." In "El feminicidio es una herramienta del capital-patriarcado: 'Vivas y organizadas hasta derrotar el monstruo machista.'" May 2, 2016. http://pueblosencamino.org/?p=2759.

Quijano, Aníbal. "Colonialidad del poder, cultura y conocimiento en América Latina." *Dispositio/n* 24, no. 51 (1999–2000): 137–48.

Quijano, Aníbal. "Colonialidad del poder y clasificación social." *Journal of World-Systems Research* 6, no. 2 (Summer/Fall 2000): 342–86.

Quijano, Aníbal. "Coloniality of Power, Eurocentrism, and Latin America." *Nepantla: Views from South* 1, no. 3 (2000): 533–80.

Quijano, Aníbal. "Estado-nación y movimientos indígenas en la región andina: Cuestiones abiertas." *Revista del Observatorio Social de América Latina: Movimientos sociales y gobiernos en la región andina: Resistencias y alternativas* 8, no. 19 (2006): 15–24.

Quintero Weir, José Ángel. "La emergencia de Nosotros I." Pueblos en Camino, January 18, 2019. https://pueblosencamino.org/?p=6988.

Radio Pozol. "EZLN: 'Son las artes la semilla en la que la humanidad renacerá.'" Radio Zapatista, December 15, 2019. https://radiozapatista.org/?p=32716&lang=en.

Ramos, Xavier. "Más de 150 comunidades indígenas en el Oriente del Ecuador siguen afectadas por el derrame de petróleo." *El Universo* (Ecuador), April 30, 2020. https://www.eluniverso.com/noticias/2020/04/30/nota/7827513/derrame-petroleo-afecta-mas-150-comunidades-indigenas-oriente.

Red Mariposas de Alas Nuevas Construyendo Futuro. *La muerte de Sandra Patricia Angulo no es un asesinato más, es un feminicidio.* Manifesto circulated by e-mail. Buenaventura, Colombia, April 2015.

Reinaga, Fausto. *Manifiesto Partido Indio de Bolivia.* La Paz: Fausto Reinaga, 1970.

Rengifo Vasquez, Grimaldo. "Education in the Modern West and Andean Culture." In *The Spirit of Regeneration: Andean Culture Confronting Western Notions of Development*, edited by Frederique Apffel-Marglin, 172–92. London: Zed, 1998.

Rexhepi, Piro. "From Orientalism to Homonationalism: Queer Politics, Islamophobia and Europeanization in Kosovo." *Southeastern Europe* 40 (2016): 32–53.

Rexhepi, Piro, Samira Musleh, and Romana Mirza. "Bandung Before and After: Islam, the Islamicate and the De/colonial." *ReOrient*, 2020. https://www.criticalmuslimstudies.co.uk/bandung-before-and-after/.

Río, Patricia del. "Nada más queda." *El Comercio* (Lima), February 8, 2018. https://elcomercio.pe/opinion/rincon-del-autor/violacion-ninos-menor-edad-violadores-miedo-queda-patricia-rio-noticia-495575.

Rivera Cusicanqui, Silvia. "La raíz: Colonizadores y colonizados." In *Violencias encubiertas en Bolivia*, edited by Xavier Albó and Raúl Barrios, 1:27–139. La Paz: CIPCA-Aruwiyiri, 1993.

Rivera Cusicanqui, Silvia. *Oprimidos pero no vencidos: Luchas del campesinado aymara y qhechwa, 1900–1980.* La Paz: Hisbol, 1986.

Roscoe, Will. *Changing Ones: Third and Fourth Genders in Native North America.* Basingstoke, UK: Palgrave, 1998.

Rozental Almendra, Violeta Kiwe, and Vilma Almendra Quiguanás. *Cristina Bautista: This Land's Bleeding Flight*. Cauca, Colombia: Pueblos en Camino, 2020.

Salgado, Samyr. "Utopía del Ahora." In *Pedagogías decoloniales: Prácticas insurgentes de resistir, (re)existir y (re)vivir*, edited by Catherine Walsh, 2:53–54. Quito: Abya-Yala, 2017.

Sandoval, Chela. *Methodology of the Oppressed*. Minneapolis: University of Minnesota, 2000.

Sanjinés, Javier. *Mestizaje Upside Down: Aesthetic Politics in Modern Bolivia*. Pittsburgh: University of Pittsburgh Press, 2004.

Santacruz, Lucy, and Judith Flores. "Entrevista a Lourdes Huanca Atencio, de la Federación Nacional de Mujeres Campesinas, Artesanas, Indígenas, Nativas y Asalariadas de Perú." *Flor de Guanto* 4 (December 2012): 46–49.

Santa Cruz Pachacuti, Juan de. *Relación de antigüedades deste reyno de Pirú*. 1613. Edited by Pierre Duviols and César Itier. Cuzco, Peru: Centro de Estudios Regionales Andinos Bartolomé de Las Casas, 1993.

Santiago-Valles, Kelvin A. *"Subject People" and Colonial Discourses: Economic Transformation and Social Disorders in Puerto Rico, 1898–1947*. Albany: State University of New York Press, 1994.

Sarkar, Radar. "The Alliances of Leftists and Evangelicals in Latin America." NACLA, October 2021. https://nacla.org/alliances-leftists-and-evangelicals -latin-america.

Schavelzon, Salvador. *El nacimiento de Estado Plurinacional de Bolivia: Etnografía de una Asamblea Constituyente*. Buenos Aires: CLACSO/Plural, 2012.

Schavelzon, Salvador. *Plurinacionalidad y Vivir Bien/Buen Vivir: Dos conceptos leídos desde Bolivia y Ecuador post-constituyentes*. Buenos Aires: CLACSO, 2015.

Schmitt, Carl. *The Nomos of the Earth in International Law of the Jus Publicum Europaeum*. Translated and annotated by G. L. Ulmen. New York: Telos, 2003.

Seale, Bobby. Foreword to *Black Panther: The Revolutionary Art of Emory Douglas*, by Emory Douglas, 12–14. New York: Rizzoli, 2007.

Segato, Rita Laura. "Género y colonialidad: En busca de claves de lectura y de un vocabulario estratégico descolonial." In *La cuestión descolonial*, edited by Aníbal Quijano and Julio Mejía Navarrete, 27–59. Lima: Universidad Ricardo Palma, 2010.

Segato, Rita Laura. "El sexo y la norma: Frente estatal, patriarcado, desposesión, colonialidad." *Estudios Feministas* 22, no. 2 (May–August 2014): 593–616.

Shakur, Tupac. "The Rose That Grew from Concrete." AllPoetry. Accessed May 16, 2022. https://allpoetry.com/The-Rose-That-Grew-From-Concrete.

Shaner, Bill. "A Hidden History Uncovered in Ashland." *MetroWest Daily News* (Framingham, MA), June 26, 2016.

Shaner, Bill. "Nipmuc Healing Ceremony to Usher in Ashland-Nyanza Memorial Garden." Wicked Local Ashland, June 12, 2016. https://ashland.wickedlocal .com/news/20160612/nipmuc-healing-ceremony-to-usher-in-ashland-nyanza -memorial-garden.

Shiva, Vandana. *Biopiracy: The Plunder of Nature and Knowledge*. Cambridge, MA: South End, 1997.

Shiva, Vandana. *Monocultures of the Mind*. London: Zed, 1993.

Sigal, Pete. *The Flower and the Scorpion: Sexuality and Ritual in Early Nahua Culture*. Durham, NC: Duke University Press, 2011.

Silverblatt, Irene. *Moon, Sun and Witches: Gender Ideologies and Class in Inca and Colonial Peru*. Princeton, NJ: Princeton University Press, 1987.

Simpson, Leanne Betasamosake. *As We Have Always Done: Indigenous Freedom through Radical Resistance*. Minneapolis: University of Minnesota Press, 2017.

Sithole, Tendayi. "Frantz Fanon: Africana Existentialist Philosopher." *African Identities* 14, no. 2 (2016): 177–90.

Socioambiental.org. "COVID-19 and Indigenous Peoples." Accessed February 2021. https://covid19.socioambiental.org/.

Soria, Ronald. "El país latinoamericano donde la policía mata a más negros que en Estados Unidos." *El Expreso*, June 4, 2020. https://www.expreso.ec/actualidad/mundo/latinoamerica-pais-policia-mata-negros-ee-uu-12882.html.

Sorkin, Aaron, dir. *The Trial of the Chicago 7*. Film produced by Marc Platt Productions/DreamWorks, 2020.

Spillers, Hortense J. "Mama's Baby, Papa's Maybe: An American Grammar Book." *Diacritics* 17, no. 2 (Summer 1987): 64–81.

Students for Cultural and Linguistic Democracy (SCaLD). "Reclaiming Our Voices." In *Education Reform and Social Change: Multicultural Voices, Struggles, and Visions*, edited by Catherine E. Walsh, 129–46. Mahwah, NJ: Lawrence Erlbaum, 1996.

Subcomandante Insurgente Galeano. "Between Light and Shadow." EZLN, May 27, 2014. https://enlacezapatista.ezln.org.mx/2014/05/27/between-light-and-shadow/.

Subcomandante Insurgente Marcos. "La historia de las preguntas." *La Jornada*, December 13, 1994.

Tapia, Luis. *Una reflexión sobre la idea de un estado plurinacional*. La Paz: Oxfam, 2008.

Teaiwa, Katerina. "On Decoloniality: A View from Oceania." *Postcolonial Studies* 23, no. 4 (2020): 601–3.

Telesur. "Femincidio en América Latina." July 4, 2016. https://www.telesurtv.net/news/Crimenes-impunes-el-rastro-del-feminicidio-en-America-Latina-20160704-0009.html#.

Terrazas, Bill, and Students for Cultural and Linguistic Democracy (SCaLD). "Struggling for Power and Voice: A High School Experience." In *Reclaiming Our Voices: Bilingual Education, Critical Pedagogy and Praxis*, edited by Jean Frederickson, 279–309. Ontario, CA: California Association for Bilingual Education, 1995.

Ticona, Esteban. "Eduardo Nina Quispe: El emancipador, educador y político Aymara." In *Pedagogías decoloniales: Prácticas insurgentes de resistir, (re)existir y (re)vivir*, edited by Catherine Walsh, 1:331–56. Quito: Abya-Yala, 2013.

Ticona, Esteban. *Organización y liderazgo aymara, 1979–1996*. Cochabamba, Bolivia: Agroecología Universidad de Cochabamba, 2000.

Tinsley, Omise'eke Natasha. *Ezili's Mirrors: Imagining Black Queer Genders*. Durham, NC: Duke University Press, 2018.

Toledo, Manuel. "La grieta en la Tate: Entrevista a Doris Salcedo." *Esfera pública*, October 10, 2007. https://esferapublica.org/nfblog/la-grieta-en-la-tate -entrevista-con-doris-salcedo/.

Tortorici, Zeb. "Against Nature: Sodomy and Homosexuality in Colonial Latin America." *History Compass* 10, no. 2 (2012): 161–78.

Tubino, Fidel. "La interculturalidad crítica como proyecto ético-político." Encuentro continental de educadores agustinos, Lima, January 24–28, 2005. https://oala.villanova.edu/congresos/educacion/lima-ponen-02.html.

Tuck, Eve, and K. Wayne Yang. "Decolonization Is Not a Metaphor." *Decolonization: Indigeneity, Education, and Society* 1, no. 1 (2012): 1–40.

Tuhiwai Smith, Linda. *Decolonizing Methodologies: Research and Indigenous Peoples*. London: Zed Books, 1999.

US Environmental Protection Agency. "Superfund Site: Nyanza Chemical Waste Dump Ashland, MA." Accessed January 24, 2022. https://cumulis .epa.gov/supercpad/SiteProfiles/index.cfm?fuseaction=second.Cleanup&id =0100948.

Vianna, Claudia, and Alexandre Bortolinni. "Anti-gender Discourse and LGBT and Feminist Agendas in State-Level Education Plans: Tensions and Disputes." *Educação e Pesquisa* 46 (2020): e221756. https://doi.org/10.1590/s1678 -4634202046221756.

Villavicencio, Arturo. "Hacia dónde va el proyecto universitario de la Revolución Ciudadana?" In *El correismo desnudo*, various authors, 216–31. Quito: Montecristi vive, 2013.

Walsh, Catherine. "Afro and Indigenous Life-Visions in/and Politics: (De)colonial Perspectives in Bolivia and Ecuador." *Bolivian Studies Journal*, no. 18 (2011): 49–69.

Walsh, Catherine. "Afro In/Exclusion, Resistance, and the 'Progressive' State: (De)colonial Struggles, Questions, and Reflections." In *Black Social Movements in Latin America: From Monocultural Mestizaje to Multiculturalism*, edited by Jean Muteba Rahier, 15–34. New York: Palgrave, 2012.

Walsh, Catherine E. "Decoloniality in/as Praxis." In *On Decoloniality: Concepts, Analytics, Praxis*, by Walter D. Mignolo and Catherine E. Walsh, 1–102. Durham, NC: Duke University Press, 2018.

Walsh, Catherine E. "Decoloniality, Pedagogy and Praxis." In *Encyclopedia of Educational Philosophy and Theory*, edited by Michael Adrian Peters, 366–70. Singapore: Springer, 2017.

Walsh, Catherine E. "(Decolonial) Notes to Paulo Freire: Walking and Asking." In *Educational Alternatives in Latin America: New Modes of Counter-hegemonic Learning*, edited by Robert Aman and Timothy Ireland, 207–30. London: Palgrave Macmillan, 2019.

Walsh, Catherine E. "Decolonial Pedagogies Walking and Asking: Notes to Paulo Freire from AbyaYala." *International Journal of Lifelong Education* 34, no. 1 (2015): 9–21.

Walsh, Catherine. "El desarrollo sociopolítico de la educación intercultural bilingüe en el Ecuador: Un análisis de perspectivas y posiciones." *Pueblos Indígenas y Educación* 31–32 (July–December 1994): 99–164.

Walsh, Catherine. "(Des)existir: Mi segunda carta a Aníbal Quijano." *Revista Descolonialdad y Autogobierno*, no. 3 (October 2020): 26–31.

Walsh, Catherine. "(Des)humanidad(es)." *Alter/nativas*, no. 3 (2014): 1–17. https://alternativas.osu.edu/es/issues/autumn-2014/essays2/walsh.html.

Walsh, Catherine. "El despertar de octubre y el cóndor: Notas desde Ecuador y la región." *Sobre 1991: Revista de Estudios Internacionales* 2, no. 1 (December 2019): 84–90.

Walsh, Catherine E., ed. *Education Reform and Social Change: Multicultural Voices, Struggles, and Visions*. Mahwah, NJ: Lawrence Erlbaum, 1996.

Walsh, Catherine E. *Enabling Academic Success for Secondary Students with Limited Formal Schooling: A Study of the Haitian Literacy Program at Hyde Park High School in Boston*. Providence, RI: Northeast and Islands Regional Educational Laboratory at Brown University, 1999.

Walsh, Catherine E. "Engaging Students in Their Own Learning: Literacy, Language, and Knowledge Production with Latino Adolescents." In *Adult Biliteracy in the United States*, edited by David Spener, 211–42. Washington, DC: Center for Applied Linguistics and Delta Systems, 1994.

Walsh, Catherine. "Fanon y la pedagogía de-colonial." *Revista Nuevamérica/Novamérica*, no. 122 (2009): 60–63.

Walsh, Catherine. "Gritos, grietas y siembras de vida: Entretejeres de lo pedagógico y lo decolonial." In *Pedagogías decoloniales: Prácticas insurgentes de resistir, (re)existir, y (re)vivir*, edited by Catherine Walsh, 2:17–45. Quito: Abya-Yala, 2017.

Walsh, Catherine. *Interculturalidad crítica y (de)colonialidad: Ensayos desde Abya Yala*. Quito: Abya-Yala, 2012.

Walsh, Catherine. *Interculturalidad, estado, sociedad: Luchas (de)coloniales de nuestra época*. Quito: Universidad Andina Simón Bolívar/Abya-Yala, 2009.

Walsh, Catherine. "Introducción: Lo pedagógico y lo decolonial: Entretejiendo caminos." In *Pedagogías decoloniales: Prácticas insurgentes de resistir, (re)existir y (re)vivir*, edited by Catherine Walsh, 1:23–68. Quito: Abya-Yala, 2013.

Walsh, Catherine. "Las estrategias de la(s) insurgencia(s): Entrevista a Catherine Walsh." Interview by René Olvera Salinas and Germania Fernández. *Grietas* 1, no. 1 (July 2012): 11–19.

Walsh, Catherine E. "Lewis R. Gordon: Existential Incantations That Cross Borders and Move Us Forward." In *Black Existentialism: Essays on the Transformative Thought of Lewis R. Gordon*, edited by Danielle Davis, 121–34. New York: Rowman and Littlefield International, 2019.

Walsh, Catherine E. "Life and Nature 'Otherwise': Challenges from the Abya-Yalean Andes." In *The Anomie of the Earth: Philosophy, Politics, and Autonomy in Europe and the Americas*, edited by Federico Luisetti, John Pickles, and Wilson Kaiser, 93–118. Durham, NC: Duke University Press, 2015.

Walsh, Catherine E. "Making a Difference: Social Vision, Pedagogy, and Real Life." In *Education Reform and Social Change: Multicultural Voices, Struggles, and Visions*, edited by Catherine E. Walsh, 223–40. Mahwah, NJ: Lawrence Erlbaum, 1996.

Walsh, Catherine E. "Not Just Philosophers of Existence, but Pedagogues of Existence: A Letter to Lewis Gordon and to Frantz Fanon." In *Fanon and the Crisis of European Man*, 2nd ed., by Lewis Gordon. New York: Routledge, in press.

Walsh, Catherine. "On Gender and Its Otherwise." In *The Palgrave Handbook of Gender and Development*, edited by Wendy Harcourt, 34–47. London: Palgrave Macmillan, 2016.

Walsh, Catherine E. "On Justice, Pedagogy, and Decolonial(izing) Praxis." *Educational Theory*, in press.

Walsh, Catherine. "On the October Awakening(s) and the Condor: Notes from Ecuador and the Region." *Black Issues in Philosophy*, November 28, 2019. https://blog.apaonline.org/2019/11/28/on-the-october-awakenings-and-the-condor-notes-from-ecuador-and-the-region/.

Walsh, Catherine E. "Pedagogical Notes from the Decolonial Cracks." *Emisférica* 11, no. 1 (2014). https://hemisphericinstitute.org/en/emisferica-11-1-decolonial-gesture/11-1-dossier/pedagogical-notes-from-the-decolonial-cracks.html.

Walsh, Catherine E. *Pedagogy and the Struggle for Voice: Issues of Language, Power, and Schooling for Puerto Ricans*. New York: Bergin and Garvey, 1991.

Walsh, Catherine. "Political-Epistemic Insurgency, Social Movements and the Refounding of the State." In *Rethinking Intellectuals in Latin America*, edited by Mabel Moraña and Bret Gustafson, 199–212. Madrid: Iberoamericana Vervuert, 2010.

Walsh, Catherine E. "The Politics of Naming: (Inter)cultural Studies in De-colonial Code." *Cultural Studies* 26, no. 1 (2012): 108–25.

Walsh, Catherine E. Preface to *Education Reform and Social Change: Multicultural Voices, Struggles, and Visions*, edited by Catherine E. Walsh, ix–x. Mahwah, NJ: Lawrence Erlbaum, 1996.

Walsh, Catherine. "Qué saber, qué hacer y cómo ver? Los desafíos y predicamentos disciplinares, políticos y éticos de los estudios (inter)culturales desde América Andina." In *Estudios culturales latinoamericanos: Retos desde y sobre la región andina*, edited by Catherine Walsh, 11–28. Quito: Universidad Andina Simón Bolívar/Abya-Yala, 2003.

Walsh, Catherine. "Reflexiones en torno a la colonialidad/descolonialidad del poder en América Latina hoy: Una carta a Aníbal Quijano." *Otros Logos* 10, no. 10 (December 2019): 12–19. http://www.ceapedi.com.ar/otroslogos/Revistas/0010/02%202019%20Catherine%20Walsh.pdf.

Walsh, Catherine E. "Resisting, Re-existing, and Co-existing (De)spite State: Women's Insurgencies for Territory and Life in Ecuador." In *Decolonial Feminism in Abya Yala: Caribbean, Meso, and South American Contributions and Challenges*, edited by Yuderkys Espinosa Miñoso, María Lugones, and Nelson Maldonado-Torres, 217–44. New York: Rowman and Littlefield, 2022.

Walsh, Catherine. "Shifting the Geopolitics of Critical Knowledge: Decolonial Thought and Cultural Studies 'Others' in the Andes." In *Globalization and the Decolonial Option*, edited by Walter D. Mignolo and Arturo Escobar, 78–93. New York: Routledge, 2010.

Walsh, Catherine E. "'Staging Encounters': The Educational Decline of US Puerto Ricans in [Post]-colonial Perspective." *Harvard Educational Review* 68, no. 2 (1998): 218–43.

Walsh, Catherine, and Juan García Salazar. "(W)riting Collective Memory (De) spite State: Decolonial Practices of Existence in Ecuador." In *Black Writing, Culture, and the State in Latin America*, edited by Jerome C. Branche, 253–66. Nashville: Vanderbilt University Press, 2015.

Wekker, Gloria. *The Politics of Passion: Women's Sexual Culture in the Afro-Surinamese Diaspora*. New York: Colombia University Press, 2006.

Wekker, Gloria. *White Innocence: Paradoxes of Colonialism and Race*. Durham, NC: Duke University Press, 2016.

Wikipedia. "Anti-LGBT Curriculum Laws in the United States." Last updated May 13, 2022. https://en.wikipedia.org/wiki/Anti-LGBT_curriculum_laws_in _the_United_States.

Wikipedia. "Francia Márquez." Last updated July 9, 2022. https://es.wikipedia.org /wiki/Francia_M%C3%A1rquez.

Wilson, Alex. "How We Find Ourselves: Identity Development and Two-Spirit People." *Harvard Educational Review* 66, no. 2 (1996): 303–18.

Wynter, Sylvia. "1492: A New World View." In *Race, Discourse, and the Origin of the Americas: A New World View*, edited by Vera Lawrence Hyatt and Rex Nettleford, 6–57. Washington, DC: Smithsonian Institution Press, 1995.

Wynter, Sylvia. "'No Humans Involved': An Open Letter to My Colleagues." *Forum NHI Knowledge for the 21st Century* 1, no. 1 (Fall 1994): 42–71.

Wynter, Sylvia. "Towards the Sociogenic Principle: Fanon, the Puzzle of Conscious Experience, of 'Identity' and What It's Like to Be 'Black.'" In *National Identity and Sociopolitical Changes in Latin America*, edited by Mercedes Durán-Cogan and Antonio Gómez-Moriano, 30–66. New York: Routledge, 2001.

Wynter, Sylvia. "Unsettling the Coloniality of Being/Power/Truth/Freedom: Towards the Human, after Man, Its Overrepresentation—an Argument." *New Centennial Review* 3, no. 3 (Fall 2003): 257–337.

Yampara, Simón. "Cosmovisión, Uruq-Oacha, desarrollo y/o qamaña andino." In *Educación intra e intercultural: Alternativas a la reforma educativa neocolonizadora*, edited by Freddy Delgado and Juan Carlos Mariscal, 23–36. La Paz: Plural, 2006.

Yancy, George. "White Suturing, Black Bodies, and the Myth of a Post-Racial America," Society for the Arts in Religious and Theological Studies, 2018. https://www.societyarts.org/white-suturing-black-bodies-and-the-myth-of-a-post-racial-america.html.

Yasar, Melike, and Ana Maria Morales. "El facismo no es un estado que no reconoce a la sociedad, es la ideología de la Guerra." *Revista Amazonas*, no. 1 (October 2019): 21–33.

Zaragocín, Sofía, María-Rosa Cevallos, Guglielmina Falanga, Iñigo Arrazola, Gabriela Ruales, Verónica Vera, and Amanda Yépez. "Mapeando la criminalización del aborto en el Ecuador." *Revista de Bioética y Derecho* 43 (2018): 109–25.

Zapata-Olivella, Manuel. *Changó, the Biggest Badass*. Translation by Jonathan Tittler. Lubbock: Texas Tech University Press, 2010.

Zapata-Olivella, Manuel. *La rebelión de los genes: El mestizaje americano en la sociedad futura*. Bogotá: Altamir, 1997.

Zapatista Women. "Letter from the Zapatista Women to Women in Struggle around the World." Enlace Zapatista, February 2019. https://enlacezapatista.ezln.org.mx/2019/02/13/letter-from-the-zapatista-women-to-women-in-struggle-around-the-world/

Zavaleta, René. *El estado en América Latina*. Cochabamba, Bolivia: Los amigos del libro, 1990.

INDEX

Page numbers in italics indicate illustrations.

"homonationalism," 31
homophobia, 30
Honduras, 29, 47–48
hooks, bell (Gloria Watkins), 107, 267n11,
    267n22
Horace Mann Bond Center for Equal
    Education, 85–86
Horswell, Michael, 149, 153, 172
Horton, Myles, 95
Huaco. *See* Mama Huaco
Huanca Atencio, Lourdes, 158–59
Huarochiri Manuscript, 139, 145
Huarte de San Juan, Juan, 155
Humboldt, Alexander von, 141

Illich, Iván, 76–78, 92–94, 266n5
immigrants, 182–83, 188
Indianism, 197, 199–204, 288n64, 288n70
Indigenous peoples, 96, 180, 205, 211,
    284n11; bilingual education of, 96;
    COVID-19 cases among, 45; dispossession
    of, 182–84; gender violence and,
    159–60; insurgency of, 160–64; *mestizaje*
    and, 186–87, 191; patriarchy and, 133–35;
    plurinationality and, 191, 193, 195, 216–25;
    UN Declaration on rights of, 223–24;
    World Bank's policy directive on, 215
Insunza, Omar "Gran OM," 67, *68*
insurgency, 54–55, 109–10, 234; of Indigenous
    women, 160–64; Lozano Lerma
    on, 164–65
Inter-American Commission on Human
    Rights, 45
interculturality, 213–16, 226
International Monetary Fund (IMF), 37
Inti Raymi (Summer Solstice Festival),
    210, 248
Iriarte, Gregoria, 288n60
Islamophobia, 31–32
Israeli-Palestinian conflict, 28, 31, 180–81,
    237

Jackson, Andrew, 63
James, C. L. R., 142
jineology ("women's science"), 71,
    169–72, 237, 280n130

Karakas, Ampam, 212
Katarism, 288nn59–60; Cárdenas and,
    204–5; founding of, 289n84; Indianism
    and, 197, 199–204, 288n64,
    288n70; Iriarte and, 288n60; National
    Revolutionary Movement and,
    288n64; Sanjinés on, 204
Kaya, Gönül, 143
Keme, Emil, 6
Kennedy, John F., 38
Kimmerer, Robin Wall, 230–31, 240
King, Martin Luther, Jr., 241
King, Rodney, 59
Kosakura (Ángel Burbano), 172–76, *175*
Kumar, Corinne, 1, 7, 75, 95
Kurdish liberation movements, 11, 55,
    170, 183–84, 188
Kurdish Workers' Party, 184
Kurds, 143; confederalism and, 184, 227,
    265n148, 289n72; jineology of, 169–72,
    237; liberation movements of, 11, 55,
    170, 183–84, 188; women's movement
    among, 70–71, 184, 227, 285n22. *See also*
    Öcalan, Abdullah

La Condamine, Charles-Marie de, 141
Land Back movements, 180, 228
Lander, Edgardo, 19, 113
Landless Movement (Brazil), 180
Land-territory, 180–82, 223–29, 233–35,
    237, 239; Black communities and,
    103, 180–82, 241–44, 270n50., 284n6;
    education and, 242n77; Palestinians
    and, 237. *See also* dispossession
Laqueur, Thomas, 154–55
Las Casas, Bartolomé de, 186–87
Lather, Patti, 87
Lawrence, Jacob, 63
Lawyers' Committee for Civil Rights, 90
Lenin, Vladimir, 188
LGBTQ+ community, 146–47, 152, 224;
    coloniality of, 173–76, *175*; homophobia
    and, 30; Islamaphobia and, 31;
    US laws against, 31–32
liberation theology, 34, 80
lifeworlds, 75, 132

National Association of Bilingual Education, 85

National Confederation of Peasant Workers of Bolivia, 196–97

nation-state, 184–85, 187–89; alliances against, 208–10; Coultard on, 182, 192–93; Gordon on on, 182, 227; ongoing questions of, 203–6; plurinationalization and, 185–90; Quijano on, 188–90, 286n37; self-identity and, 211–13; Zavaleta on, 188. *See also* Öcalan, Abdullah

nature, 138–40, 151; gender and, 151–64; race and, 126, 135–64; science and, 139, 140–43

Nature, 135–41, 152; coloniality of, 135–36; rights of, 18, 225. *See also* Pachamama

naturings, 142–44

Ndlovu, Morgan, 236

neoliberalism: in Bolivia, 189, 204–6, 208; in Chile, 188–90, 286n39; in Ecuador, 36–43, 215, 219, 292n123; Mendoza on, 189; neofascist, 178; Quijano on, 189–90

Netanyahu, Benjamin, 181

Nina Qhispi, Eduardo Leandro, 194–95

Nipmuc Tribal Nation, 2–4, 239, 253n2

Nishnaabewin, 182

Nova Scotia, 123

Nyanza Chemical Plant and Waste Dump, 3–4

Öcalan, Abdullah, 11, 170, 183–84, 188, 289n72

October Awakenings (Ecuador, 2019), 36–43

Olvera Salinas, René, 53–54, 233

Ometéotl (Aztec creator deity), 146

Operation Condor (1975–83), 38–41

Organization of Indigenous Peoples of Pastaza (Ecuador), 96

Oyewùmi, Oyèrónké, 7, 127, 129; on gender binaries, 136, 148; on nongender-specific words, 145

Pacari, Nina, 220

Pachacuti, Juan de Santa Cruz, 138, 146

Pachacuti Yamqui Salcamaygua, 207

Pachakamak (Andean deity), 146

Pachakuti, Santacruz de, 172

Pachakutik (Indigenous alliance), 217–22

Pachamama (Mother Nature), 48–49, 138, 225, 231, 240; Amazon de-existence and, 46; Chaski Warmi and, 167; rights of Nature and, 18, 152–53, 225

Pacto de Unidad (Bolivia, 2006), 209

palenques, 103, 270n50, 284n6

Palestinians, 28, 180–81, 237

Panikkar, Raimon, 215–16

Park, Peter, 87

Parliament of the Peoples (Ecuador), 42

pedagogies-as-methodologies, 56–57, 62, 72–73, 77, 100–102, 106, 114–17, 130, 160

pedagogy, 33–36; autonomy and, 121; critical, 85–90, 97–99; of cruelty, 24; Fanon and, 72–74; of hope, 99; as praxis, 101, 109, 112, 115–17, 168; Red, 99; as sociopolitical struggle, 25, 72, 77, 97. *See also* Freire, Paulo

Peña Nieto, Enrique, 26

Pence, Mike, 32

Penniman, Naima, 13–14, 50, 61, 238

Pérez, Laura E., 7, 8, 125

Peru, 29–31, 38, 137–38, 158

Peto, Andrea, 31

Petro, Gustavo, 33, 250

Piñera, Sebastián, 32, 35

Pinochet, Augusto, 39, 188, 286n39

Pinto, João Pedro Matos, 70

plurinational interculturality, 213–16, 226

plurinationalization, 42, 183–85, 190–94; in Bolivia, 194–205, 209; in Ecuador, 209–25; *mestizaje* and, 186–87, 191

political-pedagogical praxis, 86–92

Popol Vuh (Mayan document), 145–46

Popular Participation Law (Bolivia, 1994), 205

Porto-Gonçalves, Carlos Walter, 9, 47

posthumanism, 135, 142

Spillers, Hortense J., 162, 282n147
spirituality, 2, 125; Andean, 98, 99, 189; androgynous, 146; Blackwomen's insurgency and, 148, 164–66; feminist politics and, 11; hegemonic practices and, 4, 125, 127, 160; midwifery and, 165–66; Muslim women and, 130; Nature and, 153, 166–69; re-existence and, 246–47; relationality and, 125, 126; Rematriation and, 231; Yoruba/Lucumi, 148; Vodun, 148; Voudoun, 154. *See also* feminine power
Spix, Johann Baptist von, 277n60
"statelessness," 182, 227
Students for a Democratic Society (SDS), 80
Students for Cultural and Linguistic Democracy (SCaLD), 88–90
sumak kawsay. See buen vivir
Summer Institute of Linguistics, 34
Summer Solstice (Inti Raymi) Festival, 210, 248

Tapia, Luciano, 200
Tapia, Luis, 189, 287n41
Taylor, Breonna, 69–70. *See also* Black Lives Matter
Teaiwa, Katerina, 237
"theory uprising," 117
thought-as-theory, 237
Ticona, Esteban, 195, 288n59
Tinsely, Natasha, 154
Tiwanaku Manifesto, 197–99, 202
Torres Guzmán, María, 90
Tortorici, Zeb, 152
transfeminism, 88
transgender, 146–47. *See also* LGBTQ+ community
Trump, Donald, 32, 43, 178
Truth, Sojourner, 81
Tubino, Fidel, 291n111
Tuck, Eve, 4, 7
Tupac Amaru (José Gabriel Condorcanqui), 201–2
Tupac Katari (Julian Apaza), 195–97, 201–2, 288n59

Tupac Katari Indian Movement (MITKA), 200
Tupac Katari Peasant Center, 196
Tupac Katari Revolutionary Movement (MRTK), 200–201, 289n84
Turtle Island, 3, 70

UN Declaration on Rights of Indigenous Peoples, 223–24
Underground Railroad, 123
unionization, 196–97, 200, 201
United States, 11, 113, 124, 126, 130, 188, 197, 208, 226; femicide in, 29; Freire and, 87, 99; geopolitics of, 37–40, 42; Haitian literacy programs in, 92; homonationalism in, 31; militarization in, 178; pedagogical praxis in, 78–80, 83–94; Puerto Ricans in, 84, 85; settler colonialism in, 2–6, 124, 180; white supremacy in, 70. *See also* Black Lives Matter
Universidad Andina Simón Bolívar (Quito), 108, 250
Universidad de la Tierra, 119
University of Massachusetts, 64, 80
University of Peace, 235
unlearning/relearning, 83–86, 103–7, 267n22
Uribe, Álvaro, 35

Vásquez, Genaro, 16
Venezuela, 33, 35, 43, 186
Vietnam War protests, 80–81
Villavicencio, Arturo, 19
Villoro, Luis, 66–67
Viracocha (Andean creator deity), 146
votanes (guardian-heart of the people), 119–20

Weather Underground, 80
Weinberg, Meyer, 85–86, 87
Wekker, Gloria, 7, 154, 183; on European science, 128–29, 143
White, Rowen, 231
Wilson, Alex, 149
"women's science." *See* jineology

World Bank, 215
World Social Forum, 51
Wynter, Sylvia, 7, 58–60, 78, 142, 241, 263n121

Yampara, Simón, 290n92
Yancy, George, 4, 254n12
Yang, K. Wayne, 4, 7
Yanomami, Davi Kopenawa, 46
Yoruba, 145
Yupanqui, Inca, 197–98

Zapantera Negra project, 63–65, 67, *68*
Zapata-Olivella, Manuel, 137, 148
Zapatistas, 20, 95, 236–37; art projects of, 64, 65–67, *66*; Black Panthers and, 63–68; *caracoles* of, 63, 65, 119–20; Comandanta Dalia and, 51; on "cracks," 56–58; Escuelita of, 63–64, 66, 119–21; *El pensamiento crítico frente a la hidra capitalista* seminar of, 56, 236–37; seedbeds of thought of, 56, 236–37; Subcomandante Galeano and, 20, 28, 51, 56, 66–67, 236; Subcomandante Marcos and, 56–57, 95, 119, 269n39; Subcomandante Moisés and, 27, 56, 67, 119, 237; World Social Forum and, 51
Zapotecas, 147
Zarate, Pablo Willka, 201–2
Zárate Willka, Pablo, 194
Zavaleta, René, 188, 203–4
Zelaya, Manuel, 40